Helping Children on Their Way

Dedication

Audrey McAllen began her career as a Waldorf class teacher in 1942 and completed it as a teacher for children with special needs. She lived in Gloucester, England. Audrey taught workshops and gave lectures around the world. Her books are all related to the subject of helping children in need: handwriting, sleep, understanding children's drawings, and developing speech as a creative influence in education.

Her books have been translated into several languages. They are full of observations, insights and ideas for exercises to help children incarnate into their bodies, and to remove hindrances to allow all children to fully realize their capacities. Over the decades of her work, many teachers have been inspired to add to these skills for helping children with special needs. You will find her insights woven into the work of almost all the authors in this book, and the remedial resource training courses are informed by her guiding lights.

Audrey McAllen's work continues to provide a tower of strength for many Waldorf schools who are able to include Extra Lesson specialists on their faculties.

David Mitchell was a deeply committed and enthusiastic Waldorf teacher for 45 years. After completing two eight-year cycles in the elementary school, and spending some years as a high school teacher along the way, he turned his abundant energy to Waldorf Publications and the Research Institute for Waldorf Education. Over a span of 25 years he worked tirelessly to bring fine resources to publication for teachers, early childhood through high school. One work in particular, is *Developmental Insights*, which points teachers to the understanding of the cycles of childhood so essential to Waldorf teachers. Others covered subjects as varied as handwork, woodwork, chemistry, physics, and children's literature, the Waldorf curriculum and its results. His last publishing work, *Clothing the Play*, was sent to press just two days before he passed.

With more time on earth, David would undoubtedly have brought this book into life with his usual zest, insight, energy, and good will. We marvel at the volume, depth, and breadth of the work you left behind for us to model, and we have done out best, David, to follow your lead.

Brigitta Witteveen was born in The Netherlands where she completed her undergraduate studies in art, psychology and family therapy. Her MFA was accomplished at the Rhode Island School of Design and her MEd in early childhood and elementary Waldorf education at Antioch University New England. Her certification in Extra Lesson work and woodworking made her an indispensable faculty member at the Lexington Waldorf School for 29 years.

Brigitta Witteveen crossed the threshold unexpectedly in 2016 before this book was published. She died peacefully with her children around her. Brigitte's lifetime was dedicated to children and to education. She will be missed by many, including her school and all in the Waldorf movement.

Helping Children on Their Way

EDUCATIONAL SUPPORT FOR THE CLASSROOM

Compiled by
Elizabeth Auer

Printed with support from the Waldorf Curriculum Fund

Published by:
Waldorf Publications at the
Research Institute for Waldorf Education
38 Main Street
Chatham, NY 12037

Title: *Helping Children on Their Way*
Educational Support for the Classroom

Editor/Illustrator: Elizabeth Auer
Copy editor: Colleen Shetland
Cover art: Elizabeth Auer
Design: Elizabeth Auer
Layout: Ann Erwin

Copyright © 2017 Waldorf Publications
ISBN # 978-1-943582-02-0

Contents

Foreword 7
Elizabeth Auer

Child Development 8
Constitutional types, the temperaments,
and school readiness
Helen-Ann Ireland

Today's Child 18
An orientation
Hanneke van Riel

The Twelve Senses 34
Jennifer Kennerk

Dominance.......................... 41
Connie Helms

The Care Group..................... 56
Referrals, assessments, therapies, and
academic support
Elizabeth Auer

The Extra Lesson................... 66
First grade readiness screening and
second grade assessment
*Maggie Scott, Elizabeth Auer and
Brigitta Witteveen*

The Art of Child Observation 75
Christof Wiechert

Points for Observation and Description.. 78
For the Child Study
David Mitchell

Movement in the Classroom 80
Morning circle and beyond
Amy Lloyd-Rippe

Verses and Movement 90
For the younger grades
Carol Mannion

The Movable Classroom 96
Jennifer Kershaw

Boys and Girls in Movement 102
Stereotypes and archetypes—balancing gender
needs in the elementary school movement
Jeff Tunkey

Development and Integration
of the Human Body 110
The role of the lower senses and primitive reflexes,
signs of motor dysfunction, and reflex retentions
Hannah Jackson

The Importance of Morning Circle 126
How to create a therapeutic movement circle
Hannah Jackson

Reading and Writing 130
Linda Atamian

Music, Gym, and the Pencil Grip 144
Jeff Tunkey

Therapeutic Aspects of Form Drawing . . . 147
An introduction
Hanneke van Riel

Children's Drawings 155
What they can tell us
Elizabeth Auer

Math 164
Introducing it the right way
Colleen O'Connors

Executive or Higher-Level Function 183
One aspect of understanding day-to-day thinking
Mary Jo Oresti

Incarnational Disrhythmia 187
Hypermotoric and inattentive challenges,
cumulative stress reaction, sensory overwhelm
issues, non-verbal disorders, oppositional defiance
Kim John Payne and Bonnie River

Imagination and Memory 209
Rich or poor?
Arthur Auer

Sleep on It 220
The most important activity of the
Waldorf school day
Arthur Auer

Therapies 231
Music, art, eurythmy, and Spacial Dynamics
*Juliane Weeks, Karine Munk-Finser,
Barbara Sim and Jane Swain*

Extra Support with Music 239
Singing and recorder
David Gable

Speaking and Listening 247
A teacher's greatest tools
Robyn Hewetson

Drama 260
Does Perseus have to hold Andromeda's hand?
Dennis Demanett

Imbue Yourself with the
Power of Imagination 272
Arthur Auer

Listen and You Will Hear 279
Meditation as a way of life
Patrice Maynard

Parent–Student–Teacher Triangle 289
Night and day: Waldorf education in practice
Regine Bruehl-Shemroske

Remedial Training Programs 301

Contributors 303

Acknowledgments 308

Foreword

Elizabeth Auer

The primary purpose of this book is to support classroom teachers in Waldorf schools as they navigate their way through the elementary years with the students in their care. Our aim is to provide a basic foundation for the understanding of children as they develop over the years from grades one through eight, socially as well as academically. All of the chapters are summaries that give the teacher an introduction to the many facets that underlie the basic tenets of Waldorf education.

The intention is to give the teachers a comprehensive compendium of many of the aspects involved in observing students from as many angles as possible and to provide them with ideas on how to address those who need special attention. It aims to cover many of the situations the teacher may encounter and includes an introduction to the children of today and the healing aspects of drama.

Many children come to the classroom feeling uncomfortable in their bodies for a variety of reasons. A class of students can be overwhelming for the teacher, especially the one newly trained or who has no prior training. Students in need exhibit a number of behaviors: They may fall off their chairs, run around the room, fidget, blurt out, or push other students around; they may be unable to focus, to work with crayons or pencils, or to recognize letters and put them together in words; they may have little sense for numbers and a host of other hindrances to learning.

This book will help the teacher recognize what the students in front of them are revealing about themselves, how to remediate the hindrances, and where to look for support. There are many exercises and ideas with which to help the students become better integrated into their physical bodies so that they can focus on the activity of learning. At the end of each chapter are references further exploration.

The chapters are written by various authors, who offer their own unique insights based on their experiences working with children. The material speaks directly from the heart to the heart, all with the underlying theme of love for children.

Two chapters are specifically for teachers as they grow in their understanding of children and themselves. To conclude the book are two very important essays on the parent/student/teacher triangle and the art of meditation.

Each child has his or her own unique path to tread. May this book be a support for both the teacher and the student as they form the best possible bond and make the journey together.

Child development
Constitutional types, the temperaments and school readiness

Helen-Ann Ireland

Our birth is but a sleep and a forgetting:
The Soul that rises with us, our life's Star,
Hath had elsewhere its setting,
And cometh from afar;
Not in entire forgetfulness,
And not in utter nakedness,
But trailing clouds of glory do we come
From God, who is our home:
Heaven lies about us in our infancy!
    – William Wordsworth

Human beings are a complex interplay of physical, soul, and spiritual components that develop in stages from birth to adulthood. These are the overarching aspects of every human being to take into consideration when we consider child development. The soul itself can be divided into the etheric and astral, which leads to the fourfold picture of the human being as indicated by Rudolf Steiner. The physical, etheric, astral, and ego of the child, as each incarnates into a human form, take on ever more advanced earthly consciousness while keeping the spirit self connected to an angel and other spiritual beings who guide every child in this lifetime. Included in the soul are the activities of thinking, feeling, and willing. These multiple dimensions of the developing human are what the kindergarten teacher addresses in the classroom with the young child so that each can begin to develop all capacities for use in adulthood. Waldorf class teachers address all of these aspects of the child's development throughout the eight-year journey.

The purpose of this chapter is to give a general overview of child development and school readiness as determined by the first grade assessment for Waldorf classrooms. Later chapters in this book will delve into other aspects of the school experience and what Waldorf schools do to meet the individual within the classroom—especially those children who appear to be struggling with one or another aspect of learning. There are multiple modalities from which to describe and observe a child's development that will be discussed in this book: the twelve senses, constitutional types, temperaments, fourfold and sevenfold aspects of the human as a soul-spiritual being, and the individuality that melds all of these elements into a precious and unique human being.

Every child is a spiritual being come to earth with a particular destiny. It is our job as educators to help develop all aspects and to remove hindrances that might prevent them from developing their full potential. There is great wisdom revealed in the development of the young human being that is largely invisible to the human eye; it can be perceived only by the trained observer using tools of reflection and meditation that open one up to intuition, imagination, and inspiration. All children are unique, yet go through stages of development in a similar time frame in preparation for formal learning in a school setting and eventually for life in the world.

In order to develop a picture of what is happening to the child, descriptions will be referring to the common archetypes or ideal scenarios. (Freidson, 2001) Within each of these elements, there are myriad variations depending on heredity, destiny, and environmental factors that each child brings to bear in this lifetime.

Birth to 7:
From crawling to walking

Underlying learning to walk there is an inner adjustment, an orientation of the young child. The equilibrium of the organism, with all its possibilities for movement, becomes related to the equilibrium and all the possibilities for movement of the whole universe, because the child stands within it.
— Rudolf Steiner, *The Child's Changing Consciousness* (p.30)

Physical development

The main job of the child from birth to around the age of 7 is to take hold of the physical being. Beginning with the physical development of the child, there are several aspects to consider: the physical growth involving height and weight with which we are all familiar; gross and fine motor skills that need to develop and reflexes to be integrated as the child takes control of physical musculature; and the four lower senses (of the twelve Steiner describes) that enable the child to feel comfortable in the world if each is fostered toward healthy development.

There is a series of primary reflexes that each baby and toddler possesses and uses to move to the next stage of development. Each reflex, once mastered, is integrated into the next reflex to become internalized and used at will by the young child. The child gradually takes hold of the physical body and develops gross and small motor skills through crawling, walking, speaking, and eventually grasping a writing tool—the pencil. Reflex development facilitates grasping, stretching, rolling over, bending over, crawling, sitting up, standing, and walking. In some children, the reflexes may not be fully developed and can contribute to unintended consequences in the classroom if the reflex is not under control. For example, the symmetrical tonic neck reflex contributes to healthy eye tracking and, if not integrated, can affect the child's ability to read.

Learning to walk is one of the most profound accomplishments in the first year of life. The act of standing and taking the first steps relates the child to the whole world of physics, of statics and dynamics in the universe, which the child feels when he lifts from the horizontal to the vertical on the earth. Standing allows the arms and hands to be free for other activities. The right-left contra-lateral movements, with arms swinging, stimulate both hemispheres of the brain for future learning.

The next profound accomplishment is the ability to speak. At first imitating sounds and babbling to make words, then sentences, then able to communicate with others, the child enters the world of human interaction in a new way. Children can now ascertain the thoughts of another person and respond. The rhythms of speech relate to the cadence of walking and freely-moving arms. Young children, being sensitive to all sounds, are especially sensitive to the human voice and the language that is imprinted upon them.

At the culmination of this stage of rapid physical development is the change of teeth. The losing of the milk teeth signals changes in the child's consciousness and abilities. Memory is now present and available, pictorial thinking arises, and primary reflexes are integrated so that the child has control over bodily movements, particularly with arms and hands.

The more subtle physical developments of the child are the twelve senses (which are detailed in the chapter on the twelve senses) and how they relate to the child's overall sense of self, physical boundaries, and communication with others. What we call the "lower senses" affect a child's ability to learn. These lower senses relate to Maslow's hierarchy of needs and are the foundational senses that enable the child to function. The inner senses of health, self-movement, balance, and touch are the building blocks for a child to feel ready to meet the wider world. In order to thrive, children must feel comfortable and safe in their bodies and in their environment.

Invisible to outer perception, and yet equally important, is the young child's organ growth. The young child's job until the change of teeth is to grow organs to 70% of their adult size. If we interfere with this process and ask the child to do intellectual work, the etheric forces needed for organ development get put to use prematurely in another direction. While there have been some preliminary medical studies tracking children's organ growth in relationship to height and weight, there has been no study conducted to see if early intellectualism affects organ growth in the child. There have been no studies to date relating organ growth to change of teeth, yet Steiner indicates that this is a true relationship.

Many things Steiner pointed out are slowly being proven in the scientific/medical world. Anyone who has either had children or works with children knows that something is different in the child after the loss of the first teeth, and we can trust these observations. The trunk and limbs elongate, and these changes signal a release of some of the etheric forces from the intense focus on building the physical body to be applied to other aspects of the child's development.

Since there is so much growth going on in the child, and since children absorb everything in their environment at this stage, it is important to consider the kinds of experiences to which the child is exposed. It is important for parents and teachers to think about what kinds of visual, auditory, tactile, and nutritional substances we want the child to experience in these formative years. Are they promoting healthy development, or are they shocking to the system of this most impressionable human being?

The child is a whole-body sense organ and is influenced by everything in the environment. This whole-body sense organ can be observed when a child is nursing and arms and legs move in reaction to receiving mother's milk or when a toddler has strong reactions to food. Taste buds are heightened and some foods can be offensive to them in the extreme. Gradually this condition of early childhood diminishes and the child can begin to filter out extreme sensations in the environment. The whole body as sense organ is also noticeable in the child's imitative powers. Young children learn through imitating what they see and hear around them.

Etheric development

(W)e recognize higher supersensible members of human nature that are as actual and essential as the outer physical body. ...The human being has the etheric body, which becomes part of his organism and remains united with the physical body throughout his entire life.
– Rudolf Steiner, *The Four Temperaments* (p.23)

The etheric body is the part of the human being that is most closely connected to the physical body. It is also called the "life-force" body because it regulates the circulatory system (heart and lungs), along with all other fluid and glandular systems in the body. When the child is going through the first seven-year period of rapid growth and development, the etheric forces are exclusively tied to physical development. It is only at about the age of 7 that some of these forces are freed up, so the child will be ready for the next stage of

development—learning in school. Once the etheric body has primarily completed its work on the physical body, some of the forces are then freed up and the child has new capacities for memory, imagination (picture forming), and thinking processes. Until this time, the child's memory is localized, meaning a physical stimulus is needed to remember something. Modern medical science confirms the rapid growth that occurs at this time in a child's life but does not acknowledge an etheric body per se.

Astral development

The third member of the human being we recognize in the bearer of all pleasure and suffering, joy and pain, instincts, impulses, passions, desires, and all that surges to and fro as sensations and ideas, even all concepts of what we designate as moral ideals.
– Rudolf Steiner (1908, p.24)

The astral body is where the feeling life of the child resides. The feelings in this context include emotions and also a sensing for goodness, beauty, and truth in the world. In order for the child to thrive, there must be a sense that the world is a good and safe place to be, filled with beauty, and that the surrounding adults are truthful and trustworthy.

In a young child, the emotional feelings may come in waves, over which the child has little control. The "terrible twos" are an example of this. Gradually, the child gains control of reactions to life events and can regulate them.

Socially, children gradually move from parallel play in the social realm to directed play with others, where they need to learn to take turns, have patience, and use their verbal skills to communicate with their teacher and friends. By the time the children are ready for school, they should be able to wait their turn without a fuss, communicate verbally to indicate their needs ("Teacher, I can't find my pencil."), and be in control of their emotional reactions so that they do not need to lash out at classmates. All the control they have mastered in the feeling and reaction realms is part of establishing what modern theorists call *executive function*.

Ego development

Where do we find what works on the child as a higher Self and which belongs to the child but doesn't enter his consciousness? Astonishing but true, it is the children's play, the meaningful, well carried out play of all children, that the higher Self works on. – Rudolf Steiner (GA 61)

The ego as defined by Steiner is the eternal spirit of the human being that returns to earth for many lifetimes. It is part of the higher Self described in the quote above and is only fully integrated in each human being at age 21. At various points of child development, there are mini-births of the ego. The first is between 2 and 3 years of age when the child first refers to himself as "I." This is the first awakening to the fact that they are independent, separate individuals. By the age of 7, the child has a clearer sense of self, which will continue to develop through puberty and beyond.

Constitutional types

Rudolf Steiner introduced the idea of *constitutional types* as another way of looking at child development. The constitutional types are described as polarities of the way the soul-spiritual nature of the child relates to the world while incarnating into a physical body. Steiner named the three polarities: small-headed/large-headed, fantasy-rich/fantasy-poor, and earthly/cosmic. In a nutshell and at the risk of making broad, sweeping generalizations, the following statements can give us a clue as to what Steiner meant by these polarities.

The small-headed/large-headed polarity corresponds to how the nerve-sense organ and the metabolic system interact in the child. This is the system that indicates how impressions of the earth through sight, sound, taste, and touch are functioning. The large-headed child could have the tendency to daydream, meaning that very little impression is being made or the digestive process is overly strong and devours the impressions, while the small-headed child may appear impulsive and anxious—a bundle of energy, because too many impressions are being made too quickly and can't be digested. (A fuller description of these types of children can be found in the next chapter.) These two polarities are marked by what Steiner calls the Seal of the "I" in the physical body. As Steiner describes it, the forces of the nerve-sense organ and metabolic system are not functioning in balance and produce the effects of either dreaminess or nervousness in the young child, making it hard for the ego or "I" to find a home.

The fantasy-rich/fantasy poor polarity corresponds with the metabolic system and how the child takes in the world through the life of ideas and memory. It is about remembering and forgetting. The fantasy-poor child may have difficulty recalling the story from the previous day, whereas the fantasy-rich child may have trouble letting go of an idea once it has entered her consciousness and may fixate on a thought. In this case Steiner describes the Seal of the "I" in the astral body where the astral forces predominate, allowing the child to experience the "I" and take hold of thought and memory.

The earthly/cosmic polarity is closely related to the soul life of children, particularly the feeling life where they tend to dwell in their relationship to the earth. The earthly child is in love with the physical earth, is very interested in the everyday functioning of earthly things, and tends toward showing keen interest in the way things work. This child might show an exceptional ability with machines and, in the classroom, could be the child who can take a clock apart and put it back together without any help from an adult. This child may also have a gift for movement, but is not so strong in the area of thinking through and analyzing what the teacher has brought to the lesson. The cosmic child, on the other hand, may have a great capacity for mobility in thinking and the ability to make connections through reflection on the great moral questions of the day. The child tends to excel in history, the study of literature and poetry, and have a deep understanding of the human condition. On the other had, the child may be the one in the class who cannot figure out how to put their compass back together in geometry class or who is always late with assignments. Steiner describes Seal of the "I" residing in the etheric body for these children. Their gifts need to be balanced between thought and action in the world.

Every child has some of the characteristics of each constitutional type, and some are more pronounced than others in a particular child. Our job as educators is to help bring balance in the children so they can function in a healthy way for their adult life. Most children will come into balance with all these tendencies through the Waldorf curriculum, which is specifically designed to mediate extremes of any kind through movement, particularly eurythmy, and the arts—both visual and musical: speech and poetry, storytelling, literature, and writing.

Helen-Ann Ireland

The temperaments

The temperament balances the eternal with the transitory. – Rudolf Steiner

Yet another element to consider when thinking about the riddle of the young child is the temperament. Steiner describes the four temperaments as a bridge between the way we can describe the human being in general and the way we describe the unique individual. In between there are groupings of characteristics into which human beings can fall that reveal a type of disposition or way of interacting with the world. These are broad and general categories with an infinite variety within each one, and each person has elements of all. Young children often have a more predominant trait that helps the teacher identify what they might need for balance in their being and therefore help the teacher bring specific things into the curriculum to meet the various needs of the children in the class.

The following material will present a sample of the general ideas relating to the sanguine, choleric, melancholic, and phlegmatic temperaments as described by Steiner. He asserts that the temperaments are at the intersection of the heredity of the child and the infinite spirit of each individual who incarnates over and over again—how our spiritual nature unites with our heredity. Each child brings a multitude of previous life experiences and karma. "There must be a bond, a connecting link, between the special individual human being and humanity in general, into which he is born through family, people, race." (Steiner, 1908/1980)

As we look at the temperaments, it is important to remember that each temperament corresponds to a predominance of one of the four aspects of the human being: physical, etheric, astral, or ego. Ego in Steiner's view means the eternal spiritual being that comes to reside in a human body, not to be mistaken for the ego as defined by Sigmund Freud. Steiner calls those unconscious forces in the human being that need to be redeemed or transformed through life experiences the lower ego—not to be confused with instincts that are dealing with the satisfaction of basic needs. For example, the lower ego tendency to selfishness is the opposite of the higher ego force of selflessness and empathy. When working with the temperaments in the classroom, it is critical to remember that we look at the assets of the temperaments and appeal to the different strengths of the children. We can bring them into balance gradually over time by appealing to their

gifts first and helping them overcome any one-sidedness through the curriculum.

Below are some brief indications about the temperaments as defined by Rudolf Steiner. The descriptions are of the child and describe which "body" predominates as the child matures, along with some hints about how to balance this as an adult.

The choleric – astral forces

When the ego of the individual has become so strong through its destiny that its forces are noticeably dominant in the fourfold nature and it dominates the other members, then the choleric temperament results.
– Rudolf Steiner (1908, p.27)

In the choleric child, the astral body predominates and the child may be filled with passion that can be overbearing at times. Over time and through the curriculum, the ego forces can be strengthened to rein in the unbridled astral forces. The choleric child may seem self-centered and have a strong presence in the classroom. This child will want to be assertive in every situation and can be aggressive with other children. But cholerics can also be strong leaders when their passions are channeled into doing good deeds for others or to help the teacher. We can reach the choleric child through engendering respect and esteem for the authority of the teacher and through presenting appropriate challenges for him in the classroom. The body-type of the choleric is somewhat condensed or compact due to the astral forces overruling the other growth forces in the body. The gait is firm, the features are formed, the gaze is clear, and opinions are definite! As the child grows into adulthood, the transformation that takes place is from the predominately astral to strong ego forces. Depending on the child's upbringing, these ego forces can be used for doing good deeds in the world.

The sanguine – etheric forces

If the person is especially subject to the influence of the forces of the astral body, then we attribute to him a sanguine temperament.
– Rudolf Steiner (1908, p.27)

The constant motion of the etheric body as it regulates the flow of blood and breath is predominant in the sanguine child. The constant flow of air through inhalation and exhalation and the blood circulation tend to create fleeting interest in these children—yet interest in everything that comes into their view. This child lives in the realm of thoughts and ideas, which, if untempered, can lead to chaos of images. These children can easily flit from idea to idea and not settle on anything. Think of the butterfly. This child is usually very social and can bring great delight into the classroom. They weave between children and can be the great social equalizers in the classroom. Working with this temperament means finding something that can sustain the child's interest over a period of time. For these children it is love for the teacher. The body-type of the sanguine is lithe, and they can move with ease, expressing the mobility of the etheric body. They usually have a joyful presence, and their gaze can be darting from object to object as one thing after another catches their interest.

The phlegmatic – physical forces

If the etheric or life-body acts excessively upon the person, the phlegmatic temperament arises.
– Rudolf Steiner (1908, p.27)

In the phlegmatic child, the physical body dominates her expression in the world. There may be a complacency that develops as the child feels inwardly all is well and nothing more needs to be done. This can result in a lack of interest in vigorous activity. These children like to eat and digest their food! They can be the calm anchors of the class because of their inner balance; what they lack in physical initiative they make up for in imbuing the classroom with their quiet presence. What they need most is a wide variety of playmates to engage their interest in the other, which in turn will arouse their interest in the world around them.

In body, the formative forces of ease give rise to a certain lack of differentiation, and so this child may appear less articulated in overall form. The gait may be shuffling and uncertain, the gaze watery, and the handshake somewhat limp. Over time, strengthening the subtle etheric forces, which generate the continual ebb and flow of breath and blood circulating, can help bring more inner activity and balance to this person as she reaches adulthood.

The melancholic – ego forces

And when the physical body with its laws is especially predominant in the human nature, so the spiritual essence of being is not able to overcome a certain hardness in the physical body, then we have to do with a melancholic temperament.
— Rudolf Steiner (1908, p.27)

The melancholic child may have the lower ego too strongly present. These children may feel that the body is too heavy for them to manage and this creates a disharmony inside their being. The melancholic may seem inflexible and very sensitive to pain and sorrow in the soul-life, which may become a source of inner grief or brooding. This inner struggle may become manifest in the sad countenance, more inward gaze, and dragging gait. If this child can be brought to see the struggles of someone else, deep compassion can arise. Stories with great suffering of a character are most therapeutic for melancholics, and they will most likely be the ones who are ready in an instant to bring the bandages or ice packs to an injured classmate.

All variety, beauty and all the richness of life are possible only through the temperaments.
— Rudolf Steiner (1908, p.39)

When working with the temperaments, it is important to think of them in relationship to constitutional types and all the other influences in the children's lives, both hereditary and environmental. Working with all aspects of each child helps us see all children in their totality and keeps us from making stereotypical judgments about them. These are the tools we can use as parents and teachers to better understand children as they develop and help us find the best way to help them come into balance. Our ultimate goal is to help the children develop interest in the other, find compassion, and fulfill the mission of the human being on the earth: to develop true human love.

The primary school-age child (7–14): School readiness

In order for a child to be ready for the formal instruction that comes in first grade, children need to have met several developmental milestones in their physical, cognitive and emotional evolution. They must be in control of their bodies, have developed small motor skills, and be ready to interact with classmates in the school setting.

They shift from learning through imitation to learning through auditory instruction from the parents and teachers.

The two outward physical indicators we look for in a child ready for first grade are the change of teeth and elongated limbs. In an entire lifetime, the most physical growth takes place in the child between birth and the change of teeth. The young child's task is to develop physically to the point of controlling the body. The body elongates and grows more coordinated, and the limbs come under the control of the child. The change of teeth indicates that a certain physical stage of development has ended and the child is ready to take up new tasks that do not involve as much rapid physical growth. It is as if the losing of baby teeth signals a new stage of development, which will continue for several years. Children begin losing their baby teeth at slightly different times, but usually between 5 and 6 years old, there is a noticeable difference in the child's physical appearance, including more defined facial features. After the change of teeth, there will be physical growth spurts and brain growth spurts alternating from now until puberty. (Coulter 2005)

The lower senses of touch, balance, self-movement, and well-being should be established. This includes a robust sense of health and the strength to manage a full day of school. The senses of touch, balance, and self-movement are considered in that the child is able to control bodily functions and musculature, has mastered a level of spatial awareness, and senses personal boundaries. Spatial awareness applies to the visual as well as body awareness. The child must be able to discriminate between similar shapes in order to form letters and to place them on the page in a manner that can be discerned by another person for reading.

The first grader must be able to follow rhythmic patterns, learn songs, and recite poetry with gestures and movement. The child should be able to jump rope, hop, skip, gallop, stand on one leg, and throw and catch a ball. The child must also be able to stop without falling or bumping into another child. In fine motor skills, the pencil grip should be developed so that the child can hold a pencil or paintbrush for writing, drawing, and painting.

The first grader should be able to accept the authority of the teachers, look to them for direction, and accept redirection if needed. The first grader needs to be able to concentrate on a task for ten to fifteen minutes, hear and follow oral directions, listen for ten to fifteen minutes to a story, and be able to recall the story orally when asked by the teacher the next day. The first grader should have a willingness to learn and be able to cooperate with teachers and classmates, follow classroom rules, help with chores, be respectful of others, and care for their belongings. These are all signs that the child is "school ready."

Every child is different and some or all of these indicators may not be there when the child is chronologically ready for first grade. In American schools, most children start school at age 6, which is actually earlier than what Steiner recommended. He indicated that, for the healthy physical development to come to its first stage of completion, seven years are needed. So we are already moving the children into formal learning before it is advisable. Hence many first grade teachers introduce letters and numbers slowly and in picture form so that the child's imagination is stimulated and there is a minimum of intellectual strain on the child. American children seem physically ready for this transition at 6 years of age, and therefore it is especially important to make sure that strong daily rhythms are followed to foster their sense of health and well-being, that learning comes through pictures and living concepts to stimulate the imagination, and that there is plenty of movement, music, poetry, games, and rich language to augment the lessons.

REFERENCES

Berk, L. & Meyers, A. (2016). *Infants and children: Prenatal through middle childhood*, Eighth edition. New York: Pearson.

Coulter, D.J. (2005). "What's up: Important brain rights of passage and how to support them in the classroom." Article from the author. http://www.originalmindbrilliance.com

Diamond, A. (2016). Executive function information, http://www.devcogneuro.com/research.html.

Freidson, A. (2001). *Professionalism: The third logic.* Chicago: University of Chicago Press.

Gesell Test of School Readiness (1980). New Haven, CT: Gesell Institute of Human Development.

Ginsburg, I.H. (1982). *Jean Piaget and Rudolf Steiner: Stages of child development and implications for pedagogy*. Teachers College Record, 84(2), 327–337.

Glöckler, M. & Goebel, W. (1990). *A guide to child health*, English translation. Edinburgh: Floris Books.

Goddard, S. (1996). *A teacher's window into a child's mind.* Eugene, OR: Fern Ridge Press.

Healy, J. (1999). *Endangered minds: Why children don't think and what we can do about it.* New York: Simon and Schuster.

Maslow, A.H. (1970a). *Motivation and personality.* New York: Harper & Row.

_____. (1970b). *Religions, values, and peak experiences*. New York: Penguin.

McLeod, S.A. (2014). *Maslow's hierarchy of needs.* Retrieved from www.simplypsychology.org/maslow.html

Ogletree, E.J. (1985). *An interpretation of Rudolf Steiner's theory of child development and school readiness.* https://eric.ed.gov/?id=ED259827

Steiner, R. (1923/1988). *The child's changing consciousness and Waldorf education.* Great Barrington, MA: Anthroposophic Press.

_____. (1924/1998). *Education for special needs: The curative education course.* Forest Row, UK: Rudolf Steiner Press.

_____. (1908/1980). *The four temperaments.* Great Barrington, MA: Anthroposophic Press.

_____. (1924/1982). *The kingdom of childhood.* Forest Row, UK: Rudolf Steiner Press.

_____. (1909–11/1999). *A psychology of body, soul, and spirit: Anthroposophy, psychosophy, and pneumatosophy.* Great Barrington, MA: Anthroposophic Press.

_____. (1912/1995). *Self education in the light of spiritual science.* (GA 61).

Today's child
An orientation

Hanneke van Riel

This child has come down to you from the spiritual world. You must solve his riddle, day by day, hour by hour. – Rudolf Steiner

Approaching the riddle

Rudolf Steiner presented this thought of the child as "a riddle" on different occasions in his many lectures to teachers. With these simple words Steiner brings our attention from the onset to the sacredness of human life, and to our task as educators.

All educators will have had an encounter with a riddle-child. Parents and professional caretakers alike will have heartwarming and heartbreaking stories to tell of their successes and their failures working with these children. At times the teacher might raise her eyebrows in puzzlement, or even throw up her hands in exasperation: How can this riddle be solved? Who is this child? What can I do with this child?

Teachers realize they have to solve the riddle in order to develop a relationship. They know that without a loving relationship, there will be no progress. That is easy to agree on. But how to go about building a relationship with a child that is difficult to understand is not so easy.

The intent of this chapter is beautifully expressed in these words, "My teachings are a finger pointing at the moon. Do not get caught in thinking that the finger is the moon. It is because

of the finger that you can see the moon." (Zen Inspiration)

The teacher has to "study the moon" herself. There is no How-to-Build-a-Relationship handbook. Teacher and child will have to find their way to each other.

Solving a riddle

What does it take to solve a riddle? In a riddle the facts often don't seem to add up. Yet this does not discourage the puzzler. She carries on, trusting that the puzzle can be solved; moreover, she has a suspicion that the solution might be right in front of her. She creatively looks for new ways to work with the given facts in anticipation of great relief for the moment when the puzzle finally comes together: "Now I see!"

Putting the pieces of the puzzle together is easy when it concerns a "knock-knock" riddle or a jigsaw puzzle, but how is it for understanding the riddle in the child? The facts will be more bewildering and confusing, potentially misleading the teacher more and more. In the case of a riddle-child, the teacher is at risk of getting discouraged and giving up. Somehow that creative problem-solving mindset is more difficult to access when it concerns solving the mysterious riddle of a child.

When working to solve a puzzle or a riddle, it is accepted that the solution will "trick" us. The game is designed to take us by surprise. The gamer signs on for that. When faced with a child with puzzling behavior, however, this trickery may rouse reactive feelings in the teacher such as irritation, frustration, exhaustion, doubt, or helplessness. Disorienting feelings like that mask a clear view of the clues that could bring the teacher closer to an understanding. When they go unchecked these negative feelings will settle in the dark recesses of the teacher's soul and color and distort her observations. When that happens, out goes the interest in solving the puzzle, and sometimes along with that, sadly, out goes the child.

So long as the teacher meets the situation with any kind of bias, so long as it can arouse irritation or excitement—so long will he remain incapable of making any real progress with the child. Not until the point has been reached where such a phenomenon becomes an objective picture and can be taken with a certain calm and composure as an objective picture for which nothing but compassion is felt—not until then is the necessary mood of soul present in the astral body of the teacher. Once this has come about, the teacher is there by the side of the child in a true relation and will do all else that is needful more or less rightly.
– Rudolf Steiner (1981, p.41)

When irritation casts a shadow over genuine loving interest in the child, progress is highly unlikely. Teachers and parents know this, but that does not make the feelings go away. No one but the teacher herself can escape this destructive cycle. The teacher must take herself in hand by engaging in the practice of self-reflection to gain control over her reactive feelings. Rudolf Steiner spoke with urgency about this aspect of the soul life of the teacher in his regular education courses, but he put even more emphasis on this in his lectures to the educators who had taken up the work with children with differences. Unchecked negative feelings create a distance between teacher and child. With the child distanced, teacher and child will remain outside of relationship.

The healing journey

Necessary preparations

To make progress with a child, the caregiver must temper the logical mind that wants to analyze, categorize, and objectify the child. Patience is called for. Knowing, understanding, and compassion need time to develop and ripen. Evelyn Keller writes in her biography of the Nobel Prize-winning scientist Barbara McClintock about how Barbara was able to make her discoveries in the field of genetics: Over and over she tells us one must have the patience to look, the patience to "hear what the material has to say to you," the openness to "let it come to you." (Keller, 1983, p.198) McClintock was a scientist working with corn. How is this for a teacher working with children?

Education is the art of "hearing what the child has to say to you"; it is the art of "bringing out" the child. In order to bring out, or to draw forth the child, one must first enter into a relationship. Again, there is no manual with step-by-step instructions for how to do that. It is the inner attitude of the educator that will make all the difference. If we approach the child with the inner attitude to "fix" him, it implies the assumption that he is broken. But we are not in the human repair business. The child is whole, the child has integrity, the child is unique, the child is part of life, and life is a sacred mystery. Educators who can make this thought their point of departure for the journey with the child will have a healing influence. In an online article, Dr. Naomi Remen expressed it like this: "When we see the wholeness in another, we strengthen it. They then may be able to see it for themselves for the first time." With this preparation completed, the gate to the Path of Healing is open.

Priming our vision for the journey

There is more the successful "teacher-puzzler" needs to know. The teacher needs to have a strategy for how to keep her eyes open to see what's essential. Preconceived judgments will block the view, and the child will continue to elude us. On this journey toward the mystery, the teacher must leave conventional ideas behind and learn how to perceive with the heart, "for only with the heart one can see rightly." (Saint-Exupéry 1943, p.70) With the heart open, the teacher is ready to embark on a healing journey.

Arriving at the first destination

If as teachers we can enter into the child's being, then, out of our knowledge of the child, there will spring up a perception of the way in which we must act. – Rudolf Steiner (1982, p.8)

Diagnosis is the first landing place on this part of the journey. Diagnosis means: to know thoroughly, to recognize something for what it is. Heart-warmed interest and careful observation will guide the teacher to knowledge, knowledge will bring understanding, and understanding will bring the teacher to the point of diagnosis. He is now in a good place to begin the next part of the healing journey together with the child. A relationship has been forged.

The healing power in being recognized

The diagnosis announces itself with a joyous: NOW I see you! As in hide-and-seek, the child has been called out from hiding. Do you remember playing hide-and-seek? I remember one such game I played outside, in the dark, on a warm summer night. I hid myself well, but upon realizing how well I was hidden, I began to lose my nerve. Here I was, hidden in the dark, without a clue for the child who had to find me. Anxious thoughts took over. "What if 'It' will give up looking for me? What if they forget about me? What if I am not found!?" This fear alone was enough to start acting out!! I gave myself away.

So it is with the special child in the classroom who feels "unseen." She will act out to make sure that the teacher will not forget about her; her acting out is a plea to the teacher to find her out, to see her, to recognize her.

In the hide-and-seek game the existential human need to be recognized is acted out—by your recognition of me, I exist. This basic need makes itself known at a very early age. Think of one of the first games babies love to play, the game of peek-a-boo. How delighted baby is to be seen, and then to disappear again. How happy she is to hear over and over again, "I see you!" By being recognized, the baby's existence is affirmed. In this acknowledgment lies the mystery and magic of love between educator and child.

It is not only in children's games that the human need for recognition is evident. The often-quoted Zulu greeting, *Sawubona*, meaning "I see you" comes to mind. The response is *Ngikhona*: "Now I am here." Because you see me, I exist. This simple greeting is so moving because it expresses in a few words the all-important human respect and dignity implied in recognition.

Additional tips for solving riddles

All skilled puzzlers are knowledgeable; they know lots of facts. Teachers need to know the human being. They need to know about normal and abnormal human development. Rudolf Steiner has given Waldorf teachers a wealth of knowledge and insight. Throughout their careers they need to continue to build their knowledge by observing the children in their care.

Puzzle enthusiasts solve puzzles all the time; they have developed a special brain muscle for this work. With a trained puzzle-solving mindset, it gets easier. Teachers too can train their "puzzle muscle" when it comes to children. With training and practice, pedagogical intuition will develop and guide the teacher more easily toward insight into the child.

Successful puzzlers develop a strategy. What is the strategy for solving the riddle in the child? Children present such a wide-ranging variety of symptoms, that it can be bewildering. For example,

— If the child is restless, cannot sit still, and cannot focus on given tasks, does it follow that he has ADHD (Attention Deficit Hyperactivity Disorder), or could these symptoms result from living in a highly stressful situation?

— If a child is inattentive and dreamy, not really present, does it follow that she has ADD (Attention Deficit Disorder without the Hyperactive component), or could it be that she is suffering from petit mal seizures? (Healy 2011, p.90)

— If a child does not cooperate and listens poorly, does it follow that he has Oppositional Defiant Disorder (ODD), or could it be that he is hearing or language impaired? Could he be a child on the autism spectrum who tries hard to comply, but does not comprehend our language?

There are many conditions that co-occur and share symptoms. Jumping to conclusions before all aspects of the child's being have been carefully examined can lead to misdiagnosis. The key sometimes lies hidden in the least conspicuous fact.

Orientation

How do we recognize the essential nature of a child? The child is not a static entity: she is always in the process of growing and becoming. The symptoms are sometimes better or sometimes worse depending on age or the environment of the child, or even the time of day. A child may be easy-going in one teacher's care, and a little tyrant in another's. Something in the child though, is always there. For example, in the case of a hypersensitive "thin-skinned," child we see an initial panic reaction to a new challenge: "I can't do it!" She wants to do it, and she will eventually do it, but inwardly she cringes with discomfort. New situations are met by initial withdrawal. Even though the symptoms may ease in the company of a trusted teacher, the condition is always there. Her sensitivity is the essence, the constitution of this child, the vessel for her soul life.

Normal variations and extreme cases

Steiner opened his first lecture to doctors and curative teachers (1924) with the comment that studying extreme cases can provide insight in the normal variations. "What is living in the normal child is more plainly expressed in the abnormal child." (Steiner 1981, p.15)

Let's explore this with our example of the thin-skinned child. The extreme manifestation of the thin-skinned nature can be seen in autism. The thin-skinned child's emphatic, imagined, "I can't do it!" becomes true in the child with autism: he absolutely cannot do it. The child with autism lives in a state of constant pathological withdrawal. In the same way that we would not tell a child with autism, "You can do it! Don't make a fuss, just give it a try," we should not tell the thin-skinned child. "I know you can do it! Stop fussing, just do it, you'll be fine!" Both children will respond in panic mode. The thin-skinned child may throw a tantrum, the child with autism may have a total meltdown. I have seen both variants: the furiously stomping, screaming thin-skinned child responding to an ill-prepared transition, and the child with autism experiencing a total neurological breakdown* because of a simple change in the rules of a game. Both children were having difficulty adjusting to a change. In essence the same event, they differ only in degree.

If the teacher punishes either child for his misbehavior, the relationship will be in serious jeopardy. The only person in this situation that should be reprimanded is the teacher. And yes, there will be consequences for the misguided teacher! She will have a very difficult-to-handle child on her hands. This situation could have been easily avoided with pedagogical tact, with understanding. If the teacher had known the child from the inside out, she would have felt the panic reaction of the child within herself. She would have responded with a protecting gesture rather than further challenging her. Clearly, punishment is completely counter-productive.

Rudolf Steiner provided a valuable orientation by presenting opposing pathologies on either side of a continuum. Normal is the center area where the extremes are toned down and more or less kept in balance. If we know in which pathological direction the disturbance lies, we are well positioned to come to understanding.

In the opposite direction of the thin-skinned condition lies the condition of the thick-skinned child with epilepsy at the far end of the line. We will discuss this condition later in the chapter.

Exploring the opposites

The orientation explored here is based on the work of the late Dr. Holtzapfel. His book, *Children's Destinies* (2006), is a treasure trove of pedagogical insight. In the last chapter of this book Holtzapfel presents his thoughts on finding an orientation by placing the human being in relationship to space: what is above us and below us, what lives inside us and what exists outside us, our space to the left and to the right, and the space in front and behind us. What follows is an exploration of the first three of these polarities.

Above and below

The child comes to us from above, from non-physical realms, and needs to connect his soul-spiritual reality with the physical reality of earth. This is literally a balancing act and the first step of this process is mastered as he learns to stand up.

Above is the world of concepts, of thought, of imagination. Below is the world of sense perceptions, of doing. How well the child is able to bring these two spheres into harmony determines how awake he will be, how well he will be able to mediate his attention between thought and action.

Right away one can see two types of children emerging: the more dreamy types who like to think and are less inclined toward action, and the more sensory-seeking types who act impulsively without much forethought.

---

*Or neurological storm, a rage attack completely beyond the control of the child.

Extreme manifestations

Pathology on this continuum is reflected in the physical body as microcephaly and hydrocephaly: small-headedness and large-headedness. The shape and size of the head reflect whether the child is more strongly oriented to the upper pole or to the lower pole. In the beautifully-shaped domed forehead of the hydrocephalic child one perceives something cosmic, something regal. Significantly less developed limbs and narrower, longer hands and feet accentuate this impression. In its full-blown manifestation, children with hydrocephalus are unable to move due to stunted limb development and the size of the head.

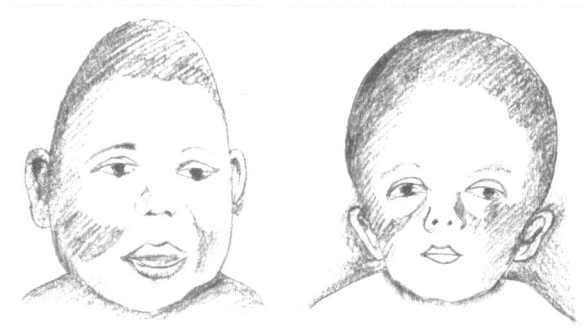

On the opposite side one can see the pull to earth in the more strongly-developed lower part of the skull of the child with microcephaly. Everything in this child's physical organism is directed toward the earth. Well-developed limbs with strong broad hands, big feet. One of the symptoms is increased movement of the arms and legs.

Teachers may never see the full manifestations of these polarities. Hydrocephalus is treated surgically by placing a shunt to normalize the circulatory process of the brain fluids. Microcephalus was rare until a recent spate of children were born with this condition across the Americas. The cause of this increase is still under investigation at the time of this writing. In normal children we see tendencies in either direction. Both types will have problems with attention. Each type will need a different approach.

The large-headed child

The attention of the large-headed child is inclined toward thinking, toward dreaming away; she is reluctant to move. Maybe you have seen her at the edge of the ballfield telling other players what to do, developing brilliant strategies but not participating in the running around. Or maybe you have worked with a child who is strong in mental math activities, but who fails the sums he has to do on paper. The activity of writing it down seems redundant to him. He will resist, and get himself in trouble with the teacher. Telling him he simply must do as he is told, will worsen the situation. In his mind it is the teacher who is wrong by telling him to do something as tedious and unnecessary as writing down the work already completed in the head. The cosmic, princely nature of the large-headed child feels this like an insult. The child is frustrated to comply with an order that in his experience is as absurd as being told to "dig a garden with our noses." (Holtzapfel 2006, p.42) The situation can easily escalate in a confrontation between teacher and child. The key to avoid that is to meet the child where he is. The teacher is well-advised to honor the princely nature in the child. With tactful acceptance of that, the child can be invited to come into motion.

A full child study should always include a study of the biography of a child. It will add pieces to the puzzle that may complete the emerging picture. Late birth, a reluctance to grow up, early speech, and late walking are common themes in the biography.

This type of child in the mainstream literature may be labeled ADD. However there is no deficit of attention. The child is so busy concentrating on his own thoughts that he resists being interrupted by the teacher. No wonder these children are often irritable.

Dr. Weihs, in his book *Children in Need of Special Care* (1979), refers to these children as "children of the morning." They seem to be "just waking up" from their dreams, all day long.

The small-headed child

These children are action-oriented, so much so that they get into all kinds of mishaps, and are used to hearing: "Think before you act!" This is not helpful because they think with their hands and feet. Action and thinking are completely bound up. One of my students could not sit down to listen to a story; he would have to get up and act it out, all the while enthusiastically commenting on the adventures of the hero. This lack of impulse control will land these children often in a time-out to think about their actions. In the worst case, they will be sent to the hall to do their thinking by themselves. By isolating the child, unfortunately, the teacher has created the next problem. The child will be doing everything he can to get back into the classroom. All the action is now happening by the classroom door. This is even more distracting than having him in the classroom!

Isolating the child from the group is not effective, and not just because the child will try to come back into the room. The punishment of isolation is always severe, but this is especially true for these overactive children. What drives them to be so actively involved with everyone and everything is a powerful force of love for all things earthly. Rejection is his greatest fear. Their very sad plight is that they often get punished for loving too much.

These children are happy to serve and they will jump at the occasion to do something for the teacher or the class. To be invited to help is an affirmation of love. The teacher would do well to have preplanned tasks for this child. Morning chores are done in good cheer; being the teacher's helper is a joy. A page of sums to solve will not frustrate this child.

In the biography study the mother may report that her child "could not wait to be born" and was already very active in the womb. From an early age the child learned by doing, and acted like an enthusiastic explorer of his world with a great eye for observing detail. Speech may have come in more slowly, but walking was accomplished early on.

In the mainstream literature these children are diagnosed with ADHD. "Deficit" again, is a misnomer. The child has too much attention. He is too awake. Symptoms can be so severe that treatment with psychoactive medications is deemed necessary. The constant fidgeting, the impulsiveness, the lack of organization, can frustrate the teacher to the point where she cannot see a way forward with the child.

If observations of behavior line up with physical characteristics and biography information, one can be fairly certain that clues to understanding the child can be found on this continuum of above and below. If there is very poor agreement between the facts, the attention differences may be secondary to other imbalances in the child or in the child's environment.

Some facts concerning children with attention differences

- ADD and ADHD are also referred to as Executive Dysfunction.
- It takes 28 years for the executive brain (pre-frontal lobe) to develop.
- The Centers for Disease Control and Prevention estimates the occurrence of attention disorders to be at 11% of children from 4–17 years old. This represents 6.4 million children.
- Boys (13.2 %) are more likely to receive this diagnosis than girls (5.6 %).
- Preferred treatment in the mainstream is a combination of the drugs Ritalin (methylphenidate) or Adderall (amphetamine) and behavioral or cognitive therapy.
- According to the United Nations, the United States produces and consumes about 85% of the world's methylphenidate (Ritalin).
- Drugs administered to control ADHD have high potential for abuse and may lead to severe psychological and physical dependence.
- Psychoactive drugs are not recommended for children under 6 years old, yet prescriptions are given to children as young as two years old. An estimated 10,000 toddlers are taking these drugs.
- The causes of ADHD are not well understood.

What the teacher can do for the child with ADHD

It is important to remember that these children do not come to school with the intent to disrupt the classroom or to make life difficult for the teacher. They are not oppositional; to the contrary, they

come from a place of sympathy with the world. The problem is that they are not able to control their behavior. They are at the mercy of their condition. The teacher must accept them for who they are. They will not fit the profile of the "perfect" Waldorf student. If teachers can move from wanting to control the hyperactive child's behavior to true acceptance and an honoring of his unique being, there is hope for the child. Köhler (2001) asks, "How do you expect to produce patience and reverence if you are upset all day long and run around with the feeling that your child ought to be different than he or she is?" (p.40) Teachers will have to let go of the idea that their reputation is endangered when a child behaves out of line. (Köhler 2001) Maintaining humor about the often impossible situations created by the child is the lifeline.

Teachers should remember that punishment is completely ineffective. Of course the ADHD child breaks the rules all the time, because the problem is an inability to remember the rules.

To address the disorganization problem that both types struggle with, telling a child to get organized will not have the desired effect. They are willing, but they simply have no idea how to do that! Teachers must patiently show how to get organized. Providing a list of steps can be helpful (if the list is secured somewhere on the desk, because the child will undoubtedly lose the list within the first five minutes).

The child with ADHD lacks the ability to self-monitor her behavior. Inner speech, the tool for self-monitoring, is poorly developed. It will help her if the adult models planning by talking through all the steps he plans to take, or talks about what he is doing. Talking with the child about the day gone by and planning the next day together, will be helpful. "Conversation builds the Executive brain." (Healy 1999, p.182)

Köhler (2001) writes extensively about the sense of life in light of hyperactivity in his book *Working with Anxious, Nervous, and Depressed Children*. He posits that it is an injured life sense that causes the need to constantly be in movement. His recommendation for treatment is to nurture the sense of life: Food, warmth, sleep, and touch will bring the comfort to the body the child craves.

What else can we do?

Large-headed children need to be more aware of the hands and feet. Simple blindfold games in which the child has to recognize objects with the hands are helpful. Origami is great for the older children. Thought is brought right into the fingertips as a complicated design is created. Writing with a pencil held between the toes is good, but a strong relationship between teacher and child is imperative before this should be attempted.

This child learns by grasping the concepts first. The more we can imbue his heady ideas with feeling, the more success we will have to get this child into motion. Subjects like history and geography for example must be presented with real feeling by the teacher. Balance between thinking and willing for this child is brought about by moving the activity in the head through the feeling realm to the will.

For the small-headed child learning goes in the opposite direction. Their learning begins in the limbs. When the child does something over and over again, the head eventually wakes up. Repetition and practice do not bore these children. They learn by doing. If the teacher can imbue activity with beauty and purpose, he has served this child well.

The child in relationship to the environment

The relationship of inner to outer develops during the second and third years of life when speech and language are developing. The child engages in dialogue with the world. This allows the experience of selfhood. The child will refer to herself at some point during this time as "I." If the child does not succeed in achieving a healthy balance in this sphere, she will suffer emotional adjustment problems.

There is a contracting and expanding nature to this sphere: She can be locked within herself, or she can lose herself by flowing too far out. Both are beyond the control of the child.

Extreme manifestations

Steiner placed hysteria and epilepsy on opposite ends of this continuum. In his discussions of children, he is not using the diagnosis of hysteria as it was commonly used in his time (a condition of emotional excess in women). Rather he used it as the diagnosis of children who experienced uncontrollable outbursts of emotion. In this context, hysteria describes a child who is so hypersensitive that interaction with the world is very painful and paralyzes the child's ability to act.

In epilepsy the imprisonment of the self becomes unbearable, and the soul is released in a fit, or an epileptic seizure.

Tendencies in either direction on this continuum are referred to as "thin-skinned" or "thick-skinned" constitutions. It is the skin that forms the boundary between our inner life and the world. The child's emotional health is determined by how comfortable he feels in his skin.

The thin-skinned child

Rudolf Steiner's description of the constitution of these children in *The Curative Education* lecture cycle (1981) is gripping. He speaks of a "soreness of soul." Contact with the external world is as painful as "touching something with a grazed hand." (Steiner 1981, p.76) It hurts! It is no surprise then to see how the child reacts with hypersensitivity to the world. We can see the child writhing in discomfort just by thinking of having to act in the world.

Thin-skinnedness is a soul condition, but one can sometimes see a physical reflection of that in the delicate skin of these children. Everything in these children expresses a flowing out. Often the children sweat easily, and have moist hands. The mother may report a problem with bed wetting, and a problem with falling asleep or nightmares. Falling asleep is a huge letting-go of the self. They wear their clothing loose, and their hair flowing out. To find reprieve, these children love to crawl into small, enclosed spaces. Crawling under the blankets or hiding under the desk in the classroom provides coverage, to compensate for the painful exposure they experience.

This constitution can be understood by picturing oneself being in a moist tropical forest. The heat, the humidity, the fullness of the forest can leave us feeling out of control. It is too much all around; we feel lost in this overwhelming world! The pressure could lead to a panic attack, at the least a breaking out in a sweat! The irritability one would feel is similar to the irritability we see in the thin-skinned child.

Because of the strong inner connection with what surrounds them, these children are very perceptive in detecting subtle soul moods of others. This does not mean that they are sympathetic toward others. We can see a contradiction in these children of a great sensitivity for what comes to them on the one hand, and a lack of sensitivity when it concerns understanding the effect they have on others, on the other hand. A frown, a tone of voice, or the smallest criticism from the caretaker can set off a potent emotional reaction. Thin-skinned children have this response also to their own self-expression. They feel they have left a part of themselves "out there" without protection. This is why it can be so difficult for them to get over the initial "I can't do it" response to a task, no matter how accomplished the child is at performing this task. Something as simple as starting a new drawing on a blank page can make the child physically uncomfortable, feel a panic reaction entirely unrelated to the task. The panic, however, is real. The teacher must make this child feel that he is not alone, that she is right beside him. Holding his hand to guide the beginning of the drawing, starting the drawing for him, putting her hand on his shoulder, will be a tremendous help. By doing it together the child no longer feels so exposed. Once the picture is started in this way, the fear usually subsides. So it is with all tasks. This child must feel patience, warmth, and companionship in the teacher. Over time, trust will build. Symptoms are likely to decrease the longer the child is in the same environment. Change will undo her again. Preparing the child for the new day can prevent many hysterical outbursts.

Skin care, massage, dress, tying up the hair, warmth, comfort, and holding the child are helpful suggestions for the parents. The child's sense of touch needs to be nourished. Providing a space for the child to calm down after a panic attack is also very helpful.

The thick-skinned child

These children are less sensitive to their surroundings. They appear quite unaware of others. They resemble in some ways the kind of person sitting next to you on a crowded airplane without consideration of where his chair ends and yours begins.

The astral body of the thick-skinned child is too strongly encapsulated by his physical bodies. He has trouble relating to the external world. An unexpected event, a new situation, or a surprise can help him to come out of himself. The child feels that as a relief from his soul imprisonment.

When left to his own devices for too long, he may act aggressively as a result of feeling cut off. This aggression is directed toward the self more than to others; it has a self-destructive quality. When teachers address the behaviors of these children, they need to use utmost care to avoid condemning the child. Some children may act like the class clown. Silliness can release the imprisoned soul. This requires a great deal of understanding from the teacher. The teacher can avoid most problems by calling on the child frequently to keep him engaged.

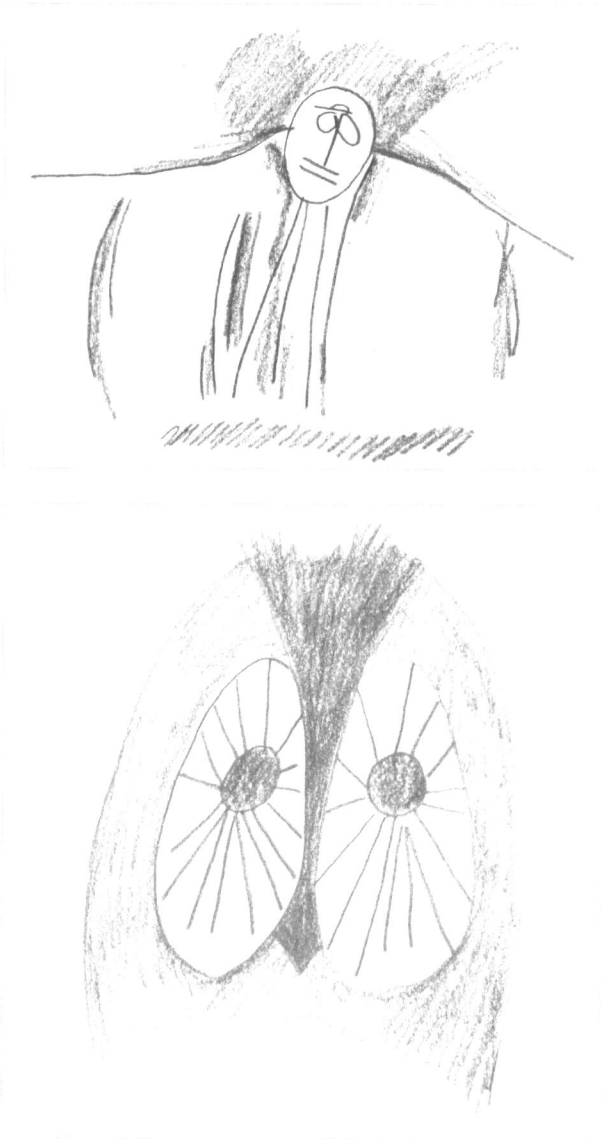

Physical activity will help this child, especially activity addressing balance issues. A small trampoline in the classroom will be much enjoyed, and it helps to keep him, literally and figuratively, in balance.

The two children's drawings above illustrate the contrasting soul conditions dramatically. The top drawing, done by a thin-skinned child, shows the flowing out into the environment; the arms stretch out as if to feel the environment. The drawing below expresses the enclosed, imprisoned experience of the soul life of the thick-skinned child.

The child with autism

Children with this condition experience a distorted relationship between self and the environment. The innermost aspect of the self, the ego, cannot effectively regulate the development of the child in all areas of his being: social/emotional, physical, or intellectual. The child with autism does not recognize himself or a fellow human being as an independent ego being. This is apparent in the fact that he does not use the word "I" appropriately, and confuses "I" and "you."

These children perceive the world, but cannot perceive meaning in what they experience. The ability to synthesize their perceptions is lacking: they lack "central coherence." The world is a frightening place of meaningless, unconnected, random, and unpredictable events and objects. The most unpredictable objects are other human beings. He will try to organize this chaotic world by putting objects into order with a preference for geometric shapes or patterns that will be obsessively repeated. Any change to this ordering will bring great distress. This obsessive need for sameness can be understood if we imagine ourselves living in a world without coherence.

For a child with autism, all human interaction is impeded. Eye contact is avoided, facial expression is flat, the voice has a mechanical monotone quality, and language expression and comprehension is limited. The child does not smile, which is a barrier to contact beginning very early in his life. These children may be affectionate, but it appears to be self-serving. They cannot interpret what is communicated with voice inflection, with facial expression, with gesture, or what is said between the lines. In severe cases children with autism display a speech pattern called echolalic speech. They merely echo the speech of others; it is devoid of meaning.

Another most devastating interaction breakdown for the child with autism is his lack of ability to live into another person's mind. He cannot put himself in someone else's position. They are left communicating at the world, not with the world. They live in a world of their own, sometimes completely isolated from the world we know.

Other than echolalia, these children do not imitate. This, along with the absence of pretend play, is an early indicator. Children with autism have impaired mirror neurons. These neurons make us unconsciously mimic each other during interaction: Your smile is reflected in the mirror of your listener, who cannot help but smile also. These neurons were identified only in 1990, and may be the basis of all learning. They make it possible for us to be tuned in to one another. (Healy 2011)

These children, like the thin-skinned children, have a fear of contact with the world. They learn to say "No!" and "Yes" may never be used. I worked with a little girl whose entire conversation consisted of a long string of no: "No, no, no, no, no, no, …" repeated rapidly, over and over again. After two years of working with her, I never once heard her say "Yes."

Autism has increased to epidemic levels. The Center for Disease Control and Prevention currently cites a 1–68 ratio for autism in children, and the number of affected children is increasing every year by more than 10%.

There is no cause and no cure for autism that everyone can agree on. Autism is a pervasive lifelong affliction.

The child with Asperger syndrome

Autism is a spectrum disorder with symptoms ranging from very severe to mild. Children with Asperger's are functioning on the higher end of this spectrum. They will attend regular classes at school and find work and a meaningful life after school. Their cognitive abilities have a range similar to normal children: from highly intelligent to intellectually challenged. They may have additional problems like all other children: attention issues, mood disorders, or learning differences. But it is the Asperger syndrome that will be their greatest challenge during their school years. Often they are not diagnosed until much later, and much emotional damage may have been done because of being misdiagnosed.

The teacher will be challenged to integrate these children in the group. They are easy targets for bullying. They do not easily engage in play, they do not listen well, they cannot read the cues from other children to change their behavior. Their obsessive talking in a professorial pedantic monotone manner about subjects that may not interest the listener at all is off-putting for the other children. There is a lack of understanding on his part that he is bothering others. He does not understand all the unwritten rules of socially accepted behavior. For example, he does not realize that he is always standing uncomfortably close to others. He may appear rude or unkind. The child with Asperger's has no intent whatsoever to be rude, annoying, or unkind. On the contrary, they try hard to please. The problem is that they cannot identify with what the other person is experiencing. They have only their own perspective.

We don't make it easy for them. Our language is confusing to the child on the spectrum. To illustrate, an example: I asked one of my students with Asperger's to "give Sonia a hand," meaning, to help her. He walked over to her and in all sincerity, took her hand in his hand. He did exactly what was asked of him, and of course, it was all "wrong" and "weird" to his classmates.

Another example: When the teacher asked the children to write down a given analog time in digital time notation, this child wrote the number 2 instead of the expected 7:45 when the given problem was "a quarter of 8." The teacher told him he was wrong. The upset this caused was unfortunate and could have been avoided. The child was convinced he was right, and the teacher should have been flexible in seeing that he was not wrong. With tact she could have helped him to see that she meant another way of understanding the problem. So much of what we say has implied meaning. To make it worse for the child on the spectrum, 65% of communication is non-verbal. All they have to go by is the words they hear, and these words do not always mean what they say.

This constantly trips up a child with Asperger's. It does not really rain cats and dogs, and we are not really fishing when we put up the sign "Gone Fishing," or when we are fishing for a compliment. Jokes are the most difficult to process; trying to make a difficult situation better with a little joke adds fuel to the fire. They just don't get the gist of it.

The child with Asperger's craves friendship. His plight of being isolated from the others without a clue for how to break through that barrier is painful. Especially during adolescence, when his awareness of being different is acute, this becomes a deeply troubling reality for him and for all around him.

Educators must be prepared to meet these children in their classrooms. Their numbers are on the rise.

What the teacher can do to make this child feel welcome

- Talk with the class about Asperger syndrome. If the class is to welcome this child, they need to understand him.
- Make classroom life rhythmical and predictable. Prepare the child for change, even a very small change. Use concrete language. Say what you mean.
- Explain to the child what certain unspoken hints mean, for example, "When I flick the lights on and off, it means: almost time to stop working."
- Do not force the child to make eye contact. If he can look at your chin, that's good. If he cannot do that, start at the shoulders. Eye contact may never happen. The child is more comfortable with you by his side, than being opposite him. Approach him from the side.
- Provide a written list of what the child is expected to do.
- Do not use the word *inappropriate* to describe a behavior; say *unexpected* instead. Be explicit in teaching the child what is and what is not expected behavior.
- Educate awareness of the body: body geography.
- Keep the child warm. The ego lives in warmth.
- Be calm. The child is trying hard to please.
- Provide a place for the child to go when the classroom is too overwhelming, preferably in the room, but an enclosed space away from the group. The child should not be told to go there, he may choose to go there if he feels the need.

- Validate the child's interests, even if unusual, by helping him find a way to constructively pursue it.
- Educate the senses of life, movement, touch, and balance.

Our right and left orientation

The brain

This polarity takes us to a discussion of learning and the brain, the cognitive realm.

The human brain has differentiated right and left sides, each side operating in a different mode and with specialized functions. This lateralization begins at age 3 along with the development of language and thought, and this development extends well into the twenties to fully mature. Learning difficulties are not the result of one area or another not functioning well, but they result from how well the different areas of the brain communicate with each other. With something like 100 billion brain cells that connect and reconnect in hundreds of trillions of different ways, we see at once the massive learning potential and the possibility of problems in building efficient networks. (Healy 2011)

The brain and the rest of our body are totally interdependent. For example, the brain determines how we move, and movement in turn changes the brain; the brain determines how we learn, and learning in turn affects the brain.

Dominance

The right/left differentiation of the brain is reflected in the rest of our bodies. We have a right and a left hand, eye, ear, foot, and so forth. Here too there is differentiation in function. We have a preference for one side over the other: one side is dominant. How this dominance corresponds with the dominant side of the brain facilitates learning or hinders learning. The system works most efficiently if there is a crossing over of signals from the brain to the part of the body that is activated. To illustrate, if a right-brain dominant child is right-handed, there is a slight inefficiency in the neurological messaging between brain and hand. Under normal circumstances this may never be an impediment, but it can become so under stress. As all new learning has an element of stress, it can benefit the child if the teacher is aware of this potential problem. Timed tests, for example, introduce stress, and are not beneficial for learning, whether the child has a learning difficulty or not. The only difference is that the child with the learning difficulty will be more hindered by it.

School

The brain too has a dominant side and a non-dominant side. This determines how we think. The left side of the brain is better attuned to working with details. This makes working with sounds and numbers more easily accessible. The right brain is better equipped to see the gist of the matter: Estimation, pattern recognition, and an ability to size up a situation are its strengths; in short, a more wholistic style of thinking. (Healy 2011) Our educational practices are tuned more to the left- dominant brain: Analytical thinking is favored over synthetic thinking. Sir Ken Robinson, in his humorous and profound TED talk, quips, "Truthfully, what happens is, as children grow up, we start to educate them progressively from the waist up. And then we focus on their heads. And slightly to one side." ("Do Schools Kill Creativity?" 2006) Schools lose the gifts of the more global, intuitive-type thinkers by putting too much value on the analytical thinking process.

So far we have identified two potential causes for learning problems. The first one indicates that the neurological makeup of a child could disadvantage him; the second points in the direction of teaching methods causing the problems. There is more to consider.

Gender

Learning difficulties are diagnosed more than twice as often in boys than in girls. In general, boys and girls experience different rates of development for the different regions of the brain. At the beginning of school, girls are in a better position for success than boys, with the left hemisphere already further developed. We may lose boys early in their school years due to this delay in brain development. It takes significantly longer for them to develop all the functions of the left hemisphere. On the whole, boys do better when they start formal schooling later.

Many other causes can be identified for learning difficulties: toxins (lead, mercury), stress (poverty, abuse), a genetic link, problems during pregnancy, substance abuse during pregnancy, a poor language environment, nutrition, childhood illnesses, lack of movement, and the list goes on. The more we can find out about the possible cause for the child in our care, the better we will be able to address the problems.

Problems children with learning differences experience in school

- Difficulty following instructions. Speech and language delays.
- Lack of organization skills, including organizing thoughts. Poor sequencing and planning.
- Low self esteem. Negative perception of their ability to learn.
- Auditory, visual, and sensory processing disorders.
- Difficulty performing school tasks: learning to read, and/or difficulty with math.
- Paper-and-pencil tasks. Dysgraphia (difficulty getting thoughts onto paper; illegible handwriting).

About reading

Reading is one of the most complex tasks we ask the brain to do. Maryanne Wolf, professor of child development at Tufts University, in her fascinating book, *Proust and the Squid* (2008), explains how reading is a relatively new accomplishment for human beings, and that the ability to read is not genetically wired into us. Each human being has to acquire this skill afresh. She writes, "It took our species roughly 2000 years to make the cognitive breakthroughs necessary to learn to read with an alphabet. Today our children have to reach those same insights about print in roughly 2000 days."

Only very recently did the expectation that all children learn to read become part of the culture. And yet, we ask our children to start at a very young age with this highly sophisticated task. The brain needs at least seven years of maturation before reading is possible without doing damage to other aspects of brain functions. Nations that start later with teaching reading, boast higher literacy rates than the U.S., where the belief is held that earlier is better.

Reading difficulties

How do we determine if the child has true reading difficulties or when more maturation time will take care of the problem? Learning to read takes place over time, and each child is on his own time schedule. The following are symptoms, however, that should raise concern from an early age on:
- The baby or the toddler does not take delight in playing with speech sounds.
- The young child is not interested in looking at books or listening to stories.
- The child does not enjoy rhyming, and cannot recognize rhyming words (a skill that should be accomplished by the age of 4 or 5).
- Speech delays and unusual word pronunciations (pasghetti for spaghetti). By age 5 or 6 children should have little difficulty with pronunciation.
- Difficulty learning the letters of the alphabet.
- Word-finding problems (ehm…like…you know…).
- Confusion about right and left orientation.
- Inefficient eye movements (tracking, focusing).
- Relatives who experienced learning difficulties in school.

If these red flags are indicated in the biography of the child, or observed by the teacher in the classroom, the child's progress in reading should be carefully monitored. His problems very likely will not go away with maturation, and intervention is warranted.

The dyslexic child

Failing to learn to read can lead to emotional scarring for a lifetime. Failing to diagnose the problem may lead to teachers and parents telling the child to try harder, to show how smart he is. Trying harder makes the situation worse, and the child eventually concludes that he just isn't very smart.

Matters are complicated by the fact that there is no universal definition of dyslexia. The reasons for its occurrence are varied and cover a vast area of possibilities. So our best bet is to observe the child in front of us, and take our cues from there. If by third grade the child is turning away from books instead of turning toward them because he hates reading, something is amiss, and the child needs help. Teaching a dyslexic child to read is a matter of finding an approach that works for this child. It is highly individual. Teacher and child need to find their way. The teacher needs to be able to present different approaches, based on knowledge of the child gained through observation.

You need to tell yourself with courage and with energy—not just saying it at some particular moment, but carrying it continually in your consciousness, so that it determines the very quality and content of your consciousness: "I can do it."
– Rudolf Steiner (1981, p.177)

What the teacher can do

Rudolf Steiner tied development and curriculum together from the inception of the Waldorf School. He gave indications for how to avoid teaching too intellectually, too abstractly, in the younger grades. The introduction to reading follows a similar course the human species followed: from story to sound to picture to symbol. From the whole to the part. Writing and reading go hand in hand: the children read what they write. This approach is nurturing the developing mind of the children.

Children need to move to learn. Speaking is movement. Young readers need to read out loud, and they should be allowed to read out loud for as long as they need to do that.

Reading is about story. Teachers need to select reading material that is beautifully written and tells a story. The phonetic readers especially designed for beginning readers are often devoid of meaning and beauty. Material like that makes the children into decoders, but not into readers.

Children are still learning to speak and to master their mother tongue. The teacher needs to speak slowly and articulate clearly. Steiner spoke about this emphatically in his lectures to teachers. This will make the class better readers and spellers!

In addition to telling stories, read stories to the children as well. It helps build vocabulary and presents the children with complex thought. Choose literature of the highest quality.

One of the major problems children with reading difficulties encounter is a lack of facility with the manipulation of the sounds of the language. The teacher should bring a fun-with-sounds activity every day. A few minutes daily of phonological and phonemic awareness activities will sharpen the children's ear for the units and sounds of the language, and prepare them for reading. This ear training should precede phonics (sound-symbol connection).

Form drawing is an excellent activity for all children, but for the dyslexic child it is especially helpful. Mirroring (symmetry) exercises can help to alleviate the stubborn reversal problems these children are struggling with (b/d; m/w; p/q).

Do everything you can to improve the acoustics in your classroom. Children with dyslexia have great difficulty distinguishing speech from background noise.

Although children with dyslexia benefit from practice and reinforcement through intervention, more homework, more practice, more pressure concerning the classroom work may be counter-productive.

Everything we can do to bolster self-esteem in the dyslexic child is very helpful. Let him do more of what he is good at!

Have a plan for helping the child. Share it with the parent. Do not tell a parent who is concerned about her child's reading development that the problem will resolve itself with time, unless you can substantiate that statement by your observations. Without the substantiation it will not take away the concern. It will make it worse. The teacher needs to build trust with the parent based on her sound professional knowledge, insight, and judgment.

And now you will be wanting to say to me: It looks as though the education of [special] children is going to take up all one's time; ...no time in fact to do anything else whatever! ...What is wanted is not that you should all day long be constantly on the watch—not that at all, but rather that you should acquire a quick sense for characteristic happenings. ...It does not at all depend on the length of time one devotes to the matter, but wholly on the degree to which one is able to unite oneself inwardly with the act of perception.
  – Rudolf Steiner (1981, p.171)

REFERENCES

Healy, J.M. (1999). *Endangered minds: Why children don't think—and what we can do about it*. New York: Touchstone.

_____. (2011). *Different learners: Identifying, preventing, and treating your child's learning problems*. New York: Simon & Schuster.

Holtzapfel, W. (2006). *Children's destinies*. Spring Valley NY: Mercury Press.

Keller, E.F. (1983). *A feeling for the organism: The life and work of Barbara McClintock*. New York: Freeman.

Köhler, H. (2001). *Working with anxious, nervous, and depressed children*. Chatham, NY: Waldorf Publications.

Remen, N. https://www.uc.edu/.../HelpingFixingServing.pdf

Saint-Exupéry, A. (1943). *The little prince*. New York: Harcourt, Brace & World.

Steiner, R. (1982). *Balance in teaching*. Spring Valley, NY: Mercury Press.

_____. (1981). *Curative education: Twelve lectures for doctors and curative educators*. Forest Row, UK: Rudolf Steiner Press.

Weiss, T.J. (1979). *Children in need of special care*. New York: Schocken Books.

Wolf, M. (2008). *Proust and the squid*. New York, Harper Perennial.

The twelve senses

Jennifer Kennerk

These four senses provide the foundation children need in order to achieve academic, social, and emotional success.

One of the most important contributions Rudolf Steiner made to spiritual science was that of the twelve senses. Steiner saw that the human being is utilizing a much more complex system of sense impressions in her interaction with the world than the traditional five senses allow for. The traditional five senses provide for only a very superficial understanding of the human experience, and if we wish to gain a deeper insight into humanity, then it is necessary to expand our knowledge of the human senses and how they work. Steiner identified the twelve senses as touch, life, self-movement, balance, smell, taste, sight, warmth, hearing, speech, thinking, and ego.

The four lower senses

The first four of these twelve senses are known as the lower senses, or the foundational senses. They are the senses of touch, life, self-movement, and balance. These four senses are of the utmost importance to parents and educators alike, as they provide the foundation children need in order to achieve academic, social, and emotional success. We regularly see children in the grades who are struggling academically, socially, or emotionally, and we may be at a loss as to how to help them. Whether you are a parent or a teacher, you should first look to the lower senses. The lower senses build three capacities in children:

Spatial Orientation – knowing where you are in space, and how to relate to it.
Body Geography – knowing the geography of your own body and how to use it.
Dominance – established dominance on either the right or the left side of the body.

These three capacities are the foundation for all academic, social, and emotional growth. Any type of learning requires the acquisition of skills, and skills cannot be acquired without foundational capacity. The four lower senses provide the capacity from which all skill is built. When they have not been fully developed, children often struggle.

Sense of touch

The sense of touch is not merely about the sensation that we feel when we touch something. For instance, when I touch an ice cube I think and feel many things. I think, "This is cold!," or I feel how the ice is wet, or hard. I may even feel pain if I hold the ice for too long. However, none of these thoughts are feelings are derived from our sense of touch. The sensation of cold actually comes from the sense of warmth (or temperature). The awareness of wet or hard has more to do with our sense of self-movement than with the sense of touch. The experience of pain is linked to our sense of life. So, what then do we mean by the sense of touch?

It is not the sensations that I experience when I touch the ice that represent the sense of touch, but the boundary that I come up against. It is the sense of touch that informs us that we are all individuals, separated from the outer world, with our own evolving consciousness and self-awareness. It is the sense of touch that separates us from each other, and separates us from the outer world.

Touch is the foundation of all the lower senses because what we experience through touch is also felt in these other lower senses; life, self-movement, and balance. When we touch something, an experience is had, and life, movement, and balance then interpret this experience. So we can see that touch is a kind of space where we can experience and interpret the other three, either separately, or in combination. When this sense is underdeveloped, a child may require additional support. Signs of this can be seen in children (or adults) who seek deeper amounts of pressure in order to feel to feel a boundary. A child may seek out excessive, rough contact with friends, or need bigger hugs to feel that they are being hugged at all. In contrast, normal amounts of touch and pressure may also invoke a fearful reaction in these individuals, and they will avoid it at all costs. Certain clothing may even be felt as too restrictive for these children, and there may be other forms of sensory integration issues as well.

Sense of life

The life sense (or the sense of well-being) is the next of the foundational senses. The life sense refers to our ability to understand our state of well-being. Dr. Steiner explains the life sense as the general perception of how our organs are functioning; of whether they are promoting life, or obstructing it.

When everything is as it should be, we pay little attention to the sense of life. When we are warm, fed, and healthy we simply feel normal, and are free to go about the day in ease. It is when something is amiss that the sense of life comes to the forefront of our consciousness. When we are dehydrated, we have an awareness that we need to supply our bodies with more water. When we are in need of fuel, we feel hunger. Sensations of warmth and cold inform us of what clothes to wear. Without the sense of life, there would be nothing prompting us to attend to our own self-care; it is a means of preservation. The sense of life is a guide. It constantly runs in the background, steering our behavior in a way that promotes health.

Because we have an awareness of our own well-being, we can have insight into the well-being of others. The life sense provides the experience of pain (and therefore the polarity of pleasure), providing the foundation of empathy. The sense of life gives us an awareness of who we are within the confines of our bones, organs, and skin. It sets us on the path to health and well-being.

Sense of self-movement

The sense of self-movement is the third of the foundational senses. The sense of self-movement is often referred to as the proprioceptive system. This is our inner sense of our own self-movement, as it relates to the muscles, joints, and other parts of the body as they move and provide information about where we are in space. This does not mean our ability to move! Of course we are able to move, and we can observe another person and see that they are in movement, but this is not what we are referring to. It is the ability to perceive one's own movement that we are concerned with here.

When working with the sense of self-movement, it is also necessary that we look at the development of the will. This is the desire to plan and to take action. If the will is underdeveloped, then a child will not have the intrinsic motivation to become a master of body and space. Children of today commonly lack proper development of the will. One of the most important things parents can do to strengthen the will is to provide their children with chores. Having daily activities that are required of us (whether we want to do them or not!) is essential to healthy will development. Ideally, this is done as early as possible to ensure that is it part of a daily routine, but chores can be added to a child's day at any age. Dishes, laundry, animals, garbage, and compost are all chores that can begin as early as five or six. Of course the younger ones will need some assistance at times, but do allow them as much responsibility as possible. Sweeping is another chore that all children should engage in regularly. This particular activity is wonderful for left-brain/right-brain integration and midline issues.

Sense of balance

The sense of balance is the last of the four lower senses that play a role in building the foundation for all learning, and is twofold. First, there is our physical balance—our ability to remain upright and centered, giving us security in relation to gravity. This physical manifestation of balance is what we are all familiar with, and is tied to the vestibular system. The vestibular system is located within the inner ear, and is made up of canals containing fluid, which send feedback to the brain about our spatial orientation. When this system is strong, we are able to maintain appropriate balance and make adjustments when necessary. When this system is not functioning properly, incorrect messages come from the brain and can result in vertigo, dizziness, or just poor balance in general. Steiner also said that the sense of balance is connected to our spiritual identity. This relationship between our inner and outer worlds not only allows us to move freely within our earthly, gravitational field, but also provides the basis for healthy social interactions and relationships.

It can also be said that the balance we experience between inner and outer worlds enables us to experience a sense of justice within the world. We naturally have a desire to weigh and balance many things in our environment. We even speak of our emotions in this way (for instance, a person

who behaves erratically may be referred to as "unbalanced"). When we have a firm place to stand in the world, we can then have an understanding of where things stand in the rest of the world. The concept of "right or wrong," or "good and evil" stem from our sense of balance. The fact that we have this kind of discernment is a product of the balance of soul. Not only is the sense of balance responsible for anchoring our standpoint within our earthy gravitational field, but, as Steiner tells us, it is also responsible for our spiritual identity. When we are unbalanced physically, we are likely to be unbalanced spiritually and emotionally.

Each of these lower senses sets the stage for healthy academic growth. Whenever we have children that struggle in the classroom, we should always pause and assess whether these foundational senses are properly developed. They can be worked with and remediated at any age, and will allow any further intervention to fully take root.

Classroom observations, modifications and interventions

Hyper sense of touch

Classroom observations
— Tactile defensiveness (sensitive to clothing, to being touched by other children, etc.)
— Defensive, aggressive
— Does not have an awareness of boundaries, space between people and objects
— Sound, speech intensity
— Dresses a season behind, takes clothes off
— Has difficulty with certain foods
— Doesn't like slippers

Classroom interventions
— Calm the tactile defensiveness with warmth, eye contact, and voice
— Cocoon wraps in blankets with firm pressure
— Games that incorporate touch (place variously textured items in bag and have child guess what they are)
— Wide range of sense possibilities: rough and soft, heavy work, gardening, baking bread, strips of velcro placed under a desk to provide tactile stimulation
— Use of large heavy bean bags or weighted balls
— Jumping from desks during a game or lesson (mountain math)
— Rolling down hills at recess, and plenty of time for play
— Layers of clothing
— Give enough personal space
— Wrestling
— Approach from the side

Hypo sense of touch

Classrooms observations
— Intrudes into other children's space
— Likes other children piling on top of him
— Talks constantly, blurts out, makes noises, comments, calls across the room through others' conversations
— Does not get deeply involved in activities

- Lacks concentration
- Does not hear, poor eye contact
- Rough play; no sense of own strength

Classroom interventions
- Deep pressure (sandbags, burrito wraps)
- Massage
- Define desk space with tape
- Stand near child and apply touch
- Give special tasks
- Have them feel objects with eyes closed
- Pedagogical stories
- Deeds that encourage empathy, community service
- Finger and string games
- Woodwork and gardening

Sense of life

Healthy signs
- Rosy cheeks, bright eyes
- Joy and interest, enthusiasm, stamina, and confidence
- Healthy rhythms of digestion, appetite, and sleeping
- Awareness, thoughtfulness about what is eaten
- Able to interact well with peers
- Can have a good fever, aware of own illness

Unhealthy signs
- Pale, needy and clingy, slumped posture, low stamina
- Lethargy of will, depression, fatigue, poor self-image
- Overly sensitive, agitated
- over- or underweight; not sleeping or waking properly
- Poor peer interaction; not forming secure attachments
- Lack of trust, breathing disruptions
- Confused in language, hesitancy, holding back, non-communicative, fear of engaging, not making connections
- Physical complaints: hot, cold, headaches, stomach aches
- Crankiness, moody, irritable

Home interventions
- Warmth, tea, massage
- Diet of healthy, whole foods
- Nutrition baths
- Pets to look after
- Medical/constitutional consultations

Classroom interventions
- Music, singing, joy in classroom
- Stories to engage feeling life
- Warm clothing (no exposed midriffs and plenty of layers)
- Rhythm in the classroom (daily, weekly, yearly)
- Healthy challenge in the classroom, spiritually and physically

Sense of self-movement

Classroom observations
- Odd posture in head
- Floppy hands
- Wooden, stiff or floppy walk
- Lying all over desk, leaning in chair
- Lacks fluidity in movement
- Poor visual perception and eye tracking; bumps into things
- Unawareness of time and space
- Lack of coordination in hands, feet, or speech

Home interventions
- Jumping jacks, jumping rope, obstacle courses
- Snow angels, snowshoeing, hiking, swimming
- Rolling, digging, walking to school

Interventions for classroom
- Lifting and carrying heavy things
- Movement games (crabwalk, wheelbarrow, crawling, etc.)
- Moving forward and backward in space (recite verses or times table forward and backward while walking forward and backward)
- Adding speech to any rhythmic movement
- Threefold walking
- Musical instruments
- Form Drawing

Sense of balance

Healthy signs
— Confident, at ease, freedom in movement
— Upright posture
— Healthy spatial orientation
— Fluidity in walking
— Coordinated movement

Unhealthy signs
— Uncoordinated, unbalanced movement
— Falling out of desk, often upside down at desk
— Holding on to things for balance, timid
— Fear of heights
— Bumps into things
— Can't skip or jump
— Emotional outbursts

Classroom interventions
— Bean bag on head, juggling
— Yoga ball, Hippity-hop ball, rolling on floor
— Balance challenges in circle/lessons
— Balance beam, climbing on chairs
— A teacher's calm, balanced ego will work on the child's balance

The middle senses

The next four senses are known as the middle senses, and are associated with our feeling life. These middle senses allow the human being to reach out into the world and experience it, and manifest in the rhythmic system. In the grade school, we work on these senses through the arts and imagination, which enable us to engage the feeling life of the children.

Sense of smell

The sense of smell is strongly linked to memory. This can be an important tool in teaching, as we can engage this sense by bringing aromas into the classroom for a particularly memorable lesson! Even describing scents and smells to the students can engage this powerful memory maker. When not functioning properly, it is wise to suspect illness.

Sense of taste

Teachers can engage this sense on physical and emotional planes. Tasting foods from other countries or traditional foods from stories can help create deep connections to the curriculum. Experiences can be "sweet" or "sour." Like the sense of smell, if the sense of taste is not functioning properly, this can indicate illness.

Sense of sight

It is often in the early grades that vision problems are first recognized. If children are struggling in your classroom, suggest an eye exam. It is a good practice to recommend to all parents that they have their children's eyes checked toward the end of second grade. Protect the eyes from media in the early years. Form drawing works wonders to strengthen this sense.

Sense of warmth

The sense of warmth is not very well developed until the age of 9, and is not fully developed until the age of 12. This sense involves a child's being able to express sensations of warm or cold, but it also fosters creativity and flexibility in thinking. Warmth involves not only physical warmth, but also warmth on a soul level. Children need help in protecting their warmth, and parents and teachers

should be quite adamant that proper clothing is worn. No child should be able to decide this for himself until the age of 12. All children in my class must come and ask permission before they are able to shed layers of clothing (and usually my answer is no!).

The higher senses

The next four senses are known as the higher senses, and develop during adolescence. It is important to note that the higher senses are dependent on the healthy development of the lower and middle senses in order to properly mature. While the middle senses allow us to begin to experience the outside world, the higher senses allow us to experience the "other."

Sense of hearing

The sense of hearing is strongly associated with the lower sense of balance. If balance is not properly developed in the early years, hearing is often affected. If you have a student who has trouble hearing, strengthen the sense of balance.

Sense of speech

The sense of speech is associated with the lower sense of self-movement. Movement and speech go hand in hand. This is why the curriculum in a Waldorf school pairs these two together as much as possible. Clear speech will often work on clumsiness, and the other way around.

Sense of thought

The sense of thought is associated with the sense of life. This sense allows us to perceive the thoughts of others and have an understanding of them. Rhythm and repetition set the groundwork for inner quiet, which helps us listen during a conversation, instead of waiting to talk. Having rhythm and predictability in the classroom works deeply on both the sense of thought and the sense of life.

Sense of ego

This sense allows us to have an understanding and appreciation of the individuality of another human being, and is associated with the sense of touch. In order to truly recognize the essence of another, we must first be able to understand where our own boundaries lie. When the lower sense of touch has not been properly attended to, it is nearly impossible for a human being to truly have reverence and respect for others.

REFERENCES

Eikenboom, Joep. (2007/2015). *Foundations of the extra lesson*. Fair Oaks, CA: Rudolf Steiner College Press; Fryeburg, ME: Threefold Press.

Kennerk, Neal and Jennifer. (2015). *Out of the garden and into the desert: The nine-year change through the stories of the third grade curriculum*. CreateSpace Independent Publishing Platform.

Köhler, Henning. (2001). *Working with anxious, depressed, and nervous children*. Chatham, NY: Waldorf Publications.

Soesman, Albert. (1999). *Our twelve senses*. Stroud, UK: Hawthorn Press.

Dominance

Connie Helms

Dominance refers to the innate preference we have for using one side of the body over another in performing movements and receiving sense impressions. Ideally dominance is fully on one side of the body; the eye, ear, hand, and foot favored will match up either all on the left or all on the right side. Most of the world's population is right-handed and many of these people are fully right-side dominant. We live in a world where tools and implements such as scissors and pants with front zippers are often made to accommodate a right-handed user. Although statistics vary, about 51% of humans are fully right dominant, about 4% are fully left dominant and the remaining 45% or so are mixed dominant. (König 1989, p.56) Examples of mixed dominance are someone who favors the right hand, ear, and foot but whose left eye is used to look through a camera lens or telescope tube. Or, a person may favor the right foot, eye, and ear but use the left hand for writing and daily motor tasks.

The importance of dominance

To understand the importance of dominance, we need to remember that the child's task in the first seven years of life is to become well incarnated into the physical body. The buildup of the structural body is universal; the same skeletal framework supports human organs, skin, and tissues. We all have 206 bones accompanied by muscles for moving them, plus sensory organs and a nervous system that assist us in perceiving and moving. Conversely, the life body or etheric body will be molded individually for each child. This is the constitutional side of each child's makeup. An individual blueprint is formed in the organs, so that a child's liver is not her father's liver, and so on. Childhood illnesses and fevers, along with nurturing life experiences in the first seven years, allow the child to mold her life body in a way that releases heredity patterns that no longer serve the organism. A useful paradigm of structural versus constitutional aspects is found in *Foundations of the Extra Lesson.* (Eikenboom 2007)

To make the structural physical body as efficient as possible is the task every child is attempting to undertake in the years before formal schooling begins, so that the body is self-sufficient and the brain is freed up for thinking, memory, and cognitive activity. Imagine if we had to mentally talk ourselves through every common motor action in everyday life, we could spend ten minutes brushing teeth or getting into the car to begin driving. By practicing motor movements from infancy to age 7, we are forming physical pathways that create the groundwork for body-free thinking, in order to meet our own personal destiny. Navigating the steps sequentially is the most efficient way to achieve an optimally functioning structural body. As Joep Eikenboom states, "These developmental steps have an objective and archetypal hierarchical order, common for every human being." (2007, p.11) Going back to recapitulate missed steps is the main reason for doing Extra Lesson exercises. These exercises revisit experiences the child missed.

The universal developmental motor sequence

Ages 0 to 2.5 years

Practice the early movement patterns so that each reflex has its unique timeline to allow for development of the central nervous system and motor skills. The body becomes ready for the forward motions of creeping, crawling, and then standing upright freely in space. With crawling, the baby experiences bilateral integration in the horizontal plane. When the child stands, the arms are freed from the pull of gravity. Three dimensions of space are now at play: left side/right side, front/back, and above/below.

Age 2.5 to 5 years

The arms are free for lifting up together, moving apart and coming back to the vertical midline. A period of symmetry ensues, building up the inner orientation of two sides, along with a strengthening of the body geography and spatial orientation begun in the previous stage.

Age 5 to 7 years (up to age 8 in some children)

Bilateral integration increases. Arms may cross the vertical midline at will. Through play, imitation, chores and use of tools, laterality (the choice of one side as dominant) becomes the norm because it is most efficient for one hand (or foot) to perform specialized motor tasks. With laterality, using tools such as a toothbrush, scissors, or utensils helps us to choose a preferred side for the hand (and kicking a ball or going up stairs with a leading foot). A result of vertical midline integration is that the preferred hand, which ideally matches the preferred or stronger eye, is able cross an entire page from left to right without the child's needing to switch hands halfway across a page to draw or write. Hand preference, along with foot, eye, and ear preference, becomes our dominance profile.

Hemispheric dominance

We also have an innate affinity for either our left or right brain hemisphere for receiving and processing information. Due to our neural wiring, the left hemisphere controls movements and receives sensory impressions from the opposite side—the right side. Likewise, the right hemisphere has the same relation to the left side of the body. For decades, medical research has found that our left brain is the language and logic brain which excels at details, temporal sequencing, linear thinking, and verbal language production, and that approximately 98% of all people have the speech center in the left hemisphere regardless of their handedness. Although only a very small percentage of humans have the main language/logic hemisphere on the right side, each hemisphere does have a language center; the one on the right side is associated mostly with emotional language, rhythm and intonation/musicality. (Goddard 2002)

Many people who are fully or mostly right-sided tend to be left-brain thinkers. The left hemisphere's affinity for language production works well with the flow of written language by the right hand, as the left hemisphere controls right-side motor function and vice versa. It is believed that most people are right-handed as opposed to left-handed because the left hemisphere is the main language center. With new learning, whether assimilating a math concept, a poem, a recipe, or how to play an instrument or a game, their sense of sequential logic will help them learn one step at a time. If holistic learning

is not incorporated however, they may not be able to intuit a sense of flow, rhythm, and the whole gestalt of what stands before them. In a stressful situation, the left-brained person may process and act immediately as logical thinking can prevail, but the emotional components may take a back seat.

Conversely, gestalt (right-brained) learners will have an intuitive sense for the inherent emotion and beauty or flow of dance, music, art, a story or lecture, to name a few experiences. Their learning may need to be more experiential by doing actions; their creativity is nurtured by experiencing and sensing rather than analyzing the steps. A child who is more right-brained will learn the times tables more easily with melodies. One can imagine many of the world's highly creative people as being very much in "their right mind," their gestalt brain. Our right hemisphere excels at seeing the gestalt or whole picture, and is more adept at working with images, colors, emotions, and our intuitions. Many people who are left-side dominant are more right-brain thinkers; these people tend to be creative, artistic, and intuitive. Albert Einstein, Maya Angelou, and Leonardo DaVinci come to mind as people who felt or sensed the big picture and then created the details afterward.

Working with the concepts of time and space, the left brain has an affinity for time, as in sequencing, while the right brain has a relation to space and the immediate or big picture. When facing a stressful situation, the gestalt-brained person may react first with emotion, and if able to respond, may use action rather than executing a sequential plan to solve a problem. As Carla Hannaford points out, Gestalt learners, more than logic learners, are affected by the early push in academic kindergartens to learn linear functions both in language and math. (Hannaford 1995) These children may develop poor self-esteem by the early grades because they perceive themselves as stupid in comparison to peers who seem to learn easily. For these reasons, she appreciates holistic education methods such as Waldorf education.

Historically, education in the United States has presented a sequenced, "logic" style as a teaching method. Mainstream education often ignores the science of the surge in gestalt hemisphere development from ages four to seven compared to the later logic brain surge in growth from ages seven to nine. In holistic education practices, including Waldorf education, a balance of teaching is the goal so that the teaching style varies between a linear presentation and a holistic one, ideally helping each type of learner to be met with both gestalt and logic methods. Experiencing both styles helps to strengthen the integrated brain by increasing the myelination of nerve fibers that cross at the corpus callosum. (Hannaford 1995, p.79)

Cross dominance

By definition, cross dominance means that hand, foot, eye, and ear are not fully dominant on the right side or the left side. While some children and adults can successfully navigate mixed dominance, experience shows that mixed or cross dominance may be a factor in some learning and behavior problems. This can decrease learning efficiency and thus affect self-esteem at an early age.

Observations on which cross-dominant situations tend to be more problematic can vary, yet teachers can assist in a child's learning efficiency by determining whether the child's hand, foot, eye, and ear dominance are on the same side and if they are opposite the dominant brain hemisphere. If the left brain and right eye are dominant, vision is facilitated. The left brain controls the muscular movements of the right eye, thus optimizing the efficiency of three-dimensional and two-dimensional focus, tracking and peripheral vision. The same might be true for right-brain/left-eye dominance.

When a left-brain person has left-eye dominance, vision is less efficient for several reasons: 1) the dominant left brain is not controlling the muscular movements of the dominant eye because the right side controls left eye movement; 2) the left eye tracks from right to left (Hannaford 2011, p.28) which can cause perception of reversals in letters and letter order in words; and 3) the left eye surveys space and form. This last characteristic matches with the right hemisphere's specialty of seeing the gestalt. If this person is also right-handed (and therefore the eye does not match the hand for the physical task of writing), in some cases the child may be seen tilting her head to the left so that the dominant left eye can survey what is being written. It is most efficient, in our left-to-right literate culture, that the right eye and right hand are teamed together. Further in this article there will be suggestions of how to facilitate changes in cases of mixed dominance.

In most people, the left hemisphere initiates verbal language and also written expression in the right hand. When both the left hemisphere and the left hand are dominant, communication may become less efficient because the language circuit cannot directly proceed from the left language hemisphere out the opposite hand for flow in written communication. The most important concept in understanding cross dominance is for the teacher (and by sixth grade, the student) to know how to maximize learning efficiency, for example, by setting reasonable expectations for visual, auditory, kinesthetic, linear, and gestalt learning, and even by knowing where to sit in the classroom.

Dominance profiles

Dominance profiles vary worldwide; while a preferred sense on one side or the other is often established in utero, in the case of hand and foot choice, there may be a cultural component. Historically in many cultures, use of the left hand was and in some cases still is considered inappropriate. Imitation can also be a factor in hand or foot choice; in cultures where soccer is played at an early age, a child may adopt the kicking foot she has seen an older child use, or adopt the left hand for writing in imitation of a parent. Such imitation does not mean the child has changed his or her intrinsic dominance, but it can cause a teacher to question whether a child is truly left-handed or just uses the left hand to draw and write out of imitation.

An excellent reference book to consult is *The Dominance Factor* by Carla Hannaford, PhD. Over thirty years ago she began to use the Dominance Profiles paradigm developed by Paul Dennison (developer of Brain Gym) to help students and teachers understand how to improve the learning process. By identifying one's dominance profile, one can begin to understand how the brain and nervous system function best and how they can be accommodated when under stress. She works with the five areas of hand, foot, eye, ear and brain hemisphere in any combination, creating 32 different profiles. For example, my profile is a common one of right hand, foot, and ear, but left eye and brain hemisphere. This combination explains why I sometimes misread a sign at first glance because the left eye, my dominant eye for perceiving, naturally tracks from right to left. My logic/left brain corrects the image, but if I am tired, it does not correct itself quickly. Although letter, number, and word reversals are common attributes in children ages 6 to 7, they may be more common in a child with left-eye dominance. (Hannaford 2011, p.28)

In the auditory realm, the right ear is more adept at receiving and processing the sounds of language. As most people have the main language center in the left brain hemisphere, the pathway from the right ear to the left brain is direct. In the case of left-ear dominance, there is a more circuitous route: The sounds travel into the left ear, over to the sublanguage center in the right brain, then must travel back through the corpus callosum to the left brain for processing. This explains why it seems to take a bit longer for a left-ear dominant person to process auditory information, especially that of a sequential nature. (Goddard 2002, p.66) However, the left-ear dominant person is able to intuit underlying meanings and emotions more skillfully than a right-ear dominant person.

One of the many helpful aspects of Hannaford's work is her recognition that when learning new information or when under stress, our dominant senses or body parts are most active for receiving and processing information. This understanding is key for a teacher's consciousness about where to place a student in the classroom and what to expect in terms of attention and focus for new learning. For example, a student who is left-ear dominant will need to have her left ear more accessible to the teacher in terms of seating arrangement. If this student is placed on the left side of the room in frontal teaching, her left ear is away from the teacher. By placing her on the right side of the room, her left ear is toward the teacher to better assimilate new information.

An example of vision skills in reaction to stress is a person's loss of proper eye focus after a stressful life event. This is often caused by pupil dilation; the eyes must be on high alert to see the periphery and the big picture; focusing on the details is less critical. It can take months or longer for the system to calm itself enough to regain accurate focus skills, and sometimes even taking a break from reading print is found to be helpful. Exercise, music, and working with color such as in art therapy are a few ways to lessen stress. It can be helpful for teachers to remember this aspect of teaching children who may be under stress.

Hannaford also describes how certain dominance profiles lean toward a visual or auditory strength. In the case of someone who can take in information best via the auditory over the visual channel, looking directly at the teacher will not serve the student to assimilate the concept or information. This learner needs to look away, perhaps to the side, to register and imprint what is being said. If too many channels are operating at once, we cannot receive and store the sense impression, so to be efficient we must access the stronger sense in the moment. How many times do we pause, look away, and let our mind create an image to recall what was said? Our visual system in the present moment needs a rest so that our auditory sense impression can process what was said a few seconds earlier or recall something from the past.

An auditory learner may also need to maximize the kinesthetic (bodily) sense in order to take in information. This student in a class can be allowed to knit or to hold a sensory "fidget toy" or a small piece of string or beeswax, for example. Sometimes the child who fidgets with various small objects in the desk is telling us that he needs to bring something together with his hands at the midline: The activity satisfies a kinesthetic sense and the hands working together at the midline help to activate the corpus callosum, uniting the two hemispheres in processing and understanding. I once met a woman at a kindergarten conference who knit during two whole days of Georg Kühlewind's lectures. She described herself as dyslexic and was grateful to her own Waldorf school class teacher who let her knit her way in classes through eight years to stay focused. [Some teachers prefer to help a child strengthen single-activity focus by avoiding hand activity during a teacher's presentation. –Ed.]

Checking simple dominance

Simple dominance can be assessed in the following manner.

HAND – Check which hand reaches for an object held at the child's level in the middle of her torso. Which hand is preferred for tasks of pointing, drawing, writing, tossing a small ball or object, and also receiving an object?

EYE – Have the child look through a telescope tube and kaleidoscope. Also, poke a hole in a piece of paper and see which eye she brings the paper toward. Have the child overlap hands at

the fingers with thumbs parallel below to create a small triangular space. Hold out the crossed hands at arm's length and look through the opening at an object a foot or two away. Close one eye, then the other. The eye that maintains the image is the dominant eye.

(Merely having the child close one eye with the eye muscles does not always indicate a clear eye dominance, as a child may just have stronger eye muscles on one side.)

EAR – Have the child pick up one shell at a time to listen to the sound. The choice of ear may vary, so also have her place one ear against a door to listen for people talking on the other side. Beware of earwax buildup that can block hearing on one or both sides; a preferred ear may not be the dominant one.

FOOT – Check which foot the child uses first to step up on a chair. Roll a ball, have the child stop it with her foot and kick it back, repeat three or so times. Have child stand like a log, say "timber" and have the child pretend to fall forward and then catch herself. Which foot extends forward first?

BRAIN HEMISPHERE – Have the child repeat a common story such as "Goldilocks and the Three Bears"; listen for either a more gestalt summary or a very detailed, sequential one. Also ask the child which subjects she likes best in school. Often a teacher has indications from the child on which brain hemisphere is dominant, based on the indicators mentioned. It is often easy to tell which children may be more inclined to linear thinking and learning compared to holistic and gestalt learning. A left-brain dominant child may be more adept at spelling and remembering sequential number and letter patterns, whereas a strong right-brain learner will memorize the gestalt configuration of a word, confusing *dragon* for *dragging*. Right-brain learners may memorize multiplication tables best if they sing them, through association with melody, in the same way that many children recite the alphabet best if singing the familiar melody. Another indicator is to check balance on one foot. The foot supported for the longest time correlates with the stronger opposite hemisphere.

The path to established dominance

The developmental pathway from infancy to around age 7 must be traveled before a child can establish a clear dominance. Mastery over one neurodevelopmental skill at a time allows the emergence of a higher skill level to build upon a secure foundation. A good overview of the motor development pathways has been described by Dr. P. Mesker, a Dutch neurologist, and can be found in the *Second Grade Development Observation and Assessment: Background and Manual*. Published in the Netherlands in 1986 by teachers, and included Else Göttgens as a consultant, it is available in PDF format at http://www.movementforchildhood.com/uploads/2/1/6/7/21671438/dutch_manual.pdf

Stage 1: Oppositional movement or trunk stage

The identifying feature of the first stage is oppositional movement or left/right antagonism. Mesker named it the "trunk stage," comparing it to an elephant's trunk: the trunk lifts but the tail is generally relaxed. The muscles on one side flex or contract while the opposite side relaxes or expands. A very clear example is when the baby makes a fist or grasps with one hand and the opposite hand will relax or even extend. Likewise one leg stretches way out while the other contracts with a knee bend and this action may switch back and forth if the baby is in a contented but excited stage. Contraction and expansion are the salient themes of this stage, most of which occur while still in the horizontal plane.

As muscle groups flex and are opposed by extension or relaxation, the hands, feet, arms, and legs are in a process of maturation. Within several months after birth an infant ideally develops stability in the core and neck, leading to rolling over around 4 to 5 months old. Consider how a baby might be on her back, raising just one arm and one leg. Suddenly she has plopped over onto her tummy. Then, with raising and reaching one arm, she plops over again—this time onto her back. The limbs gain more control because separately each limb has had the opportunity to stretch and reach, with relaxation in between movements. Clearly babies are ambidextrous, as either hand reaches to the mouth or stretches out as a random movement.

Sufficient floor time establishes our internal map of directionality: We begin to have a sense of front and back and one side versus the other side. During the whole process of floor time, eye convergence and eye-hand coordination are developing as well as near-point and far-point vision. Eventually the limbs and core are strong enough to support motion forward, but in some cases a baby creeps backward.

After experiencing and integrating many primitive reflexes on the horizontal plane, a baby is able move the torso forward by creeping on the belly, then lift the torso up to a four-point position to begin crawling at around 8 months. There is a period of about a month when the baby simply rocks back and forth while on her hands and knees with the head lifted up. There is no forward or backward motion; the body is merely perfecting stability without toppling over. One day the arms stretch forward to reach, and the opposite leg—the opposing muscle group—will also go forward. With the onset of crawling, there is still no handedness established. This is nature's way of exercising both brain hemispheres: Motor function on each side stimulates the opposite brain hemisphere; it's the beginning of bilateral integration. The language center in the left is stimulated, as well as the gestalt center in the right brain.

By pushing the hands against the floor when crawling, hand development is strengthened (this will have an impact on fine motor control leading to successful handwriting) along with increased opportunities to be more vertical. Eventually the baby pulls herself up … and she stands. This is a hallmark of the first year—coming into standing with no assistance. This achievement is a deed of the will.

Soon after standing, forward motion begins. The legs are spread wide for stability, and there is very little bend in the knees—one whole leg swings forward at a time. It can appear as though the child's whole body is lurching forward as this is a new way to navigate gravity and maintain one's balance so as not to fall forward. When there are falls, the baby, now officially a "toddler," will fall back on her bottom, or else both her hands go forward to the ground as she goes down. The oppositional movement stage is adjusting to using the two arms and hands together.

Stage 2: Symmetrical movement

Once the baby is able to come into aspects of verticality, her arms are freed up for lifting—and they can lift at the same time. Picture a toddler saying "uppy" to be picked up as she raises her arms up together. Mesker refers to this as the "symmetry stage." The arms can move away from the body or move back toward the body together. The legs can also do this, moving out and in as in snow angels or sand angels. Picture a toddler clapping hands together at the midline. Maybe the hands miss an exact meeting in the middle, but the movement is symmetrical.

If a child is in the symmetry stage, a squeeze to one hand makes the other hand also clench. The same applies to stretching out the fingers. In the symmetry stage, a child uses the two arms or two legs to walk, run, jump, climb stairs (one foot always in lead with toddlers) reach, push and pull—universally this is a chance for all children to exercise muscle groups and strengthen both limbs, hands and feet. Young children can toss a ball, carry a heavy object a good distance, build a sandcastle or snowman. Some young children can even downhill ski and ride a tricycle or a very low standard bike.

A typical 4- to 6-year-old is using tools and objects with both hands and also with one hand. Usually the left hand and the right hand each do their own task on respective sides of the body. Yet by age 4, a preference for using one hand over the other may appear; this is a classic age when children begin to use a pair of scissors. In most cases, the child will show a preference for holding a tool in the right or left hand while the other hand has a supporting role. With tasks like drawing and playing with toys, however, the choice of which hand to use is not always clear. It is often the case that a child will draw with either hand in the same picture. This generally happens because the vertical midline has not yet integrated and the child's hand may not easily draw across a whole page. Functionally, the result is that the left hand draws on the left side and the right hand on the right side. Not all children do this, but when it occurs after age 5 or 6, it is best to encourage use of one hand only.

Vertical midline barrier

The vertical midline barrier is a protective barrier that prevents a baby and young child from using just one side of the body. For example, using only the right hand to reach for toys would not allow the other side to engage. It requires the child to use the left and right sides equally, especially the hands, so that both sides may develop. With this symmetrical use of the body, both brain hemispheres are fully activated. However when the child is around age 6 (it varies), this barrier should disappear as hands can cross easily over the vertical midline. The actual activity of crossing helps to end the symmetry stage and strengthen bilateral integration. Now hand dominance becomes established. This is a critical time in brain growth as the two hemispheres connect more strongly at the corpus callosum and they further specialize: the left even more so in language and logic while the right more in musical and spatial abilities and also seeing the whole picture. The child is now ready for formal learning.

Retention of the vertical midline barrier after age 7 can be cause for difficulty in reading, copying, and carrying or borrowing in math since the eyes are unable to track accurately across the page and the hands are unable to cross freely at the child's will. A colleague told a story once of a boy in class who had his lunchbox on his desk. Rather than reach with one hand across to the other side of the lunchbox, he got up from his chair and walked around to retrieve the item; this is an extreme example of a retained vertical midline. The child with a residual vertical midline is in need of more activities such as handclap games, crossing games with arms and legs, plus sweeping, raking sideways across the front of the body and even canoeing. Many timeless chores and childhood games encourage crossing over.

Stage 3: Lateralization

If a child can pass smoothly through the stage of oppositional movement, which then is incorporated into the symmetry stage, her body geography and the sense of awareness in space continues to develop. Bilateral coordination in three-dimensional space is a hallmark of this stage: Picture a kindergarten-age child running, skipping, or marching with an arm lift opposite the leg that is moving. This bilateral coordination was also experienced in crawling, although in the horizontal plane.

With maturation around age 7, the child progresses to an understanding of left and right and conscious awareness of one side as the dominant side. This is then the stage of lateralization, the use of one side of the body as the leading side in daily motor tasks such as writing, using cutting tools, doing kitchen work, and lifting a cup or utensil when eating.

A quick reference check for observations about where a child is on the developmental path is to shake a child's hand:

a. In the first stage of *oppositional movement*, the child will stretch out the opposite hand because the other hand is contracting.

b. In the second stage of *symmetry,* the opposite hand will also contract.

c. In the third stage of *lateralization*, the opposite hand will remain relaxed as there is no need for any associative movement triggered by the handshake.

Challenges in trunk and symmetry stages

When educators know about stages of motor development and the importance of successfully traveling the developmental pathway, what follows is better understanding about establishing clear dominance. Mesker stated that when a child shows disturbances in language, it is possible she remained in the trunk stage too long, not having lifted herself freely into space of her own accord at an opportune moment. König stated, "The whole organism of movement is characterized as the necessary foundation of all speech." (König 1998, p.30) Brain development and central nervous system function are inherently included in this picture, yet the driving force is movement.

The experience of standing freely leads to proper walking. Coupled with the emerging symmetry phase, walking propels speech development at an astounding rate, with a common peak time from 18 to 24 months. At this stage, one-word exclamations blossom into fuller sentences with nouns, verbs, and adjectives. Pediatrician Dr. Edmond Schoorel commented, "Children who suffer from a disturbance in their motor development will also face a speech problem." (2004, p.197) If walking freely based on healthy movements is not at her disposal, speech does not develop easily. She may sense that others are different, creating a closing off and subsequently less imitation of and inclination toward speech as a social gesture.

Difficulties in the symmetry stage are due to either insufficient length of time or staying in the stage too long, with the results being left/right reversal issues and lack of differentiation of feelings, as everything is the same, much like a "b" appears the same as a "d." Left versus right does not matter to the child. This is appropriate before first grade, but by age 6 or 7, once in school, lateralization should help the child to differentiate left and right. Indeed it does matter that the child uses only one hand for writing. Without a designated hand, signals to the brain are mixed, causing confusion. In order for the child's ego to penetrate the organism in a healthy manner, there must be a chosen hand whose willed activity is written expression.

To take the question of ambidexterity to a soul level, Dr. Thomas Weihs, a Camphill Scotland physician in the last century, has captured the deeper essence of lateralization. "It is known that dominance development is closely associated with language development, and its first signs appear in the second year (as speech development surges forward)." (1979, p.55) He goes on to say that dominance truly becomes established in the early school years after a latency period between ages 3 and 5. Later he adds that the lateralization of the brain hemispheres is a consequence—not a cause—of speech development. Thus, the two hemispheres are in play with one another. One becomes dominant as the main language center, usually the left hemisphere, and the right holds imagery, the whole picture, and more connection with emotion.

Between our two sides, however, are several identifying polarity characteristics: Universally we know the right side of our body has a Mars quality of action, while the left side of our body has Venus qualities of passivity and receiving. Dr. Weihs speaks of the right as day and the left as night, ending with "Right is the sword; left is the shield. Every child needs to develop these polar qualities in a decisive yet harmonious way." (p.56) The characteristic of decisiveness is key here, for when a child chooses deliberately, she is able to discern between left and right. Dr. Weihs's statement on the morality of ambidexterity contains food for thought for parents and professionals: "The problem is simply that left and right have never differentiated, and with this, truth and falsehood and right and wrong have remained vague and undifferentiated." (p.61) The pliable window of opportunity to effect change is before puberty; after puberty it can be difficult for the child's neurology and soul life to make any change. (Many anthroposophic doctors agree on this point.) While Dr. Weihs is not indicating that every learning or moral issue is tied to lack of established dominance, he does state that when we observe a connection between behavior or learning issues and lack of dominance, it is to be taken seriously. His chapter "Left and Right" on this topic is well worth reading and keeping handy.

Ambidexterity is something that some children are proud to claim because they have heard the term. Yet with tact we might say, "You are so clever with your hands! Now let's make this hand [be it left or right] your strong hand for writing. And which hand will be very good at flipping pancakes or stirring the batter? Then each hand has its special tasks." Ideally one will work on having the right hand be the writing hand regardless of a child's use of the right or left for other tasks. Regardless of dominance, many people are successful in sports with an unexpected hand choice due to arm strength or personal preference.

Left-handedness

A comprehensive 21st century view, which is much needed on this topic, is the explanation given by Dr. Michaela Glöckler. Her lengthy reasoning is found in *A Guide to Child Health* and also in *Developmental Insights,* edited by David Mitchell. From a review of Rudolf Steiner's indications, she states that he advised children who are left-handed to be taught to use the right hand. These earlier statements can lead one to believe that Steiner was dogmatic, yet this was not the case. Steiner advised that we have young children up to their ninth year use their right hand as much as possible in school, but not to force this if it seemed stressful for the child. Today in many early childhood programs and in family life, we may consciously encourage the putting on of the right sleeve or right shoe first. A child who is strongly left-sided will generally end up maintaining left-sidedness, while others will become accustomed to using the right side first and more often, based on our gentle guidance of these habits. Note that up to the ninth year means the time of the eighth birthday. After this, it is not so easy to have a child do tasks with the right hand if the leaning is strongly left.

Dr. Glöckler qualifies that Rudolf Steiner, very much invested in the science of his day, based his indications on the assumption that the speech center in the brain was always in the opposite hemisphere from the dominant hand. Modern research has shown this is not the case, as a small minority of people have their speech center fully in the right hemisphere. The right hand works well in conjunction with the flow of language generated by the left hemisphere where most people have the speech center. Regardless, her explanation of the outward and active quality of writing with the right hand matches well with the active soul quality of the right side as opposed to the receptive and introspective left side. Even physiologically, the right side of the body is more active. The lungs have three lobes on the right side but only two on the left, making lung capacity stronger on the right. The liver, the largest gland in the body and second largest organ, is also on the right side.

The right side then is more favorable to carry the "sword" or the "pen," as the case may be. By using the right hand for language expression, it matches well with the left language hemisphere, and the direction of writing for a right-handed writer is away from the body, again an active gesture of going out into the world. Dr. Glöckler states, "Using the left and right sides of the body in accord with this original design helps us to use our energies economically and avoid one-sided overexertion."

Left-handedness is a topic that "could fill a book" wrote Audrey McAllen in *Teaching Children Handwriting*. She cited research that identifies the main causes of left-handedness as injuries to the structural or nervous system, unresolved ambidexterity, or a fully left-sided dominance. The question about whether to guide a left-handed child to use the right hand for writing only is to be treated on an individual basis depending on the child's overall situation. In this century of children and adults who are independently minded, we can respect the wishes of parents and children by providing them with information and letting the family make the decision. It is commonly noted that those within Waldorf education discussing this topic recommend seeking the advice of an anthroposophic physician, who would provide a neurological opinion and assessment. After looking at a child's unique situation, it might be decided by the parents and aided by teacher input to embark on this process. A doctor would recommend therapeutic eurythmy if available, to help the child's etheric forces stay healthy and balanced in such an undertaking and to strengthen the right side. Besides therapeutic eurythmy, exercises from the Extra Lesson are helpful. These will be mentioned later on.

For a sense of how families can explore this topic, Dr. Glöckler offers anecdotal stories of left-handed children approaching or in grade one, each of whom was given the opportunity to experience writing with the right hand. In all of these cases, there is never a complete switching of all left-sided activity to the right side, which is a common misconception; there is never an attempt to fully change dominance. All other activities, whether cooking, painting, using scissors, playing tennis or baseball, can be executed by the left hand. Left-handed piano players have no trouble being accomplished in their skills at various levels. The right hand plays the melody while the left works hard to maintain the patterns and beat in many musical pieces. With many stringed instruments, the left hand holds the neck for fingering, while the right hand uses a bow. Similarly, we have to use our left foot in holding down the clutch in vehicles; the left foot adapts to this task regardless of foot dominance. Thus with writing, the right hand can do this one particular task related to language production and flow generally with more ease than the left side. The left-to-right flow of this direction works well for the right hand but can be difficult for the left hand to execute as it becomes a pushing across rather than a flowing outward movement. The left hand must push from left to right yet in many people, the left hand makes a "hook" above the writing area to create a flow.

The most important factor in presenting the idea and helping a child to try the right hand for writing is always to work with the concept of free will. This means not pressuring a child in any way; the child must show us an inner drive, curiosity about what the right hand can learn, and participation to try something challenging. Also it would be unfair to ask a child to complete the same workload in the same time frame as others in a class.

As this would usually be undertaken in the early grades, the amount of writing would be minimal and should be preceded by many form drawings that start large and progress to smaller ones. Taking up any new motor skill involves new neural pathways being formed in the brain. The laying down of new tracks can happen, but if stress arises, it would be counterproductive. A child must be given time, praise for the effort, and a chance to reflect on progress or setbacks. In the end, it is really up to the family and child to determine what seems to be working best, and the option is always there in later life to make a switch of the writing hand. There are cases of adults who through their own volition have changed their handwriting to the right side. Their inner motivation is crucial in the success of this endeavor. The many tales of nervousness, flightiness of ideas, and emotional difficulties in the case of changing the writing hand have a common thread of coercion by an authority without the free will of the individual.

Rudolf Steiner's indications are most helpful when we employ an updated mindset: We honor a child who is fully left-side dominant by respecting her use of the left hand in all activity; yet we may also make an effort to educate the parents to consider the use of the right hand for writing only, based on the outward active quality of the physical right side of the body. Sharing Dr. Glöckler's comments and anecdotes is strongly recommended. Another excellent source is an interview conducted with Else Göttgens. (Wilby 1998, p.264) Else (as she was known) advocated strong parental participation and inquiry, cautioning that the likelihood of learning problems is unfounded. "Writing is a learned skill, and one is no more making a child cross-lateral by writing than by expecting him to play scales with his right hand on the piano. The right-hander acquires many skills with his left hand without causing problems, so a skill where the left-handed child uses the right hand is the same requirement."

Since 1945, six of the past twelve U.S. presidents have been left-handed: Harry Truman, Gerald Ford, Ronald Reagan, George H.W. Bush, Bill Clinton, and Barack Obama. It is fair to say that several of these people have given eloquent speeches, although assisted by speech writers. Yet Barack Obama wrote out his two inaugural speeches on yellow legal pads, with his adept left hand.

Working with cross dominance

We live in an age where the children today are strong willed and expressive. Cross dominance is a situation whereby we can make an attempt to help a child achieve lateralization without forcing anything. We are not out to "fix something" that is not even broken. Our intent is to hold the attitude of making learning more efficient by attempting to strengthen dominance, be it all toward the right or all toward the left side, with the hopeful possibility that the hand for writing is the right hand alone. Dr. Karl König advised, "… (you can) attempt to orient the 45% who are not decidedly either right- or left-handed to the right side…if you do, you pull them out of their instability and bring about a certain consistent direction in their existence…" (1989, p.57)

As the path to dominance entails passage through the symmetry stage, it is advantageous to include symmetry activity for children with a cross dominance especially, even up to age of 12 or more. Practicing several times a week for a month or so may be sufficient for many students to recapitulate the symmetry stage while for others it may take longer. Here are some symmetry activities.

Games and movement activities

Clapping Games: Many handclap games from varied cultures are taught by Jaimen McMillan (founder of Spacial Dynamics®) and have traveled widely. Simple games have a sequence of slapping one's thighs, clapping one's hands at the midline, and then clapping both hands directly across to a partner's hands. Fists, fingers, and feet can also come into play with symmetry activities.

"Hot Cross Buns" and "Pease Porridge Hot" (excellent for nursery and kindergarten): Use the above sequence whether seated or standing; and also do with the feet and foot taps on floor while seated on bottoms.

For "Double Double," the ulnar sides (little finger side) of the fists are tapped across to a partner's and then the hands meet at the palm or back of the hand.

DOUBLE DOUBLE

Double Double This This
Fist ends meet twice, back of hands twice.
Double Double That That
Fist ends meet twice, front of hands twice.
Double This
Fist ends meet once, back of hands once.
Double That
Fist ends meet once, front of hands once.
Double Double This That
Fist ends meet twice, back then front.

ARRIBA ABAJO
Four people stand in a square, facing across.
Arriba
Pair A claps above across to partner, pair B claps under and across.
Abajo
The pairs switch so that the As now clap below, Bs clap above.
Al lado
Everyone extends arms to clap person's hands on the side.
Yo contigo
Pair A persons each turn right and clap across to side neighbor.
Tú conmigo
Pair A persons each turn left and clap across to other side neighbor.

THREE – SIX – NINE
(CS means clap own hands – "clap self")
Three – six – nine
Left hand up/right hand down/switch, CS
The goose drank wine
Left hand up/right hand down/switch, CS
The monkey chewed tobacco
Left hand up/right hand down/switch, CS
On the streetcar line.
Left hand up/right hand down/switch, clap twice across

The line it broke,
Left hand up/right hand down/switch, CS
The monkey got choked,
Left hand up/right hand down/switch, CS
And they all went to heaven
Left hand up/right hand down/switch, CS
In a little row boat.
Left hand up/right hand down/switch, clap twice across

Weighted Balls are amazingly therapeutic. These can be found in stores that sell health and fitness items or online. Three or four pounds are versatile. Sit or stand closely with a young child and toss to a simple song. Whether aware of it or not, the child makes an association of this ball with her arm muscles which learn to work hard to lift up. If a young child cannot toss it underhand, practice rocking the "baby" to "Rock-a-Bye Baby," as you swing it yourself several times, then the baby gets tossed over to the child. Then she must rock the baby several times before sending it back to you. This provides ample practice in symmetrical lifting movements of the arms.

Stand farther apart as skill level increases to toss with a child ages 5 to 8, and by age 7 into adolescence, a student can toss it up herself and say a poem or skip count. For an added challenge, stand on a balance board. Tossing this much weight gives the arms a strong experience of lifting out of gravity into levity. Work upward in skill level and do not overdo. It's good if the child has sore arms!

Rod Rolling: Eurythmists and Extra Lesson teachers are familiar with using a copper rod to roll gently up and down the arms. One can have the older child do this herself but with a child age 8 or 9, it is soothing to do this with the "Skye Boat Song" chorus many times and keeping to just the first two verses.

Bean Bag Exercises: Many of these have a quality of using the arms in symmetry or in bilateral coordination, without crossing the midline. *Take Time: Movement Exercises* is one resource.

Handle Exercise: The seated or standing clapping game is also excellent for bilateral coordination.

Age 10 and up

The Extra Lesson exercise known as the Copper Ball exercise contains elements of symmetry with the arms either being parallel or working in bilateral fashion.

Form drawing with both arms

A form drawing developed by Mary Jo Oresti is done on a chalkboard or else on a large vertical piece of paper taped to a wall or door. The child stands directly in front of a vertical line or an imagined one. She draws a form with a large chalk in each hand (or stick crayon if using paper) simultaneously on both sides of the line. It is a mirrored form. This can be done in groups or individually.

GOING TO GRANDMA'S (for grades 1 & 2)

Say this poem while making circles with both hands. Child makes a circle on each side of the line starting at the bottom, moving "away" from midline: Right side circle goes clockwise and left side circle goes counterclockwise. The hands go round and round.

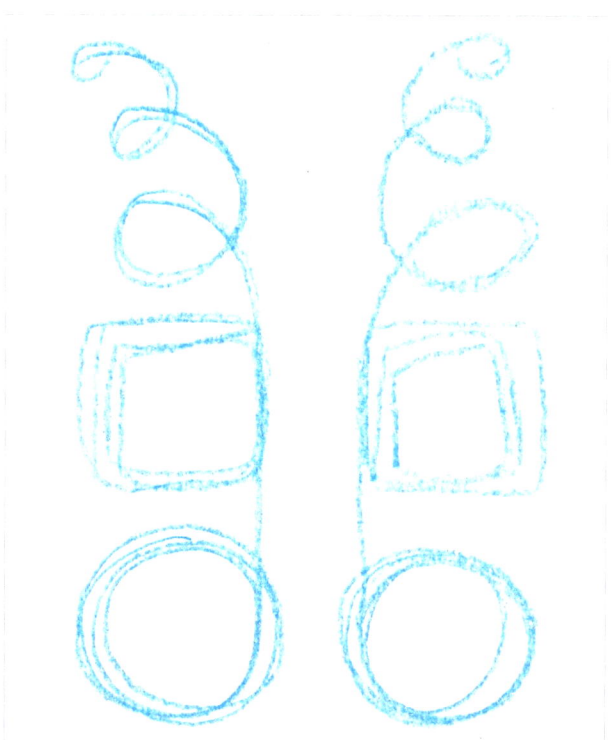

The wheels in the car go round and round (repeat)
  They take us over the bumpy ground.

Next, make squares on each side of the line above the circles, again going up by the center, then outward on the left counterclockwise and clockwise on the right.
The boxes in the trunk they rattle all around (repeat)
  We take them to Grandma who lives across town.

Pause –
STOP !! Here comes a train on the track.
  Child makes straight lines, drawing up.

You can see lots of cars when you look back.
  Child turns head to look, then resumes drawing upward spirals of smoke.
Whoo Whooo... see the smoke coming from the stack!!

Allow for good stretching upward and balance by encouraging them to go on their toes. One can make up lots of simple movements and poems. Also the children may draw down from the top, such as a poem with falling, swirling leaves.

Exercises to strengthen the right side

Rudolf Steiner gave indications to teachers and eurythmists to be used for children with an undecided dominance or ambidexterity. One exercise is found in *Learning Difficulties: A Guide for Teachers.* (Wilby 1998, p.266) It involves using the eyes to track a finger that slowly travels up and down each arm, with a specific color on the left versus right side. A variation of this exercise is provided by Rachel Ross in the *AHE Resource Teacher's Developmental Exercise Manual* vol. 1 along with the Red Star exercise. The Red Star exercise is for the right hand, foot, and eye. Materials needed are a large, red, five-pointed star about 5" in diameter. The red star is made of red copy paper, adhered to a piece of lavender copy paper and laminated. Instructions are in the manual and involve strengthening the right side with focused activity while the left hand is engaged in holding a copper ball or special stone behind the back. There are several parts to the exercise and it is done on an individual basis.

More adaptable to a classroom is the Dominance Form from *The Extra Lesson*. It is also called the Red Snail Trail. It is a large form drawn on a poster board in red block crayon and adhered to a wall or back of a door at ground level. The student sits on the floor and traces it with a sequence of body movements geared all for the left side or all for the right side to strengthen dominance on one side. The directions are found in *The Extra Lesson.* This exercise is indicated for grades one through four and is easy to include in activities set up in a standard classroom with minimal monitoring from an adult or a child from an upper grade. It takes no more than five minutes per child to do this and is recommended for a few times a week for a month for a total of 12 sessions.

(Please note: In the illustration below the student is shown at the side in order to show what the snail trail looks like. In actual practice, the student should sit directly in front of the trail.)

Older students, from grade five (age 11) and up, can strengthen dominance by using the Right Angle Triangle exercise. With careful instruction and monitoring it can be set up in a quiet portion of a classroom, but due to this exercise having four forms (for the left side to be strengthened or else four forms for the right side), it is best done in a more private undisturbed space. Again it is done for 12 sessions over a month or more and is very

effective in helping to establish clearer dominance as well as overall strengthening of the individual.

Specifically to help strengthen eye dominance on the left or right, indications are found in *The Extra Lesson* and through advice from a eurythmist or anthroposophic physician, using a blue lens or a red lens in simple eye frames.

Conclusion

Rudolf Steiner spoke to teachers of the hindrances each child carries at the end of lecture 4 from *The Spiritual Ground of Education*. Helping a child to achieve consistent dominance helps the ego to more fully penetrate the physical organism, which allows for more efficient actions and learning.

Our rightful place as educators
Is to be removers of hindrances.
Each child in every age
Brings something new into
The world from divine regions,
And it is our task, as educators,
To remove bodily and psychical
Obstacles out of the way,
To remove hindrances so that
This spirit may enter in full freedom into life.

REFERENCES

Association for a Healing Education. (2005). *Resource teacher's developmental exercise manual, vol. 1*. Prescott, AZ: AHE.

Eikenboom, J. (2007). *Foundations of the extra lesson*. Fair Oaks, CA: Rudolf Steiner College Press.

Glöckler, M. (2002). *Education as preventative medicine*. Fair Oaks, CA: Rudolf Steiner College Press.

Glöckler, M. & Goebel, W. (2003). *A guide to child health*. Edinburgh: Floris Books.

Goddard, S. (2002). *Reflexes, learning and behavior*. Eugene, OR: Fern Ridge Press.

Hannaford, C. (1995). *Smart moves*. Arlington, VA: Great Ocean Publishers.

_____. (2011). *The dominance factor*. Salt Lake City, UT: Great River Books.

König, K. (1989). *Being human: Diagnosis in curative education*. Great Barrington, MA: Anthroposophic Press.

_____. (1998). *The first three years of the child*. Edinburgh: Floris Books.

McAllen, A. (2004). *The extra lesson*. Fair Oaks, CA: Rudolf Steiner College Press.

_____. (2002). *Teaching children handwriting*. Fair Oaks, CA: Rudolf Steiner College Press.

Mitchell, D., ed. (2002). *Developmental insights*. Chatham, NY: Waldorf Publications.

Nash-Wortham, M. & Hunt, J. (1997). *Take time: Movement exercises for parents, teachers and therapists of children with difficulties in speaking, reading, writing and spelling*. Stourbridge, England: Robinswood Press.

Schoorel, E. (2004). *The first seven years: Physiology of childhood*. Fair Oaks, CA: Rudolf Steiner College Press.

Steiner, R. (1922). *The spiritual ground of education*, lecture 4. http://wn.rsarchive.org/Lectures/GA305/English/APC1947/19220819p01.html

Weihs, T. (1988). *Children in need of special care*. London: Souvenir Press, Ltd.

Wilby, M.E., ed. (1998). *Learning difficulties*. Fair Oaks, CA: Rudolf Steiner College Press.

The care group
Referrals, assessments, therapies, and academic support

Elizabeth Auer

For many years it has been recognized that students in the classroom often need extra support beyond the regular curriculum and the time and availability of the class teacher. In many schools committees have been formed to coordinate this support as a service to the classroom teacher and the students in need.

What is a care group?

The term *care group* has been adopted over time by many support committees in a considerable number of schools all over the nation. In the first Waldorf School, Rudolf Steiner held faculty meetings where students were discussed, and since then students with various needs have been brought up for discussion in faculty meetings, either as a class/group or as individuals. These studies have frequently been referred to as child studies and, depending on the school, take place on a frequent basis throughout the school year. (see "The Art of Child Observation") Over time it was felt that a committee of teachers was needed to take the recommendations from the faculty study and to organize the support needed for the student.

The constellation of the care group

Depending on the unique school situation, the care group can consist of three or more individuals who have a special interest in academic or therapeutic support and who represent the various age groups in the school. Typically the early childhood program, the lower school, and the middle school are represented. If the school's

budget permits, a trained remedial Extra Lesson teacher will be part of the group and may also be the chairperson. Whenever possible responsibilities are shared, with a chairperson taking care of the organization and delegation of different tasks.

Tasks of the care group

This varies from school to school but could include the following:
- Meet at regular times and frequency
- Take minutes of each meeting for future reference
- Support class and subject teachers that could include observing students in and out of the classroom and making recommendations
- Receive and process referrals from teachers and parents
- Organize and lead child studies in faculty meetings
- Follow up on faculty input and organize/arrange for educational support

- Meet with school district educational support teams for local public school assessments, independent education plans (IEPs), and funding
- Invite speakers/experts to present to the faculty or the care group
- Meet with parents and teachers as needed
- Create forms that can be use for parent meetings, referrals, assessments, educational support and invoices, etc.
- Monitor educational support
- Communicate with the members of the support team, create schedules, and organize spaces for them to work
- Organize the first grade screenings and the second grade assessments; facilitate the follow-ups with the teachers
- Develop an up-to-date referral list of independent evaluators, doctors, therapists, and tutors and present them to the faculty for general awareness.

Child observation

Teachers begin observing children from the time they first become acquainted with them, from early childhood on through the grades. If the teacher is taking on a new first grade, the first meeting will usually be at the first grade readiness assessment when the student visits the school for the first time as an applicant. Upon acceptance of admission, the second meeting may take place at the family's home, generally referred to as a home visit. The teacher can observe and get to know the child as well as the parents in the home setting and begin to create the special bonds between both student and teacher and parent and teacher. Once school begins, observation of students happens on a daily and weekly basis and a picture of the child gradually emerges. (see "The Art of Child Observation") Teachers may also make home visits to new students who join in subsequent years.

Referrals

A class teacher or subject teacher who recognizes a student's needs above and beyond the classroom setting can refer the student to the care group chairperson. The form will have the student's name, date of birth, grade, class teacher's name and a brief description of the student's needs. The members of the care group who receive the referral discuss the student and determine whether a child study is needed before it is decided what type of support may be appropriate. A further referral may be made for an assessment by a remedial support teacher or with the local school district support team.

Therapies

The therapies available are given once per week (except for therapeutic eurythmy, twice per week for a shorter duration of time) and either for six or seven consecutive weeks, depending on the school's arrangement with the therapist. This allows the student a break, and allows the therapist an opportunity to give other children a turn. The referral may be repeated later on in the year or in the following year. Results of therapies are not always immediately apparent as the therapies work slowly and deeply on the individual and are not always tangible. The overall desired result is that the child unfolds at her own pace in development, becomes more comfortable in her body, and grows in confidence in her social and academic endeavors.

What follows is an outline of what the various therapies address. For further reading please see the chapter on "Therapies."

Therapeutic eurythmy works on:
- spatial orientation, coordination, movement in space, forms on the floor
- crossing midlines, working with copper rods
- body awareness, grace in movement
- concentration, focus, rhythm

Extra Lesson works on:
- balance
- crossing midlines
- anxiety, nervousness
- body geography
- incarnation process
- eye-hand coordination
- eye tracking
- spatial orientation

The care group

- relationship to numbers
- writing, spelling, and reading

Speech therapy works on:
- clear pronunciation
- relationship to the spoken word

Art therapy works on:
- individual stories/biographies
- immersion in colors
- behavioral concerns

Music therapy works on:
- auditory processing
- sharpening the senses to tone, etc.
- nervousness and anxiety

Spacial Dynamics works on:
- the enhancement of the relationship between the human being and space

Screenings and assessments

There are several different assessment options for the class teacher and the students:
- the first grade readiness screening (see "Child Development")
- the second grade assessment (see "Extra Lesson")
- an Extra Lesson assessment (see "Extra Lesson")
- a school district assessment (see information on the IEP later in this chapter)
- or a private assessment with a specialist.

Other options include an ophthalmology assessment, and an auditory or speech evaluation.

The care group can help determine with the teacher which direction to follow. In addition, Once the assessment is completed, it is reviewed by the teacher together with the care group, and a decision is made as to further steps that need to be taken.

Support programs

Support programs can come in a variety of forms once the need has been determined. In the lower school years, the type of support recommended is often movement that works with the lower senses to strengthen the foundation for learning. (see "The Twelve Senses") This might include therapeutic eurythmy and Spacial Dynamics, as well as occupational therapy and sensory integration. Music or art therapy may also be recommended. Some of these therapies may take place at the school during the school day, such as therapeutic eurythmy. Other therapies, such as occupational therapy, would be scheduled for after-school hours and at the therapy office location.

Tutoring in math and language arts typically may be provided in the later years beginning in fifth grade, sometimes as early as fourth grade. Tutoring can be scheduled during school hours at the school, or after school hours at the school or in the tutor's work location.

Craniosacral therapy

Craniosacral therapy is a gentle, hands-on approach that releases tensions deep in the body to relieve pain and dysfunction and improve whole-body health and performance. It was pioneered and developed by osteopathic physician John E. Upledger in the late 1970s.

The craniosacral system is made up of the membranes and fluid that surround, protect, and nourish the brain and spinal cord. A craniosacral practitioner uses a soft touch to release any restrictions in the soft tissues in the central nervous system. It is effective for a wide range of medical problems associated with pain and dysfunction. The practice is increasingly used as a preventive

health measure for its ability to bolster resistance to disease. It has proven effective in working with the following conditions:
- migraines and headaches
- chronic neck and back pain
- autism stress and tension-related disorders
- motor coordination impairments
- infant and childhood disorders
- brain and spinal cord injuries
- chronic fatigue
- fibromyalgia
—and more.

Sensory integration

Sensory Integration therapy is the result of the life work of Jane Ayres, an occupational therapist and educational psychologist. Her work indicated to her that children who have irregularities in sensory processing can develop challenges and problems such as inattention, over- or under-sensitivity to sensory stimulus and input, lack of muscle tone and coordination, as well as speech and language problems and behavioral concerns. Dr. Ayres developed a series of tests to assess the basic components of sensory integration, such as touch reception, balance, spatial orientation, hand-eye coordination, bilateral integration and motor planning.

Sensory processing is the neurological process that organizes sensations from the body and the environment to enable the body to be used effectively in the environment. The typically developing child does not need specialized therapy because play naturally provides her with the sensory experiences her brain needs and allows her to respond in a meaningful way to stimuli. Each child is unique and has different neurological needs. Sometimes the encoding of the sensory information does not function efficiently, causing a Sensory Processing Disorder (SPD) that can cause postural control problems, poor motor control, and sensory modulation disorder.

Sensory Integration therapy is most commonly used together with occupational therapy programs and is one of the approaches used by the specialists who treat children with autism, attention deficit disorders, and other learning disabilities.

Therapies vary widely, and many of the suggested exercises dovetail with those for occupational therapy. For instance, therapies for the vestibular system (balance) include movement on swings, spinning, rolling, somersaults, and cartwheels. Therapy for the proprioceptive system (body position, spatial orientation) involves bouncing on a trampoline, skipping, and pushing large objects. Typically the sensory integration therapist has a wide variety of equipment for all kinds of activities to provide for the child all sorts of opportunities for full body movements as well as finer movements such as manipulating objects.

Occupational therapy

The term *occupation* refers to activities that may support the health, well-being, and development of an individual. For children and youth, occupations are activities that enable them to learn and develop life skills (school activities), be creative and/or derive enjoyment (play), and thrive (self-care and care for others) as both a means and an end. Occupational therapy practitioners work with children of all ages (birth through young adulthood) and abilities to promote active participation in activities or occupations that are meaningful to them. Recommended interventions are based on a thorough understanding of typical development and the impact of disability, illness, and impairment on the individual child's development, play, learning, and overall occupational performance.

Occupational therapy practitioners provide services by collaborating with other professionals to identify and meet needs of children experiencing delays or challenges in development; identifying and modifying or overcoming barriers that interfere with, restrict, or inhibit a child's functional performance; teaching and modeling skills and strategies to children and their families to extend therapeutic intervention; and adapting activities, materials, and environmental conditions so children can participate under different conditions and in various environments.

Developmental needs

The primary occupations of young children are play and interacting with caregivers. Occupational therapists evaluate children's development and provide intervention to improve skills and/or modify environments when concerns arise about a child's functional performance. Some examples are:
- Facilitating movement to help a child sit independently or crawl
- Helping a child learn to follow 2- or 3-step instructions
- Helping a child develop the ability to dress independently
- Helping a child learn to cope with disappointment or failure
- Reducing extraneous environmental noise for a child who is easily distracted
- Building skills for sharing, taking turns, and playing with peers
- Helping a child develop the ability to use toys and materials in both traditional and creative ways

Educational needs

Occupational therapy practitioners work with students in preschool, and elementary, middle, and high school to support successful learning, appropriate behavior, and participation in daily school routines and activities.

Academic support

Academic support is usually for language arts and math. The process of reading and writing can be augmented by a specialist in the Orton-Gillingham and/or Wilson method, where the student is usually seen on an individual and weekly basis as a supplement to daily work done in the classroom. With math, processes and times tables are supported and practiced in the lower grades, as well as a focus on number awareness, depending on the need of the student. In the middle school, students can receive tutoring by math specialists.

The Orton-Gillingham method

The Orton-Gillingham philosophy is based on a technique of studying and teaching language and on the understanding of the nature of human language, of the mechanisms involved in learning, and of the language learning processes of individuals. Inherent in the language acquisition process is emphasis on the meaning and comprehension of the material that is written and read.

The Orton-Gillingham method is a program that was developed for the student to acquire skills through a multi-sensory approach that is phonetically based, structured, sequential, cumulative, and rational. (see "Reading and Writing")

The Wilson Reading System

This is an intensive Tier 3 program for students in grades 2–12 and for adults with word-level deficits who are not making sufficient progress and have been unable to learn with other teaching strategies and require multisensory language instruction; or who require more intensive structured literacy instruction due to a language-based learning disability, such as dyslexia.

As a structured literacy program based on phonological-coding research and Orton-Gillingham principles, The Wilson Reading System directly and systematically teaches the structure of the English language. Through the program, students learn fluent decoding and encoding skills to the level of mastery. From the beginning steps of the program, students receive instruction in:
- phonemic awareness
- decoding and word study
- sight word recognition
- spelling
- fluency
- vocabulary
- oral expressive language development
- comprehension

The Lindamood-Bell program

This is an individualized instructional or tutorial program used in a therapeutic setting. This approach can be used with poor readers of all ages who are dyslexic or otherwise severely disabled. The program emphasizes three sensory-cognitive functions that underlie reading and comprehension:

- Phoneme awareness—the ability to auditorially perceive sounds within words
- Symbol imagery—the ability to create mental imagery for sounds and letters within words
- Concept imagery—the ability to create mental representations for the whole: actions, scenes, movement, and so forth.

The school district assessment and the Individual Education Plan (IEP) process

This is a summary of the assessments available in local school districts and how the process of obtaining an IEP for a student works. The availability, the application process, and the criteria for receiving an IEP will vary from state to state.

What is an Individual Education Program?

An individualized Education Program (IEP) describes the educational plan that has been designed to meet the student's unique needs. Each child who receives special education and related services must have an IEP. The IEP process creates an opportunity for teachers, parents, school administrators, and related service professionals to work together to improve education for children with learning disabilities.

Legal document

The IEP is a legally binding document that establishes a plan for an individual student. The eligibility criteria for an IEP include the following:

- autism and Asperger's disorder
- Pervasive Developmental Disorder (PDD)
- emotional impairment
- physical impairment
- communication impairment
- developmentally delayed learning disorder
- sensory impairment
- limited cognitive function
- specific learning disability
- health issues

A summary of what is contained in the IEP (when appropriate and needed):
- the student's disability
- a vision statement of the student's long-term goals
- description of how the student's disability affects his or her progress in the classroom
- how the student's progress toward these goals will be measured
- accommodations
- a program designed to address emotional and behavior issues
- summer services
- transport needs
- type of placement

When to refer a student for a school district assessment

- A student is struggling academically, or not performing at the same level as the other students in the class. A student struggling to read is one of the major reasons students are referred for an IEP.
- There are behavior difficulties at home or at school. The student may exhibit unusual stress or anxiety.
- The student may exhibit attention issues such as Attention Deficit Disorder, (ADD) or Attention Deficit Hyperactivity Disorder (ADHD)
- Depression
- The student has memory difficulties, short term or long term.

The IEP Team

The Federal law, or Individuals with Disabilities Act (IDEA), defines the IEP team as a group of people who are responsible for developing, reviewing and revisiting the IEP for a student with a disability. The team includes:
- parents
- teacher
- school system representative
- special education provider
- a professional who can interpret the instructional implications of the evaluation results

Types of evaluations

There are several types of evaluations/assessments that can be done by the school system or by an independent evaluator. The school system evaluations assess all areas of suspected disabilities. An independent evaluator may evaluate only one aspect, such as speech. A school system assessment include:

Educational Evaluation – an assessment of reading, written language, spelling, math. The reading evaluation includes assessment of word analysis skills (word decoding, word recognition, oral reading rate, and comprehension).

Psychological Evaluation – an intelligence test measuring general cognitive ability. Sensory, motor, language, perceptual, attention, cognitive, affective, attitudinal, self-image, interpersonal, behavioral, interest, and vocational factors are evaluated in regard to the student's maturity, integrity and dynamic interaction within the educational context. The assessment is based on the student's developmental and social history, diagnostic observation of the student in familiar surroundings (such as the classroom), and psychological testing as indicated.

Neuropsychological Evaluation – provides a profile that tells the parents and teachers how the student approaches learning and doing things, based on patterns of strengths, weaknesses, and integration among a range of neurological measures. (ADD, autism, PDD or specific learning difficulties are assessed in this evaluation.)

Functional Behavioral Assessment – a problem-solving process for addressing problem behaviors. It is used to create behavior plans that contain strategies and skills the student needs in order to behave in a more appropriate manner, or that provide motivation to conform to required standards. The plan should be pro-active with positive intervention plans that teach new ways of behaving and should address both the source of the problem and the problem itself.

Speech and Language Evaluation – an assessment of receptive language, expressive language, phonological processing, articulation,

Elizabeth Auer

voice, auditory memory, and pragmatics (ability to use language with others).

Auditory Processing Evaluation – an evaluation by an audiologist who identifies, measures, and treats hearing disorders as well as loss and central auditory processing issues.

Occupational Therapy (OT) Evaluation – assesses gross and fine motor skills, visual motor integration and visual perception or visual processing.

Physical Therapy (PT) Evaluation – assesses physical activities such as sitting, standing, crawling, walking, running, and climbing. It looks at the student's body strength, coordination, balance, and symmetry as she moves and controls her body, and how she plans new motor activities.

Assistive Technology (AT) Assessment – determines if devices can assist the student's learning process.

Transition Assessment – may include independent living assessments, aptitude tests, intelligence tests, achievement tests, and measure of self-determination.

Home Assessment – by an authorized social worker, nurse, guidance counselor, teacher or psychologist to ascertain pertinent family history and home situation factors including, with parent consent, a home visit.

Teacher Assessment/Observation – an assessment by the teacher to include current information on the student's present level of performance in the general curriculum.

How does the process begin?

The process begins with a referral from the teacher or the parent of a student to the care group. In most cases the care group will already have an awareness of the student's challenges, and remedial work will have taken place or have begun. There may or may not be in place an informal in-house IEP that has been carefully planned for the student by the student's teacher together with the care group.

The care group serves to help the teacher and parent create the best possible conditions for their students to learn to his/her best capacities. It may take several years for an IEP process to be initiated from the date of the student's enrollment at the school. Typically, students are given a chance to develop and mature into school-ready children. Some students in the first years of school benefit from therapeutic eurythmy to help them feel at home in their bodies and orient them in the space around them. The second grade assessments done during the second half of the year may indicate challenges, and Extra Lesson will be recommended. Typically around grade three (and usually not before), it may become apparent that the student is unable to keep up with his or her peers for certain reasons. Tutoring begins mostly in fifth grade. An IEP process, if and when needed, may be implemented at this time. (There are cases of young students coming from other schools who already have IEPs established by their school districts. In this case the IEP would be reviewed by the admissions team in conjunction with the teacher and the care group.)

This process toward an IEP then typically serves both students who are unable to keep up with their academic work in the classroom and students who may need help beyond the regular help that the school can provide. The IEP process is carried out under the overview of the Student Administration Unit (SAU) of the local school district, both for public and private schools.

The IEP process follows specific steps in sequence:

1. *Identification of the student and referral process.*

    The teacher and the case manager (or care group chairperson) of the student meet with the parents to determine the need. Parents are asked to sign a permission form for the assessment/ evaluation if the need is determined. (Parents may initiate the meeting with the teacher.)
    The case manager of the student at the school then communicates with the special education teacher at the local school and sets up a pre-evaluation meeting for the team. This can be followed up with a written referral explaining what the learning challenges are. Any report from a professional, such as a developmental optometrist or a neuropsychological evaluation, is copied and submitted for review before the second meeting.

2. *Pre-evaluation meeting*

    Parent or teacher can request a pre-evaluation conference to talk with a school professional about the five Ws: Who, What, When, Where and Why—
    - Who will conduct the evaluation,
    - What evaluations would be helpful,
    - When the student will be taken out of class to be evaluated,
    - Where the evaluations will take place,
    - Who will explain Why the evaluations are happening.

    The team members meet and review the referral material submitted and any pre-existing submitted materials. The evaluations decided upon depend on the individual student. Testing will be conducted by trained, licensed evaluators. The testing is usually done within school hours at the school in the privacy of one of the small rooms that are made available for this purpose.

3. *Determination of eligibility – post-evaluation meeting*

    The team meets this time to review the results of the testing and to determine whether the child is eligible for special education services. To be eligible, the child must have a disability and require special education or special education and related services to benefit from education. The child will then be identified or coded with a specific classified disability. Parents are asked to sign a document stating that they agree with the findings of the testing. Without the parent's signature, further IEP planning cannot take place. Parents have the right to waive the signature and end the process. If parents disagree with the results of the testing, conflicts can be resolved through discussion and information sharing. If issues cannot be settled informally, formal dispute resolution procedures can be implemented. A list of organizations/agencies that help parents understand the special education process and resolve disputes should be available.

4. *Development of the IEP*

    Within 30 days after the student is found eligible for special education, the team meets to develop an individualized education program for the student. Once a student has an IEP, it is reviewed, revised annually, and put in place at the start of the school year. The IEP becomes effective once the parents have signed the document. The team meets once more to determine the least restrictive environment in which the child can receive educational services described in his or her IEP.

5. *Monitoring*

    Once the IEP is in place and implemented, the educators involved monitor the student's progress on an ongoing basis to ensure his or her educational needs are met. If concerns arise about the student's progress, a meeting of the team may be requested. The IEP is typically reviewed after three years to determine if services need to be continued.

Services

Services for support by the school district vary from district to district, state to state. They are mostly available only if the student attends the school where the assessment took place. If this is not deemed advisable, the care group team with the parents can devise an in-house IEP with accommodations in the classroom. Parents with a student who has an IEP can also opt to have tutoring services done at the Waldorf school that are paid for by the state, such as a Title 1 program. In this case the tutor, who is often a reading and/or math specialist comes to the school during class time.

Note: Currently the school district stresses that the student referred needs to be receiving adequate instruction, and teachers need to be prepared to explain and defend the Waldorf methods of teaching reading, writing, and math. You, your care group chairperson, and your school administration may need to provide the school district with a document to this end, in order for the school district team to agree to have the student tested.

In the case of a newly-admitted student, a careful checking of prior school records and reports will need to be made to determine if the student has had adequate instruction prior to being admitted.

In addition, the student needs to be failing to make adequate progress academically, even though supports and modifications have been tried before the referral is made. Many students have needs, but they do not necessarily have a learning disability and will not always be granted an IEP.

The 504 Plan

Congress passed a civil rights law in 1973 that protects people with disabilities by eliminating barriers and allowing full participation in areas of life such as education and the workplace. Executive function, ADD/ADHD, and memory issues fall into this category. A physician must make a diagnosis and then the student can be eligible for modifications that support him/her with this disability. This is known as Section 504 or the 504 Plan.

The purpose of a 504 Plan is to level the playing field and allow a student to get the accommodations and modifications needed to access the curriculum at the same level as his or her peers.

The 504 Plan is based on the student's medical disability, for students who have a disability, have a record of a disability, or are treated as having a disability but do not qualify for special education services under IDEA. For example, let's say that a child has cerebral palsy. While it does not interfere with the student's progress in the general curriculum, it does require the child to use special equipment to access his/her education. Therefore, this child would qualify for a 504 Plan.

Before deciding whether a student is eligible for this type of plan, the child must be assessed and the school team must agree that the child has a substantial and pervasive impairment in order to be eligible under this federal law.

RESOURCES

Autism Research Institute, San Diego, CA, https://www.autism.com/

"Definition of Occupational Therapy Practice for the AOTA Model Practice Act," http://www.aota.org/-/media/corporate/files/advocacy/state/resources/practiceact/model%20definition%20of%20ot%20practice%20%20adopted%2041411.pdf

"Guide to the Individualized Education Plan." U.S. Department of Education, https://www2.ed.gov/parents/needs/speced/iepguide/index.html?exp=0

Institute for Multi-Sensory Integration, Orton-Gillingham approach. https://www.orton-gillingham.com/

Oresti, Mary Jo and Ross, Rachel. *Care group manual*, Association for a Healing Education, Southfield, MI.

The extra lesson

First grade readiness screening and second grade assessment

Maggie Scott, Elizabeth Auer and Brigitta Witteveen

The capacities needed for learning lie in the developmental process of the first seven years of a child's life. Normally, through the development of the lower senses, early childhood provides for the child: movement coordination, spatial orientation, and the visual perception to move between two and three-dimensional images effortlessly. These, along with good body geography and established dominance, form the foundation for learning. The Extra Lesson addresses the needs of a struggling student by first assessing what areas of development might be weak or missing, and then offering a series of exercises to further develop those areas.

The Extra Lesson was developed by Audrey McAllen in England, during the early 1970s. She was an experienced Waldorf teacher had been inspired by Rudolf Steiner's many lectures on the developing human being and by her own work with children with learning difficulties. It was out of her teaching experience, her deep study of Steiner's work, and her observation of children with needs that Ms. McAllen developed first an assessment and then a curriculum of movement, speech, drawing, and painting exercises to support the further development of children who are struggling in the classroom.

The Extra Lesson is meant to be used as one part of a solution with other interventions, which might include: nutritional/diet support, osteopathy, therapeutic eurythmy, art or music therapy, and for older children, academic support. Ideally, an individual student will have an Extra Lesson once or twice per week for an hour, as well as a short daily home practice. A typical lesson consists of floor exercises, speech work, form drawings, bean bag and ball exercises, and working with copper rods and balls, and concludes with a painting lesson.

The Extra Lesson is not just for individual children; it can also greatly benefit an entire class. Much of the Extra Lesson work can be used in addition to other exercises such as "Take Time" in the classroom to support every child's ability to learn, focus, and engage socially. Many of the exercises can also help a teacher bring focus and concentration to a class when needed. If possible, it is helpful to have another teacher come and be an extra set of eyes to help observe a class while doing the exercises to come to a clearer understanding of what a class teacher might want to focus on.

Not all schools are fortunate enough to be able to employ an Extra lesson specialist full time. Some schools have an Extra Lesson teacher on a part-time basis, for example, for two days a week, or they arrange for a specialist to come for a block of time to do the screenings for first grade readiness and the second grade assessment.

Exercises

In the classroom with the whole class

Note: Some of these exercises can be done with the students standing behind their chairs or in a circle. Others will need more space for movement, especially the exercises for integrating the early movement patterns.

To support the development of body geography:

"Simon Says": Ask the students to touch parts of the body with both hands, right or left hand crossing over, for example, place your pinky from your left hand on your right big toe.

To support the development of spatial orientation:

Bringing awareness of left and right: Two soft felt balls, blue and red. Students have one in each hand. Ask them to throw up the one in the right hand while passing the ball in the left hand to the right hand and catching the returning ball in the left hand.

Awareness of above and below: Students hold a ball in each hand and throw first the right one under the right leg and catch it with the same hand, then throw the ball in the left hand under the left leg and catch with the same hand. When rhythm is established, students walk forward and backward while saying the times tables.

Awareness of forward and backward: Students each grasp a copper rod vertically, with the right hand above the left at arm's length, and walk forward and backward counting out loud or saying a chosen sentence, stepping on each number or word. They change the position of the rod to behind the back, with the same walking and speaking. For very bad posture holding the rod horizontally across the shoulders is effective.

To help establish dominance:

For the hand: games such as looking-aim, skittles, throwing rings over a hook. *For the foot:* hopping and stamping with the dominant foot. (see "Dominance")

To integrate early developmental movement patterns:

These exercises can be done with the whole class taking turns on the mat on the floor, lining up to take their turn. Working with half the class is best while the other half is busy with something else; otherwise it may take too long for the children to have their turn. (This of course depends on how large the class is.) In some schools the movement teacher incorporates these exercises into the movement lesson. Or the school employs an Extra Lesson teacher who works with the class, maybe once a week.

Creeping on the floor like a lizard, using both arms and legs with stomach on floor

Caterpillar crawl, lying on the back and pushing with heels backward along the floor without the help of the arms

Crab walk: forward, backward and sideways, keeping bottoms off the mat

Circus seal: Students lie on mat and roll along, keeping their bodies straight and hands up above head. You can make this progressively more challenging by placing a bean bag between the knees or feet, and as they roll along the bean bag needs to stay in place.

Eagle: Students lie down on their stomachs and first place their arms at the sides. Ask them to slowly raise their arms up with hands under their shoulder blades as though spreading their wings, lifting head and also lifting their legs that need to be kept straight.

Roly poly: Students lie flat on their backs, bring their knees up toward their chins, clasp the knees around with a two handed clasp, and rock the body back and forth, while keeping their balance.

To integrate the horizontal and vertical midlines:

Wool winding, skein twisting, braiding and modeling with beeswax, juggling, table tennis, sweeping

Other exercises for the whole class:

Stretching and lifting: With the students gazing straight ahead, ask them to lift the toes as high as they will go without the soles of the feet lifting from the floor. Now ask them to lower the toes and press them hard against the floor, gripping it as strongly as possible. Repeat twice more, then raise the heels and stand on the toes with the ball of the foot up from the floor. The hands should remain at the side of the body. This exercise helps to release tensions and to experience the lifting element in which the will forces are working. It also helps the students with spatial orientation.

Bouncing balls: Each student has a ball in each hand, bounces the ball from the one hand on the floor, and turns the hand to catch it with the same hand, then repeat with the other hand. Alternating hands, the students count forward to a given number and then back again. This exercise brings great flexibility between the stretching and lifting elements and requires will forces and concentration.

An obstacle course: For the young children an obstacle course is a wonderful way to get them to crawl under and jump over objects, as well as squeeze and wriggle through a narrow tunnel. You can include a station where the students have to use fine motor skills such as turning pennies or buttons over from one side to the other. Include also the bunny hop, hopping through rings, balancing along a balance beam—whatever you can come up with that challenges the students. In the very early years a story to go along with the journey through the obstacles is ideal. (Try pairing up children and have one lead his blindfolded partner through the course.)

Writing with feet: This is a wonderful exercise and can be done in the classroom while the students are seated at their desks. Each student has a slate on the floor in front of the feet, and a white piece of chalk between the big toe and second toe. Students practice writing their names on the slates in front of them. This can be very challenging for some who will need encouragement as you circle around the room.

Finger walking on a rod: Each student holds a rod horizontally with two hands, and the fingers move to the side and back again to the middle. Variations include holding the rod vertically with one hand and moving the fingers up and down. (see "Music, Gym, and the Pencil Grip")

Painting the lemniscate (figure eight): This is a painting that can be done in a regular painting lesson and is a marvelous exercise. First paint a large figure eight, horizontally, in yellow. Then fill in the left center loop with cobalt blue and take this across the yellow to surround the outside of the right-hand loop of the figure eight. Next fill the right-side center with red and paint this across the yellow to surround the outside of the left-hand loop. The painting movements should be from above to below.

Form drawing: There are many forms that can be drawn (see "Therapeutic Aspects of Form Drawing"), but one of the special forms that McAllen created is the flower rod exercise. This form is also a lemniscate, drawn vertically with a centering line. McAllen stated that "in this exercise we can see if the student has the capacity to move inwardly from the convex to concave mirroring and the willingness to be receptive."

IMPORTANT NOTE: There are many other exercises that are best left to the Extra Lesson specialist who can work with the students individually. For further reading and understanding of the above exercises, see *The Extra Lesson* by Audrey McAllen.

Home program:

Here are some activities that support a child's capacity for learning at home or at recess.

Activities for vestibular stimulation:
- Play with a large beach ball: lie on it, under it, place feet on top while holding a push-up position (with supervision)
- Rolling and sliding in a box down a hill, wheelbarrow rides
- Balance boards, trampoline jumping
- Merry-go-rounds, swings, slides, teeter-totter, jungle gym
- Climbing up stairs and jumping down with feet together

- Hammock play
- Jumping rope games

Activities to improve tactile perception:
- Play with varied textures: sand, clay, paint.
- Draw on a carpet square with chalk: numbers, letters, shapes, tic-tac-toe; erase chalk with hands, feet, and forearms.
- Find common household items such as a key, paper clip, marble, silverware, cork, pencil, nail, etc. (can use pairs of items) and hide them in a box of millet, having the child identify or match each object while blindfolded. Also provide a box of mixed beans for the hands and feet to sift through.
- Draw in the sand with hands or feet.
- Massage with lotion or a firm pressure rubdown after bath time and before bed.

Activities to improve gross motor skills:
- Crawling on all fours through hula hoops, under tables, etc.
- Hitting a balloon on a string
- Swimming
- Shaking sheets/towels out for spreading and folding
- Drawing/writing upright on a chalkboard or easel
- Chores such as carrying trash, raking, carrying and washing dishes, moving furniture
- Jumping over obstacles, lines, and cracks
- Jumping with one or both feet
- Ball throwing and catching
- Hula hoop
- Balloon volleyball
- Games: "Simon Says, "Follow the Leader," "Tug of War"

Activities to improve fine motor skills:
- Kneading dough and mixing batter
- Using a hole puncher
- Wringing out clothes, face cloths
- Hanging up clothes using clothespins
- Using cake decorating tools
- Stretching rubber bands around an object
- Stringing beads, macaroni, Cheerios, straws, paper clips

- Finger puppets
- Paper folding/origami
- Flicking coins or ping pong balls into a cup
- Turning over/shuffling cards, checkers, and coins

Activities for perceptual skills:
- Sorting a deck of cards, beads, buttons, or shells by shape, size, and color
- Sorting laundry socks
- Copying designs with pipe cleaners, toothpicks, popsicle sticks, coins, play dough
- Picking out items on a grocery list
- "Itsy Bitsy Spider" song with hand movements
- "Simon Says"
- Construction toys such as Legos, waffle bricks, Lincoln Logs
- Pin the tail on the donkey

Activities for visual motor skills:
- Using a paint brush or giant chalk on slanted surface
- Cutting with scissors
- Using a squirt bottle
- Using an eyedropper with colored water to paint on paper
- Rolling, tearing, and crumbling colored tissue paper to stick onto clear contact paper

- Stringing beads, macaroni, straws, paper clips, Cheerios
- Picking up rice, popcorn, or other small objects with tweezers
- Using chopsticks
- Pinching clothespins with thumb and fingertips
- Sealing ziplock bags
- Crawling on all fours, rocking back and forth in this position
- Swinging on swings and playing on monkey bars

The Extra Lesson assessment

A general Extra Lesson assessment may be requested at any time during the elementary school years. Students may be referred in any of the grades, especially as they arrive in the middle school years when the work becomes more challenging. New students are given some time to settle down in the class and their new school environment and often have to catch up on their artistic work as well as academic work. At times teachers will refer a student for a school district or a private neurological/cognitive evaluation that goes beyond the Extra Lesson assessment.

A general Extra Lesson assessment looks at the student's physical development, gross and fine motor skills, dominance, integration of early movement patterns, body geography awareness, spatial orientation in space and time, finger grip and posture, writing, reading, spelling, math, form drawing, listening and hearing, speech, eye-tracking, and short-term memory, and usually finishes up with asking the student to draw a Person, House and Tree picture. (see "Children's Drawings") Observations are made as to how the student cooperates, follows instructions, relates to the assessor, moves around in the room, and manages all the assignments. (see additional notes on criteria for observation)

There are two mainstay Extra Lesson assessments that take place every year—one for first grade readiness and the other for a general development progress check.

First grade readiness screening

This screening is provided for children who are chronologically ready for first grade and who have been deemed by the kindergarten teachers to be ready for formal instruction. (see developmental milestones in the chapter on "Child Development") It is also an assessment for prospective students who come from non-Waldorf schools. Over the years Waldorf schools have developed various modes and processes for this assessment, and the way it is handled and organized will vary from school to school. The following process is an example of how it can be organized.

The kindergarten teacher(s) present the class of children to the faculty in January and give an outline of the potential students who are ready to move on to first grade. This is followed by the organization of the assessment by the care group chairperson and a team consisting of the lead teacher and observers. The eligible students are split up into groups of four or five, and a suitable time is set for the assessment.

The assessment

Students are fetched from the kindergarten in small groups and led to the eurythmy room or other suitable space where the lead teacher and the observers are waiting for them. They have prepared and set up the room with a balance beam, rings on the floor, jump ropes, bean bags, crayons and paper at a bench in the corner, and so forth. The lead teacher greets the children and begins the storytelling while the children travel around the room, balancing over the bridge, tossing bean bags, hopping on one foot along the rings, bending over to go under a chair, stepping up and over a chair, and so on. The observers each have a couple of students to watch and they take notes on each. They look for various criteria: dominance, fine and gross motor control, listening and focusing ability, crossing midlines, being able to touch the left ear with the right hand stretched over the head, ability to move with the group, the Person, House, Tree drawing as well as a Form drawing, and other aspects.

The follow-up

A meeting is arranged as a follow-up to the assessments, and the team members discuss the findings together with the admissions director. It can happen that a particular student is deemed not quite ready and the request may be made for another follow-up assessment in May with some physical exercises, such as jumping rope, suggested for the student to work on before the reassessment. Most often the kindergarten teachers have a fine sense of which children are ready, and for the most part the assessment is a confirmation of the students' readiness. There are times when parents deem their child ready and the teachers feel he or she needs more time—this needs careful mediation between the parents and the kindergarten teachers.

Students from other schools

At times it is possible to have students from other schools that are applying for first grade to be assessed with the group from the in-house kindergarten(s.) This can be coordinated with the admissions director. Some teachers prefer to do the screenings individually, other teachers prefer to do the screening in small groups so that the social interaction of the student within the group can be observed.

The second grade assessment

This assessment is also under the purview of the Extra Lesson and takes place during the second half of second grade. After giving the students time to settle in to the class and to be introduced to writing and reading as well as all the other subjects, it is time to evaluate how they are developing their physical and academic skills. The assessment is similar in some ways to the first grade readiness assessment, with the addition of assessing for early (primitive) reflex retentions and the newly acquired skills such as spelling, math, reading, and writing. The other big difference is that the students are each assessed individually and not in a group. Typically the assessor is an Extra Lesson specialist who schedules an hour for each student.

Criteria for observation

Dominance: Is it established? Is it mixed? Are their signs of ambidexterity?

Gross motor skills: jumping rope, running/accelerating/dead stop, high jump, long jump, throwing and catching a ball, kicking a ball, hopping on one foot, hopping on two feet, balancing on a beam or rope

Fine motor skills: threading a needle, turning pennies over

Toe dexterity: picking up jewels with toes, writing name with pencil between toes

Spatial orientation: backward, forward, sideways, centered, diagonal

Time of year: season, weekday, yesterday and tomorrow

Sense of symmetry: form drawing, simple vertical and horizontal symmetry, crossing midlines

Math: simple computations showing understanding of all four processes

Writing: alphabet in order in capital letters and lowercase—any reversals? Hesitation? Repeatedly having to start all over again from the beginning?

Numbers: any reversals?

Finger grip: correct, poor?

Writing a sentence: Does it have a verb and a noun? Hesitation?

Spelling: list of typical words covered in class

Reading: list of typical words covered in class

Person House Tree drawing: Are all three elements there? Is there a ground and a sky/sun? Is the figure threefolded? Does the house have windows, a door with a handle? (see "Children's Drawings")

Reflex retention check: Does the neck move freely sideways and the head up and down, bilateral integration etc. (see "Development and Integration of the Human Body" for more on reflexes)

The follow-up

The care group team meets with the class teacher to discuss their observations and any resulting concerns from the individual assessments. This discussion may also include any behavior or social concerns in the classroom or during recess. Recommendations may be made for students who are showing challenges with any of the criteria assessed. Also included can be recommendations for music or art therapy, therapeutic eurythmy, or Spacial Dynamics. (see "The Care Group" and "Healing Therapies")

The observations on each student are written up and stored in the student's file, and generally kept as in-house information.

A chart for recording class-wide screenings

In this article, AHE alumnus Brigitta Witteveen explains how she developed a useful chart to monitor progress of the capacities we want to see developed in children in order for them to be successful in school. Sharing the charts with the class teachers and subject teachers over the years has been a successful process at her school, The Waldorf School of Lexington. – Connie Helms

The history

My interest has always been the healing aspect of Waldorf education. When I became the Extra Lesson teacher at The Waldorf School of Lexington, MA, in 1996, I had completed my training in Association for a Healing Education's educational support program (AHE). Previously I completed the early childhood and elementary Waldorf training at Antioch University New England in Keene, NH, and later the Waldorf high school training at Rudolf Steiner College in Fair Oaks, CA.

My first task in the job was to complete assessments with the new incoming students and the students going from kindergarten to first grade. I started using the format of assessments created by my former colleague, following indications from the Extra Lesson plus input from colleagues and fellow AHE students. Over time, the order and content of the assessments changed and solidified with use.

The exercises I use with the children from the Extra Lesson make up the header of the chart: ball playing, jump rope, bean bag, drawing, form drawing, checking reflexes, writing and others.

With all the information gathered about the children, my question became how to best communicate the information to my colleagues. Sitting down with each teacher and going over the assessment itself is my primary way.

I started to create on paper what would become the prototype of a chart, listing the names of students in an alphabetical order on the left side of the paper, making check marks after the individual student's name. This was all done by hand in black and white. Later, I started using colored pencils to indicate the levels of the students' work: green, red and orange, with green showing competency in an area, orange being a "watch," and red signifying difficulty with mastery. Soon I realized I needed a computerized changeable chart, one that could follow the students through their years in school.

At the suggestion of my older daughter, I headed for the Apple store. She suggested a MacBook Pro with some specific applications: pages, numbers, AND a year of one-on-one tutorials with Apple computer professionals. That summer was a very rainy one—a perfect opportunity to take a class several times a week. Learning how to use formulas, I revised the chart with colors in numbers: The chart took shape.

 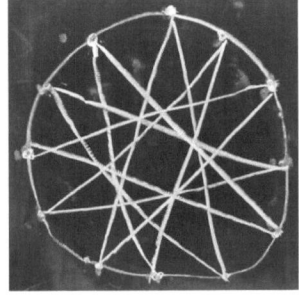

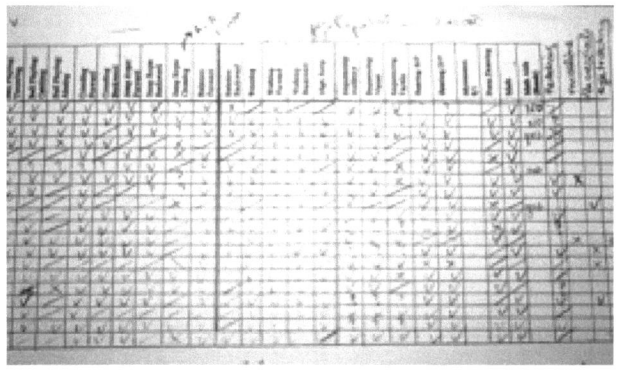

The use of the chart

The Spacial Dynamics teacher and I have worked closely together with the chart over the years. Through its use, we are able to see an individual student's progress and get a picture of the whole class situation, both strengths and weaknesses. Out of that information the movement teacher, the classroom teacher, and the subject teachers can observe which activities may help individual students and what would support a class as a whole.

Eventually it became clear that the Extra Lesson components that made up the base of the chart could be used in any of the subject classes. The Extra Lesson exercises could be done before a German, Spanish, reading, math, or handwork class. I showed the exercises to the subject teachers so they could do them themselves. Gradually I added some subject classes to my chart. I now check in with those teachers and add their input to the chart as well.

This allows for research over time and shows how the developmental stages noted in the chart impact the students' work in school. One can also use the information to see trends and changes over the years. For example, some years a class may need more work in balance. This year I see a need for more work in spatial orientation and eye tracking.

Once the chart is made from the screenings with the kindergarten students, I share the results with the kindergarten teachers, the incoming class teacher, and the educational support group. In these meetings we share suggestions for activities, some of which can happen in the classrooms while others are done individually or in a small group.

When meeting with parents, I take notes from the chart and show them exercises that will benefit their child. I never share the chart itself with a parent (as that would expose confidential information about other students), just the content of their own child's evaluation. I explain that my findings capture that moment in time when I saw their child and that changes can happen. Each student is unique and has his or her own timeline for progress.

Presently I am in communication with one of our kindergarten teachers about how to further involve the parents in their child's development. Sharing in a class parent evening, I will go over some of the work I do with the students during the assessment and suggest that the parents take this up at home. We can see the effects of the extra support at school, which may encourage the parents to provide more support at home.

The timeline

After seeing the students in the kindergarten, I see them again in first grade. I chart the progress from one year to the next by having an extra empty line underneath the preceding year's. One can then read if there is change, progress or not. As I noted earlier, the chart records a moment in time. Even the way I chart in the kindergarten versus first grade is different; I can expect more skill mastery in first grade. The same activity is looked at with that time change in mind. It is moving and changing with the children.

I have developed two basic charts: the standard chart and the second grade assessment chart. Depending on the need, I can share these via the computer or in hard-copy format At the 2014 summer AWSNA conference, I gave a keynote presentation, going over the components of the chart, sharing the history of it, the different formats and colors, and explaining how I store the hard copies through the years: rolled up in a cylinder with the date at the top. Sharing the charts with the class teachers and subject teachers over the years has been a successful process at our school. It can be used from K–8. In later years check-ins can be done.

The extra lesson

Following are some other comments from our teachers who have used the charts:

The chart is an easily digestible, graphic representation of the whole class that also provides detailed information about each individual child. As a second grade teacher, I use it to guide my selection of exercises for my class and also to enhance my understanding of the children. For example, very verbal or intellectually advanced children's needs may not be fully appreciated without aids like this "snapshot." It's also very satisfying when we "check in" later with certain children and find there has been improvement.

— Lauren Smith, second grade teacher

Our school curriculum contains two periods per week each for grades 1, 2, and 3 for students to receive developmental exercises as a group. As a Bothmer-trained movement teacher, I have used the charts as a comparative tool: When the chart shows that several individuals present the same issue, then I bring specific exercises for a few weeks to the whole class. Using the charts in collaboration with the class teachers and Brigitta has been extremely useful in helping the children to develop more harmoniously.

— Catherine Steiner, movement teacher and second grade assistant

As an incoming first grade teacher I found the color charts to be a helpful introduction to the physical capacities of my students. I could see at once where the group as a whole needed to work. Likewise, it was useful to be able to see where each student was in his individual development. This information could then be shared with parents at conference time, homework assigned, and goals set. As student progress was assessed at regular intervals from the end of kindergarten through third grade, the color charts were good indicators of the progress we made over that time. I found the charts to be innovative and invaluable in determining the movement activities for our early years as a class.

— Karen Weiland, eighth grade teacher

One can tailor a chart to meet individual needs. I hope that we will continue to share ideas and discoveries about the chart that may help us serve our students and faculty as best as we can.

To access and download a copy of the template Brigitte Witteveen developed in collaboration with Catherine Steiner, visit the Book's Place on the Waldorf Publication's website, www.waldorfpublications.org/helpinghchildrenontheirway

The art of child observation

Christof Wiechert
Translated by Genie Sakaguchi

Is it possible to learn the art of child—or student—observation? There are two answers: yes and no. Yes, as a human being, one can learn everything. No, because one can never be finished with learning it. As soon as one believes one can do it, one is in a risky situation, comparable to an artist who is completely relaxed before a concert, feeling he is already able to do it. Either it is successful, or it is nothing. It is also like this in the case of a child study. One never knows whether it will be successful; one is rather tense, as when one has stage fright. Will we really be able to recognize this child in his true being and, through that, be able to help him?

Conditions for a child study

An essential feature of this art is that it takes place in a community. A colleague has a question about a student. The student doesn't respond as expected, or doesn't achieve what the teacher had hoped for him. The teacher would like to understand the student, for he realizes that without this understanding, he will not be able to reach the student, and learning will become difficult.

He knows: Education requires relationship. So he turns to his colleagues and asks for guidance. The faculty meeting actually has no more important work than to enable these mutual discussions on pedagogical matters. What is necessary for such a conversation to be successful?

A community

There must be a community, a circle without gaps. If a person is not interested in this work, it would be better for him to stay away. If a person cannot feel sympathy toward the student, he should stay out of the circle. For the conversation depends on the active interest of all participants; it is the high school of interest. Thus the parents can take part, as well as colleagues who do not know the student. Through their neutral interest they can bring up important questions. It is helpful when the colleague who is presenting the student does not also have to facilitate the conversation.

Breathing

The child study requires breathing. Once one has practiced this art for a while, one will need at least an hour. It makes a difference who belongs to the circle. The true activity lies not so much in the presentation by the colleague but rather in the quality of listening. Where does one perceive what light begins to bring into the darkness of the events portrayed? When do the described situations begin to speak, bringing light for understanding the child?

Peace

An important condition is a situation of peace in the social life. These are lofty words that one does not use or like to hear very often any more. However, they are true. A College that has been damaged from debates over structure or similar problems will not easily find itself ready for a child study—for the child study needs a certain mood. A conversation that consists only of reports and information will not be able to bring about such a mood.

Coming to an agreement

At the end of the conversation, the group should strive to come to an agreement on one or more supports for the student. After eight weeks or so following the child study, the group can look back and ask the questions: Have we done what we agreed to do, and has it helped? If this can take place, the child study will become one of the strongest instruments to ensure the real quality of the school. In this activity, the College not only helps the child, but it also learns a very great deal. Many complain that Rudolf Steiner's *Study of Man** is just theory. But [in practicing this method of] child study, the study of man becomes really practical. Whoever participates in these conversations can feel them to be a fortunate experience [*Glückserlebnis*].

The child sets the priorities

Basically there is no given model or protocol for a child study. In this work, the priorities are set by the child himself, as he becomes recognized. However, one can differentiate three stages. These have existed since the time of Hippocrates: *anamnese* (medical history), *diagnose* (diagnosis), and *therapie* (therapy). In the case of a child study, we can speak of description or characterization, of understanding, and of help or support, which would be found through intuition, through the process of the child study.

Speaking and listening – inclusive

The class teacher or class sponsor presents the student as he experiences him, as the student presents himself. The teacher tries to describe the student's physical characteristics, features,

---

*Translator's note: Readers familiar with Steiner's pedagogical writings will know that *Allgemeine Menschenkunde* is a specific book, published in English as *Study of Man*, also under the title *Foundations of Human Experience*. But there are other places in this article where the author refers to Steiner's *Menschenkunde*. This can mean the particular book, but it could also refer to many other instances in Steiner's writings where he expands on the nature of the human being. In these cases, I have used "study of man" with lower case letters.

and behavior, and shows examples of his work: in short, builds a picture of the student. This also includes a developmental picture of the student over time [*Zeitgestalt*]. The picture is expanded by other colleagues. If possible, the school doctor will bring any relevant history of the student. Those who are presenting the student practice the art of inclusive speaking, and the others practice the art of inclusive listening, listening not only with the ears, but also with the heart. The one who is presenting is furnishing building stones for discovery of the truth; he should not speak out of long-pent-up frustrations of the soul. Naturally, this part often goes on too long. Everyone has something to say, even if one says the same thing as the person who spoke before. It is the only opportunity for one to speak out of experience, but one need not know everything.

A feeling for evidence

Now it becomes conspicuously quiet in the room. Who has something to say? Who is able to interpret the picture [of the child] appropriately? Here it becomes evident how far the members of a College have been able to make [Steiner's] study of the human being their own. For an interpretation or understanding arises out of this way of understanding a human being. The person who speaks merely of what he has read has a different effect than the person who has taken the study of man into his own inner understanding. Here one must have a feeling of colleagueship that is capable of recognizing the capacities of one's colleagues. Listening and holding oneself back are both necessary. A refined sense for the evidence [indications] will arise: what is coherent, what is not. Rudolf Steiner gave many indications for such interpretations that a College should work through in its meetings. According to my view, Steiner's study of man provides everything one needs to understand even the phenomena of today.

In the course of the conversation, this is also the right moment to ask oneself with empathy: How would I feel if I were described in this way? How does it feel to experience from within the urge to impetuous movement, for example? How about stuttering? Or dyslexia? Such questions can help overcome shortcomings in one's general understanding of the study of man, but they should not become an end in itself. The person who listens carefully will notice that the child, the student is gradually revealed.

The most decisive thing – the will to help

And how do we help now? To begin with, we look for means of support among the teachers and the pedagogy. After that it can be determined whether or not specialized help is needed. What kind of subject matter helps with which kinds of problems? What effect does math have on a student? What about drawing or even form drawing? How does a foreign language work on a child? What about stronger intellectual demands, or perhaps a more picture-like approach? What [kind of effect does one find] with musical activities or with graphic or plastic arts? Could the child be supported with exercises that work on building the memory or though speech exercises? The possibilities are legion. Rudolf Steiner said that education, instruction is gentle healing. Here the will to help has a greater effect than the correct point of view. In essence we are all helpless and can only try to prepare ourselves to be helpful. The child study concludes with the determination of who will do what for the child. After eight or ten weeks there should be a review, asking: Have we done what we agreed to do, and has it had an effect?

Parent participation – a question of tact

Following a basic ethical feeling, one would seek, as far as possible, for the parents' consent for the child study, and one would say why one believes it is advisable. In principle there is nothing against the parents participating in the child study, if they so wish. However the College of Teachers should ask itself whether the relationship between the parents and the school would support or allow this participation. The answer is a matter of tact, not of principle. And tact is generally healthy human understanding with feeling. The child or student study is a quality instrument which, wisely used, has no equal.

Points for observation and description
For the child study

Compiled by David Mitchell

History of the child
From conception and birth and events from early childhood

Pregnancy: normal, difficulties, maternal illness, stress, accidents

Birth: normal, breech, caesarean, complications

First three years: crawling, walking, speech, memory, complete sentences, when did the child refer to him- or herself as "I"?

Childhood diseases and any other health problems

Teething

Accidents

Play

Physical description of the child
(only observations are noted here, not interpretations)

Skull: Head: large/small, round/angular

Forehead: high/low

Eyes: wide/narrow, large/small, color

Nose: large/small, snub/beaked

Cheekbones: high, flat

Mouth: small/large, thin/full

Chin: weak/strong, split/receding

Ears: small/large, primitive/complex, flat, standing off/set at an angle/upright, set low/set high (ears are usually located between the end of the nose and the eyes in a frontal view)

Earlobes: attached/free-floating, fleshy/thin

Neck and Shoulders: thick/thin, long/short

Trunk: broad-chested/narrow-chested/pigeon-breast/hollow back/too short/too long—compared to rest of body

Arms: too long/too short

Hands: large/broad/thin/delicate, easily bent back, flabby/hard, dry/sweaty

Legs: long/short—relative to body

Knees: knock-kneed, knees form a hollow

Feet: pigeon-toed/pointed out, large/small, narrow/broad

Perception and movement

Senses: Go through all 12 senses and describe any peculiarities

Movements: gross and fine motor movements—characterize the movements if appropriate, such as a nervous, hoppy, placid, flighty, heavy, determined, tentative, abrupt, cautious, and so forth

Gait: toe/heel first touching floor, rhythmic/uneven, shuffle/springy

Dominance: determine left/right dominance in eye, ear, hand, and foot

Aspects

Related to the etheric body

Temperament: sanguine/melancholic/ choleric/ phlegmatic/mixed

Memory peculiarities: What is the relationship to time? Always too slow, too fast, just right, or rolling along (Time-relationship is an excellent indication of temperament.)

Healthy/unhealthy looking, easily flushed/mostly pale, low/ high pain threshold

Relationship to modeling: clay/beeswax

Related to the astral body

Characterize thinking/intellectual capacities: picturing/abstract conceptualization/ relationships/sequence/logic/etc.

Characterize feeling and emotional capacities: sensitive/insensitive, deep empathy/ callousness, tempers/always calm, cruel/ sympathetic

Characterize will nature: instinctive mode of action/ deliberate mode of action, follow through/ leaves things unfinished, difficult to start/ difficult to finish, gets stuck easily/able to ask for help, able to plan action/always needs guidance before beginning action, leader / follower

Characterize imagination: strong/weak/bizarre/ artistic/visual

Social and ego relationships

What are the relationships and interactions with classmates/siblings/parents/ teachers/ strangers?

What is the social behavior? Temperament?

What is the relationship to nature, to plants, to pets, etc.?

What is the relationship to work: Does she/he take responsibility? Does she/he take pride in good work? in completion? In beautiful work?

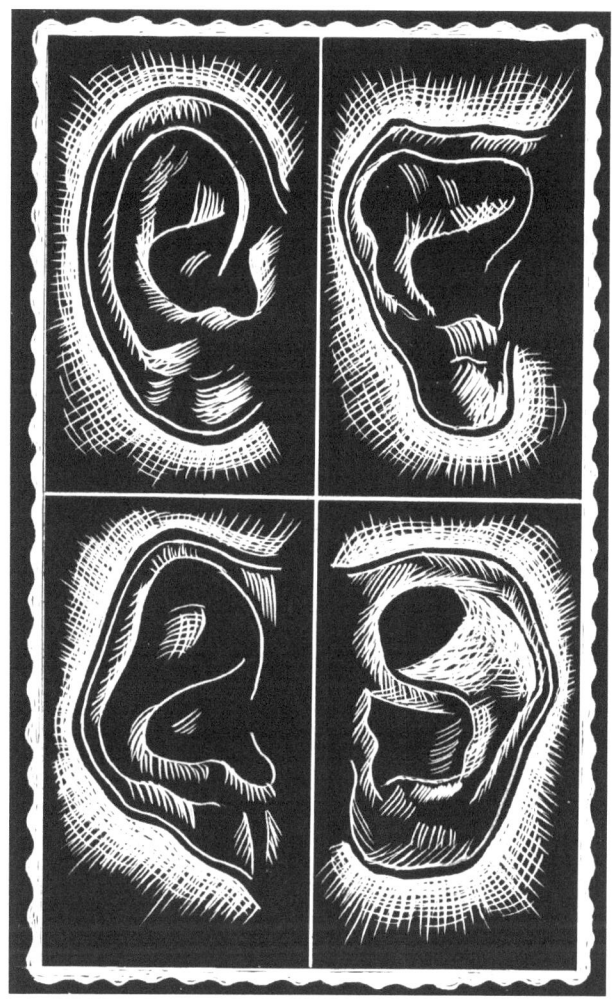

Artistic capacities

Describe work in modeling/ drawing/painting/ music/speech/drama/eurythmy

Learning profile

Type of memory: visual/aural/tactile

Relationship to music: learn by imitation/by figuring out by self/by being talked through/by acting out the relevant patterns/by repetition

Movement in the classroom
Morning circle and beyond

Amy Lloyd-Rippe

"All bodily activity arises, soul-spiritually, from the will—is indeed an out-streaming of will-impulses into the organism of movement. Even in purely mental activity, the will is active and is flowing into the limbs."

– Rudolf Steiner, *A Modern Art of Education,* Lecture 7

We are creatures of movement—from the obvious external movements of our bodies to the inner movement we experience hearing the cadence of human speech. As teachers in a grades classroom, we consciously create and shape movement experiences for the students. These experiences not only concern the physical movements arising during morning circle activities, but also include how the will is engaged in gestures, intonation during recitation, and in intentional activities such as class chores and how we transition from activity to activity throughout the school day.

When working with a class from grade one through to grade eight, teachers, guided by Rudolf Steiner's indications for child development, bring the curriculum alive through the warmth of our engagement and interest. Our journey through the grades rests on the foundation of both Steiner's pedagogy and our own observations of the children in our care. Sensitive observation guides how we design the class activities, as we note the phases of development that the children enter, work through, and leave behind. The children will meet these developmental phases at different times. It is good to recognize that any child may be challenged by one or more of these developmental phases during his or her school years.

As students progress through the grades, we need to ask ourselves how our role as class teachers evolves to meet their age-appropriate movement needs over and above what they receive through their eurythmy and movement classes. How do we recognize and address the struggles some children experience? How do we enliven our teaching through our own research in the classroom and our own sense for the art of education? In *A Modern Art of Education,* Rudolf Steiner helps clarify the form of this art: "Rhythm, measure, even melody must be there as the basic principle of the teaching, and this demands that the teacher have this musical quality in himself, in his whole life." (1972, p.121)

Diverse facets of movement in the classroom

As we endeavor to remove hindrances to assist the body in becoming a "suitable instrument" (Steiner, p.186), we need broaden the definition of movement. Although in general children have achieved basic gross and fine motor skills by the age of 9 years old, the honing and mastery of more complex skills continues throughout the elementary school years. As the children transform through the years, so too should the movement activities reflect their evolving relationship to themselves and to each other. Using soul economy, we can develop movement games in the early grades that can evolve as the students move through the grades, as well as ones that address specific individual needs.

The rhythms implied by the term *movement* encompass a broad spectrum of human involvement in daily activity. We can point to the structural rhythms established for each day, week, and month of the school year and to their beneficial effects on the developing etheric of the students. Free play, games, and activities during morning circle work clearly address the child's increasing mastery of his physical being through conscious repetition, effort, and sheer joy in movement. Less obvious are the movements occurring within the child during recitation, singing, form drawing, language studies, watercolor painting, math, and any rhythmic memory work. We strengthen each child's sense of comfort in his or her own body by assisting in the integration of both these inner and outer qualities of movement.

The musical flow of language, whether the mother tongue or a foreign language, resonates as movement within the child. In *Teaching as a Lively Art,* Marjorie Spock notes that, "Yet in spite of ourselves every word we speak is a thing of movement, a little dancer dancing out our inmost characteristics." (1985, p.38) We can reflect on the teacher as an artist by shaping and creating our own speech, movements, and gestures, recognizing that the students unconsciously perceive everything we do in the classroom. These perceptions cause a corresponding inner form to arise within them. The implications require that we consider the overall physical flow within the classroom and of the school day as a part of the movement experience for the class. Awareness of how we light a candle, erase a blackboard, organize students to line up and maintain order in all areas of the classroom all impact our ability to influence the rhythm and flow of the daily experience.

Just as we physically move through the day, we also move socially among others. Lively attention to the flow of conversation during class discussions encourages flexibility of thinking and is another expression of movement—this time a movement of ideas and feelings. A child who is able to clearly express thoughts about a story told in class will become a child able to write about that story. Children who are unable to recall the previous day's story or who tend to give one-word answers need guidance in articulating inner experiences. Teaching moments occur throughout the day. You can bring attention to something you see during a walk in nature, and, through casual conversations, encourage these children to talk about what they saw and experienced that day. Particularly in grade one, guiding some snack or lunchtime conversation in the class allows an opportunity for shy children to talk about something with confidence. Assisting and encouraging children to speak in full sentences from grade one on strengthens their capacity to articulate intangible inner images in words, giving them a new life shared with their classmates.

Eye-hand coordination

Eye-hand activities can involve either gross and/or fine motor control. Eye-hand coordination develops through the routine skill-building found in tying one's shoes, using scissors, manipulating a paint brush, crayon or pencil, sweeping with a broom, pouring water from a pitcher into a glass and endless other examples from the daily and weekly routines of a classroom.

Creating chores in the classroom develops a strong sense of community. It is equally important for the teacher to take the time to demonstrate how to complete a chore. Even the simple chore of passing out crayons requires the child to maintain awareness of each desk, to create a system of walking from row to row, and to ensure that everyone has the requisite colors. Thus, vital organizational skills develop and become a part of the child's habit body. Often it is in the realm of chores that the teacher can provide a movement activity specifically needed by a particular child. A wiggly child who tucks a leg under him, who half stands, half sits, or who kneels on a seat can benefit from a chore that works with constant movement and shifting balance, such as sweeping, delivering attendance to the office, erasing and washing the chalkboards, or perhaps assisting in setting up a balance beam for a class obstacle course. A dreamy child who struggles to remember story recall can benefit from a passing-out chore that requires that she remember and identify each child's placemat, crayon bag, or other item with a unique color or pattern characteristic. With a chore such as erasing or washing a blackboard, teachers should model a system that crosses the midline and that is regular in stroke: top to bottom and left to right, for instance. Working to match particular chores with your observations of the children in your class is an additional way to incorporate beneficial movements, while accomplishing the needs of the daily routine and strengthening each child's eye-hand coordination.

We can follow a specific fine motor eye-hand skill as it evolves throughout the grades, gaining complexity. Beginning in first grade, the class can practice folding a single sheet of art paper, used as a card or for a symmetry form drawing. This is actually a difficult task for many children, aligning the top and bottom corners, holding the paper steady while using an index finger to crease the fold. Sometimes, the task of folding the paper is the activity. This skill can evolve into creating multiple folds to make a fan or to divide a sheet into four, five or more columns for place value math work in grade two, and for spelling or math dictation problems in grades three and up. We use the simple fan fold in creating simple moving pictures to illustrate a fairy tale, using "pop up" clouds, tree canopies or flying birds. Using waxed colored paper, students can learn to create beautiful folded translucent stars for gifts or class decoration, using multiple folds to make pointed shapes. This is the beginning of simple origami, which can be a wonderful activity for grades four and up; the shapes increase in complexity as the students hone their skills. The moving picture books, which in the lower grades incorporate string pulling, levers, folded pop-ups, and turning wheels, can evolve into true pop-up gift and thank you cards for grades five and up. The simple folded sheet of grade one reaches perfection in the creation of accurately scribed, cut, folded, and glued Platonic solids in grade eight. The work involved in paper folding calls upon each hand to work independently and for the eye to assess alignment and symmetry of form. The final shape lives first in the child's imagination, and creating the shape from paper is a true expression of the child's will. Repetition of activities works deeply on the child, strengthening her capacity to connect an inner picture with an outer reality.

Eye-hand coordination plays a vital role in modeling beeswax, in learning to play the pentatonic flute, and in form drawing. It is often in these three activities that you will notice who struggles to match their own work with what the teacher is modeling. Moving through the grades, we also help the children gain proficiency in observation, a skill that will be necessary in the middle school science and arts curricula. Steiner notes, that "...if a child is to learn to observe aright, it is a very good thing for him to begin, as early as

possible, to occupy himself with modeling, to guide what he has seen from his head and eyes into the movements of his fingers and hand." (p.192)

In a similar fashion, gross motor eye-hand activities involving throwing, catching, weaving dances, hand-clapping games, and even jump rope turning, should be continued through grade eight with appropriate enhancements for each succeeding grade. For instance, mixing individual bean bag work with either small group or whole class bean bag activities hones individual skills, as well as each child's awareness of his classmates in space and time; bean bag activities can also become increasingly complex, building on earlier skills and class interactions. Bean bag games in the lower grades expand from simple tossing from hand to hand to more complex sequences that include crossing midlines, rhythmic foot work, and rhythmically passing the bag behind, around, in front, above and below. Children should toss underhand and catch with a single cupped hand—they should not snatch the bag from the air in a downward gesture. The gesture is always that of giving and receiving.

Working in twos, children progress to working in rhythm with another, tossing one or two bags simultaneously in a pattern or as part of the poetic rhythm of a verse. Using these skills, students in grades four and five can work in groups of eight with partners moving to the next station in a pattern—all while tossing the bags to the appropriate person. From grade one on, the class, working in a circle, can start with one bean bag tossed from one student to the person opposite, who tosses it to the neighbor of the first person. They continue tossing to the neighbors of the previous person until the bag is back at the first person or the teacher. Students not only focus on accurate tossing and catching, but they also need to remember to whom they toss and from whom they receive the bag. Once the class can make it around the circle without dropping a bag, a second bag is added shortly after the first bag is tossed. By grade five, the class can become so skilled that many bags can be tossed successively, perhaps as many as seven bags. Beginning in grade four additional complexities can be added, such as a clap before catching the bag and seeing how many claps everyone can achieve and still catch the bag.

Morning circle time does shift away from rhythmic movement activities beginning in grades six; however, these earlier bean bag games are still wonderful to include in increasingly complex ways. The circle toss can return but with the whole class walking in a circle while tossing the bags. By grade eight, they can be jogging while tossing a succession of bags. Grades seven and eight children can use the simple circle toss to include a full 360° turn prior to catching the bag or they can toss from behind their backs. The variations are endless; working with your movement instructor, you can identify new enhancements on an old activity that will meet the age and developmental needs of the class.

A relatively new approach to integrating the brain and body in movement is Bill Hubert's *Bal-a-Vis-X* (Norsworthy 2009), which uses rhythmic ball bouncing exercises. These balance, auditory, and vision exercises increase in complexity, challenging and strengthening the lower senses of touch, movement, and balance. It is best to introduce these exercises to a class through the movement teacher, but after a class has learned a few bounce-and-catch exercises, the class teacher can incorporate them into morning circle activities.

Ball bouncing, jacks, and hopscotch all involve tossing and/or catching and are activities that can be incorporated into recess and free play periods during the week. The goal is to introduce and teach these movement activities during a class and then to make the balls, jacks, and hopscotch materials available for the children to play with on their own, increasing their own play repertoire.

Body geography

In the lower grades, body geography orients the children in space and in relation to their own bodies. Steiner also indicates the relationship between the child's ability to combine ideas in his mind with the ability to coordinate outer movements using his inner being. (pp.189–190) The game of "Simon Says" immediately engages the children; the anticipation of the teacher's next set of directions, "Simon says touch your left index finger to your right ear" is coupled with the increased attention needed to note whether Simon gives the direction or not. The complexity and number of directions given at one time should increase throughout the lower grades. Many body geography and other movement exercises found in *Take Time* (Nash-Wortham & Hunt 1994) can be adapted for full class use as well as for working with individual children.

In grades four and five, body geography expands to include a child's sense of human movement as compared to the movement of animals or plants. Enliven the Human and Animal block with exercises exploring how it might feel to move with the languid musculature of a lion or with hooves rather than articulated feet; experience the different points of view of the snake and the giraffe. Returning to the upright stance of the human, students can reconnect to the immense freedom of moving through space with arms and hands free for activities arising from their own inner will.

The curriculum of grade five, highlighting the creation myths of the ancient cultures, is an opportunity to blend recitation and movement. Visually evocative poetry lends itself to dramatic enactments. An excellent poem for this type of physical movement is "Light and Shadow" found in the Live Education curriculum for the *Ancient Cultures, Persia* (Bischof & Rosenbloom 2000). Dividing the class into the polar opposites of light and dark, the teacher can express the drama of the birth of light by Ahura Mazdao through dance, gymnastics, and eurythmy accompanying the recitation.

Entering the pre-adolescent phase, students experience a shift in their center of gravity, and indeed begin to sense weight in their own bodies, in addition to the many other physical and emotional changes maturing within them. Socially, their need to relate to classmates increases at the same time that they become most self-conscious. Classroom movement activities and games in the middle school years can assist the students in regaining confidence in living in their changing bodies, in honing all the skills of earlier grades, and in meeting or relating to each other in a way that overcomes their new self-consciousness.

Early grades obstacle courses can evolve into a full class exercise—but with blindfolds. Create a pathway in the classroom with simple obstacles, one child waits outside the door and another child ties a blindfold around his or her eyes and will lead that child into the room. Inside, the others determine the path and the goal for the blindfolded student to reach. A classmate guides the child to the starting point. Students, in turn, guide their classmate through the obstacles with verbal directions. The obstacles can include crawling under desks, over a chair, and so forth.

In her book, *Improvisation for the Theater* (1985, p.73), Viola Spolin outlines the Three Changes game, which is great for grades six and up. The class observes a classmate for 30–40 seconds, after which that student leaves the classroom and makes three changes to his outward appearance: hair, clothing, or accessories. The student returns to the classroom and everyone attempts to identify the changes. You can adjust this game to have students work in groups of two as well, and the number of changes can increase as they improve in their ability to observe. Although this exercise does not involve outward physical activity, it does activate inner movement through the observation of change. It also gives an outlet for the middle school student to have a valid reason for looking at another student!

The Simon Says game of the early grades also gains complexity in the middle school. Working in pairs, the teacher calls out two directions, for instance right index to left shoulder and left foot to left ankle. However, students are performing the actions on their partner's body not their own.

In grade seven or eight, joint strategy challenges are a lot of fun and highlight cooperative work to achieve success, as well as a sense of where your body is at all times. Tape out a space of 12 or 13 linear feet, and give the whole class the challenge of moving everyone from one side of the space to the other. However, within that taped space their bodies may touch the ground at only three points. How will they achieve this? They balance, use each other as bridges and counter-balances, and have a great time working together as well. This exercise helps the students reconnect to the shifted center of gravity that they are experiencing.

The curriculum in motion

In these older grades, even grammar offers the opportunity to combine thinking with body geography movements. Adapting the game of Twister to grammar is a great addition to language arts practice.

The class or teacher creates a simple sentence, such as, "Whales swim in the ocean," and writes it on the board. The teacher determines the specific language arts skill to work on, and the grids of the Twister "board" on the floor refer to those skills. For instance, a grid of six down and four across will have four columns each of a color. Each color will represent a part of speech or grammatical construction: Red means add a participle phrase, green means add a gerund phrase, blue means add an adverb, and so on. On each flick of the spinner or roll of a die, the teacher calls out the indicated body part (right hand, left foot) and the color. The two students on the board find and place their hands or feet. Each student must now restate the sentence on the board, adding the part of speech or grammatical construction. You can have the sentence increase in length as they add complexity, requiring them to remember all previous sentence

additions, or have them always start from the sentence as written on the board.

The flows of peoples, of our blood circulation, and of ocean currents are all aspects of the middle school curriculum. The study of the migration of the barbaric hordes in grade six, transported onto the playing fields outside, becomes a physical reenactment of the invasion of Rome. In this activity, the class and teacher establish the general breadth of the Eurasian continent, marking the mountain ranges, bodies of water, and lowlands. The teacher divides the class into the major invading groups: Goths, Gauls, Huns, and Visigoths. The various groups gather in their regions of origin and the teacher guides the flow by calling out a timeline of the major thrusts of each group. The groups move across the field, bringing geography, the movement of peoples, and history together spatially.

Enrich the study of ancient Rome by teaching the students various Roman marching drills using Latin military commands. Experiencing the precision needed, students develop respect for the discipline, timing and rhythm, and unity of the Roman soldiers. After a few routines have become familiar to the students, you can increase the complexity by repeating these drills on stilts.

Students in grade seven move into the rhythm of the circulatory system following the flow of blood through the heart, and the carbon dioxide–oxygen exchange in the lungs on a huge taped-out heart on the floor. All the veins, arteries, valves, and chambers should be indicated; blue and red tape can indicate oxygenated and depleted blood flow,

and so forth. The teacher taps out a rhythm on a small drum, while the full class begins at one entry point and continues along the flow path multiple times; soon many students are swirling in, through and out of the heart in pulsing motions.

In *Awakening Intelligence*, Magda Lissau describes a wonderful activity for eighth grade geography, moving the whole class in the patterns of ocean currents around the student-delineated continents. Half the class remains still as the other half follows the wind and currents around the globe. Then the groups switch and repeat the exercise. Again, students internalize the vast global movements, awakening the relationship between the wind, water, and land. (2004, p.14)

Keeping the students moving during the middle school years counteracts the lethargy that tends to creep in at this age.

Math and number work

Each child stands before us with a unique relationship of him- or herself to the world around. To varying degrees, each child holds an inner sense of the straight line, the curved line, and the harmony found in equal sides of a square or triangle or in the roundness of a circle. The lower grades classes experience morning circle activities, but for many a student the act of seeing and feeling the rightness of a circle develops slowly. This first grade activity is the first step on the pathway to the artistic geometry of the middle school and the logical understanding of geometry in high school. In *Education as an Art*, the essence of the Waldorf approach to number sense is captured in their statement, "Geometry is first experienced as motion." (Barnes & Lyons 1986, p.2) It is in this realm of movement that the children can experience a sense of the spatial harmony in geometric forms, of the rhythm and intervals between numbers, and of the sense of wholeness or unity in the circle.

Henning Andersen's *Active Arithmetic!* (1995) is one of the best resources for helping teachers develop their students' number sense through movement. Working from the whole of the circle, children step-count in unison, silently or chanting the numbers, linking auditory beats of the counted numbers with the physical stamping of their feet and clapping of their hands. We observe who is able to make discrete steps for each number and who shambles along without recognizing the one-to-one connection between steps and numbers. In grades one to three in particular, repetition of movements is vital in counting rhythms or in times table patterns, and in developing the spatial awareness of moving in geometric patterns, facing forward rather than following your nose.

Counting in sequence, whether starting from one or from any other number, lays the groundwork for all future number-pattern recognition. Repetition and variation are key words here. After the students are confident with the sequence of 1–10, you can toss a bean bag to a student while calling out a number; each student will respond with the next number, the previous number, or the appropriate number in any other pattern you are working with. You can count, marching in a circle, changing the dynamics and approach: slowly, quickly, in a pattern, on a rhythm, silently, loudly, forward, backward, foot to the side alternating or step count, hopping every time you reach 10, and so forth.

Active Arithmetic! also contains numerous games for transitioning from the first ten numbers through all the following decades. Being solid on sequence and position of each of the first ten numbers, children will recognize what is to come after 20, 40 or 90.

Starting from the whole and working to the parts, children can skip in a circle, dividing into specific groups using a singing rhyme. We engender flexibility of thought through many variations of this activity, whether using physical movement in circle or using manipulatives at their desks. Students develop an inner sense that any whole can be represented in a variety of ways.

"Dancing 'Round the Fir Tree" is an example of recombining parts from the whole. Children skip in a circle while singing:

Chorus
We dance around the fir tree in every kind of weather.
Twelve little gnomes are we, dancing all together.

Then they divide into groups:
Two big groups of six are we,
Two big groups of six.
Two big groups of six are we,
Two big groups of six.
Chorus

Three little groups of four are we... Chorus
Four little groups of three are we...Chorus
Six little groups of two are we...Chorus

In grade six, the sequential step-counting of the early grades develops into a more complex game. In a circle, students will be stomping their feet in a one-two-three pattern. However, the count will flow from the first person to the next person in line, and then back to the first person, only to return to the second person and so on!

Person #1 steps right foot, left foot (1–2).
Person #2 steps right foot (3).
Person #1 steps left foot (1).
Person #2 steps right foot, left foot (2–3), then right foot, left foot (1–2).

Movement then passes to person #3 and repeats the above sequence with each succeeding person in the circle.

This sounds easy to the sixth grade students at first, but they quickly discover that they truly need to concentrate on starting with the right foot, on remembering to stamp "1" with their left foot and on making the movement flow around the circle as if it were one person stamping.

In the early grades, movement provides auditory, visual, and kinesthetic reinforcement of quantity and sequence of numbers, and of the intervals between numbers. Shifting movement from the feet up into the hands, student exercises make use of hand-clapping games, individual and partner bean bag or ball tosses, and stick clacking games with the stressed number punctuated by a toss, clap, or clack. Children are tailor-seated opposite a partner, each child has either one or two 12"–14" straight sticks of roughly 1" diameter. Counting in threes, children would tap their legs with the bottom of the sticks on "one, two," and make a diagonal clack with their partner on "three." On the next sequence, they would clack using the opposite hands on "six." Many variations and complexities can be added over the first three grades, as they experience the change in intervals between numbers in patterns, establishing the unique patterns between sets of numbers and for each times table.

In grades two and up, students can experience the common unity between times tables in a rhythmic way. The class is divided into inner and outer concentric circles, marching, either in the same or opposite directions, to the teacher's light claps or drumbeats. The inner group will clap on the twos table and the outer group will clap on the threes table, noting when they are all clapping at the same time. By the fourth grade, students can generally handle dividing the class into four groups to find the common unity within the 2's, 3's, 4's and 5's tables simultaneously.

With the introduction of fractions and formal strings instruction in grade four, the teacher works with the students' hands and feet clapping/stamping in differing rhythms. While feet are

Movement in the classroom

stamping whole notes, the hands are clapping half notes. This is a challenge and great fun to do while singing well-known 4/4 rhythm songs. Eighth, quarter, half, and whole notes can all be used, with the teacher calling out "switch," when hands and feet swap rhythms.

Studying Africa in either seventh or eighth grade, the teacher can bring any of a variety of African dances such as the Gumboot Dances of South Africa. These typically involve varying rhythms of hands and feet as well as stomps, claps, slaps, and so forth. Sources for these dances include summer training programs, your school's movement teacher, and even Waldorf YouTube sites. These are very social dances and yet they rely heavily on powerful rhythms, utilizing complex motor skills, in harmony with everyone in the class.

Just as geometry in the lower grades connects children's physical bodies to an inner experience of a form, from grade five on, the imagined movement of geometrical forms within their minds strengthens the capacity to concentrate and to envision. In grades five through seven, these exercises remain in the two-dimensional realm; in grade eight, they progress to the three-dimensional realm. The teacher has all the students close their eyes and imagine a horizontal line. Quietly talking them through the exercise, she then briefly and clearly describes an identical new line appearing on top of the first. This new line pivots at the point where both lines end, creating a perpendicular line. The description grows and completes a geometric shape. The teacher asks the class what shape they see in their minds. All the geometric shapes you have studied can grow and transform in many ways through this exercise. Imagine the complexity of working through any of the Platonic solids in grade eight! Students at that time can develop the inner picture of an octahedron and then rotate the whole form to identify the number of vertices and faces of the solid. This requires intense concentration and is a true accomplishment.

"Whenever students are engaged in bodily or movement practices, they are engaged with their whole being, because our body is closer to us than any outside abstraction….It is the bodily engagement in a learning activity that integrates the physical with the mental into one coherent experience." (*Awakening Intelligence*, Lissau 2004, p.90). As researchers in the classroom, teachers are most alive when they unite their observations with a broad range of movement activities designed to help the children overcome their individual obstacles.

Motor skills checklists

The following checklists for grades one–four have been adapted from *A Handbook for Waldorf Class Teachers* compiled by Kevin Avison. (2003)

Grade 1

The goal is that all the children in the class join in circle activities. Student competencies:
- Good body geography
- Throwing bean bags, balls to oneself
- Throwing and catching to one another (age 7 onward)
- Clapping above and below legs (sitting, standing, walking)
- Singing and action games and dances
- Skipping: both as basic dance steps and rope skipping
- Writing with the foot (legible by grade two)
- Jump rope games that include jumping over the rope at increasing heights
- String games (cat's cradle)

Grade 2

The goal is that all children can do the exercises well, in both small groups and as a class. Student competencies:
- Clapping in front and behind body
- Exact rhythmic clapping
- Catching bean bag with different parts of the body (under chin, below other arm, between legs, etc.)
- Walking a balance beam or on stepping stones
- Following a line on the floor while balancing a bean bag on head
- Writing legibly with the foot (also picking up acorns with toes and placing in a bucket)
- Walking on toes and heels; developing a sense for placing of the foot
- Aiming games (throwing balls or bean bags into a container, rings onto sticks, etc.)
- Hopscotch, jacks, tops, etc.
- More complex string games

Grades 3 & 4

The goal is that every child can do exercises properly both independently and in groups.
- Walking on a balance beam with a bean bag or rod on head
- Passing one another on a beam or tree trunk (without pushing one another off)
- Movements in sequence (skip, hop, twirl, etc.)
- Team games involving cooperation
- Clapping complicated patterns (cross-clapping in pairs)
- Walking on stilts
- Marching in patterns (four steps forward, turn to right, take one step, turn left…)
- Doing the crab walk and other zoo exercises

BIBLIOGRAPHY

Aeppli, W. (1955). *The care and development of the human senses.* Forest Row, UK: Steiner Schools Fellowship Publications.

Andersen, H. (2015). *Active arithmetic!* Chatham, NY: Waldorf Publications.

Avison, K. (2003). *A handbook for Waldorf class teachers.* Forest Row, UK: Steiner Schools Fellowship Publications.

Barnes, H. & Lyons, N. (1986). *Education as an art.* Chatham, NY: Waldorf Publications.

Bischof, B. & Rosenbloom, R. (2000). *Live education: Ancient cultures, Persia.* Aptos, CA: Live Education.

Edmunds, F. (1981). *Rudolf Steiner education: The Waldorf schools.* Forest Row, UK: Rudolf Steiner Press.

Lissau, M. (2014). *Awakening intelligence.* Chatham, NY: Waldorf Publications.

Nash-Wortham, M. & Hunt, J. (1997). *Take time: Movement exercises for parents, teachers and therapists of children with difficulties in speaking, reading, writing and spelling.* Stourbridge, England: Robinswood Press.

Norsworthy, F. (2009). *The illustrated Bal-A-Vis-X.* Wichita, KS: Bal-A-Vis-X, Inc.

Riccio, M. (2002). *An outline for a renewal of Waldorf education.* Mark Riccio.

Spock, M. (1985). *Teaching as a lively art.* Great Barrington, MA: Anthroposophic Press.

Spolin, V. (1985). *Improvisation for the theater.* Evanston, IL: Northwestern University Press.

Steiner, R. (1997). *The essentials of education.* Great Barrington, MA: Anthroposophic Press.

_____. (1981). *A modern art of education.* Forest Row, UK: Rudolf Steiner Press.

_____. (1965). *Waldorf education for adolescence.* Forest Row, UK: Steiner Schools Fellowship Publications.

Verses and movement
For the younger grades

Carol Mannion

The whole later life depends on whether the child in school breathes in the right way and whether he is taught to speak clearly and with good articulation.
— Rudolf Steiner

Rudolf Steiner speaks at length about movement in young children. Children develop through movement. In this modern world, the Western child is often thwarted in his quest for self-development by well-meaning adults and the pace of everyday life. All too often, he is given too much help and not permitted to strive to develop himself. Lifted upright too early, he is not allowed sufficient time to crawl or stay on the floor. Prams, car seats, shopping carts, bath seat retainers, bouncy chairs, and so forth, all keep the child from the floor. Self-development is hampered.

The results of this can be seen in the elementary grades from kindergarten on up through the years. Audrey McAllen speaks of this in her chapter in the book *Learning Difficulties*. The class teachers can do much to remedy this situation through the use of speech and movement.

Speech

Speech has a very powerful effect on the body and, coupled with movement, can bring about change and healthy breathing in the children.

In the kindergartens the dreamy time is often elongated, and the children are encouraged to move quietly, and songs and rhymes are in the dreamy realm.

Normal child development is based on the natural healthy self-implementation of pyramidal developmental movement, a broad base on which all other movements are built up one on another. In some children these may have been incomplete or missed completely. With movement sound and rhyme, we can reverse this. Through observations the teacher can pinpoint where a child needs extra help and provide rhymes and movement to help them overcome their handicaps.

The waistline area in some children is very flaccid, and they seem to be made up of three parts: upper, middle and lower. In some children these parts seem to be separate and do not move fluidly.

The following movement and rhymes can be incorporated into the circle time for all the children, as all can benefit, including the teacher. A great variety of movements, using all the parts of the body, are incorporated into the exercises, including bouncing, crawling, creeping, stomping, stooping, crossing the midlines, and more.

MORNING HAS COME
Morning has come,
> *Bend down, arms held open, then bring them to cross over the chest.*

Night is away.
> *Push arms out, palms outwards.*

Rise with the sun,
> *Rise up onto toes, raise arms over head, gradually opening and then lowering them to waist.*

And welcome the day.
> *Bring arms in and then cross over chest.*

LONDON TOWN
That is the way to London Town.
> *Standing with feet slightly apart, one foot up and the other foot down, lift leg up in front of body.*

Glad go up,
> *Alternately lift and drop legs; knees should be raised as high as possible.*

And glad go down
> *Arms at sides. Watch for hands that turn or arms that lift with the leg.*

To see the sights of London Town.
One foot up, and the other foot down:
That is the way to London Town.

WHAT THE ANIMALS SAID
> *Children make the sounds of the animals and accompanying movements.*

It's four o'clock,	
Said the cock.	*Cock a doodle doo!*
It's dark,	
Said the lark.	*Whistle and flap wings.*
What's that?	*Open both hands in question.*
Said the cat.	*Miaow*
I want to sleep,	*Hands together at side of head*
Said the sheep.	*Baaa*
A bad habit,	
Said the rabbit.	*Twitch nose.*
Of course,	
Said the horse.	*Neigh*
Let's have a spree,	
Said the bee.	*Hold finger and thumb together and make zzzz sound.*
But where?	*Hold hand out in questioning gesture. Then hands up sides of head for long ears.*
Said the hare.	
In the barrow,	*Point index finger down.*
Said the sparrow.	*Whistle and flap arms as wings.*
I'm too big,	*Arms in a large circle*
Said the pig.	*Oink, oink*
In the house,	*Point down finger tips together to indicate roof of house.*
Said the mouse.	*Squeak, squeak*
But the dog said,	*Wiggle hand as wagging tail.*
Bow, wow, wow,	*Woof, woof!*
It's too late now.	

FEE FI FO FUM
> *Hold hand out, palm up, then close fingers.*

Fee fi fo fum	*Start with little finger on "Fee," unfold fingers one at a time.*
See my fingers	*Show fingers,*
See my thumb	*Then thumb.*
Fee fi fo fum	*Repeat first movements.*
Fingers gone	*Hide fingers.*
So is thumb.	*Hide thumb under fingers.*

PIPPERTY PIP
> *Do actions to suit words; enunciate clearly using lips.*

Pip, Pip, Pipperty Pip	
Slid on the lino	
Slipperty slip,	
Fell down the stairs	
Tripperty trip,	
Tore her knickers	*Point to knickers.*
Ripperty rip,	
Started to cry	*Pretend to cry and rub eyes.*
Dripperty drip.	
Poor little Pippa Pipperty Pip.	

Verses and movement

WINDSHIELD WIPERS
Standing up, hands in front, palms facing out, move them from left to right at the pace of the rhyme; start slowly, pick up pace, then slow down for last line.
Flicker, flicker, flack,
Flicker, flicker, flack.
The wipers on the car go
Flicker, flicker, flack, flick.
And the rain goes flack,
And the wipers on the car go
Flicker, flicker, flack
FLICK, FLACK.

GREY SQUIRREL
Standing up, hands in front, palms facing out, move them from left to right at a steady pace on the words.
Grey squirrel, grey squirrel,
Swish your bushy tail.
Grey squirrel, grey squirrel
Swish your bushy tail.
Hold a nut between your toes,
   Hold hands at midline, pinch fingers together.
Wrinkle up your little nose.   *Wrinkle nose.*
Grey squirrel, grey squirrel,   *As first lines*
Swish your bushy tail.

CANOE
Sitting on the floor with legs in front as if in canoe; hold paddle to one side, and dip in and out of water; suit pace to words.
Dip your paddle
And pull with a will.
The river is quiet
And sleepy and still!
The blade cuts deep   *Dip paddle strongly.*
And the ripples spread wide *Hold arms out at waist height and open them.*

So rest on your paddle *Rest arms on paddle.*
And drift with the tide. *Slow the words down for the last two lines.*

DWARVES
Tramp march heavily with whole foot.
Tramp, tramp, tramp, tramp
Tramp, tramp, tramp,
Every little digger dwarf
Is holding up his lamp   *Hold one arm up as if holding lamp.*
Snoopy and Sneezy
Sleepy and Doc
All coming home again
At five by the clock.
Happy and Grumpy,
Bashful and me,
All the little digger dwarfs
Coming back to tea
Tramp tramp, tramp tramp,
Tramp tramp, tramp.
Every little digger dwarf
Is holding up his lamp.

BOOTS AND SHOES
Standing

Boys' boots are big	*Enunciate clearly.*
And when boys jump,	
Boys' big boots go	
BUMP, BUMP, BUMP.	*Jump up on each bump and come down hard on the bumps.*
Girls' shoes are dainty,	*Raise voice higher, point toes in front.*
Girls' shoes have bows	
And all the girls dance	*Dance on toes, turning around on the spot.*
On their tippy, tappy toes	

GOLDEN BOAT
Hold hands cupped in front at midline

This is the boat,	
The golden boat	
That sails on the	*Move right hand across the body in undulating waves.*
Silvery sea.	
And these are the oars	*Cup hands and interlace fingers.*
Of ivory white,	
That lift and dip,	*Lift interlaced hands on word and dip down again.*
That lift and dip.	
And these are the little ferry men	
Running along	*Hold hands up, palms out and run finger in front.*
Running along	
To take the oars of ivory white	
That lift and dip,	*As above.*
That lift and dip,	
That move the boat,	*Cup hands.*
The golden boat,	
Over the silvery sea.	*With right hand cross the body in wavy motion slowly.*

PORRIDGE
Standing or sitting; strong, slow, stirring movements

Porridge is bubbling	
Bubbling hot	
Stir it 'round	
And 'round in the pot.	
The bubbles go PLIP!	*voice higher*
And the bubbles go PLOP!	*voice lower*
Porridge is bubbling,	
Bubbling hot!	

MY FAMILY

My mummy is a baker	
Yummy, yummy	*Smile and rub tummy.*
My daddy is a dentist	
Aahhh, Aahhh!	
My sister is a show-off	*Put hands on hips and swing them in a show-off way.*
Honky Ponky	
Honky Ponky	
My brother is a cowboy	
Turn around	*Turn around, touch the ground, and point finger on Pow!!*
Touch the ground	
Pow!	

BOBBY, BOBBY
Hold hand out, palm down. On each word, bounce the hand down and then up.

Bounce the ball,	
Bounce, bounce,	
Bounce big ball.	*Hold hand out, palm down.*
Bounce up high	*On each word bounce hand down and up.*
Bounce down low,	*Raise hand up, lower hand down.*
Bounce, bounce	
To and fro.	*Take hand across body and back bouncing hand as you go.*

GOBLINS WALKING
Start the rhyme softly and creep.

Goblins, little goblins,	
They are creeping on their toes	
Down the fairy meadows	
Where the magic mushroom grows,	
Searching for a rabbit	
With an itchy, twitchy nose.	*Twitch nose.*
Faster, little goblins,	*Tread lightly and quickly, getting faster.*
Faster and faster you must tread	
In your little shoes of green	
And your little coats of red,	
Or the itchy, twitchy rabbit	
Will have run away to bed.	

Verses and movement

OWL

Make circles with thumb and forefinger of both hands.
There's a big-eyed owl
Who sits in a tree   *Close hands as claws on a branch at waist height.*
With two pointed ears   *Point index fingers up and place hands at side of head.*
And a nose like a V.   *Bring index finger together at side of nose in a V shape.*
He sit in his tree   *Close hands as claws.*
And he looks at you   *Make circles again.*
And he flaps his wings   *Spread arms out to sides and flap slowly up and down.*
And says, "Thwit, thwoo, thwit, thwoo."

MRS PECK PIGEON

Mrs. Peck Pigeon   *Nod head up and down.*
Is picking for bread.
Nod, Nod, Nod,
Goes her little round head. *Make a circle with thumbs and index finger.*
Tame as a pussy cat   *Hold left arm out; stroke it with the right hand.*
In the street   *Lift feet up and down and step.*
Step, step, step
Go her little red feet
With her little red feet   *Step up and down.*
And her little round head *With index fingers and thumbs brought together to form a circle.*
Mrs. Peck Pigeon
Is picking for bread.   *Nod head.*

SWINGING

Start swinging movements gently, gradually getting stronger and higher.
Swing me over the water,
Swing me over the sea,
Swing me over the garden wall,
And swing me home to tea,
Swing me up the stairs,
Swing me into bed,
Hear me say my prayers   *Put hands together.*
And kiss my little head.   *Make a kiss.*

MISS ERMYNTRUDE

Oh, dear Miss Ermyntrude,
Do not let your tongue protrude   *Stick out tongue.*
That is rude, so very rude.
Please don't let your tongue protrude.

COUNTING

Can be used for bean bag throwing alone or with partner; hold hand up and put one finger up for each number. On number 7, hold hand to lips and whisper for last line.
One for sorrow,
Two for joy,
Three for a girl,
Four for a boy,
Five for silver,
Six for gold,
Seven for a secret,
That's never been told

Carol Mannion

TIP TOEING
Tip toe, tip toe,
That is how the pixies go,
Tip toe, tip toe,
Tripping lightly to and fro.
Tip toe, tip toe,
They can hear the daisies grow,
Tip toe, tip toe,
Softly come and softly go.

ELEPHANT WALK

Plonk on this foot,	*Movements to match*
Plonk on that,	*the words*
Swinging my trunk,	
Swinging my trunk,	.
I'm out in the jungle	
Without any hat,	
Plonk on this foot,	
Plonk on that!	
I'll go to sleep	
In the shade of the tree,	
Nose on knee,	*Nose on knee*
And no one will know	
That it's only me.	
Nod and nod,	
Sleep and sleep.	

DOG AND CAT
Christian Morgenstern

Pick, pack, pull,
Will the pail soon be full?
Hinka, hanka, hat,
Where is the dog, and where is the cat?
The dog is lying near the hearth
Giving himself a nice clean bath.
The cat is sitting by the window
Licking her fur and each little toe.
Hinkety, pinkety, heckety hairs
The lady is coming up the stairs.
What's she bringing to the kitty?
A ball, a ball, ball so pretty!
A woolly, white ball in the big house
That looks just like a little mouse.
And to her doggy what does she bring?
A handsome collar with a golden ring.
A handsome collar of a special kind
With doggy's name in front and behind.
Hinkety, pinkety, heckety hout,
Now my tale is all told out.

The movable classroom

Jennifer Kershaw

Introduction

Let's begin with an understanding about what we mean when we're talking about a "movable classroom." The movable classroom, or the Bochumer model, was developed by a committee of parents and educators from Germany.[1] Early in 2000, this group gathered together to discuss the growing needs of today's children. These educators and parents agreed that the children of today are facing new challenges unlike those seen in previous generations. The culture of fast-paced business, technology, and the modern world is sweeping modern children along in its stream. As a result, these children seem to have more challenges with attention, focus, movement, and sensory stimuli (such as noise and touch) and with navigating social boundaries and situations. This is not an issue of parental neglect; it is simply a symptom of the modern culture of today. As a result of this meeting, the movable classroom was designed to help modern children fully develop their capacities.

Our modern world makes it difficult for children to get enough of the right kinds of movement experiences to develop themselves. Movement is an essential element for a child's development and capacity for learning, but to achieve these

objectives, a child must have opportunities to explore varied movements both simple and challenging.[2] For instance, most children spend a great deal of time in cars rather than walking on varied surfaces and balancing along a log or across a series of stones. Family life is so hectic that schedules with a balance of unhurried free time for exploring, day dreaming, and messing about are luxuries that few children experience on a regular basis. A Waldorf classroom already has many of these opportunities built into its daily structure from circle time to movement classes. But what if a teacher had an ability to alter the learning environment so that more of these necessary skills can be developed easily? What if the space and materials are supportive on a deeper level? The movable classroom aims to create some of that "open space" within the school day by allowing flexible opportunities with space, time, and varied movement in the classroom.

How does it work?

The movable classroom works in two realms: a physical one and a philosophical one. In the physical realm, desks and chairs are removed (to return in later years); and they are replaced by long, wide benches and cushions or smaller slanted benches for sitting. First, let's talk about the benches. The benches are made of natural material and provide a workstation where two children can work side by side. This seating arrangement immediately calls for collaboration and cooperation. Instead of "mine," the conversation between children shifts to "ours." This may seem very simple, but I found that the attitude of the children did change. In speaking with two other colleagues who have also used the movable classroom, they concur with my observation. However, some children do need a larger space or are not yet able to share a work space with another. My colleagues and I did experience this in our classes, and the use of a single bench for one child allowed for an accommodation that helped to keep the focus on learning in more than one situation.

The benches also offer a creative opportunity for teachers. Benches can be turned upside down, to be used as a balance beam or bridge or walkway of discovery. In my classroom, I observed that I had two children who were not able to crawl. Crawling! Think of the many skills developed through crawling: vision, proprioception and balance, learning to work in a new way with gravity, integration of the left and right sides of the body, and hand-eye coordination.[2] All of these skills ware needed in learning, so I created a tunnel of the benches as part of an obstacle course. The children went through in pairs, so I matched up a child who could not crawl with one who could so that they could work together on the skill. There were many variations of this "tunnel" in first grade, and I was able to build in imaginative elements that made the adventure fun and engaging for the students. I found that the children's ability to be creative with the benches far surpassed my own. The imaginative world of the kindergarten found an appropriate home in the first and second grade where children could use the benches and cushions as a creative tool in learning and play.

What about crayons, main lesson books, and all of the other things? In first and second grade, I simply passed these things out as we needed them. This is already a common practice among many educators in the early grades. Before switching to the movable classroom in the middle of first grade, the children did keep things in their desks. But I found that the desk (especially inside it) was a constant challenge for many of the children in my care. There were many redirections and time spent talking to children about the stuff in the desk. This lack of focus added to distractions, and children with behavior or impulse control challenges had an especially difficult time with managing space and objects. The benches simply took all this out of the equation.

There are two possible options for seats. Instead of chairs, the movable classroom uses cushions or small, slanted benches. These cushions are filled with natural materials, buckwheat hulls for example, and form to support the pelvis and core muscles.

The core of our bodies provides us with stability and security in balance and movement.[3] The child sits on the cushion like a saddle on the floor. Why is this important? What does this provide? Educators have found that there is a direct connection between the executive function of attention and a child's ability to maintain postural control.[3] The authors (Reilly, Donkelaar, Saavedra and Woollacott) of a study, completed by the Department of Human Physiology in Eugene, OR, looked at the connection between dual activities involving postural balance and cognitive tasks. They found that in many situations, when a demanding cognitive task was given, an individual had a difficult time maintaining an upright posture. While their results were not conclusive, they found that the cognitive performance of a young child could be enhanced by "appropriately sized desks and chairs or by use of an alternatively less demanding position."[3] The movable classroom provides an option for the latter. The floor helps to relieve some of the pressure needed to maintain an upright posture in a chair. The child can use the cushion as a support. It is soft, it is close to the floor, it is weighted. In my own class, some children reported that it was comforting to sit on.

While the cushion worked very well in first grade, I did find challenges with some children in second grade. As limbs grew, some children found the floor hard on their knees and ankles. A colleague had created a small, meditation bench for himself and thought it could be useful in the movable classroom as an alternative to the cushion. These meditation benches are built out of wood and are approximately 18" in length. The slant on the seat is about a 15–20 degree angle. The bench has two side pieces so that the child sits on the surface, the pelvis is tilted slightly forward and the child stretches his legs out behind. While some children loved this bench, I had a couple who found the position of the legs confining, so I allowed for choice as the children grew.

Maintenance of posture

Many children have difficulty maintaining a proper posture in a chair. While this is a skill that needs to be developed, many children work so hard to keep themselves upright in a chair, that all of their focus goes to maintaining this posture. When learning challenges are present, many children compensate to hold the form, and their attention is entirely on that, not on the learning.[3] They slouch, they lay their heads on the desk, they lean over, they sit on their feet, they wrap their legs around the chair legs, they rock their chairs, and they do many other positions to compensate. They can be so focused on their posture, or lack of, that they simply aren't able to attend to the lesson. We have all seen this happen. The child lays her head on the desk, but seems to be listening to the lesson. Then the teacher asks the child to lift her head and almost immediately, she begins to fidget, play with pencils, tap, poke her neighbor.

Now, the movable classroom does not fix posture. In fact, it doesn't "fix" anything. It allows for flexibility and an ability to be responsive. You will need an imagination to help the children develop the ability to sit upright on the cushion. Children who do not have core strength will flop over. Some will "W"-sit on the cushions. I used the image of an eagle on its perch to create an imaginative picture for the children. My colleague sang a simple song and had a horse and rider image for his children. The pictures in this article were not imagined. They come from real world images taken in my classroom and that of a colleague before and after the movable classroom was integrated.

The environment is also simplified. In a world often cluttered with objects and busy schedules, the environment of the movable classroom simplifies the environment. I went to a wonderful talk a few years ago called "Behind the Label" by Kim John Payne.[4] In this talk, Mr. Payne discussed the challenges facing educators today. Children come into the classroom carrying the day—the morning, the rush, the fever-pitched pace of today's world and they bring it all into the classroom. In this talk, one of the things recommended was the ability to simplify the environment so that children have the space to find balance and calm. While we, as educators, don't have control over all the environmental and learning challenges facing our children, we can have an impact on the classroom environment.

The philosophy

The movable classroom allows a teacher the creative opportunity to implement and focus the Waldorf curriculum in ways that expand children's experiences so they can develop all of the capacities needed to be vital, active, enthusiastic students. Young children who feel their way through the world have opportunities for expanded use of the lower senses. Children need a strong foundation for the development of these senses of touch, life, movement, and balance.[5] When these are in place, then there is a base for the learning that needs to take place in school.

As a teacher, I found I had a new opportunity to play within the curriculum, whether my students were moving benches to build a boat or creating a perch for a recall of the "Fox and the Crow." In addition, the movable classroom allows for remedial movement activities such as obstacle courses to be created with ease and flexibility. Stability and balance activities could be easily integrated. Form drawings were done while the children sat on

cushions and benches—designed and built in the physical space before a crayon was even picked up.

What can we see?

Let's think about some of the things that one could see in a movable classroom. The day may start with benches facing front in a traditional frontal teaching model, or they could be in a circle. In a circle, there is one, big front row. A teacher can easily move to any child based on the needs of the day. There is flexibility with the physical arrangement of the classroom. The benches can be repositioned for bridges, walkways, or other "tests of courage" to develop a child's sense of balance and self-movement. For written work, the benches can be arranged in a frontal way, or the children can sit on cushions behind benches in a circle formation. This circular way of working is wonderful for group work and promotes cooperative learning and social skills. In math classes with manipulatives, I found that the benches allowed me to differentiate the instruction by varying the groupings of children. Children looking for more challenging problems could sit together, while children who needed more one-on-one instruction could too. There was also the chance to intentionally place varied skill abilities together for the purpose of academic growth. In class, there was a collaborative nature to our counting of gems or seashells or other items. The children sat together to work on problems.

Our handwork teacher arranged the benches in collaborative groups so that children who were working on the same skill sat together. The foreign language teachers preferred the benches to be in a frontal mode with the children facing the front of the classroom.

In the afternoon, the benches were often organized for crafts or for cooking. I have a wonderful picture of my second graders gathered in one, long table of benches making hot cross buns at Easter. The benches can also be put together to form lunch tables where children can practice social skills and collaboration.

There are many games and activities that are possible with benches and cushions in the movable classroom, but the real focus is on how the children move and the ways in which space can be utilized to bring life to the Waldorf curriculum.

Having taught in a movable classroom for two years, I found that the furniture became a part of what we were doing in the learning environment. I was able to teach through the furniture and not around it. In the two years, I felt that I had simply scratched the surface of what is possible. I found the model enjoyable and inspiring.

It is important to note that the furniture itself is not a movable classroom. Rather, the movable classroom is a way of thinking about teaching through movement. Children still need to find stillness, and form is still established using the movable classroom. Good teaching is good teaching whether you are movable or not; one is not indicative of the other. When researching the movable classroom, I spoke with a trainer from Germany who said that mandating this style was not productive. In fact, these mandated movable classrooms were where the system itself had not been successful. It is the skill and passion of the teacher to bring a more mobile method of instruction to his students that brings success.

In the beginning of this chapter I talked about the challenges facing modern children. I found that the movable classroom allowed me the creative space to meet these challenges head-on. They were not pushed to the side, but were incorporated into the teaching style of the class. The curriculum was brought in such a way that these hindrances were worked with on a daily basis. I found that the creative opportunities were limitless. It allowed me to bring a class of strong individuals together as a group in a very short period of time.

Things to think about

However, it is not perfect. I did say that I feel that the teacher must have a passion to work in this way, creatively through movement as a way of teaching. I use a lot of movement and imagination in my teaching and found that this method was a match for my own teaching style. I don't think it is for everyone. Children who don't sit upright at desks still have this difficulty on cushions. Some children flop over and have to learn to sit upright. However, there are fewer ways to compensate on the cushion. In a chair, they can rock or slouch or sit on their legs or feet; on a cushion, you are either up or over—sometimes over is what happens! You still need form. As in any class, you have to think through your transitions, your form, how you will move the children in the space, and how this model will enhance your teaching. Don't think that a change in furniture is going to do your work for you!

Some teachers have come to me as thinking the movable classroom is an answer to a problem. I have discouraged those teachers from looking at this model in this way. It is not an answer; it is a possible option. I believe that you have to look at yourself and your children. Who are the children coming to you? What gifts do they have? What challenges do they face or are they working with in this life? What hindrances do they need to overcome either as a karmic group or individually? Would this model support the children in their growth? How will you use the movable classroom in your teaching? Does using benches and cushions allow you to bring your best to the children? Are you willing to seek out your own growth? The answers to these questions may help you to figure out if this path is one that is best for you and for the children in your care.

Making the move

In 2011, the Pine Hill Waldorf School (Wilton, NH) introduced the movable classroom. Today, it is not a mandatory form, and teachers are encouraged to think about their students and themselves when choosing between traditional desks and chairs versus benches and cushions. Some teachers chose to be movable in grade one and then transitioned to desks and chairs in grade two. Some teachers waited until the end of second grade. I transitioned my class in first grade and remained movable until partway into third. In looking back, I should have transitioned at the end of second grade. When the children arrived in third grade, I knew that it was time to transition. The children had changed and something different was needed. So, I moved out the benches and cushions and brought in the desks and chairs. I did keep two benches and four cushions in the back of the room. I had a couple of children who would self-regulate, by this point in time, and would simply move to the benches during bookwork. By fourth grade, these children were in their desks the entire time. I also did not have a need for one-legged stools. Once the desks came in, the children were ready for them and the transition was smooth and easy. I will tell you that there are still days (we are in sixth grade) when my students talk about missing their benches.

When the initiative was first introduced, during a parent discussion on the movable classroom several parents stated that they found it comforting and simple. One parent said that it "seemed like a natural transition from kindergarten to first grade." There were other comments about allowing a young child to move freely and that it felt more like home. A parent was quoted as saying that he chose our school for his child because he felt that the movable classroom would help his child work with sensory integration issues. As one teacher of the movable classroom said so beautifully,

There is a modern necessity to move that children bring with them that can no longer be pushed off to the side, that all of their being must be developed in education. Children learn with both legs standing on the earth. They experience that they are needed. They grow in their skin and become comfortable in it. They become skilled in their movements. They learn it all, painting, math, form drawing, writing, reading, well-articulated speech, and they learn much, much more.

– Gabriele Brons in *Erziehungskunst* October 2005

ENDNOTES

1. In Germany, one-third of the 222 Waldorf schools have movable classrooms, known as the Bochumer Model 2000.
2. Blythe, Sally Goddard. (2005). *The well balanced child: Movement and early learning.* Stroud, UK: Hawthorn Press.
3. http://www.ncbi.nlm.nih.gov/pmc/articles/PMC2586927/ "Interaction between the development of postural control and the executive function of attention."
4. Payne, Kim John. (2013). "Behind the label," a talk given at Antioch University New England.
5. Auer, Wolfgang-M. (2010). Article on Bochumer model, www.waldorf-ideen-pool.de

Boys and girls in movement
Stereotypes and archetypes–balancing gender needs in the elementary school movement

Jeff Tunkey

You may have noticed the recent popularity of news from the gender front. Books, magazines, newspapers, and online news sites seem to be playing up the good news and the bad news about changing gender roles, expectations, and fortunes.

In January 2014, *The New York Times* carried across two pages a report on the abiding biases parents express in favor of their sons.[1] Harvard-trained economist and writer Seth Stephens-Davidowitz analyzed Google searches and found, among other things, that in the U.S. for every 10 searches for the phrase, "Is my daughter gifted?" there were about 25 searches for the phrase, "Is my son gifted?" For the phrase, "Is my (blank) overweight?" for every 10 searches for "son" there were 17 for "daughter." (Because of the nature of Google, comparative statistics from past decades are not available.)

News outlets gave prominent play in December 2013, to the results of a groundbreaking brain imaging study by a team of University of Pennsylvania Medical School researchers, led by professor Ragini Verma.[2] "These maps show us a stark difference—and complementarity—in the architecture of the human brain that helps provide a potential neural basis as to why men excel at certain tasks and women at others."

Many news outlets reported in November–December on a preschool in Sweden that replaces the Swedish pronouns for *him* and *her* in favor of a newly-minted gender-neutral pronoun, *hen*.[3] *Time* magazine titled its article "In Sweden, Boys Won't Be Boys."[4] Indeed, the new news seems to be about how much of this publishing wave focuses on the topic of challenges faced by boys—and maleness in general—in the 21st century. Book titles in this newly popular niche include *The War against Boys*, *Boys Adrift*, *Men on Strike*, *The Minds of Boys: Saving Our Sons from Falling Behind in School and Life*, and many others.

A common love of he-can/she-can tales (and publishers' love of publishing) may be part of the reason for this shift in focus, but there is much more than a grain of truth behind the rising concern for boys in schools today. Realities include statistics from the U.S. Department of Education,[5] which predict that by the next decade, 60 percent of college degrees will be earned by females (see Figure 1); and from the National Honor Society, which states that nearly two-thirds of the high school students it recognizes for academic excellence are female.[6] In the U.S. and elsewhere, fear seems to be the driver behind many educational changes, leading us down the steps from No Child Left Behind to mandates for a Core Curriculum, taking schools to an ever-narrowing definition of their academic aims and, at the same time, circumscribing time allotted for, and play activities allowed in, the classroom, gym, and schoolyard.

Without question, we can only feel relief that the millennia of unrelenting female disempowerment (to say the least) are finally being stepped back in many areas. It subtracts nothing from this feeling to suggest that in the light of the above, it may be necessary to take stock of the latest attitudes and see what might need to be rebalanced. Let us consider: Are there learning-

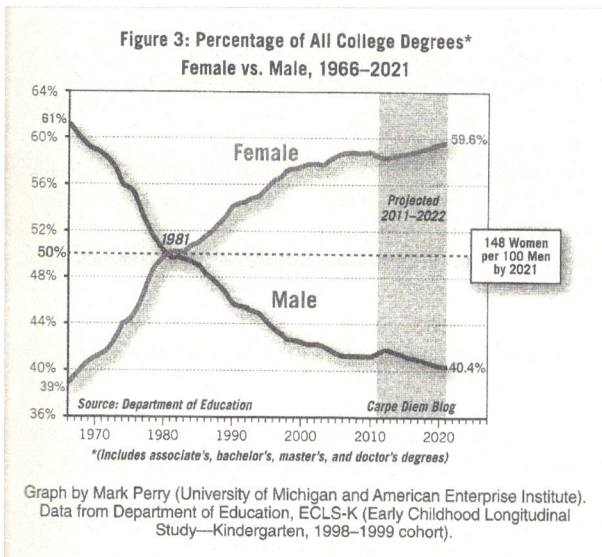

Figure 1. The ratios of college degrees – a reversal over 70 years

style differences between boys and girls? And if so, might the academic ascendance of girls be, to some degree, the result of changes in mainstream educational approaches during recent decades. Are schools now, in general, more suited to girls' learning styles, and less suited to boys'? Has there been a downside to the rightful movement to empower girls, such that typical "boy behavior" has been in some circles defined as a problem to be disciplined away? I think many teachers would answer "yes!" to these questions. And finally, what is the situation in our Waldorf schools? Is it more balanced?

I believe that boys and girls do have different developmental movement needs, needs that should be addressed in our Waldorf classrooms, schoolyards, and games classes; that while boys and girls have many developmental movement needs in common, there are also important differences in the ways they use movement to structurally organize their perception of and contact with the world. My goal in writing is to review perspectives on this vital topic from a number of informative sources; to see how these seemingly disparate sources might be connected; and, I hope, to inspire further research and discussions at your school.

Differences indicated by Rudolf Steiner

During a cycle of eight lectures he gave to teachers in Stuttgart in June 1921, Rudolf Steiner devoted himself to the topic of differences between boys and girls.[7] His comments on how these should be addressed during the elementary years were quite general:

We must consider the differences between girls and boys in our education leading up to this age [leading up to adolescence]. We must make the effort to develop the girls' moral and ethical feelings in a way that they are directed toward the aesthetic life. We must take special care that the girls especially enjoy the moral, the religious, and the good in what they hear in the lessons. They should take pleasure in the knowledge that the world is permeated by the supersensible. ... In regard to boys, it will be necessary to provide them with ideas and mental pictures that tend toward strength and affect the religious and ethical life. With girls, we should bring the religious and moral life to their very eyes, while with boys we should bring the religious and beautiful predominantly into the heart, the mind, stressing the feeling of strength that radiates from them.

And about movement:

[W]e should encourage the inner experience the children's physical nature asks for in other areas— in the movements of arms and legs, in running, and so forth... But this kind of physical education should be based on the development of movements not from the mere experience of the physical/corporeal but rather from the experience of soul and spirit, by letting the children adapt the physical/corporeal to their experiences.

I haven't found specifics given by Steiner on addressing gender differences in early childhood or elementary school settings. However, the fifth lecture in *Education for Adolescents* does provide us with guiding thoughts for middle school and beyond. Permit me to offer a few samples:

What we see initially is that the astral body has a stronger influence in girls than in boys. Throughout life the astral body of women plays a more important role than that of men. The whole of the female organism is organized toward the cosmos through the astral body. Much of what are really cosmic mysteries is unveiled and revealed through the female constitution. The female astral body is more differentiated, essentially more richly structured, than that of the male. Men's astral bodies are less differentiated, less finely structured, coarser.

If we bear in mind these differences between boys and girls, we shall understand that the blessing of coeducation allows us to achieve much by a tactful treatment of both sexes in the same room. A conscientious teacher who is aware of his or her tasks in approaching such a coeducational situation will still differentiate between girls and boys.

Naturally, we must not take these things to an extreme, should not think of making the girls into aesthetic kittens that regard everything merely aesthetically. Nor should the boys be made into mere louts, as would be the inevitable result of egotism being engendered through an unduly strong feeling of their strength—which we ought to awaken, but only by connecting it to the good, the beautiful, and the religious. We must prevent the girls from becoming superficial, from becoming unhealthy, sentimental connoisseurs of beauty during their teenage years. And we must prevent the boys from turning into hooligans. These dangers do exist. We must know the reality of these tendencies and, during the whole of elementary education, must see to it that the girls are directed to experience pleasure in the beautiful, to be impressed by the religious and aesthetic aspects of the lessons; and we must see to it that the boys are told: "If you do this, your muscles will grow taut; you will become strong, efficient young men!" The sense of being permeated by the divine must really be kindled in boys in this way.

In an era when gender/career roles were more stereotyped, Steiner also said that:

Our curriculum should be such that it allows the children to become practical in life; it should connect them with the world. Our curriculum for the tenth grade class will, therefore, be based on the following: We must, in order to do justice to the social life, have girls and boys together in the room; but we must differentiate by giving them activities suited to their sex. We must not separate them. The boys should watch the girls during their activities and vice versa.

Since we know from many lectures by Steiner that he considered the astral body to be also the body of movement and emotion (and also the "faith body"[8]) and that he identified the astral body as central to thinking, the above, happily, gives us two quests. First, it provides us with a starting point for further observation and meditation, so that his recorded words become for us more than received wisdom. Our second quest must be to find a modern science parallel, not because we need modern science to validate its truth or falseness per se, but rather because when we can find mainstream parallels to anthroposphic findings or concepts, we add to our individual understanding and, even more importantly, strengthen our readiness to communicate with and build bridges to parents and others beyond our classroom walls.

Differences demonstrated by modern science

The pioneering University of Pennsylvania study mentioned earlier has shown for the first time that the brains of men and women are "wired up" differently, which scientists have said could explain some of the stereotypical differences in male and female behavior. Researchers found that many of the connections in a typical male brain run between the front and the back of the same side of the brain, whereas in women the connections are more likely to run from side to side between the left and right hemispheres of the brain. (see Figure 2)

"On average, men connect front to back [parts of the brain] more strongly than women," whereas "women have stronger connections left to right," said Ms. Verma. But she cautioned against making sweeping generalizations about men and women based on the results.

The study found that this difference in the way the nerve connections in the brain are hardwired is established during adolescence, when many of the secondary sexual characteristics such as facial hair in men and breasts in women develop under the influence of sex hormones. The researchers believe the physical differences between the two sexes in the way the brain is hardwired could play an important role in understanding why men are in general better at spatial tasks involving muscle control while women are better at verbal tasks involving memory and intuition. Psychological testing has consistently indicated a significant difference between the sexes in the average ability to perform various mental tasks, with men outperforming women in some tests and women outperforming men in others. Now there seems to be a physical explanation.

Professor Verma noted, "What we've identified is that, when looked at in groups, there are connections in the brain that are hardwired differently in men and women. Functional tests have already shown that when they carry out certain tasks, men and women engage different parts of the brain."

The research, which involved imaging the brains of nearly 1000 adolescents, found that male brains had more connections within hemispheres, whereas female brains were more connected between hemispheres. The results, which apply to the population as a whole and not individuals, suggest that male brains may be optimized for motor skills, and female brains may be optimized for combining analytical and intuitive thinking.

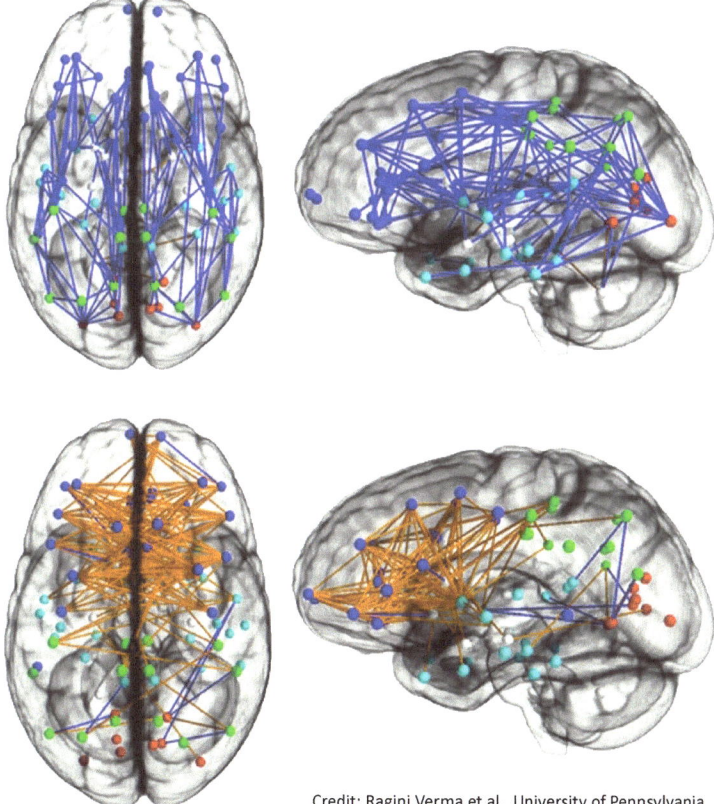

Figure 2. Brain networks showing significantly increased intra-hemispheric connectivity in males (upper) and inter-hemispheric connectivity in females (lower). Intra-hemispheric connections are shown in blue, and inter-hemispheric connections are shown in orange.

Credit: Ragini Verma et al., University of Pennsylvania

Differences in play stereotypes

Boys

When I've asked workshop groups to name or briefly describe stereotypical play of elementary-age boys, it has never taken very long to come to consensus on the phrase "rough and tumble play" for a wrestling/tussling activity.

There is considerable research on the topic of rough and tumble play and its connection to social and mental development. *The Art of Roughhousing* is a wonderful book that I recommend to all parents of young children.[9] In it the authors state the following:

Rowdy, physical, interactive play is by far the most common type of play in the animal kingdom. It occurs in every species of mammal and in many non-mammalian species as well. We've all seen videos of lion cubs wrestling, but you'd be amazed by the vast number of species that enjoy rowdy play—elephants, whales, even ants.

Play—especially active physical play, like roughhousing—makes kids smart, emotionally intelligent, lovable and likable, ethical, physically fit, and joyful. We're not exaggerating (much). Roughhousing activates many different parts of the body and brain, from the amygdalae, which process emotions, to the prefrontal cortex, which makes high-level judgments. The result is that every roughhousing playtime is beneficial for body and brain as well as for the loftiest levels of the human spirit: honor, integrity, morality, kindness, and cooperation. The authors also assert that roughhousing is not just for boys.

Almost all children love and benefit from roughhousing, but boys engage in rough-and-tumble play much more frequently than girls. Of course, many girls roughhouse and many boys don't. Boys, as a group, tend to tease, shove, and hit more than girls, even when they're having fun and being friendly. Girls, meanwhile, are famous for what is called "relational aggression": cruelty through gossip, dirty looks, or a cold shoulder. Roughhousing can in fact help break this mean-girl pattern. Through roughhousing, girls learn to be more direct about their feelings.

There is a continuing growth of attention deficit and hyperactivity diagnoses, especially for boys. Why? It may be partially due to a past under-recognition of the symptom cluster. I would assert, however, that the increase is largely due to culture shifts, especially perhaps in schools, toward defining typical boy behavior as a problem that must be restricted everywhere, forbidden on the playground, or even seen as evidence of a pathology that it would be appropriate to medicate away.

Fergus Hughes, author of *Children, Play and Development*, states the following in this regard: There is a correlation between the appearance of this activity and the maturity of the frontal lobes of the brain. The executive functions of the frontal lobes include reflection, imagination, empathy, and play/creativity, and when these develop, they allow for greater behavioral flexibility and foresight, for well-focused, goal-directed behavior. As the frontal lobes mature, the frequency of rough and tumble play goes down, and damage to the frontal lobes is associated with a higher level of playfulness. In fact, surgical reduction of the frontal lobes of young rats results in an increased level of playfulness and hyperactivity.[10]

Whether or not a neural disorder is present, however, findings from animal research suggest that rough and tumble play not only reflects frontal lobe development but also promotes it. In other words, active, energetic, spontaneous physical play may facilitate neurological development.

Girls

When I've asked the same workshop groups to then name or briefly describe stereotypical play of elementary-age girls, it usually takes a little longer to reach a conclusion, but the discussion always leads to "spinning" (for example, cartwheels, dancing) and the phrase "expressive movement," which covers both gymnastics and dance. Interestingly, Karl König emphasizes that folk dance is an important activity for the development of math capacities.[11]

Googling the phrase, "Why do boys like roughhousing?" produces over 110,000 results. But while phrases like "Why do girls like gymnastics?"

(or dance, spinning movement, and so forth) produce millions of results, the first several pages of link results, at least, include no pointers whatsoever to developmental reasons for this preference.

A different way to look at the polarities

I contend that there is a developmental reason for these typical play characteristics: boys' love of rough-and-tumble, and girls' love of spinning, expressive movement reflect two poles of human growth and perhaps even neurologic organizing. I've reached this conclusion by looking through a sort of "binoculars" that combines ideas from Rudolf Steiner with a gem of an insight from the 20th century physician and therapist Alfred Tomatis. I offer this lens on the polarities of boys' and girls' movement not as a definitive answer to all questions, but rather as a theory I've followed with some success in my movement program and as food for thought and research by others as well.

Doctor Tomatis notes that the sensory cells of the inner ear and the tactile cells of the skin have the same origin. According to him, the skin and ear basically evolve from the same embryonic tissue, the ectoderm. Thus the skin is differentiated ear, and we listen with our whole body. Tomatis called the ear "the Rome of the body" because almost all cranial nerves lead to it and therefore it is considered our most primary sense organ.[12]

Rudolf Steiner indicated that humans have twelve senses; that the four physical senses are touch, life, movement, and balance.[13] Isn't it so that in rough and tumble play, the touch and life senses are most engaged and affected; and that in expressive, spinning movement, the movement and balance senses are most engaged?

My theory is that, (a) through rough and tumble play, all children can work to develop (a1) their frontal cortex with its modulating of executive function and (a2) one of the modalities humans (mostly boys) use to establish their places in social hierarchies. And (b) through spinning/expressive movement, all children can work to develop (b1) their vestibular system and language centers in the brain, and thereby (b2) one of the modalities humans (mostly girls) use to establish their places in social hierarchies. Figures 3 and 4 depict how I visualize these interrelationships.

POLARITY	BOYS (stereotypically)	GIRLS (stereotypically)
Physical structure/organ	SKIN	EAR
12 Senses	Touch sense, also Life	Balance sense, also Movement
Play characteristics	Rough and tumble play Strength	Gymnastics, spinning, dance Beauty
Type of movement	Im-pressive movement (i.e., pressing in, not "awesome!")	Expressive movement
Neurologic development	Executive function	Neurology of language
Multiple intelligences model	Spatial & Math	Language & Interpersonal
Learning style	Right brain; whole to part Visual and Kinesthetic learners	Left brain; linear-sequential Auditory and Reading-Writing learners
Learning difficulties	"On the surface" - evident in early grades Attention Deficit - Hyperactive Dyslexia	"Hidden secret" - may not manifest until upper grades Attention Deficit - Inattentive Type Dyscalculia

Figure 3.

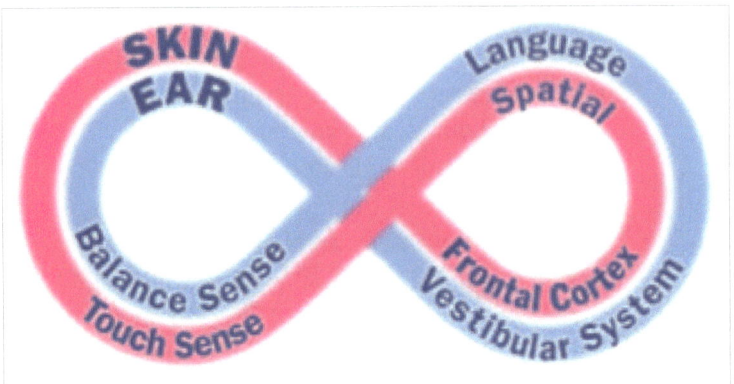

Figure 4. Two interrelated developmental loops that can be strengthened by two polar opposites of childhood play: rough and tumble and spinning/expressive movement.

In summary

When we consider changes in elementary movement programs over the past several decades, perhaps the forms of movement which have been most reduced are rough and tumble, and gymnastics. It may be that opportunities for spinning, expressive movement have not been diminished to the same degree as those for rough and tumble; although most schools have cut gymnastics, there is still plenty of dance in most PE programs. Fears are probably the main motivations for the drastic change.

Fear of student injuries is of course appropriate for administrators, school boards, parents, and teachers; both gymnastics and wrestling are sports in which injuries occur. I think that in the case of rough and tumble, there is also fear that boys will take the roughness too far; in some cases, there is general discomfort with the way that boys work things out; and fear that this kind of play looks a lot like bullying (or might look that way to others, in hindsight). To the contrary, true rough and tumble play is, at heart, play: You know it's happening if the contestants are playful. They're laughing, they can meet each other eye to eye, and there is flexibility and frequent reversal of winning and losing.

In my experience, both gymnastics and rough and tumble can be part of a relatively safe program, and they are vital ingredients for any program that aspires to meet the true developmental needs of young human beings. By bringing these back, in a thoughtful way, we can rebalance children's readiness for classroom success. As a plus, they can both also contribute mightily to students' athletic foundations. While not a great many boys nowadays go on to pursue gymnastics in adolescence or beyond, the positional and postural control built up in either gender through elementary gymnastics transfer readily to skateboarding, snowboarding, diving, cheerleading, and other more popular activities. Similarly, although only a minority of boys (and a rarity of girls) will pursue wrestling in high school or beyond, the basics built up through rough and tumble can transfer to all contact sports such as football or lacrosse, to semi-contact sports such as soccer and basketball, and to all arenas of life in which there is a test of wills, a need for always thinking one move ahead, and a real awareness of one's own strengths and vulnerabilities.

I have found that by starting a progressive program for these two "bookend" sports in first grade, a culture of safe and playful engagement can be created and nurtured. There are many resources for such activities, available in numerous PE books from the last century. The Resources section ofmovementforchildhood.com contains pdf files of a number of out-of-print books and suggestions for further reading.

ENDNOTES

1. Google, "Tell Me, Is My Son a Genius?" Available online at http://www.nytimes.com/2014/01/19/opinion/sunday/google-tell-me-is-my-son-a-genius.html?_r=0
2. See http://www.uphs.upenn.edu/news/News_Releases/2013/12/verma/ for the University of Pennsylvania's news release on the research. News outlet reports included, for instance, in *The Independent*, Dec. 3, 2013, available at http://www.independent.co.uk/life-style/the-hardwired-difference-between-male-and-female-brains-could-explain-why-men-are-better-at-map-reading-8978248.html
3. See, for instance, the Nov. 13, 2013, *The New York Times* article available online at http://www.nytimes.com/2012/11/14/world/europe/swedish-school-de-emphasizes-gender-lines.html?_r=0
4. Dec. 16, 2013, *Time* magazine.
5. Sommers, Christina Hoff. (2015). *The war against boys: How misguided feminism is harming our young men*. New York: Simon & Schuster. See also Richard Whitmire. (2011). *Why boys fail: Saving our sons from an educational system that's leaving them behind*, New York: AMACOM, a division of American Management Association.
6. As noted in a March 10, 2010, op-ed by article titled "The boys have fallen behind" by Nicholas D. Kristof in *The New York Times*. Available online at http://www.nytimes.com/2010/03/28/opinion/28kristof.html
7. Steiner, Rudolf. (1996). *Education for Adolescents*. Great Barrington, MA: SteinerBooks. A pdf file of this book is available at http://www.steinerbooks.org/research/archive/education_for_adolescents/education_for_adolescents.pdf.
8. Steiner, Rudolf. *Faith, love, hope: The third revelation to mankind*, lecture of December 2, 1911. Great Barrington, MA: SteinerBooks. Available online at http://wn.rsarchive.org/Lectures/FaithLoveHope/19111202p01.html
9. DeBenedet, Anthony and Cohen, Lawrence. (2011). Philadelphia: Quirk Books.
10. Hughes, Fergus. (2009). *Children, play and development,* fourth ed. Thousand Oaks, CA: SAGE Publications, Inc. A copy of Hughes' earlier doctoral thesis on this topic is available at http://www.movementforchildhood.com/uploads/2/1/6/7/21671438/play.pdf
11. König, Karl. (2009). *Discussions with teachers: Conferences and seminars on mathematics, with zoological considerations.* Available online at http://www.waldorfresearchinstitute.org/pdf/Arithmetic.pdf
12. Tomatis, Alfred. (2004). *The ear and the voice*, Lanham, MD: Scarecrow Press, Rowman & Littlefield.
13. See *Working with the Twelve Senses* on movementforchildhood.com for additional background on this topic.

Development and integration of the human body

The role of the lower senses and primitive reflexes, signs of motor dysfunction, and reflex retentions

Hannah Jackson

By virtue of being born to humanity, every human being has a right to the development and fulfillment of his potentialities as a human being.
— Ashley Montague

In utero the baby is already developing its first senses and reflex movements. As a pregnant mother moves about, she is helping her unborn baby develop both the proprioceptive sense (the sense of self-movement) and vestibular sense (the sense of balance).

When a child is born vaginally, it comes through the birth canal, which provides a deep pressure massage, activating the early reflexes, stimulating the nerves, and giving the child its first sense of self. The development of the sense of touch starts here, a sense that allows us to establish boundaries, interact with the external world, connect with other human beings, and give us the sense of where we end and the outer world begins. The sense of touch works closely with the proprioceptive sense.

Upon birth, we see the baby go into a full extension of its body, with arms, hands, and legs extending out from the body. The baby has a quick intake of breath, freezes momentarily, and then totally contracts into a fetal position releasing its breath, which often results in a cry (Moro/startle reflex). This cry is important because it helps clear out the lungs and gives them a kick start, allowing the baby to breathe. The baby is then swaddled, kept warm and held close, giving it a sense of well-being/life in its new environment.

When the baby's cheek rubs up against something, it immediately starts to root (rooting reflex) around for a source of food. Once it finds the nipple, its sucking reflex is engaged.

Each developmental stage plays an important role in our physical and brain development. During the first seven years of a child's life, the child goes through necessary milestones. When done in a way that completes the stages of development, these milestones or gateways create the foundation for unencumbered learning. Hindrances in these developmental milestones can contribute to anxiety, depression, ADD, ADHD, autism, learning challenges, developmental delays, sensory integration disorders, vision and hearing problems, behavior challenges, lack of confidence, and constant feelings of being overwhelmed.

Early movements help free our bodies and ready them for more complex movements and tasks (the development of the higher senses). Once we learn to stand up and walk, the whole world is opened up to us and new movements are explored. Imagine if we hadn't learned to stand. We certainly couldn't learn to jump. As one of my mentors likes to say, "You can't make a flower grow by pulling on it." We need to provide the appropriate support and time so that our children will not only grow, but grow in such a way that they will be able to blossom into their full potential.

When working with children remedially, I focus on two main things. I work on many more, but these two things I have found are the foundation to supporting all the other areas. These are the healthy development of the lower senses (I work most closely with the proprioceptive system and the vestibular system) and the integration of the early reflexes.

To provide a quick and easy reference, I have drawn up lists of what a developed and integrated sense or reflex looks like and what an underdeveloped or un-integrated sense or reflex may look like, along with lists of activities to promote healthy development.

Proprioceptive sense

The proprioceptive sense or the sense of self-movement gives us the ability to know where parts of our body are in space (body geography) without having to look at them. We receive this internal knowledge of self-movement through the stretching of the muscles and compression of the joints. Having a healthy proprioceptive sense allows us to throw a ball with the correct amount of force to a friend, hold a pencil, pick up an object, and move around skillfully.

Providing a child with regular opportunities to receive healthy proprioceptive stimulation can help with the overall development of the nervous system and may help with any integration difficulties. The proprioceptive sense works closely with the sense of touch.

When we have a healthy lower sense of proprioception/movement, we are able to develop a healthy higher sense of speech/language.

Healthy sense of proprioception/movement
- Ability to stop and start movement with control.
- Having the appropriate muscle tension in a task (i.e., lifting a cup of water with the correct amount of force, throwing a ball at a target/basket with the right force)
- Achieving uprightness
- Sense of the parts in relationship to the whole
- Sensitivity to subtlety
- Imitation of healthy purpose-filled movements
- Individual strength
- Ego deepening
- Connectedness to body and earth
- Knowing where one's own space begins and ends
- Knowing where other's space begins and ends
- Relationship to gravity/levity, front/back, left/right

Unhealthy sense of proprioception/movement
- Unaware of where limbs and body are in space
- Often in other's space / need for physical closeness with others, clingy
- Bumping and crashing into things
- Inferiority, hopelessness
- Fearful
- Fixed concepts, rigidity of thought
- Failure to pick up social subtleties, blandness
- Failure to pick up verbal subtleties
- Little respect for adults
- Loss of biography line – Who am I becoming?
- Depression and inwardness
- Desensitization to the other
- Inattentiveness
- Fidgety
- Speech problems
- Prefers or seeks deep pressure—swaddling, bear hugs, deep massage, bumping/crashing

- May apply too much pressure to pencils/crayons, toys, etc., and break them
- Stiff/uncoordinated and clumsy movements
- Tripping and falling
- Hard foot fall when running, skipping, jumping, walking
- Constantly stretching, cracking knuckles, neck, fingers, etc.
- Sitting on feet/legs
- Falling out of chair or bed
- Difficulty falling asleep and staying asleep
- Chewing on clothes, necklace, collar of shirt, other things

Helpful activities/suggestions
- Play
- Tumbling
- Crawling games
- Jump rope
- String games
- Blindfolded games
- Ball-bouncing games
- Jacks
- Wheel-barrow walking
- Playing on monkey bars
- Any lifting, pulling, pushing
- Opportunities where the child can impact the environment
- Help the child be aware of his actions.
- Engage the child in purposeful work.
- Provide rhythm and predictability.
- Play with different elements (sand, water, clay).
- Sustained movement that builds endurance
- Movements that involve change of direction
- Practice and repetition
- Allow child to rock slowly when sitting and needing to concentrate. Allow for flexible seating arrangements (on the floor, bean bag, cushions, pillows).
- Provide squeezing items such as a squish ball, to provide proprioceptive stimulation.
- Have child jump rope or jump on a trampoline before and after learning activities to help with attention to the task as well as with retention of the material.
- Allow for flexible seating arrangements. Allow child to stand at his/her desk or sit on his legs. Perching on a "physio ball" may be beneficial.
- Allow chewing gum or a crunchy snack. These are excellent sources of proprioceptive stimulation. Have child chew gum while doing homework or when doing tasks where he/she needs to focus, e.g., chores.

Helpful home activities

It may be beneficial to recommend home activities for parents to support their child just before starting homework (to focus his attention) and just afterward (to help integrate the information). Have him do bending and stretching types of exercises and activities. An occasional backrub from mom or dad can also provide child with the proprioceptive stimulation he is craving. Including proprioceptive and body-kinesthetic types of activities, such as activities that require balance, coordination, bending, and stretching prior, during, and after a learning activity can stimulate the brain and help significantly with integration and retention of the information. Activities that might be beneficial include:

Massage. Deep pressure massage to the extremities and joints provides both tactile and proprioceptive stimulation. This helps integrate the nervous system and will improve attention, concentration, and, hopefully, retention. A regular massage program that can be part of the daily routine (before and after homework or after bath, before bed) would likely be helpful in the overall development of his nervous system.

Jumping on a Trampoline. A kid-sized trampoline may be a good investment. This provides both vestibular and proprioceptive stimulation.

Perching on a Physio Ball. Get a large therapy ball for him to sit on while doing homework, deskwork, or listening to a story. The ball's diameter should equal the distance between the child's buttocks and the floor when his knees are bent at a right angle and his feet are flat on the floor.

Carrying Heavy Loads. Have the child carry a filled laundry basket or grocery bags filled with non-breakables. He can also carry a load of books, a bucket of blocks, or a pail of water from one spot to another.

Pushing and Pulling. Have the child drag heavy loads. Let her push the wheelbarrow (stroller, vacuum, rake), push heavy boxes, tow a friend on a sled, or pull a loaded wagon.

Pillow Crashing. Pile several large cushions, bean bag chairs, or downy comforters in a corner. Invite the child to dive, jump, roll, stretch, and burrow in the cushions.

Bear Hugs. Stand behind child and give her a big squeeze. Lift her off the floor to also stimulate the vestibular system.

Roughhousing. Pushing, pulling, rolling, and tumbling with an adult or friend can feel good all over, but this activity must be carefully supervised so no one gets hurt or overloaded with sensory stimulation.

Lifting and Carrying Chores. At school, have the child help lift chairs up and down from the tables at the beginning and end of each day. Encourage the child to carry several books during cleanup.

Jumping. Jump rope is a good activity.

Sports and Gymnastics. Sports such as wrestling, swimming, basketball, and soccer provide proprioceptive stimulation. Gymnastics, rock climbing and martial arts can also be excellent sources of proprioceptive stimulation.

Have the child use both arms, suspend the body from overhead parallel bars and swing freely without feet touching the ground. Monkey bars are good. Swinging first with hands facing the body and then with hands facing away from the body.

Rocking, swinging, spinning, twirling, skipping, running, hopping, jumping, and playing on a see-saw can enhance awareness of body position in space.

Log rolling. With hands down at her sides, the child rolls starting with the head, with the body following. (Set up a target for her to roll to.)

Brushing. Use a dry soft sponge, wash cloth, paintbrush, or soft baby brush and lightly pat or brush over the child's body as he lies flat on his stomach with eyes closed. Rub downward firmly following the direction that hairs grow. Keep sessions short. When the session is finished, supply the child with a large piece of paper and crayons and ask him to draw his body. The ability to picture one's own body can affect that individual's ability not only to picture geometric forms, such as alphabet letters and numerals, but also to manipulate them in his head.

Vestibular system/sense of balance

The vestibular system helps develop an inner sense of orientation and equilibrium. This system is based in the inner ear and responds to body movement through change in head position. It gives us the experience of stability and security in relation to gravity and the basis for attention. It coordinates the movement of our eyes, head, and body and is central in maintaining muscle tone, coordinating the two sides of the body, and holding the head upright against gravity. It is the foundation for spatial orientation and balance.

When we have a healthy lower sense of balance, we are able to develop a healthy higher sense of listening/hearing skills.

Hypersensitive – movement sensitive (avoiding movements)
- Does not engage in swinging, spinning, rolling, tumbling, inverting the head, etc.
- Overreacts and/or startles easily to movements or unexpected movements
- Dislikes fast movements such as biking, running, sledding, downhill skiing, surfing
- Hesitant and cautious with new/unknown movement activities
- Easily motion-sick
- Fear of falling

Hyposensitive – movement seeking
- Always spinning, rolling, tumbling, rocking, etc.
- Never gets dizzy
- Daredevils
- Needs constant movement/stimulation in order to know where the center of balance is, in order to have a sense of "stillness"
- Enjoys inverting head

Healthy vestibular sense
- Sense of middle ground
- Confidence moving and interacting with environment
- Sense of calm and control
- Healthy rhythmic system
- Healthy sense of self
- Sense of appropriateness
- Sense of timing
- Ability to maintain balance
- Experience of gravitational security
- Ability to quiet oneself and actively listen
- Ability to come to stillness
- Ability to show concern for the welfare of others
- Ability to attend and respond to all the other senses we encounter daily
- Ability to move between tension and release, concentration and relaxation, reverential and practical, rhythm and predictability

Unhealthy vestibular sense
- May be under-responsive or overly sensitive to movement
- Clumsy/uncoordinated
- Excessive movement or avoiding movement at all cost
- Difficulty planning and coordinating motor tasks
- May appear weak or floppy, always leaning on things
- Eyes may have difficulty focusing from one distance to another and tracking smoothly.
- Vertigo
- Disorientation
- Motion sickness
- Inability to read or write cursive
- Inner agitation
- Spontaneously falling down
- Appears to be "driven by a motor"
- Constantly aroused
- Difficulty maintaining attention
- Inability to sit still and listen without moving or rocking
- Head banging
- Impulsive
- Blurting out
- Cannot take turns
- Babbling and fidgety
- Decreased auditory processing

What we can do to support this
- Gymnastics
- Rolling, rocking, twirling/spinning
- Outdoor play that allows for exploration and movement
- Swinging, sliding, sledding
- Cycling
- Skating, roller blading, skateboarding, riding a scooter
- Climbing on rock, playground equipment, trees, etc.
- Hanging upside down on playground equipment
- Dancing
- Playing on a rocker board
- Jumping on a trampoline, pogo ball or pogo stick
- Balancing on a balance beam, railroad ties, river rocks, a sidewalk curb
- Put child in a "burrito wrap" or blanket roll.
- Provide rhythm and predictability.

- Create balance through interweaving humor and seriousness.
- Celebrate festivals that recognize seasonal changes.
- Provide daily and weekly rhythms (mealtimes, bedtimes).
- Tell stories that demonstrate polarity and resolution in the middle ground.
- Model our own inner balance through self-care and maintenance.
- Focus on a task with enthusiasm and risk (i.e., jumping, diving, riding a bike).
- Help our children find the right balance between being too fearful of life and over-controlling vs. being foolhardy and reckless and always hurting themselves.

The primitive reflexes

Reflexes are involuntary movements made in response to a stimulus. Think of when a doctor hits your knee and your leg automatically kicks out, or when our eyes start to feel dry or have something in them, and they start blinking more frequently. These are both examples of reflexes (automatic involuntary movements).

Our first reflexes are called primitive reflexes, and they are formed in utero. These early reflexes help the baby position itself for birth and assist in the birthing process. An infant is born with a variety of different reflexes to help strengthen and develop the central nervous system and to help the baby survive—to eat, breathe, grasp, and then eventually to develop more complex, coordinated movements. Coming from a fluid environment to a gravity-bound environment is a huge change. Yet, our bodies are miraculously prepared for this new milieu. For example, some of the early reflexes allow the infant to keep its head upright, which allows it to keep the breathing passages open. Other reflexes help the infant roll over and eventually attain a vertical position.

In addition to these early milestones, reflexes provide rudimentary training for many later voluntary skills. When you think about it: To walk, you have to be able to stand; to stand, you have to have the ability to hold your trunk upright; and to hold your trunk upright, you have to be able to hold your head erect. The earlier skills must be attained in order for the later skills to develop.

Primitive reflexes have a limited life span. If a child is given the opportunity for plenty of movement, these reflexes become integrated or taken up into the body and they can no longer be stimulated. These reflexes are integrated by doing movements over and over again until they reach their peak and release from the brain stem, allowing the central nervous system to mature, so new and more developed movements can come about. By late in the first year or early in the second year of life, these primitive reflexes should be integrated. Retained reflexes (the continued presence of these primitive reflexes after the first year of life) cause blockages and interfere with the work of postural reflexes, which should follow. The postural reflexes allow the body to have static and dynamic balance, as well as head and body alignment. Without the full development of these higher-level reflexes, voluntary movements cannot develop, and we will see a weakness in the functioning of the central nervous system that influences behavior, healthy growth, and efficient learning. Retained primitive reflexes can lead to developmental delays, ADHD, sensory processing disorder, and learning disabilities. The persistence of primitive reflexes contributes to issues with coordination, balance, sensory perceptions, fine motor skills, sleep, immunity, energy levels, impulse control, concentration, and all levels of social, emotional, and intellectual learning.

Some children may differ slightly in sequence and timing of development and movement skills due to their environment, parental handling, their physical characteristics, and their experiences. Only when a reflex persists after several months past the average should one be concerned. We should be aware, however, that these reflexes can be reactivated due to trauma, injury, toxins, and stress.

Other possible causes of retained reflexes
- Stress of mother during pregnancy, breech birth, induced labor, birth trauma, caesarean birth
- Lack of enough proper movement in early childhood—plastic play disks, play pens, walkers, jumpers, being carried around and restrained constantly in a car seat, TV and computer use—these all restrict critical movements required for brain development.
- Placed prematurely in a position that it would not naturally get into by itself deprives a baby of the time it needs to develop the control of the posture.
- Delayed or skipped creeping and crawling
- Lack of tummy time
- Chronic ear infections
- Illness, trauma, injury, cranial compression, chronic stress
- Environmental toxins, complications with vaccinations
- Dietary imbalances or sensitivities

Reflexes can be integrated/reintegrated at any age through slow, repetitive, and specific movements. When doing these movements, we are rebuilding the foundation of the nervous system by going back and repeating more of the movements that are needed. In this way, the reflexes can be released and the body can have greater ease and freedom of movement.

The reflexes outlined below are reflexes that, if not integrated, may affect the child's success in the classroom.

Moro reflex

Should be integrated 2–4 months after birth

The Moro is a reflexive response to sudden stimuli (bright light, change in body position, temperature, loud noise, intense odor, touch, and so forth). This response is the baby's first attempt to protect itself from harm. The baby first extends its arms and legs out, arching its back and head, has a quick gasp of breath, and then totally contracts, curling back into itself for protection, and often releasing the breath as a cry.

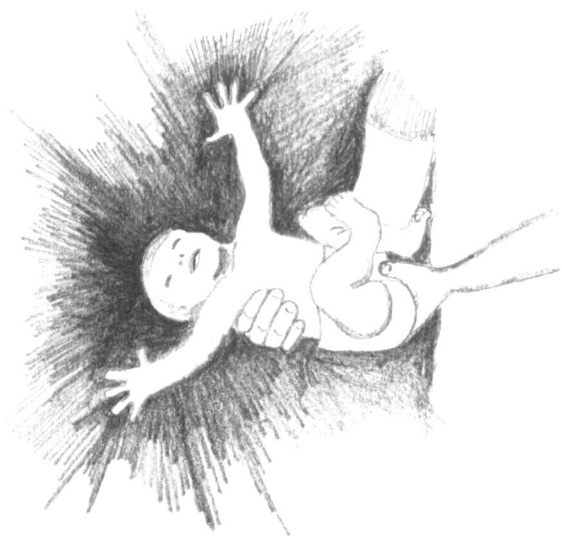

The integration of the Moro allows for a more mature startle reflex to develop. In response to sudden change or perceived danger, the baby will raise its shoulders seek the source of the stimulus, then either pay attention to it or ignore it. This helps develop the more mature nervous system skill to filter out unwanted stimuli and selectively attend.

Triggers of the Moro reflex
- Bright or sudden change of light
- Loud noise
- Temperature change
- Sudden movement
- Sudden rough touch
- Sensation of falling
- Change in body position
- Intense odor

Response to the Moro reflex
- Flushed face, reddened ears, increased heart rate
- Uncontrollable overreaction
- Fearful
- Angry
- Withdrawn

Retained Moro reflex
- Experiences stimulation to the senses as too intense
- Oversensitivity to light, noise, temperature, movement, touch, textures, odors

- Experiences the world as too bright and too loud
- The eyes will be drawn toward changes in light and to every movement in visual fields.
- Eyes become fixed in the periphery and unable to come to the midline for near-point focus work such and reading and writing.
- Difficulty with visual perception
- Often cannot ignore irrelevant visual material within a given visual field, so the eyes tend to be drawn to the perimeter of a shape, much to the detriment of perception of internal features
- The ears may receive too much auditory information.
- Possible auditory confusion resulting from hypersensitivity to specific sounds. The child may have poor auditory discrimination skills and difficulty in shutting out background noise.
- May habitually tune out to the more high-pitched sound frequencies, e.g., *f, s, th, ph*, and possibly confuse phonemes on the same scale, e.g., *p-d, t-d, c/k-g, f, th*. His spelling may also reflect this confusion.
- Unable to filter out extraneous stimuli; becomes easily overloaded.
- Easily distracted
- Dislikes busy/stimulating environments
- Sleep disturbances, difficulty settling down to sleep
- Has difficulty catching a ball
- Usually has a low tolerance to stress and/or continuous anxiety seemingly unrelated to reality
- May be fearful and/or socially withdrawn
- Tends to be very emotional: anger, tears, mood swings
- May be unable to accept or demonstrate affection easily
- Dislikes change or surprise, poor adaptability
- Dislikes participating in games or activities where eyes have to be closed or blindfolded
- Has difficulty making decisions
- Weak ego, low self esteem seen as either insecurity/dependency or need to control or manipulate and/or dominate events
- May be overactive, aggressive, highly excitable
- May have problems reading other people's body language
- May appear violent and use abusive language
- May have problems conforming to rules
- Has poor stamina; may have cycles of hyperactivity followed by excessive fatigue
- Has reduced muscle tone
- Allergies and lowered immunity, e.g., asthma, eczema, a history of frequent ear, nose, and throat infections
- May suffer from hypoglycemia and/or crave sweet food because he burns up so much sugar to cope with the Moro
- May have digestive problems, especially as adults
- Has poor balance and coordination, particularly seen during ball games
- Colic

Helpful activities/modifications for the Moro

- Provide predictability and consistency.
- Keep noise levels down.
- Keep general movement levels down so eyes can stay focused on what is of immediate concern.
- Seat child at back or side of room, preferably with back against a wall or near a door or window.
- Permit a water bottle on the desk/table when doing school work.
- Avoid putting her in situations where she might fail, mentally or physically. She lives constant and silent fear of this.
- Never put a child with a retained Moro into a timeout area or room. Other suitable forms of punishment will need to be considered.
- Ensure that the student knows you are approaching by saying her name and wait for her to acknowledge you before going any closer.
- These children usually respond well to gentle relaxing massage and music.
- Follow a routine/rhythm. This will allow the child to feel more secure. She will actively avoid unfamiliar situations and is wary of surprises.
- Allow a small snack often to restore blood sugar levels. It is important that these snacks be of

the sustaining and lasting kind, rather than those that will give an overabundance of instant energy for a very short period.
- Appreciate that sight-reading aloud can have extremely embarrassing results for such a child, especially if the child has not been allowed any time beforehand to be able to read the passage.
- Allow blank spaces to be left on "busy" walls near where the child sits to allow for periods of visual relaxation.
- Copying from the board will be an arduous task, so supplementary notes will certainly make life easier for such a child.
- Be aware that any bright sunshine shining on her work may distress the child. She may choose more dimly lit situations in which to work.

Symmetrical Tonic Neck reflex (STNR)

Should be integrated by 9–11 months after birth

The STNR is not really considered a primitive, hyper reflex, but rather a transitional reflex that is short-lived. Integration of this reflex prepares a baby for crawling, using automatic movements for raising up on all fours. It allows the baby to go from lying on the floor to a crawling position.

The STNR links the movements of the head with the movements of the arms and legs. When the child's head goes up, the legs flex and the arms straighten, and bottom goes down. When the head goes down, the arms bend and legs extend, and bottom goes up. The STNR develops hand-eye coordination, binocular vision, as well as the ability of the eyes to refocus from one distance to another. The STNR also develops bilateral movements and allows the body to integrate upper and lower portions of the body.

The horizontal midline is related to the STNR; this midline should be integrated by age 4. It relates to the plane of feeling. This is the plane of the 0–7-year-old; it allows us to experience above and below.

Around the age of 4, the child bends at the knees or squats to pick something up, rather than bending at the waist. The child may have difficulty finding a connection between upper and lower parts of the body if this midline is not integrated.

What we will see if this reflex/midline is not integrated

- Prevents creeping on hands and knees. Child may be a "bottom shuffler" or simply omit the creeping/crawling stage.
- Poor posture; uncomfortable when sitting or standing for long, squirmy or fidgety, slouching
- Lies on desk when writing
- Poor attention and concentration; difficulty staying on task
- Headaches from muscle tension
- Poor eye-hand coordination
- Poor vertical eye tracking
- Poor binocular vision
- Difficulty writing and reading
- Problems refocusing from far to near distance; difficulty copying from the board
- Difficulty catching a ball
- Clumsy, messy eater
- Ape-like walking
- Swimming is very difficult because if the child's head is above water, the rest of his body is sinking. (To remedy this, they may be under-water swimmers.)
- Poor upper/lower body integration
- When crawling, feet come up off the floor or knees and feet are dragged along.
- "W"-sitting

Helpful activities/modifications for the STNR

- Provide a sloped surface for the child to work at so that the head can maintain a more erect posture. This can be done either by providing a desk that is slanted already or by placing a 3-ring binder under the child's work with the spine of the binder facing away from the child.
- Provide a copy of the work to be done or copied to the child to have at her desk so she doesn't have to look back and forth from the board to the desk.
- Exercises that include creeping on hands and knees
- Exercises that allow the child to rock. Rocking not only helps integrate the STNR but it is also a grounding movement.
- Tack silk or other long fabric on wall and have child toss ball up toward the top of the silk and watch it roll down and catch it. This helps develop near to far vision and eye convergence.
- Rolling and tumbling
- Have child crawl on hands and knees and bring knees to nose.
- Play between gravity and levity, e.g., prance like a deer, walk like a duck.
- "Ring around the Rosie"
- Play on the slide, see-saw, swings.
- Sit and bounce on a hoppity-hop or yoga ball.
- Climbing/jumping
- Finger knitting
- Sewing; up and down motion
- Bending over at waist to pick items up or to touch toes, knees, ankles, etc.
- "Pitter-Patter-Polt": doing exercise as above, bending knee up and touch it with elbow
- Have child go through a hula-hoop.
- Play leap frog.
- Specific form drawings
- Tumbling activities
- Cartwheels

It is important for children to hang upside down once a day. It gets blood flowing to the brain (especially good for breech children).

Row Your Boat – Facing partner, sit with legs slightly bent at knees with feet touching partner's feet; grasp partner's hands. When one child leans back, he will pull the other forward and vice versa. This can also be done sitting back to back with your partner, elbows interlocked, and bodies rocking forward and back.

Wicket Walk – Simple: With knees straight, bend forward touching floor with hands; walk forward and backward with small steps, keeping legs and arms close together. Advanced: Grasp ankles and walk without bending knees.

Bouncing Ball – One child is the ball and another the bouncer. Try to achieve the feel and rhythm of a bouncing ball.

Monkey Run – On all fours scamper nimbly, imitating a monkey; put down both hands, then both feet.

Thread the Needle – Clasp the hands in front of the body, bend the trunk forward and step through clasped hands with right foot, then left foot. Return by stepping backward with right, then left foot.

Inchworm – Bend over with hands on floor. Keep hands stationary and walk feet to hands and walk back with hands to starting position keeping legs straight.

Jumping Rope

Bean Bag Exercise – Hold the bean bag in the right hand; then, toss the bean bag under the right leg and catch it with the left hand. Toss the bean bag under the left leg and catch it with the right hand. Establish a rhythm; have child count numbers or say the times tables out loud.

Tonic Labyrinthine reflex (TLR)

The TLR has two forms and is a primitive response to gravity, forward and backward. Forward – When lying on the back, as the head comes up and is tilted forward, the legs, knees and arms come up and curl in toward chest into fetal position. The TLR in frontal form should be integrated by 4 months after birth. Backward – when lying on the back, as the head goes down or is tilted back, the legs and arms extend. The TLR in backward form should integrate gradually from 6 weeks to 3 years.

Integration of the TLR allows one to have head control and correct alignment of the head with the rest of the body. This alignment is necessary for balance, visual tracking, auditory processing, muscle tone, coordination, and spatial skills, which are all important for the ability to focus and pay attention.

The frontal midline is related to the TLR. This midline should be integrated by age 3. It relates to the plane of the will and time. This is the plane of the school-age child, ages 7–14. It gives us experience of the difference between what is in front and what is behind.

What we will see if this reflex/midline is not integrated
- Standing for any length of time may be difficult.
- Poor posture due to having to adjust in an attempt to accommodate the reflex; tendency to grip ground with feet to maintain equilibrium
- Toe walking after 3½ years old
- May have floppy or tight muscle tone
- "W"-sitting on the floor
- Holding arms up, as in raising a hand, will be tiring quickly
- Poor balance and coordination
- Vestibular related problems (poor balance, tendency to motion sickness)
- Dislike of sports activities, PE, running, etc.
- Visual-perceptual difficulties; difficulty judging distance, depth, space and speed
- Spatial perception problems
- Tendency to reverse and flip letters (b/d, p/q)
- Poor sequencing skill
- Difficulty following directional or movement instructions
- Difficulty walking up and down stairs
- Poor organization skills
- Stiff and jerky movements
- Fear of heights
- Tires easily
- Poor sense of time and rhythm (no sense of self in space, no sense of outer environment)
- Residual TLR will prevent the complete establishment of head control and balance.

SOMETHING TO THINK ABOUT

According to my notes from my training course, when astronauts are put into a gravity-free environment, they start to write from right to left, to reverse numbers and letters and to produce mirror-writing, demonstrating the significance of gravity and balance for all levels of functioning. Studies have shown that weightlessness causes several key systems of the body to relax, as it is no longer fighting the pull of gravity. The astronauts' sense of up and down gets confused, NASA said, because the vestibular system no longer can figure out where the ground and the ceiling are.

Crew members also experience a disruption in their proprioceptive system, which tells us where arms, legs, and other parts of the body are oriented relative to each other. "The first night in space when I was drifting off to sleep," one Apollo astronaut said in a NASA interview, "I suddenly realized that I had lost track of ... my arms and legs. For all my mind could tell, my limbs were not there." See more at: http://www.space.com/23017-weightlessness.html#sthash.ky1RY4i0.dpuf

Helpful activities/modifications for the TLR
- Use graph paper to help line up math problems.
- Use a place-marker or a finger to help with tracking when reading.
- Rolling and rocking exercises, done initially with eyes closed
- Stretching and flexion exercises performed on floor in both supine and prone positions, with eyes closed

- Play on scooter; lie on belly and push off wall with feet to see how far he can go.
- "Swim" motions on scooter
- Have child lie on belly on scooter and you "fish for him." Throw a rope to him and he has to reel himself in.
- Fly on stomach on a swing.
- Drink through a curly straw.
- Chew gum or suck on hard candy.
- Fingerplay: bean pods, pea pods, seed pods, poppy pods split when they ripen and open with a pop (hands together, separating fingers when saying each line and clap for pop)
- Riding a bike/scooter
- Skateboard/snowboard
- Surfing – paddling out while on stomach
- Stand-up paddle boarding
- Walking on a balance beam, going forward and backward
- "Pitter-Patter-Polt": touching opposite hand to opposite foot in front of body and in back of body
- Tumbling activities, frontward and backward rolls
- Cartwheels
- Games to play: "Red Light/Green Light," "Mother, May I?"
- For children who are too much in their frontal space (tripping, falling), bring awareness to their back space.
- Wear capes and tails
- Crab walk
- Play horse with reins
- Walk backward
- Jump rope, dodge ball

Row Your Boat – Facing partner, sit with legs slightly bent at knees with feet touching partner's feet; grasp partner's hands. When one child leans back, he will pull the other forward and vice versa. This can also be done sitting back to back with your partner, elbows interlocked, and bodies rocking forward and back.

Churn the Butter – Back to back, elbows locked with a partner, one child bends forward from the hips and the second child leans back and lifts feet from the floor. Repeat changing tasks.

Human Rocker – Lie face down, bend knees, arch back and grasp right foot with right hand and left foot with left hand. Rock forward on chest and back on thighs. Rock in open position, holding arms and legs tightly together.

Egg Sit – Sit on floor with knees bent close to chest. Grasp ankles, rock back, and extend legs.

Asymmetrical Tonic Neck reflex (ATNR)

Should be integrated by 6 months

This reflex facilitates movement in utero and assists in the birth process. Limbs straighten as the head turns toward them and bend as head turns away from them. Integration of this reflex allows the body to go from homolateral movements to cross-lateral movements, and lets the body have separation of right and left. The ATNR also trains early hand-eye coordination. When the baby sees something it wants, it reaches out to grasp it.

The vertical midline is related to the ATNR; it gives us the experience of right and left. This midline should be integrated by age 7. The ATNR relates to the sagittal plane, which is the plane of symmetry, focus, and thought. This is the plane of the 14–21-year-old. Children with ADD have difficulty in this plane.

What we will see if this reflex/midline is not integrated

- Poor balance
- Poor handwriting
- Reading, listening and spelling difficulties
- Difficulty with math

- Poor expression of ideas in written form
- Difficulty retrieving information learned
- Horizontal eye tracking problems, which affects reading ability. A lack of tracking ability means that the head, instead of the eyes, moves to take in text line by line. Punctuation, letters, small words or even whole lines might be omitted.
- Child seems to have poor short-term memory for things just read. All concentration goes to the process rather than the product of reading.
- Difficulty crossing midline. The child experiences her body as being split into two separate halves (homolateral). This will also show in her writing, slanting away from the left hand margin.
- When drawing a line across the page, the child may start with one hand and then switch to the other.
- Wherever the head goes, the arm goes. The child may have her arm and paper way out to the side or in front of her to write.
- Mixed laterality/confused handedness
- Children who have not developed a stable reference eye or hand will have difficulty with the orientation of letters (*b/d, p/q*) or words (*saw/was, on/no*) or may write in mirror images. Some children try to compensate for this by covering up one eye with their hand or by resting one side of their face on their arm.
- They may do homolateral movements, instead of normal cross-lateral movements, as when walking, marching, skipping, etc.
- Have hard pencil pressure and/or awkward pencil grip. This is an attempt to keep her grasp on the pencil and the pencil in contact with the paper, i.e., her hand wants to extend out.

Helpful activities/modifications for the ATNR
- Provide the child with extra space when writing in order to accommodate the reflex movement of the arm.
- Be sure not to seat right- and left-handed children next to each other, since a child with the ATNR often pushes the paper to the far side of the working surface.
- These children may experience difficulty expressing ideas in written form. Allow them to give information orally.
- In class discussions, condense ideas into key words or phrases to use in an outline for an essay or short piece of creative writing.
- Teach the child to underline salient points when reading.
- Perhaps allow the child to type her work on a computer and later copy it into her books. This allows her to get her ideas out.
- Provide a place marker for reading to prevent frequent loss of place due to eye tracking difficulty.
- Give child something to hold in hands to bring hands to midline, helping her to focus.
- Allow the chewing of gum, sucking on hard candy, chewing of crunchy snack. Having something in their mouths helps them focus.
- Balancing games
- Hand clapping games
- Fingerplay: bean pods, pea pods, seed pods, poppy pods split when they ripen and open with a pop (hands together, separating fingers when saying each line and clap for pop)
- Ride a bike or scooter, skate, cross country ski
- Swimming, rock climbing, stand-up paddle boarding
- Weight bearing activities are really important. They enliven, strengthen, and elongate muscles to bring children back to focus.
- Finger knitting, carding, felting, sewing
- Beeswax modeling
- Woodworking: sawing, hammering while holding nail, using screwdriver while holding screw, sanding, rasping, whittling
- Winding wool into a ball (clockwise: with the non-dominant hand holding the ball, dominant hand winding the yarn from the bottom up nearest the body, out and away from the body, then down and around toward the body again.)
- Tying shoestrings
- Washing dishes
- Sweeping and raking
- Digging and weeding
- Folding laundry

- Kneading and shaping dough
- Grating veggies (Dominant hand grates as non-dominant hand holds grater)
- Origami
- Cutting with scissors
- Tearing and pasting paper
- Threading large beads on leather thong to make necklaces
- Clapping hands alternately on knees to a song or verse
- Stomping feet alternately on floor
- Crawling
- Walking on a balance beam or doing tight rope walking with rope on floor
- Climbing a ladder
- "Pitter-Patter-Polt": touching opposite elbow to opposite knee in front of body
- Walking like a hermit crab
- Wheelbarrow walking
- Form drawing
- Cartwheels
- Weather Vane: Stand with feet apart, hands on shoulders, elbows up. Turn from side to side.
- Stepping over copper rod. (This can be done to the song "Jump down, turn around, pick a bale of cotton.") Child places rod in front of feet, jumps over it, bends waist and twists to pick up rod, stands up straight, and replaces it in front of toes. This is also good for horizontal midline.
- "Counting Stars" exercise found in the Extra Lesson work.
- Bean bag exercise. Holding one bean bag in each hand, toss one bean bag up and pass the other bean bag into the empty hand. Catch the returning bean bag in the first hand. Continue. After a period, reverse the direction with the other hand tossing the bean bag up.
- Eye tracking exercises: dot-to-dots, mazes, word searches
- Cross-crawl exercises
- Roll out on physio ball with feet and ankles still on ball. Throw pennies or bean bags in the wishing well/basket. (Vary this with bigger or smaller balls, throw the bean bags to child to be caught or to make it easier, have bean bags on floor near child.)

Spinal Galant reflex

Should be integrated by 3–9 months after birth

If the baby is placed in the prone position, and stroked along the spine, it will rotate its hips outward toward the stimulation. This movement helps increase the range of movements needed in the hips in preparation for crawling and walking.

What we will see if this reflex is not integrated

- Fidgeting
- Bed-wetting. A high percentage of children who wet the bed past age 5 have a present Spinal Galant reflex.
- Very ticklish around back area
- Poor concentration/attention difficulties
- Poor short-term memory
- Hip rotation to one side when walking/scoliosis
- Loose, easily sprained ankles
- Toe walking
- Flatfooted or walks on sides of feet
- Fatigue
- Tactile defensive; experiences things more intensely
- When retained, this reflex acts as a constant stimulation to the back, so the back of the chair, clothing labels, and elastic waistbands may be annoying.
- A withdrawn sort of stance with waist cocked out to side
- When seated, child has a slanted posture; looks almost like he is "beside himself."

Helpful activities for the Spinal Galant
- Exercises done lying on the back
- Snow angels. Do these slowly so the child becomes aware of where her body is in space. Have the child make "snow angels" on different textures.
- Provide opportunities to balance. In righting themselves, they are working on integrating the Galant.
- In a table-top position, place a small bean bag on one of the hips. Have the child look over her shoulder to see the bean bag and move the hip toward the head, squeezing the waist and exhaling for 7 seconds. Do this about 6 times on each side. The slower the movements, the better.

Rooting reflex

Should be integrated by 3–4 months

This assists the baby in breastfeeding. It is activated by stroking the baby's cheek, which makes it turn its head and open its mouth.

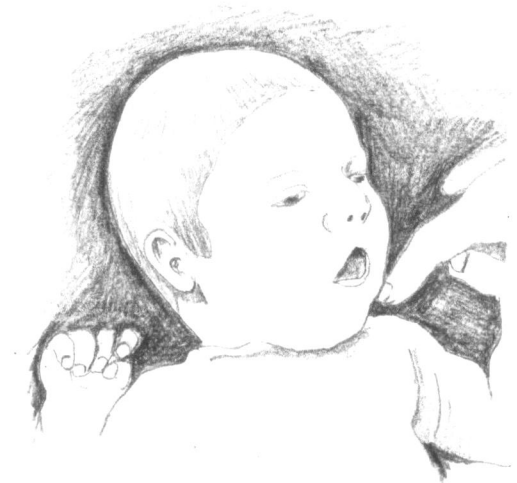

What we will see if this reflex is not integrated
- Trouble eating solid foods
- Messy eater
- Dribbling
- Dislike of certain textures of food
- Speech and articulation issues
- Oral fixations: pencil, hair, clothing chewing/sucking
- Tactile sensitivity around the face
- Dental issues/poor tooth alignment from pushing tongue forward against teeth
- Thumb sucking

Helpful activities for the rooting reflex
- Drink through a twisty crazy straw.
- Integrate the Moro reflex.
- Strengthen the proprioceptive sense.

Palmar grasp reflex

Should be integrated by 2–3 months

When the palm is stimulated, this reflex causes an automatic flexing of the fingers to grab and hold onto an object; this reflex is replaced by the pincer grip around 9 months.

What we will see if this reflex is not integrated
- Difficulty with fine motor tasks
- Poor pincer grip causing issues with writing and using utensils
- Messy handwriting
- Speech and articulation difficulty due to hand-mouth connection
- Tongue/mouth movement when writing and drawing
- Tactile sensitivity in palm of the hand
- Poor manual dexterity, difficulty with independent thumb and finger movements
- Poor control of grip tension, may hold pencil too tight causing fatigue in hand
- Difficulty with fine motor skills like buttoning a shirt, tying shoes, holding a utensil
- Child may handle (pick at, touch) food while eating, may be a messy eater, nail biter

Helpful activities for the Palmar grasp reflex
- Hand clapping games
- Creeping and crawling activities
- Beeswax/clay modeling
- Climbing on playground structures: monkey bars, ladders, jungle gyms
- Fine motor activities
- Doing activities with toes and feet: drawing pictures, writing, digging, and picking up things with toes

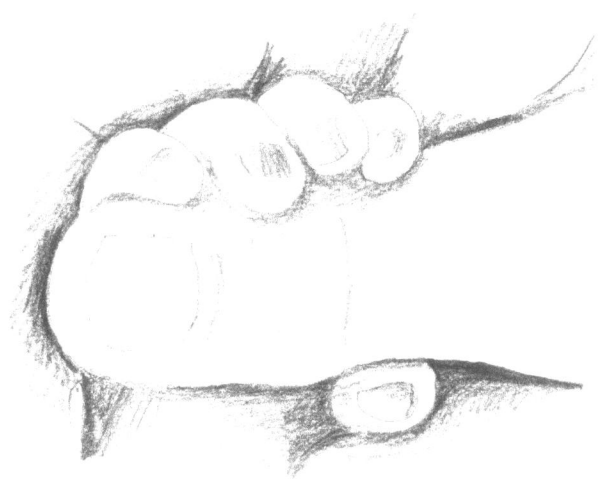

REFERENCES

Blythe, S.G. (2005). *The well-balanced child: Movement and early learning*. Stroud, UK: Hawthorn Press.

Eliot, L. (1999). *What's going on in there*? New York: Bantam Books.

Goddard. B. (1996). *A teacher's window into the child's mind*. Eugene, OR: Fern Ridge Press.

Hannaford, C. (1995). *Smart moves*. North Carolina: Great Ocean Publishers.

Kranowitz, C.S. (1998). *The out-of-sync child.* New York: The Berkley Publishing Group.

_____. (2003). *The out-of-sync child has fun*. New York: The Berkley Publishing Group.

Kranowitz, C.S. and Newman, J. (2010). *Growing an in-sync child*. New York: Tarcher Perigree, Penguin.

Miller, L.J. (2006). *Sensational kids*. New York: The Penguin Group.

IT IS NEVER TOO LATE TO HELP SOMEONE! If these primitive reflexes are not inhibited in a healthy way, the more mature movement patterns are not supported later on and developmental problems may occur. Any of these reflexes can reappear when we have had an injury, are sleepy or sick, have an ear infection, or have been abused in some way. They are protective patterns.

The information I've presented in this chapter is a compilation of my notes from trainings, workshops, lectures, and my experience working with children remedially for the past 11 years. I am grateful to my many mentors and teachers—Rachel Ross, Joan Treadaway, Mary Jo Oresti, Joan Ingle, Laurie Clark, Dr. Bruno Callegaro, Dr. Tom Cowan, Dr. Michaela Glöckler, Dr. Adam Blanning, Dr. Susan Johnson, Tim and Patty Connelly, Nancy Blanning, Judith Bluestone, INPP, Dr. Ron Minson and Kate Minson, Jaimen McMillan, Eugene Schwartz, Kim John Payne—and to all my colleagues and students throughout all these years. I am constantly and continually learning.

The importance of morning circle
How to create a therapeutic movement circle

Hannah Jackson

Movement is a child's first language, and it is through movement that he/she first starts to explore the world and to gain control over his/her body. The most advanced level of movement is the ability to stay totally still, and until a child has control over movement and the ability to sit or to stand still, he does not have the fundamental equipment necessary for learning in the classroom.
— Sally Goddard Blythe

In the early formative years, play is almost synonymous with life. It is second only to being nourished, protected, and loved. It is a basic ingredient of physical, intellectual, social, and emotional growth.
— Ashley Montague

Morning circle may be the most important part of the morning in the early grades. By providing healthy movement to our students, we are helping them develop foundational skills they need to be successful in all areas of their life. Through our circle work, we are helping children exercise their motor, communication, social, emotional, and cognitive skills. Too often in schools, the focus of early childhood is on the cognitive-mental development and less on the physical development. As Waldorf teachers, we understand the importance of movement and its role in helping to fully integrate and ready the physical body, so the child's physical development forces can be freed up and put into play to develop higher-level thinking.

Movement is the single most important thing for brain development. When children are allowed to go through the natural development of movement and haven't been hindered in any way, their bodies will be freed up to sit, focus and attend to tasks, think and learn. There is a strongly held misconception in our society that mind and body are separate, that movement has nothing to do with intellect. People simply find it hard to believe that physical activity can help us think. Think about when you have had to sit and focus for long periods of time and you started losing that focus. If you got up and moved around and stretched, you found that you had a clearer mind, more energy, and a renewed focus.

Teachers in Waldorf and public schools are seeing a higher percentage of children with sensory, attention, movement, and learning challenges. The number of children needing some sort of extra support seems to be on the rise. Cognitive learning and physical activity go hand in hand. Many of our children these days lack opportunities to engage in meaningful, healthy movement. They have too many structured activities and not enough play, too much screen time, always on the go, fast-paced, carted around from one thing to another, too little time outside, too little unstructured free play, poor diets, junk food, sensory bombardment—the list goes on and on. To help counteract the negative effects of all the sensory overload our children are experiencing, our focus as educators should be to provide a safe, healing, movement-rich education for them.

The morning circle can help the children engage in healthy movement first thing in the morning. It can help them wake up, get their hearts beating and breath flowing, and become more grounded in their bodies. Morning circle incorporates movements and gestures that help develop gross and fine motor skills and hand-eye coordination. The movements we do strengthen dominance; aid in the integration of early reflexes and crossing midline barriers; allow the children to develop spatial awareness, listening, and rhythmic skills; as well as strengthen their auditory, visual, and kinesthetic memory. Morning circle helps the children develop their sense of self in space and their balance. It helps them transition from one activity to another, learn to move as individuals and learn to move as a group. It helps them develop strength, coordination, concentration, and self-confidence. It gives them the foundation they need to strengthen their core so they can stand straight and tall and sit upright with ease in a chair.

Socially, circle time helps children learn to work together, to synchronize, and to work cooperatively. Circle work brings awareness of the seasons, connects the children to the curriculum being studied and helps them fully integrate into their bodies. Morning circles develop faculties that are very important prerequisites to academic learning and helps set the tone for the rest of the day.

Creating a movement circle can sometimes be overwhelming. Having an understanding of why we do morning circle work in the Waldorf classrooms may help you as the teacher better understand what is needed in creating a healthy and meaningful circle.

In Waldorf education, "circle" work can start outside of the actual circle. Before or after moving into the actual circle, speech, drama, math, and flute work can be done as part of the morning's movement work.

Coming to the circle

Most of the time, movement circles are done in an open space that is either already free of furniture or created by moving desks. Getting the children from behind their desks to standing in a circular formation in the open space you just created can be no small feat. As we know, establishing good habits is much of the work we do in the younger grades. So, deciding how you want to get your students from behind their desks to standing in a circle takes careful planning. Think of a song that acts as a signal to the children each time they hear it, indicating that it is time to move the desks away and form a circle. Decide how you would like the children to move the desks and chairs and where they need to move them. Once the desks are moved, where do the children go? Do they sit on their desks or stand in front of them and wait for you to lead them into the circle? Or do they move to the circle on their own? Do they have an assigned place to stand in circle or do they choose? I recommend having assigned places (this could be role call order, boy-girl order, or any other configuration that you feel will work best).

Physical formation of a circle

Some classes imitate beautifully and simply follow the teacher to form a beautiful, round circle. Other classes have more of a challenge with this and may need some support in order to hold a circle. You can tape a circle on the floor, draw a circle on the floor with chalk, or have a circular rug. I have found that a physical representation of a circle can help classes that struggle with finding and holding that form. Having a physical representation of the circle can also help contain and "hold" the class if they are a squirrelly bunch. I have seen some classes that cannot immediately start in a circle and need even more form to contain them. In this case, it can work to do circle behind the desks. You can still do gross motor movements by circling up around the outside perimeter, which seems to provide more structure for the children.

Sometimes too much open space can agitate children and they need external physical boundaries to help them feel their own boundaries and keep them grounded. If this is the case for your class, try doing your morning circle behind the desks and around the desks for some time, and then introduce the open-floor model of circle. The children will be your best gauge, and you will know when they are ready to move forward. With any scenario, have a verse or song that signals the start of circle.

Elements of a morning circle

- Gathering song or verse to signal beginning of the circle time
- Seasonal poems, verses, songs
- Curriculum-based poems, verses, songs, and movements
- A balance between in-breath and out-breath and the polarities, in other words a balance between activities that are more grounding, inward, quiet and calming, with activities that are more "excarnating," outward, quick and loud. You can play with polarities in tempo, fast, medium, slow; with volume loud and soft; with movements big and small; with voices: giant voice and tiny gnome, fairy or mouse voice.

In-breath: Quiet, inward, grounding, small and fine-motor activities; moving inward toward the center of the circle, circling to the left for more grounding; seated activities, activities with the feet or with the fingers and hands.

Out-breath: Louder, bigger, faster, gross-motor activities; moving out toward periphery of circle, activities in which the children have to engage with each other, such as folk dancing, hand-clapping games, and so forth.

- Movements that provide experience through all planes of space: up/down, side-to-side, forward/backward, stretching, bending, twisting, leaning. These movements help integrate the midlines and early reflexes.
- Movements that include vestibular (balance) and proprioception (sense of self movement and sense of self in space) input
- Gross-motor movements: running, jumping, skipping, hopping, throwing, catching (ball/bean bag skills), crawling, creeping, rolling, rhythm sticks, moving like different animals
- Fine motor movements: finger-play games, work with feet and toes
- Ending song or verse to signal close of circle time

Closing the circle

It is always a very good idea to end your circle with a calming, in-breath activity. This will allow the children to calm down and be ready for the ending verse or song and move on from circle to prepare for the rest of the main lesson. Repeat your song for moving desks back to their places. This can be a planned out-breath within your morning. Once the children have moved their desks back into place, allow them to get a drink of water. When everyone has had their water and is back to their seats, you will need to have another in-breath activity. You will find that your main lesson needs to "breathe" as well, and if you can do this in a healthy way, your students and lesson will flow much more smoothly. An activity that I always found helpful to do after our circle time was mental math. This brings the student's focus in.

All we do in our circles is beneficial for children and their development. We can create even stronger therapeutic circles for our students by incorporating more movements that support the development and integration of the early reflexes and the proprioceptive and vestibular systems. For further inspiration, please read my essay on "The Development and Integration of the Human Body," and see below for other resources. Be inspired and have fun!

What to look for when observing a child

How is this child in his body in this moment? How is the child moving? Does he move freely? Does he hold any tension in his body? Where does his movement appear to be stuck? Is he extending fully? Can he move comfortably/smoothly through all planes (up/down, forward/back, side-to-side)? It is important to refrain from jumping to conclusions, and simply observe things as they are.

What are the child's interactions with and reactions to the senses? This is called sensory integration: touch, smell, sight, hearing, taste, movement, balance (vestibular), and awareness of body position in space (proprioception).

Is the child hypersensitive, experiencing sensations intensely and therefore experiencing pain and feeling overwhelmed and avoiding sensations because he cannot tolerate them? Is he hyposensitive, experiencing sensations less intensely than normal and therefore needing a lot of stimulation to achieve ordinary arousal or alertness? Bumping, crashing, twirling, falling, or seeking the same movement over and over again?

What we as teachers and parents can do

Provide ample opportunity for children to explore movement. Get them out in NATURE!! Provide movements that work with the senses, balance, and spatial awareness (above/below, front/back, right/left).

REFERENCES

Andersen, H. (2014). *Active arithmetic!* Chatham, NY: Waldorf Publications.

Blanning, N. and Clark, L. (2010). *Movement journey and circle adventures: Movement enrichment with a therapeutic approach for early childhood.* Spring Valley, NY: Waldorf Early Childhood Association of North America (WECAN).

Blythe, S.G. (2005). *The well-balanced child*: Movement and early learning. Stroud, UK: Hawthorn Press.

Brooking-Payne, K. (1996). *Games children play*. Stroud, UK: Hawthorn Press.

Cole, J. (1989). *Anna banana: 101 jump-rope rhymes.* New York: William Morrow and Company, Inc.

Cole, J. and Calmenson, S. (1990). *Miss Mary Mack and other children's street rhymes.* New York: William Morrow and Company, Inc.

Reading and writing

Linda Atamian

Rudolf Steiner set the teaching of language arts in an overall sense of the structure of language and the wisdom of language.
— M.C. Richards (1980)

Henry Barnes described reading as "the art of entering with one's whole soul into an experience outside oneself. It is a gleaning of the sunlight hidden in the hard kernel of the word." (1969)

Learning to read and write is a long but magical journey. How do we support students who might need to take a slightly different route?

What are the stages of reading?

Waldorf educators will find commonality with Dr. Jeanne Chall's "Stages of Reading." The renowned Harvard professor developed these stages by keenly observing children during her clinical work and then combining her observations with child development theories. She intended the stages to be connected, overlapping, and continuous sequences, and she hesitates to link them to specific grade levels, rather she emphasizes that learning to read takes a lifetime. In her introduction to *Stages of Reading Development*, she reported that, when Goethe was very old, someone asked him when he had learned to read, and he responded that he had spent a lifetime learning and was still learning.

Chall's chronology is similar to Waldorf education's early childhood approach. **Stage 0** focuses on oral language development. **Stage 1** (grades 1–2) emphasizes alphabetic-phonics where children learn to associate sounds to letters and letters to sounds. According to Dr. Chall, "in a sense, it is as if the child has recapitulated history from… the discovery of picture writing…" (1983, p.16).

The focus of **Stage 2** (grades 2–3) is fluency. Students read what is already familiar to them to develop automaticity and confidence. "What kind of environment fosters the development of Stage 2? Essentially, it requires an opportunity for reading many familiar books—familiar because the subjects are familiar, or the structure is familiar, as in fairy tales or folktales."(p.19).

Stage 3 (grades 4–8) begins the transition to "reading to learn," but isn't it also about "learning how to read to learn"?

Stage 4 (high school) requires dealing with more than one viewpoint, and **Stage 5** (ages 18 and above) may be characterized as constructive reading: The reader builds his or her own knowledge through reading. (Chall 1983)

Reading is an extremely complex matter which plays itself out on various levels. It is not merely decoding; it is not a one-to-one transfer of symbols into information. Reading must involve the inner activity of the reader. It is never, in terms of its true character, mere intake of information. To understand the contexts of meaning within a text, I always add something of my own, something of my current knowledge of the world, my own will and my own experience. – Sam (2003)

Learning to read, write, and spell

Young children learn best when their feelings are engaged in a warm and enthusiastic manner. Rudolf Steiner reminded educators: "It is not only important what a teacher does, but who the teacher is, the attitude in his or her soul." (1998, p.237) "What we need is a certain kind of enthusiasm, a kind of inner activity…" (1998, p.400) So, let us kindle our enthusiasm as we consider ways to support students on this remarkable journey of learning to read, write, and spell.

Human beings come to earth prepared to learn to speak through interactions with other human beings: their family members and caregivers. Waldorf early childhood educators know this well! Although formal reading instruction comes later, learning to read really does begin in early childhood with its emphasis on oral language and bodily development. Stories, warm conversations, poems, songs, nursery rhymes, and circle games—all these lay a strong foundation for oral language. Children learn so much besides the meanings of words: to recognize that some words begin and end the same; that there is rhythm, tone, and pitch involved in reading; and that stories and books are entertaining and informative and can be a shared experience.

Since reading is a fairly new capacity for human beings, it takes time to become ready for formal reading instruction. What is the best teaching approach? We might ponder Steiner's indications in *The Child's Changing Consciousness and Waldorf Education* (1983). He discusses three methods as they were described in the 18th and 19th centuries (not to be confused with modern definitions): the spelling method (making words by adding single letters), the phonetic method (developing a feeling for the quality of sounds), and the whole-word method (progressing from sentences to words to single sounds). He goes on to say that "everything needs to be considered from different angles." (pp.88–89)

If the letter forms have been gained through painting, drawing, and drawing-painting, and if one has gone on to a kind of phonetic or whole word method, which is now appropriate because it leads the child to an appreciation of wholeness, and prevents him from becoming too fixed in details—if all this has been done, there is as yet something else which has been overlooked…It is this—the single sound by itself, the separate M or P…
— Rudolf Steiner (p.90)

In grade one, children learn to write their letters first. The symbols for the consonants emerge from drawing picture elements connected to stories. Steiner indicated that we should begin with the whole word: *king*. A drawing of the "kind king" evolves into an artistic representation of the letter *K*. The letters are introduced imaginatively, and they artistically connect movement and shape through a word to the sound. Today, explicit instruction is considered a best practice for teaching early literacy skills to all children (The National Reading Panel Report 2003). "The hallmark of programs of systematic phonics instruction is the direct teaching of a set of letter-sound relationships." (*Put Reading First* 2003) Class teachers explicitly link a key word with its sound and its letter: king K/k/.

Dyslexia

It is estimated that as many as one in five students in every class is apt to struggle to learn to read, write, and spell. For these students, being ready to read and write takes longer and requires an explicit, sequential, multisensory, structured language approach. It also takes soul warmth! Further, dyslexic students benefit from lots of practice and may spend a longer time in Stages 1 and 2.

The word *dyslexia* came into English from the German word *dyslexie*, from the Greek morphemes *dys,* "difficulty with," and *lex,* "word," ergo, difficulty with words. The National Institute for Children's Health and Development (NICHD) and the International Dyslexia Association (IDA) define *dyslexia* as

> a specific learning disability that is neurological in origin. It is characterized by difficulties with accurate and or fluent word recognition and by poor spelling and decoding abilities. These difficulties typically result from a deficit in the phonological component of language that is often unexpected in relation to other cognitive abilities and the provision of effective classroom instruction. Secondary consequences may include problems in reading comprehension and reduced reading experience that can impede growth of vocabulary and background knowledge.

According to the Academy of Orton-Gillingham Practitioners and Educators (AOGPE), the certifying body for O-G practitioners,

> dyslexia has its genesis in human biology. While not the result of neurological damage, it is the product of neurological development. Dyslexia commonly runs in families and varies from mild to severe. Most importantly, the use of the Orton-Gillingham approach by a skilled and experienced teacher can significantly moderate the language learning and processing problems that arise from dyslexia. Indeed, the approach, used early enough and by qualified practitioners, has every likelihood of eliminating the emergence of notable reading and writing problems.

What might signal dyslexia?

No two dyslexic students are exactly alike, but they demonstrate some common characteristics that "persist over time and interfere with learning." (IDA 2014: *IDA Dyslexia Handbook: What Every Family Should Know*). In addition, some dyslexic individuals may have related challenges such as ADHD, dysgraphia (writing), dyscalculia (math), dyspraxia (motor skills), or executive dysfunctions (for example, planning and organizing). The list below is guided in part by Dr. Sally Shaywitz from her book *Overcoming Dyslexia* and from the *IDA Dyslexia Handbook*.

In the preschool years:
Finds it challenging to
- learn new words
- retrieve known words for expressive language (rapid automatized naming)
- remember nursery rhymes and songs, recognize rhyme or generate rhyme (phonological awareness)

Shows signs of
- mixing up sounds or syllables in longer words, e.g., *pasketti* for *spaghetti* (phonological memory)

In the early grade school years:
Finds it challenging to
- blend sounds to make words or segment sounds to spell words (phonemic awareness)
- associate sounds with letters (phonics)
- spell words (orthography)
- produce consistent work

Shows signs of
- transposing sounds when reading
- omitting or misreading short words
- reading slowly and choppily (fluency)
- needing lots of repetition to learn skills and concepts

In the later grade school years and high school:
In addition to the items above, finds it challenging to
- Learn a second language

Shows signs of
- A wide discrepancy between verbal and written expression
- Avoiding literacy tasks or not wanting to attend school
- Complaining of headaches and stomach aches
- Expressing feelings of failure

How is dyslexia diagnosed?

The evaluation process begins with conversations at parent-teacher conferences as early as kindergarten. Of course, children should be assessed for vision and hearing. There will be further conversations if the child still shows signs of dyslexia in grade one or two. There may be a remedial consultation or the care group may take up the question. When parents and teachers work together, much can be accomplished. Before too long, the student will need a formal psycho-educational or neuropsychological evaluation done by a highly qualified individual or group. Some families begin with their public school district. Others opt for an independent evaluation. The evaluation will culminate with a guiding document that will usually confirm what parents and teachers have already noticed. But the document will also present the results of formal testing. A Wechsler Intelligence Scale for Children, fifth edition (WISC-V), which does not involve reading, will reveal specific cognitive strengths and challenges within the areas of verbal comprehension, visual-spatial, fluid reasoning, working memory, and processing speed. Additionally, a full-scale score will usually be reported. In addition to the WISC-V, evaluators will use other standard assessment tools to examine academic achievement or may look further at areas such as memory, phonological awareness, and so forth. Sometimes evaluators will recommend further assessments by a speech and language pathologist or an occupational therapist to attain additional insight. The document usually ends with specific recommendations. For a dyslexic student, that usually includes explicit, multisensory structured literacy instruction, such as Orton-Gillingham, with plenty of opportunity for practice.

What type of instruction supports dyslexic students?

Dyslexic students benefit from instruction taught by a highly trained teacher or tutor. The following components should be included: phonological awareness, phonics, handwriting, spelling, and fluency. Later the focus will shift toward vocabulary, comprehension, and written expression, as well as study skills and learning strategies.

Orton-Gillingham is a structured literacy approach to teaching students of all ages to read, write, and spell. It is not a method or program, though there are many commercial programs that are based on Orton-Gillingham, such as the Wilson programs and the Slingerland Approach. These programs and trainings are widely used in schools with good results.

The Orton-Gillingham approach is considered the gold standard; it requires rigorous training and practicum experience taught and supervised by a Fellow of the Academy. There are several levels.

1. Parents and teachers may get a general overview through a *Subscriber* level course (available online for a nominal fee at the Academy website: www.ortonacademy.org).

2. The *Classroom Educator* level, developed for teachers or specialists who provide whole class and/

or small group instruction within a school setting, involves 30 hours of instruction and a 50-hour supervised practicum.

3. The *Associate* level is step one on the track toward certification as an Orton-Gillingham practitioner. This level includes a 60-hour course and a 100-hour supervised practicum.

4. The *Certified* level involves another 100 hours of instruction and another 200-hour supervised practicum. After successful completion of the Certified level, teachers may apply to the Academy to become certified Orton-Gillingham practitioners.

5. The *Fellow* level qualifies individuals to provide Orton-Gillingham training to teachers and interventionists.

Orton-Gillingham remedial language specialists learn the structure of the language and how to break it down to create a personalized program that leads to success for each student. Every Orton-Gillingham lesson approaches instruction by combining a synthetic and an analytic approach; students go from the whole to the parts and the parts to the whole. Students read, write, and spell in an integrated lesson. Throughout the 40- to 60-minute teacher-created lesson, taught from two to five times per week, students follow a routine in which they receive simultaneous feedback through the visual, auditory, and kinesthetic-tactile modalities based on Dr. Orton's Language Triangle. (Gillingham & Stillman 1997) The approach is sequential, structured, systematic, and multisensory. Lessons are cumulative; skills are not taught in isolation. New information is connected to previously taught information, and practice continues until skills become automatic.

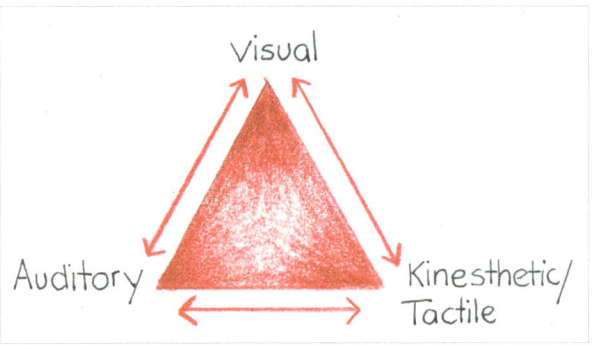

A great part of educational method depends on finding the most rational way of linking the new things we have to teach the children to what we can draw from their store of memories.
– Rudolf Steiner, *Anthroposophy: An Introduction* (1983)

When should students be diagnosed and provided with intervention?

In her book, *Overcoming Dyslexia* (2003), Dr. Sally Shaywitz, warns that

> under-identification of reading-disabled children is particularly worrisome because, even when school identification does take place, it occurs relatively late, often past the optimal age for intervention… Reading disabilities diagnosed after third grade are much more difficult to remediate. Moreover, once a child falls behind, he must make up thousands of unread words to catch up to his peers who are continuing to move ahead. Equally important, once a pattern of reading failure sets in, many children become defeated, lose interest in reading and develop what often evolves into a lifelong loss of their own sense of self-worth. (2003, pp. 30–31)

Waldorf teachers employ the oral tradition as an essential teaching approach; therefore, it may be possible for dyslexic students to feel successful during the first few grades. But before long, their peers will read books, and the sense of failure will set in quickly if they do not receive the support that they need. And even if they are exposed to sophisticated text by being read to or by listening to audio books, they are still not seeing the words that they are hearing.

It is essential to the well-being of children that Waldorf schools find ways to support children as soon as possible. Waldorf schools can forge a path that is unique to their curriculum and understanding of child development. There is an opportunity for parents, teachers, care groups, remedial teachers, school doctors, and tutors to work together to support students within the Waldorf school environment.

Phonological awareness, phonemic awareness, and phonics

Connecting the shape to the sound

Picture, movement and sound—all these lie behind the letters…. Most teachers find that children differ very much in their abilities to grasp what they learn. Some more readily relate themselves to the picture element, while others are more aware of the sound. A few can form their letters very beautifully without waking to any consciousness of either picture or sound… We should bear all these in mind, and, in the teaching of the letters, pictures, movement, and sound must all play their parts so that the different children become harmonized. (Hutchins)

In a Waldorf school, first grade children learn their letters joyfully; in fact, they often have favorite letters. Through a multisensory approach, they recognize the shapes of the letters while they feel the formations as they move them in space, skywrite them, and form them with beautiful colors. At the same time, they learn that the letter *K* makes the sound they hear at the beginning of *king*: /k/. They recite alliterative verses that reinforce the sound: "Kickamore, kackamore, on the king's kitchen door…." They may even clap or stamp their foot each time they speak the sound /k/.

We know that children learn at different rates and in different ways. Dyslexic students have a more difficult time recognizing the phonemes or separate sounds of our language. They may have trouble blending sounds to read and segmenting them to spell. They may even have trouble with broader phonological awareness: recognizing and generating rhyme and understanding that certain words begin the same or end the same. They may change the sequence of syllables in words or omit syllables in their speech. They not only take longer to gain this awareness but they do so only through explicit instruction with an opportunity to practice over time. They don't usually infer knowledge from exposure; they learn best through direct instruction with guided practice.

Circle time and transitions provide opportunities to practice phonological and phonemic awareness.

Phonological awareness

Recognizing rhyme
- Thumbs up/ thumbs down
- Say two words: *pin, chin* (thumbs up) or *pat, lit* (thumbs down)

Generating rhyme
- I'm going on a journey: Toss the bean bag to a child and say, "I'm going on a journey and I am bringing my _____ (cat)." The child who receives the bean bag tosses it to someone and says: "I'm bringing my _____ (bat, hat, mat, rat)." When you run out of words, switch to a new rhyme.

Phonemic awareness

- Elkonin cards

Materials: pebbles, picture cards (Teachers can draw pictures or use objects or just say the words.) Children repeat the whole word: *goat,* and then move one pebble down for each phoneme (smallest unit of sound): /g/ /ō/ /t/

This can be done, at first, through sound alone, with no connection to written letters.

bug: /b/ /ŭ/ /g/
bed: /b/ /ĕ/ /d/
cat: /k/ /ă/ /t/
rose: /r/ /ō/ /z/
pin: /p/ /ĭ/ /n/
fox: /f/ /ŏ/ /ks/
queen: /kw/ /ē/ /n/

(There are actually two phonemes for "x" and "qu" but it is better to teach students to recognize the sounds for these letters as one sound.)

sheep: /sh/ /ē/ /p/ (*sh* is a digraph and cannot be segmented.)
bride: /b/ /r/ /ī/ /d/ (*br* is a blend and can be segmented.)

Phonics/ decoding

Letter/sound associations

Consonants: Many first, second, and third grade classrooms have beautiful, painted alphabets above the blackboard, which offer important visual support. Including the picture elements adds another layer of support. These alphabets can relieve the working memories of children who struggle to hold information in mind while they complete tasks. Others may have trouble efficiently retrieving what they know (rapid naming); visuals will support them, too.

To prevent confusion, do not teach "b" and "d" too closely together. Additionally, teach students to form these letters very differently. Begin "b" with *bat* and end with *ball*. Begin "d" with *drum* and end with *stick*.

Vowels: What about the vowels, the singing star letters? Each vowel can be written on the point of a five-pointed golden star. Unlike most reading approaches, Waldorf educators usually begin with the long vowel sounds, the names of the letters.

When the short vowels are taught, children will benefit from a key word connected with the short vowel sounds such as *apple, egg, igloo, octopus, umbrella*.

Teach short "i" long before introducing short "e," as these sounds are easily confused. A suggested teaching sequence is to space out the teaching of the short vowels: *a, i, o, u,* and *e*.

Be careful with picture clue/key word choices:

Elephant is not a suitable picture element for "e" because students hear the letter name "l" or the sound /ĕl/ at the beginning instead of /ĕ/. In some dialects, *egg* is pronounced /āg/; in that case, *egg* would not be a helpful key word either. *X-ray* and *xylophone* are not appropriate choices for "x" since "x" usually says /ks/ at the end of words like "fox." "Y" is a double agent! It is a consonant at the beginning of syllables (*yes*) but a vowel in the middle (*gym*) or end (*my* or *happy*).

Blends are two or three consonant sounds that need to be blended together for reading and segmented for spelling. These can be taught in groups, such as the "l" blends: *bl, cl, fl, gl, pl, sl, spl*.

Digraphs and trigraphs are two to three letters that stick together to make one sound: *ch, sh, th, wh, -ck, ph,* and *-tch*. In later grades, students need to know the Greek ch /k/ and the French ch /sh/.

Vowel combinations such as *ai, ay, ee, ea, oa, ie, igh, oo, ou, ow, au, aw, oi, oy, oe, ew, eu, ei,* and *eigh*. Many of these have multiple sounds (e.g., *ea eagle* /ē/, *bread* /ĕ/, and *steak* /ā/).

R-controlled vowels such as *ar, or, er, ir, ur*.

Consonant *-le* endings such as *-ble, -dle,* or *-ple*.

Final stable syllables such as *-tion* and *-sion* /shŭn/ or *-ture* /cher/.

Word Families: In the beginning, students can learn to read words with common rhymes or word families: *-an* (can, Dan, fan, Jan, man, pan, ran, tan, van) or *-ing* (king, Ming, ping, ring, sing, wing). Create a pictorial representation for each family. Some teachers represent each member of the family "seated" at a dining room table; others draw a house for each family with their family name on the door and a list of the family members within.

While we generally think about teaching letter-sound associations in the primary grades, there are many advanced letter-sound associations that students need as they progress through the grades such as *-age* (village /ĭj/) or *-eau* (plateau /ō/). These can continue to be taught in word study or spelling lessons. All the vowels can make the schwa sound in unaccented syllables. For example, the "a" in *amaze, magma,* and *banana* is not long or short.

Jack Petrasch offers a little story for imaginatively presenting the second sound of /k/ with the letter "C." In his story, the cat brought the letter "C" to help the king. Further, his story "Noisy Nimmy," designed to introduce the letter "N," also formed a bridge to teaching the silent "K" and "G" in "KN" and "GN." (2002)

Reciting, copying, and illustrating poems with repeated elements is another way to provide practice with letter-sound associations. Margaret Wise Brown's poem "High on a Hill" could be used to reinforce the *-igh* /ī/.

HIGH ON A HILL

High on a hill
When the moon is still
In the still night sky
A rabbit
Lifts his ears high
And listens
While the crickets fight
In the bright moonlight,
Katy-did, Katy-didn't
Katy-did, Katy-didn't
Who cares!
High on a hill
When the moon is still
Up.

But teaching letter-sound associations is not enough. To decode unfamiliar words, students need to be able to segment syllables and identify syllable types. There are six syllable types:

1. closed: There is one vowel at the beginning or middle, and it is followed by a consonant. The vowel sound will usually be short (as in *inch, best*)

2. open: There is one vowel, and it is at the end. The vowel sound will usually be long. Students can create a visual for these two syllable types: *hid hi, got go.*

Many Waldorf teachers and students sing a song that can be adapted to reinforce the difference between closed and open syllables: "Now we know our singing sounds: a, e, i, o, u.

Let's put a (insert a consonant like *b*) right after them: ăb, ĕb, ĭb, ŏb, ŭb." (This forms closed syllables.)

Then reverse the placement to form open syllables: "bā, bē, bī, bō, bū /boo." (Notice that long u has two sounds: /ū/ and /oo/ depending on the preceding letter: cu- /kū/ but du /doo/)

Write the vowel sequence on the chalkboard to provide a visual support for students as you sing the song.

3. vowel-consonant-e: There is one vowel followed by a consonant and then a final silent "e" (the magic e). The magic e makes the first vowel say its name, the long sound.

Children can make magic e wands. When they place the magic e at the end of words like *cap, pet, hop,* and *cut*—abracadabra—they turn into new words: *cape, Pete, hope,* and *cute*.

4. r-controlled: Vowels can be controlled by the beastly "r" /r/ to form new sounds: ar (*arm*), or (*horn*), er (*her*), ir (*bird*), and ur (*burn*). Later, students will learn additional sounds for *ar* and *or*.

5. vowel combinations: ee, ea (/ē/, /ĕ/, /ā/), ai, ay, oa, oo, ou, au, aw, ie /ē/, ie /ī/, igh, ow /ow/ and /ō/, ey /ē/ and /ā/, ou /oo/ and /ow/, oi, oy, eu, ew, ue, ei /ē/ and /ā/, eigh /ā/

6. consonant-le: -ble, -cle, -ckle, -dle, -fle, -gle, -kle, -ple, -stle (silent "t"), -tle, and -zle

Students also need to know seven syllable division patterns:
1. VC/CV răb/bĭt
2. V/CV or VC/V tī/ny or căb/ĭn
3. -Cle bū/gle
4. VC/CCV or VCC/CV sŭb/trăct or pŭmp/kĭn
5. VCC/CCV or VC/CCCV ĕgg/plănt or sŭb/scrībe
6. V/V nē/ŏn
7. Division by word parts or morphemes: un- + lock + -ed

Morphology

Students must also be guided to think about morphemes, the smallest units of meaning in our language. They learn the inflectional suffixes quite early. For example, -s and -es make words plural or show present verb tense. -ed indicates past tense. The "s" signals possession.

Later, derivational suffixes become important; they change the part of speech: the verb *imagine* becomes the noun *imagination* or the adjective *imaginative*.

Students learn to read and spell English by recapitulating its history. In the early grades, they work mainly with words from the Anglo-Saxon layer of our language. This layer includes many of the high frequency words, some of the hardest to spell, by the way: *was, of, there,* and so forth. It includes base words and common prefixes and suffixes (*jumping, girls, backyard*). Next comes the Latin layer of the language with Latin bases, prefixes, and suffixes (*subtraction* or *flexible*). The third layer comes from the Greek and includes combining forms like *tele, graph* and *phon* (e.g., *telegraph, telephone, phonograph*). At the very top layer are words adopted from many languages including Spanish and Native American words that have been welcomed into English. English is a growing language!

High frequency words

There are many lists of high frequency words such as the "Dolch" and "100 Instant Words." Some high frequency words are phonetic (*had, she, on, it*); others are not phonetic (*the, was, of, what*). They all need to be read and spelled with automaticity. Like all other skills, they need to be taught to dyslexics through a multisensory approach, and students need to practice them over time until they become automatic. 1. Read the word. 2. Spell the word aloud while tracing/ writing. 3. Read the word. 4. Repeat three times. Tricky parts can be written in color: *too* or *was*. Various mnemonic devices can be used: (for example, *friend*: I am a friend to the end!)

Spelling

Emergent writers sound words out and spell them just the way they sound: *was* = wuz or *happy* = hape. Through exposure to words over time, students begin to infer and integrate rules and patterns, and they form visual memories for the spelling of many words. Dyslexic students "encounter the same linguistic challenges that normally progressing children do, but they fail to resolve them." (Moats, Spelling Symposium, IDA conference 2011) Dyslexic students—indeed, all students—benefit from explicit instruction with sound-to-letter associations, spelling generalizations, and spelling rules. They should not be expected to memorize long lists of miscellaneous words. But they will benefit greatly from learning high frequency words—a few at a time—and words that follow regular patterns and rules.

Spelling rules:

-ff, -ll, -ss Rule: Use -ff, -ll, or -ss to spell /f/, /l/, or /s/ at the end of one-syllable words after a short vowel (*staff, bell, grass*).

Doubling l for one-syllable words: Double the final consonant of words that are 1-syllable and end with 1 vowel and 1 consonant if the suffix begins with a vowel (jog + ing = *jogging* but film + -ed = *filmed*).

E Rule: Drop the final "e" if the suffix begins with a vowel (trade + -ing = *trading* but hope + -ful = *hopeful*).

Y Rule: Change the "y" to "i" if there is a consonant before the y (spy + -ed = *spied*). Keep the "y" if there is a vowel before the "y" (play + -ed = *played*). Keep the "y" if the suffix begins with "i" (try + ing = *trying*).

Spelling generalizations:

Students can also be guided to discover spelling generalizations for ow/ou /ow/, au/aw /aw/, oi/oy /oy/, -k/-ck /k/, -ch/-tch /ch/, and -ge/-dge /j/. For example, use *ou* to spell /ow/ at the beginning or middle of words; use *ow* to spell /ow/ at the end of words. These are "generally" true. Teach exceptions to rules and generalizations only after the rules or generalizations have been learned.

Other important clues to spelling that are worth teaching involve **meaning clues** (*health* is related to *heal*; thus, use "ea" to spell /ĕ/ in *health*), **part of speech clues** (*natural* is an adjective, so use the -al suffix versus the noun ending in *novel*), and *language of origin clues* (*chorus* is from the Greek so /k/ =ch).

Reading fluency

Waldorf teachers model fluent speaking and reading. Students need to read fluently to comprehend what they read and to find reading an enjoyable or useful activity. According to Hasbrouck and Glaser, fluent reading is "reasonably accurate reading at an appropriate rate with suitable prosody that leads to accurate and deep comprehension and motivation to read." (Hasbrouck)

Besides modeling fluent reading so students can imitate it, teachers can provide opportunities for repeated reading of what is familiar. This is the best way for students to become fluent readers. Students might reread their main lesson books. Since we know that repeated reading—to simply memorize words—is not the best approach for students, we need to provide them with practice reading decodable text.

Teachers can create decodable text for main lesson books and underline words that are not decodable: *The king was sitting on the throne*. This sentence, for example, is decodable for a student who knows short vowels, the *-ng* family, closed syllable type, vowel - consonant-e syllable type, and VC/CV syllable division pattern.

After a dyslexic student I worked with was provided some O-G instruction and was practicing reading decodable text, he told me that he used to memorize books so he could "read" them. He wondered why he had not been taught to "break the code" earlier, and he felt he had been cheated or tricked into thinking that reading meant memorizing. Schools need to create and purchase decodable text. Flyleaf Publishing offers two sets of beautiful books that are decodable. Other sets of decodable text are available for sale through various vendors.

If students lose their place, which will affect fluency, guide them to hold a line marker above what they are reading. Readers need to see the words and punctuation marks that are coming, so they shouldn't hold their line marker below what they are reading.

Dyslexic students can reread their main lesson books and decodable books in small reading groups at school as well as to their families at home. This will provide them with the safe practice they need; it will boost their confidence and lead to success.

Once their peers are reading real "books," a service such as Learning Ally (formerly Recordings for the Blind) can provide assistive technology so students can see and hear text at their interest level. This assistive technology allows dyslexic students, who need more time to learn how to read, to gain access to the same books their friends are reading. This accommodation supports their souls! We wouldn't deny eyeglasses for a student who needs them. Thoughtful use of technology to accommodate dyslexic students is worth considering.

All Waldorf schools serve dyslexic students, and these children, like all children, are eager to learn. It just takes leading them along a slightly different route.

Handwriting

If we turn now to the act of writing, we will find that it is one of the most complicated and hidden of all human activities. – Dr. Karl König

What are some ways to provide practice with handwriting?

Teaching correct letter formation is a first goal. But it must be followed by opportunities for guided practice in order to achieve fluency and automaticity.

Class teachers can focus on teaching and reinforcing proper letter formation. Steiner reminded us: "Children will not improve much when you want to make them learn to write better

Reading and writing

by improving their writing. You need to improve their dexterity; then they will learn to write better." (*Faculty Meetings with Rudolf Steiner 1*, 1919–1922, pp.99–100)

Beginning in early childhood and extending into the grades, Waldorf education supports the development of dexterity throughout the curriculum. Extra lesson or remedial work in the grades also provides supplemental on dexterity and the bodily foundation that are essential. Improving dexterity, however, won't improve accurate letter formation; that relies on direct instruction and practice with corrective feedback.

First, teachers need to make sure they know how to form the letters correctly themselves. They also need to pay attention to children's posture and pencil grip. Children should be seated with their feet flat on the floor and hold their paper stable with their non-dominant "helping" hand. They should hold their writing tool with a proper tripod grasp. Desk and chair heights matter. According to Audrey McAllen,

> the desk height should not push the arm upward so that one shoulder is higher than the other. The chair should be 10 inches lower than the desk height. The child should sit so that both feet are firmly on the floor with the knees higher than the hips. This angle between knee and hip joint is vital. The child should really be sitting in his hips so that the movement of the hand-arm can flow to the base of the spine. (1977)

She recommends presenting this to the children as a picture of a king signing a kingly decree.

Whole class practice:

Children can wear their royal crowns during handwriting practice as a gentle imaginative reminder to hold their heads aloft so their heavy, jeweled crowns won't slip off.

To begin, use unlined paper and focus on correct letter formation. Use imaginative, pictorial language cues to guide children through the correct formation. "Start at the king's crown and move straight down to his boot. Then, pick up your crayon and start at the king's hand and move to his belt buckle and then down to his other boot." For practice, group letters with similar motor movements. For example, the letters that begin like r: r, n, m, h, and b.

Sand: Provide each student with a large, sturdy red paper plate. Good quality plates can last for years. Sprinkle in some fine sand. Model the proper letter formation for the group on the blackboard, and then move from desk to desk as the children practice forming the letter correctly in the sand. Three is a magic number so children should practice each letter correctly at least three times. Writing in sand is forgiving, especially for a child who has trouble; a little shake and the mistake will disappear. The teacher can even model the shape in the child's sand and leave a path for the child to follow. Walk about and provide help as needed. This is a wonderful way to practice the letters that have been

introduced and to informally assess the children as they progress.

Main Lesson book: After the children know how to form a letter correctly, the work in main lesson books can take place with size and space considered. Some children benefit from target lines: the sky line, the bird line, the grass line, and the worm line (adapted from Wilson Fundations) or the image of a house with the basement, first, and second floors. This kind of guided practice sets children up for success. It is also easy to slip a paper with the guidelines under the main lesson book page as a support for children who need it.

Some schools teach uppercase and lowercase print letters in grade one and then teach cursive in grade two.

There are common pedagogical practices that may need to be considered further. For example, is it a good idea to write words with all capital letters when this will need to be unlearned? Or is it better to write words only after the lowercase letters have been taught?

Writing difficulties

There are children in every school who have difficulties with the art of handwriting. For them, writing can be a chore, at best, and—at worst—an activity that can cause real frustration. It can take them a lot of effort and time and result in fatigue and frustration. Children who experience these challenges need the teacher's attention and understanding, as well as intervention and possible classroom accommodations.

What is dysgraphia?

Some students are diagnosed as dysgraphic during their formal evaluation. Dysgraphia is another Greek word. The suffix *-ia* suggests "a condition." The prefix *dys-* indicates that there is a difficulty, while the base *graph* refers to both the role of the hand in letter formation and to the letters that are formed. According to IDA, dysgraphia is disabled handwriting, in which impaired handwriting can also interfere with the speed and spelling of written text.

According to IDA, "children with dysgraphia do not have primary developmental motor disorder, another cause of poor handwriting, but may have difficulty planning sequential finger movements such as the touching of the thumb to successive fingers on the same hand without visual feedback."

In addition, there may be a challenge with orthographic coding linked to working memory. "Orthographic coding refers to the ability to store written words in working memory while the letters in the word are analyzed or the ability to create permanent memory of written words linked to their pronunciation and meaning." Therefore, dysgraphia can result in poor spelling. In fact, dysgraphia can impair handwriting alone, spelling alone, or both handwriting and spelling. (IDA)

The causes and diagnosis of writing difficulties

Writing is a highly complex process that involves several senses, muscles, and areas of the brain. When there are problems with any of the areas connecting and functioning effectively, writing difficulties may arise. These may not all fall under the mainstream label "dysgraphia." For example, there may be retained reflexes that are hindering the child from writing fluently. (see "Development and Integration of the Human Body")

As the teacher observes children during early form drawing and handwriting lessons, it is important to recognize when children may need help beyond regular instruction in the classroom. Much can be done through correct identification and intervention. Effective handwriting instruction with guided practice that includes corrective feedback is critical. It is possible to teach most students, including many dysgraphic students, to write by hand through effective instruction and intervention. And, it is never too late to begin.

When not served early enough, children will struggle more during the later grades. By the time a student is in grade four and is assigned to write an animal report, it can become very apparent that writing is not going as well as it should. Instead of focusing on the expression of ideas, the student will be hindered by a lack of writing fluency. By sixth grade, frustration can mount to high levels as the writing workload increases and becomes ever more important in all the studies. Hopefully, through early identification and explicit instruction, these challenges can be minimized. In any case, even when a struggling student has learned to form letters correctly and can write accurately, the hindrances may still interfere with fluid and legible written output. What else can be done in the classroom?

Some students will benefit from extra handwriting intervention. They might begin with practice that includes "painting" the letters with a wet paintbrush on a chalkboard. Or their tutor might use Dr. Orton's folded paper technique. An unlined paper is folded into thirds. In the first column the child traces a teacher's large colorful model; and in the second column, the child makes his or her own letters with the original model in view. Column one is folded over column two and in column three, the child next makes the letter without a model. If needed, the paper can be unfolded to reveal the model. Finally, the paper is folded over so a fourth column appears from the back. Here, the child closes his or her eyes and makes the letter without looking. This enhances the kinesthetic and tactile reinforcement of the letter formation. (Gillingham-Stillman 1997)

Explicit instruction and remediation are the most important responses. But additional classroom accommodations may be needed to support students for success within the classroom setting.

- Reduce the writing workload for assignments (for homework and class work).
- Provide the student with a copy of notes or blackboard text.
- Provide speech to text software, when deemed necessary. (Few students will require this accommodation.)
- Provide a word processor as an important accommodation for written expression, especially for lengthy writing assignments. This will also require providing proper keyboarding instruction.

In any event, today's graduating high school students all need to be able to write in print (labeling diagrams or maps), cursive (note-taking), and keyboarding (essays and reports).

Successful reading and writing relies, at minimum, on the creation of a strong bridge between reading, writing, and spelling. Every child can succeed when guided by understanding, support, and, most importantly, soul warmth. Then they will be able to make the journey needed to "glean the sunlight hidden in the hard kernel of the word."

REFERENCES

Academy of Orton-Gillingham. (2010). "An Overview." Accessed February 24, 2016. http://www.ortonacademy.org/

Armbruster, Bonnie B., Fran Lehr, Jean Osborn, and C. Ralph Adler. (2003). *Put reading first: The research building blocks for teaching children to read: Kindergarten through grade 3*. Washington, DC: National Institute of Child Health and Human Development.

Barnes, Henry, Nathan Lyons and Frances McLaughlin Gil. (1969). *Education as an art: The Rudolf Steiner method*. New York: Rudolf Steiner School.

Chall, Jeanne S. (1983). *Stages of reading development*. New York: McGraw-Hill.

Gillingham, Anna and Bessie W. Stillman. (1997). *The Gillingham manual: Remedial training for students with specific disability in reading, spelling, and penmanship*. Cambridge, MA: Educators Publishing Service.

Hasbrouck, Jan. *Reading fast or reading well: Let's take another look at fluency*. PPT.

Hutchins, Eileen. "The Teaching of Writing." The Online Waldorf Library, www.waldorflibrary.org

International Dyslexia Association. *IDA Dyslexia Handbook: What every family should know*. http://eida.org

_____. *IDA Fact Sheet*. "Understanding Dysgraphia." http://eida.org

König, Karl. (2002). *On reading and writing*. Camphill Books.

McAllen, Audrey E. (1997). *Teaching children to write: Its connection with the development of spatial consciousness in the child*. Forest Row, UK: Rudolf Steiner Press.

National Institutes of Health. (2000). Report of the National Reading Panel: "Teaching children to read: An evidence-based assessment of the scientific research literature on reading and its implications for reading instruction." Washington, DC: National Institute of Child Health and Human Development.

Petrasch, Jack. (2002). *Understanding Waldorf education: Teaching from the inside out*. Lewisville, NC: Gryphon House.

Richards, Mary Caroline. (1980). *Toward wholeness: Rudolf Steiner education in America*. Middletown, CT: Wesleyan University Press.

Sam, Martina Maria. (2003). "Renewing the art of reading: Active transformation versus phrasemongering." Goetheanum: Anthroposophy Worldwide.

Shaywitz, Sally E. (2003). *Overcoming dyslexia: A new and complete science-based program for reading problems at any level*. New York: A.A. Knopf.

Steiner, Rudolf. (1983). *Anthroposophy: An introduction*. Forest Row, UK: Rudolf Steiner Press.

———. (1998). *Faculty meetings with Rudolf Steiner*. Vols. 1 and 2. Great Barrington, MA: Anthroposophic Press.

Music, gym, and the pencil grip

Jeff Tunkey

*These three friends will learn to serve—
to help me draw straight lines and curves.*

Every teacher knows there are only so many battles one can take up in a given day, and quite often the effort to steadily encourage the attainment of a nicely functioning pencil grip by all or even most students in a class tumbles down the list of priorities to somewhere below tying shoes, raising a hand to speak, and so many other small but important details that fill our careers. Attainment of a grip suitable for cursive writing, form drawing, and painting is best worked on in the early grades. Before this time, a palmar or fist grip may be more in line with the child's stage of development; after a grade or two, many occupational therapists believe, only the most counterproductive habits should lead the teacher to make an attempt for change.

The pictures below illustrate a tripod grip, the "gold standard" of pencil grips: heel of hand steadied on the work surface; pinkie and ring fingers also acting as a stabilizing base; and thumb, pointer and middle finger encircling the pencil as a triumvirate that maximizes mobility and ease. The tripod is not the only possibility for a smoothly-functioning grip. Teachers need to observe: Is the grip (and the writing) tense, or relaxed and smooth? Does the student tire, or can she write without strain for a good length of time? Remember that Doctor Steiner suggested that the first avenue to helping with tension in writing is practice writing with the feet!

To see why helping students with their pencil grips might still be a very worthy educational effort (even in the Texting Century!) and how it can be worked on with less psychological effort and more

success, let us imagine that we will be taking our writing hands "down the hall" for music class and then gym class.

When we enter the music room, the chorus lesson begins by getting the altos in one section of the riser, the tenors in another, and so forth. The teacher reminds us to plant our feet firmly, stand up in a straight and stable way… and to keep our jaw and the lower half of the head nice and loose, with the lips and tongue also relaxed. She begins the singing with some scales or other musical agilities. Through this beginning, she has helped the physical readiness of the students so they can sing on pitch and with good tone. Tight jaws, pursed lips, or tense tongues will all lead to pitch and tone problems, and weak music.

Next, it's off to the gym for our writing hands. This teacher has the students form a circle and do some pushups, situps, calisthenics and other strength and agility exercises. Then he leads some stretches. He's gathered up the class in this way so that they are not only warmed up and attentive, but physiologically better prepared for the exertions ahead.

In all of the above that our "finger students" have just experienced, we can find a rhythm between stretching and lifting movements as described by Audrey McAllen; an alternation, or breathing, between tension and relaxation.[1] This rhythm is vital to integrating the postural system, particularly the senses of balance and self-movement. And in his lectures on arithmetic, Dr. Karl König emphasizes the essential role of these senses in the development of mathematical capacities.[2]

Back to the drawing board

Looking at a proper pencil grip for writing, form drawing, and painting—and at how to help in its achievement by our students—we can find everything mentioned above. First of all, the wrist is like the feet, gliding on the working surface as a grounded base for the fingers. The pinkie and ring finger are like the legs, poised to stabilize those fingers that move the pencil. The relaxed jaw and lower head from our music warmup correspond to the open, C-shaped position of the hand shown in the sketches above. And finally, the pencil, pen or brush is in the position of the tongue, articulating the words or pictures. Only when the other members of the chorus are in their places for harmonious movement will it be possible for the thumb, pointer and middle finger to carry the most beautiful melody.

For a more practical and scientific background on the reasons this tripod or classic pencil grip is the most functional and non-tiring, there are many fine references on the internet written by experienced occupational therapists.[3]

Agilities and warmups: strengthening the foundations

Both fine- and gross-motor capacities, together with hand flexibility and a flexible attitude, must be strengthened if all students are to gain the ability for a tripod or other nicely functional grip. The series of copper rod exercises given on the Movement for Childhood website includes many such activities that can be led by a class, gym, or eurythmy teacher.[4] For example, the "Pepper and Salt" copper rod exercise.

Pepper and Salt: both hands on top of the rod, then under the rod; successively lift indexes, middles, rings and pinkies (same order both over and under!). Verse: "Pep/per and salt… Pep/per and salt… Over and under and never a fault. Pepper and salt."

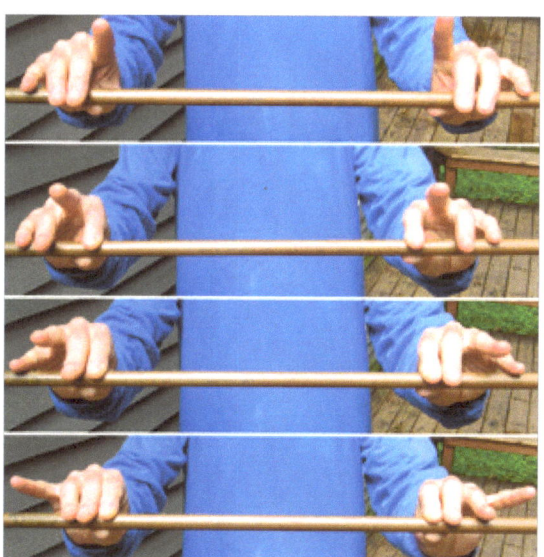

Music, gym, and the pencil grip

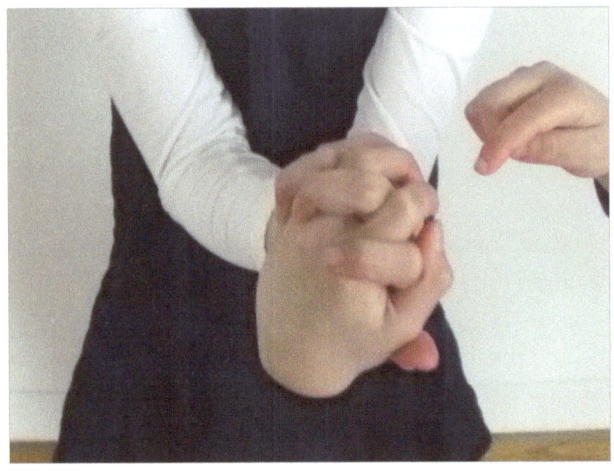

There are also many desk or classroom activities that may be done without supplies; here are two of my favorites.

Finger Finder Partner Game: "A" interlaces fingers, with thumbs pointing down, then rotates wrists so fingers are on top. "B," the partner, points to a finger without touching it, and "A" attempts to raise and wiggle the selected finger without moving any other finger.

Crab Walk across desk: Student reaches right hand to far left side of desk; stretches fingers out as far as possible; plants pinkie firmly and pulls fingers back together (leaving pinkie in place); plants thumb firmly and then stretches fingers back out so that pinkie is reaching as far as possible for the next step; and so on to the other side. Then left hand takes the same walk, from right to left. Repeat.

The **Thumb Twirling exercise** from *The Extra Lesson* is also an invaluable warmup for writing, drawing and painting. In conclusion, I think you will find that a steady diet of copper rod exercises and other finger-awareness and dexterity-strengthening activities will make the achievement of the tripod pencil grip easier and more successful. Beginning these approaches and expectations right from first grade, before other habits become implacable, will save you from many a battle in the years to come!

ENDNOTES

1. McAllen, Audrey. (2004). *The extra lesson. The extra lesson*. Fair Oaks, CA: Rudolf Steiner College Press.
2. König, Karl. *For teachers: Conferences and seminars on arithmetic*. Typescript available online at http://www.waldorfresearchinstitute.org/pdf/Arithmetic.pdf
3. Just type "importance of pencil grip" into a Google search. Three examples I've drawn on are: http://nspt4kids.com/parenting/evaluating-effective-pencil-grasps/
http://theanonymousot.com/2013/03/22/when-to-fix-a-pencil-grasp/
http://www.skillsforaction.com/handwriting/pencil-grip-overview
4. http://www.movementforchildhood.com/uploads/2/1/6/7/21671438/copperrods.pdf

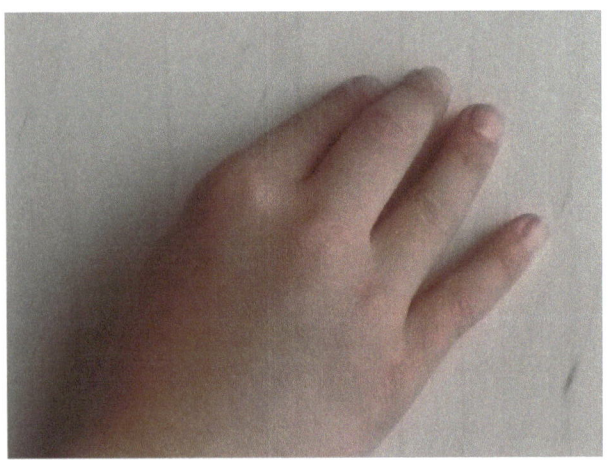
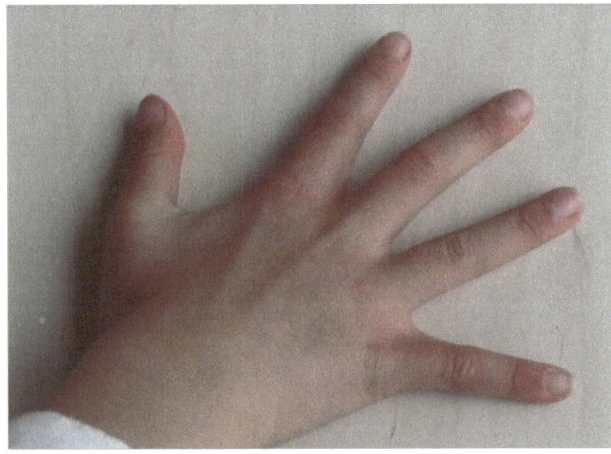

Therapeutic aspects of form drawing
An introduction

Hanneke van Riel

Thus the All-wise originated the world of form, the total essence of which is encompassed in the contrasts of the straight and the rounded line.
— Johannes Kepler
quoted by Van James, in
The Secret Language of Form

Before exploring this topic we must establish a shared understanding of the word *therapeutic*. For the purposes of this chapter we will assume the following: In a therapeutic setting two or more people are engaged in a relationship in which they affect each other. A therapeutic relationship in a school setting aims to bring about beneficial change in the child.

Our understanding of "beneficial change" for the purposes of this chapter is that, through our work the child will experience improved harmony and balance between the physical-etheric and soul-spiritual aspects of his being. Rudolf Steiner's indication to make the arts an integral part of education opens up many possibilities to support that process. When we direct our artistic activity specifically to affect the child's development, we may speak of a pedagogical therapeutic relationship.

Rudolf Steiner introduced the art of form drawing into the first Waldorf school for this specific purpose. He first spoke of it in the context of helping to bring balance to children whose temperament was overly one-sided. Form drawing could address these imbalances, Rudolf Steiner argued, and he sketched a few examples for the teachers present at that time.

The understanding of the balancing-healing power of pattern, rhythm, motif, and geometry goes back to earliest times in human history. Across all cultures one finds patterned drawings: rock carvings, sand paintings, medicine wheels, images on mosques and in church windows. Hindu and Buddhist practitioners of meditation use concentric forms representing the universe (mandalas) for

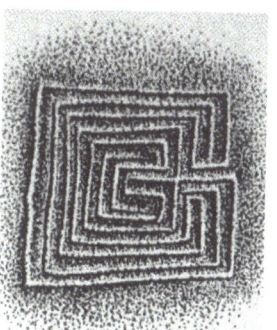

Therapeutic aspects of form drawing

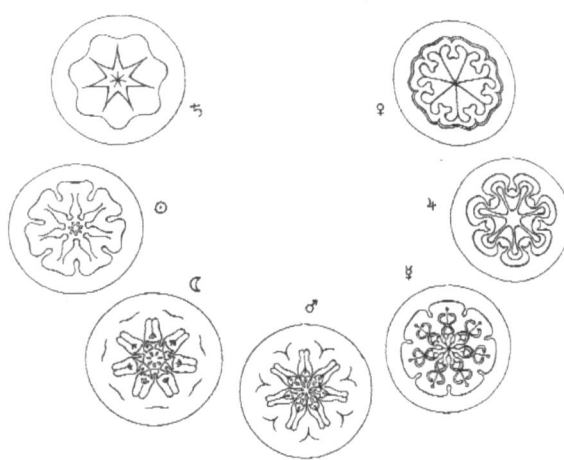

the purposes of finding unity, harmony, and peace. These mandalas are built on geometric principles; lines and spaces interact to provide balance in the visual experience. The mind finds rest in the beauty and purity of geometry.

Rudolf Steiner created seven circular forms specifically for the teachers as a meditation aid. These forms are known as the Seven Planetary Seals. Each teacher should draw these beautiful seals and experience their beneficial effect!

Engagement with any art calls for concentration of the inner forces of the creator and also of the beholder. This engagement takes place through the senses. In the case of the art of form drawing, the four lower senses (touch, life, movement, and balance), so essential for development of the four higher senses (sound, word, thought, "I"), are strongly activated.

The sense of movement (in addition to sensing one's own movement and the movement outside oneself) perceives the movement used to create forms. All forms are movement that has come to rest. If we behold a circle, our eye moves around the periphery. If the circle has a flaw, we immediately notice it: Our sense of balance has been activated We feel disturbed by the flaw, and want to fix it: our sense of life is involved. If the circle is perfect, we experience harmony, we feel well. We have been touched, we have been affected by the form.

One can easily experience the power of a line by drawing or walking many straight lines in repetition and then doing the same for curved lines. I have done this simple activity with many adult students over the years, and all report similar feelings after the exercise. The straight line tends toward creating some inner rigidity, while the curved lines tend to make us giddy. In other words, the straight line bring us into ourselves, the curved lines loosen us up. When taking the walking exercise of the curved line to an extreme, some students end up weak with laughter on the floor. The straight line taken to an extreme could lead to a headache. The straight line moves us into our heads. Drawing too many straight lines has a tiring effect. This is echoed in our language: "I am so tired, I can't think straight."

This simple exercise demonstrates convincingly that lines affect us in different ways. How can we find ways to explore this phenomenon more deeply and use that knowledge to design forms and patterns that can help children find or restore their equilibrium?

Other chapters in this book describe in detail how all pedagogical work is informed by careful observation of the child we are working with. If we use form drawing as our therapeutic tool, we can learn a great deal by observing a child's movement. A second prerequisite for using form drawing as a therapeutic tool is to penetrate this art form for ourselves, in order to use it out of a living experience of its effects. These two aspects constitute the preparation for our work with the child: developed skill with the art form and trained pedagogical observation skills. Let's explore further how lines affect us.

We have already seen that accurately drawing straight lines requires a certain level of alertness. The child must focus. A child that is dreamy, or a class that needs to wake up for a math class could benefit from drawings like these.

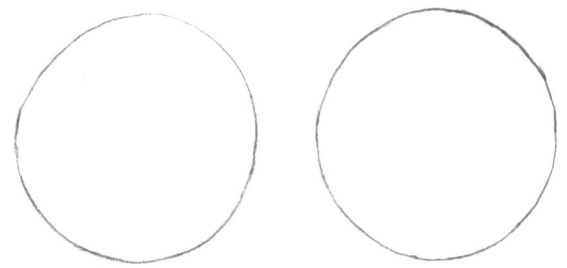

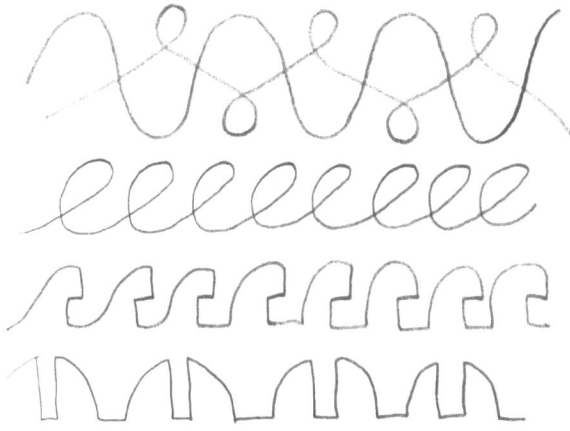

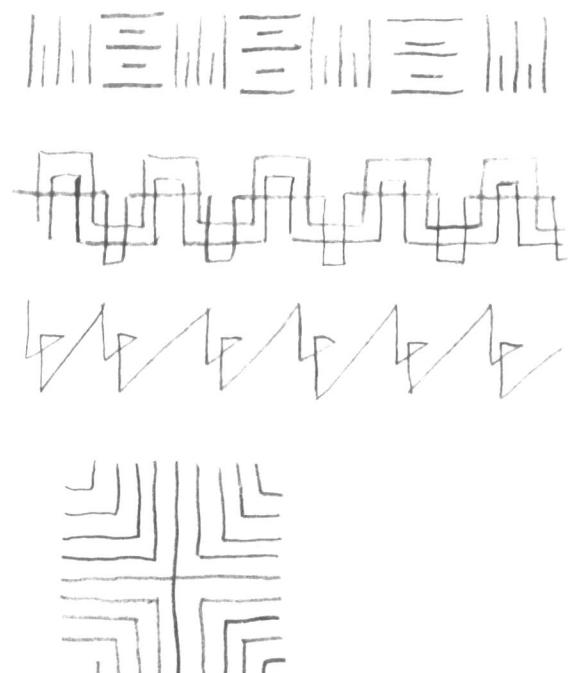

These lines are the visible traces of the movements that created them. Larger drawings are created by larger movements. In our work with children, we would work larger to achieve maximum benefit.

An overly intellectually-awake child, or a group of children who need to relax a bit after a rigorous math class or other focused head activity, could benefit from drawing curvy lines.

Hyperactive children could benefit from both straight and curved lines, or a combination of curved and straight, as for them the benefit is in bringing control to their chaotic movements. Hyperactive children often enjoy form drawing tremendously because in form drawing they can experience their movements under conscious control. Some examples:

Now take a moment and draw these lines:

What new element is introduced here? What does it take to continue with a line like that?

Did you notice that you have to be very alert, and plan ahead for the line to turn back? This planning is difficult for children who are overly impulsive, who tend to rush ahead without thinking. When a child is engaging with a movement that challenges her, then growth can happen. If an impulsive child can eventually execute a line like this, the experience of this will spill over into every day life. The key element, of course, is practice through repetition.

Children who tend toward fixed thoughts with a marked lack of imagination could benefit from exercises like the following.

Teacher and child draw this line:

Then the teacher asks the child to imagine that this is the surface of a lake on a day without wind. What would happen to the surface if a small breeze starts up? The child responds with a line like this:

The next line could be in response to the teacher saying: make the wind blow harder!

Now a storm!

Then let the storm die down by drawing the lines in reverse order. All exercises asking for transformation are great exercises to stimulate the imagination.

Another example: Here is a curvy line. Can you change the curves into straight lines?

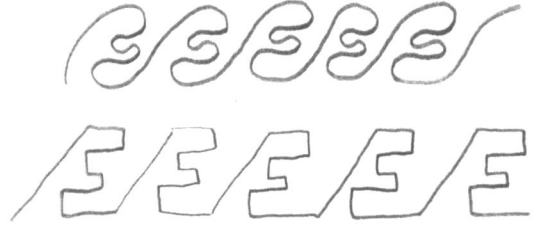

Now that the imagination has been involved, children may want to draw added features to the line drawing; a little boat may appear on the water, for example. Instead, work with the children to stay focused on the line, to let the imagination live in the movement of the line. The line itself is the subject. Form drawing is a nonrepresentational art form. And no additional drawings should distract from the line!

Some children are inclined to color in the spaces created by the lines. Instead, work with them to see the line as the main character. They can make the line as strong and beautiful as they want by retracing it, but the coloring of the spaces in between belongs to the study of geometry later in the grades.

The movement itself can be the imagination. For example: Watch how the bunny hops!

Here is a leaf falling off a tree:

Keep it simple. Elaborate stories are not necessary for form drawing. The rhythm, the beauty, the movement are enough to engage the children.

What faculties in you are called upon when you are asked to finish this form?

This is a balancing act isn't it? To complete the symmetry provides the balance in the form. Children with dyslexic tendencies have difficulty with directionality. These exercises are very helpful to perceive right and left. One may see right/left reversals in the children's writing or see the children struggling with reading because of the problem with perceiving direction (for example *b* becomes *d*). Reversals can also occur in the above/below direction (for example *M* becomes *W*). Symmetry exercises along the horizontal or vertical axis can be very helpful for these children.

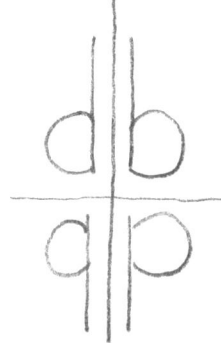

When the child is asked to draw the following form, he may struggle if he has not completed the very important developmental step of being able to cross the midline.

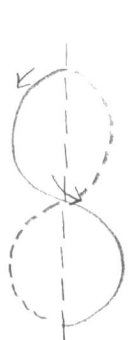 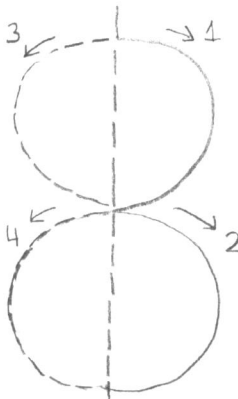

Children who are struggling with this may come up with a solution circumventing the difficulty, as shown on the right.

Human functioning is rooted in a neurological system that is based on the crossover of signals from the right side of the brain to the left side of the body and vice versa. Forms that help these children to overcome the blockage to cross over this midline are very effective and should be practiced with great frequency and regularity.

More spiral forms:

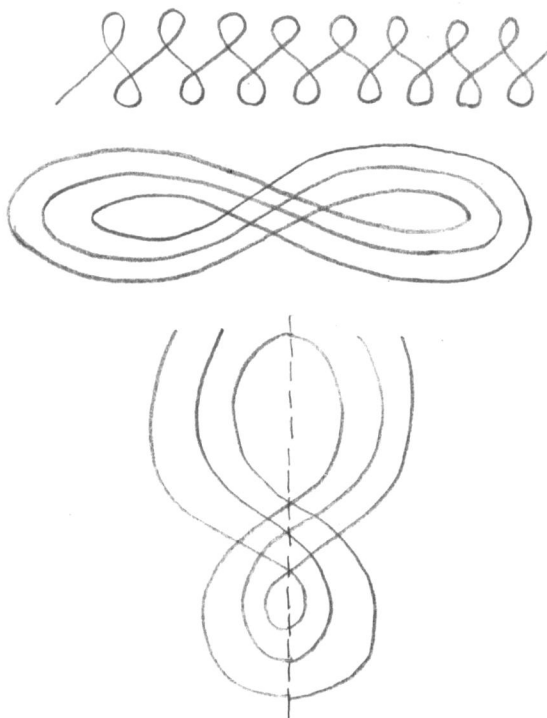

Lines that turn in a spiral are very powerful and have been used in all cultures to lead us into ourselves and bring us out again. There is the flow of breath in that experience of expansion and contraction.

Some children struggle to find a healthy relationship between inner and outer realities. Exercises that incorporate a conversation between inner and outer form can be helpful:

How will the outer ring respond to the change of the inner form?

This brings us to a discussion of the temperaments. A child who has a problem finding a balanced relationship to his environment, who is a little pusher, not always aware of the needs of others, who has a lot of energy and considers himself indispensable, could maybe learn to hold back a little by working with forms that enclose an initial freestanding form.

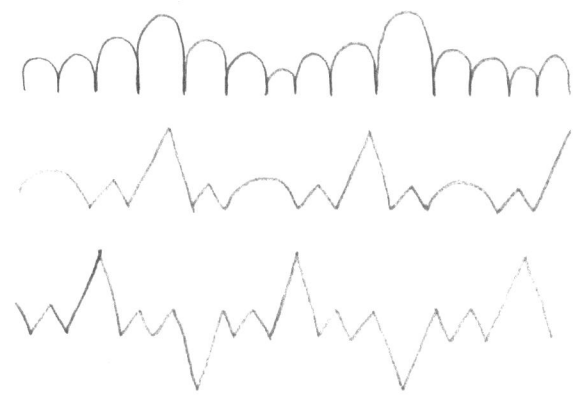

Children who like to keep things in order, who like routine, who are somewhat dreamy and unfocused, who feel best when things are at rest could benefit from exercises where the first step is a circle. The challenge comes for this child to break the perfection of the circle and bring some part of it into movement.

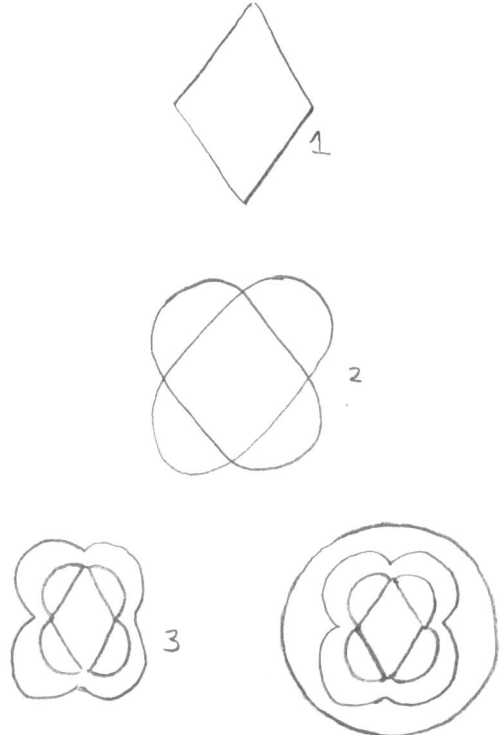

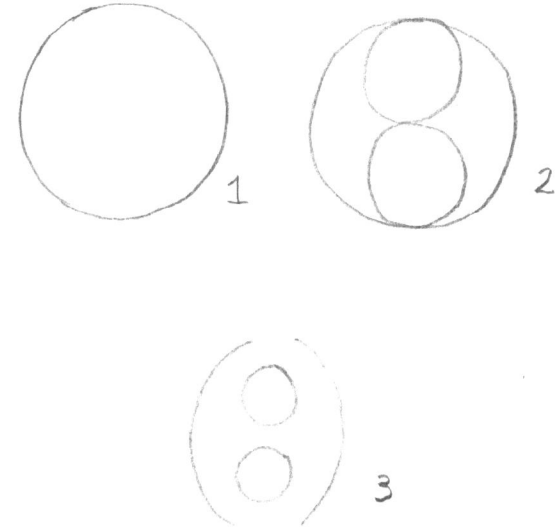

Children who struggle in the movement realm, who are so mobile in action and thought that they tend toward chaos, could benefit from rhythmical pattern drawings. Patterns that increase and decrease could provide practice in measure. Variation in rhythm can provide control by drawing flowing and stopping movements in sequence. Lines that turn back will be helpful to bring some thought into the forward rush of movement that is the natural inclination of these children.

This leaves one more type of child to discuss as part of this grouping by temperament: the child with a dominant melancholic temperament. These children have a rich inner life, sometimes so strongly developed that they can become self-absorbed. They are reflective and often artistically inclined. They look for meaning and beauty. We may see an issue with the sense of touch with these children: They can be overly sensitive to their environment and easily wounded on a soul level.

Therapeutic aspects of form drawing

Working to bring out different impressions of the same form can stimulate these children to open up to other points of view. In addition, metamorphosis, labyrinths, and spirals all require thoughtfulness and are well suited to the melancholic child. Turning forms inside out will also be great food for thought for the child with a melancholic inclination.

The teacher will be guided by his observations of the movements of the child to decide which forms will best support this child in her growth. To be beneficial for the child's growth, form drawing should be part of the child's daily rhythms throughout the year. The child's enthusiasm for this subject will be stimulating for both teacher and child.

REFERENCES AND FURTHER READING:

James, V. (2007). *The secret language of form*. Fair Oaks, CA: Rudolf Steiner College Press.

Kirchner, H. (1962). *Dynamic drawing*. New York: The Rudolf Steiner School.

Kutzli, R. (1981). *Creative form drawing*. Stroud, UK: Hawthorn Press.

Lawlor, R. (1982). *Sacred geometry*. London: Thames and Hudson.

Sheen, A.R. (1991). *Geometry and the imagination*. Chatham, NY: Waldorf Publications.

Shubert, E. & Embrey-Stine, L. (1996). *Form drawing grades one through four*. Fair Oaks, CA: Rudolf Steiner College Press.

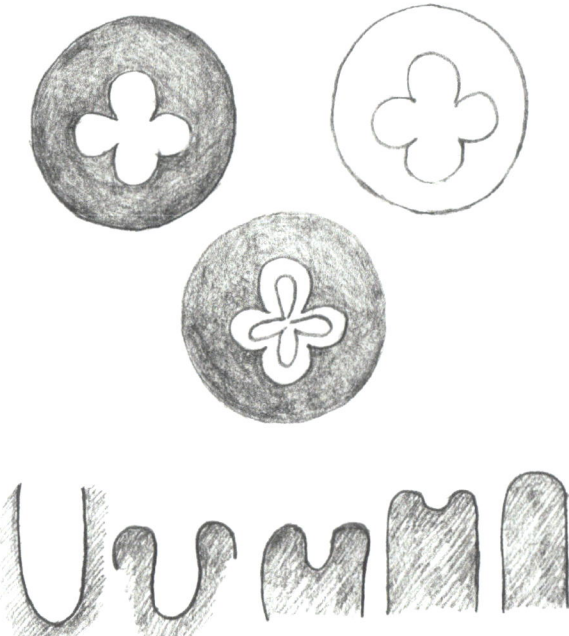

Children's drawings
What they can tell us

Elizabeth Auer

A fundamental task of teachers is to endeavor to understand the children they teach in the classroom. There are many aspects of the developing child to consider, including family history, physical description, movement, academic and artistic strengths, and so forth. The activity of drawing is also an important one, and interpretations of the drawings can be used as one of the diagnostic tools available to the teacher.

The history of analysis

Children's drawings have been the subject of many specialists dating all the way back to 1921, when research began with an emphasis on using drawings to determine intelligence levels. In the first chapter of her book, *Understanding Children's Drawings*, Cathy Malchioldi writes that this study has quite a long tradition in the fields of psychiatry, psychology, art therapy, and education. The "long-standing fascination has generated a great deal of information that clinicians, counselors and teachers who use drawings with children should know to interpret content." She also describes multidimensional approaches to understanding children's drawings, and how important they have become to finding additional ways of understanding children.

Drawing the human figure

Drawing the human figure became a popular subject of many studies during the first half of the 20th century, and analysts intuitively began to realize that drawings of human beings could provide information about the children themselves, as well

as how they perceive others. In addition, specialists started to look at the drawings to ascertain the child's development and personality.

The "Draw-a-Man" test was developed in 1926, based on the assumption that certain capabilities of drawing indicated a child's intellectual development and could therefore be used as a measure of intelligence. Eventually the "Draw-a-Person" test became widely known and a major influence on almost all research on clinical applications of human figure drawings, including that of children, and it is still used today.

Emotional aspects

During the latter half of the 20th century, the idea began to take hold that drawings could also be used to determine the emotional and internal psychological states of the child. One of the drawing tests developed was the "House, Person, Tree" drawing because of the familiarity of these three themes for young children. Audrey McAllen, subsequently in her research, changed the order to "Person, House, Tree."

No consensus

Malchioldi writes that there is "no definite consensus about the meaning and purpose of art expressions and no singular, reliable way to interpret content." Children can express themselves in drawing and in other media such as modeling, painting, handwork, and movement.

In this study I chose the modeling medium of beeswax to complement the drawing studies. I asked the children to model a self-portrait at the beginning of the third grade and again in January of the same year. The three-dimensional addition to the study added another dimension to studying the children's view of themselves.

The connection between the human being, her house, and the environment

Rudolf Steiner described in some of his literature how the child, after having been enclosed in the womb up to the time of her birth, continues to have a protective life-giving "sheath" until about the seventh year. Michaela Strauss writes that many times children return again and again to drawing a ball of whirls, even at the age of having long outgrown this early phase of drawing. She likens this to the adult's habits of sleeping in a curled-up ball in the embryonic position. The womb is the house that shuts us in, that protects us from the world outside. In drawings, the house has a variety of environmental additions and accompaniments. These additions can be an animal, flowers, a path, a swing, a fence, a pond. All the additional components accompanying the house have their own individual roles to play in the picture of the child's development.

Houses and other buildings

The archetypal house can be seen appearing very early in the form of whirls and other spherical enclosing forms and shapes, such as a beehive, a dome-like form. Gradually the roundness acquires angularity. Buildings are constructed through drawing a combination of diagrams in a variety of ways. There are countless different designs and combinations. The base of the house is often square or rectangular. In Rhoda Kellogg's research, she shows that for children by ages five to eight years, the most commonly drawn combination of shapes for a house is the square at the base, with a triangle for the roof.

Roofs

Roofs appear as a triangle or a trapezoid, sometimes shown with windows, square or round.

Chimneys

Chimneys are sometimes part of the roofline, at other times attached after the roofline is completed. A house can have more than one chimney. Smoke appears coming out of the chimney, often drawn as a swirling spiral.

Windows

Windows are primarily rectangular or square, and sometimes round. They appear singly or in multiples. They can have a single cross or multiple crossed lines. The most dominant window design for the same age span (ages 5–8) is the square with one single cross.

Doors

Doors come in shapes of vertical rectangles, triangles or a vertical half circle. Handles on doors may appear as young as age 3. The dominant door design is a vertical rectangle, with a door handle on the middle right side.

Animals

Children do not generally draw animals until about the age of 5. The child's first efforts to draw animals look very like humans. Some appear with the trunk in a horizontal or upright direction with ears coming out of the top of the head. By changing the position of the face features in relation to the torso of the human, the child suggests the image of a horizontal animal. Simple changes are required for the child to change a human shape to that of an animal.

Trees and flowers

Between the ages of five and seven, trees appear in many varieties. The straight line and the curve are created with many, varied combinations. The tops of the trees are a collection of suns, radials and mandalas, with straight lines making up the trunk.

The first tree that appears can be seen as very similar to the human figure. It has a round head on top of a trunk, and the treetop has many markings, such as circles or dots. Some trees take on the look of armless humans. Internal branches appear, in addition to divided branches without enclosing lines on the perimeter.

A frequent theme is trees drawn as Christmas art. During the ages of five to seven, the child draws flowers, primarily with a single stem and with the images of suns and mandalas constituting the flower petals.

Boats, trains, planes, and spaceships

Between the ages of five and eight, children are frequently absorbed by and drawn to objects that transport things from one place to another. Boats and planes often appear in drawings. The shapes children are able to produce at this stage are combinations of curves and straight lines, with the circle and rectangle used most often. The shapes become increasingly complex as the child develops through the years.

Ladders

Axes of symmetry are often found in pairs of straight lines running parallel to one another, with straight, short lines crossing the two vertical lines—as struts in a ladder. The ladder can be compared to a child's rib cage created in picture form. The ladders are a recurring and favorite theme of children and also appear in the "Person, House, Tree" pictures. The verticality of the ladder and the horizontal lines crossing it indicate the human being standing in space. Michaela Strauss refers to this phenomenon in drawing as the child's showing its skeleton, its architecture.

Children's drawings

Fences

Fences can appear as early as five years and can surround the house or extend from the house on the left and right sides. The fence is usually shown as a series of vertical lines with one, two, or three horizontal continuous lines running along the top half or through the middle.

Swings

Swings appear mostly hung from trees. Sometimes they are empty of figures, and other times they are occupied.

Ponds and rivers

Ponds, streams, and rivers appear between the ages of six and eight and can also appear in older children's drawings. A pond can be shown with one or several ducks or other waterfowl, or with a person fishing. Rivers appear with or without bridges.

Islands

Islands do not usually appear until the age of 12 or 13 and can indicate the onset of puberty.

Additional elements

Children may add some items to their "Person, House Tree" drawings, though they often choose not to. Whether extra elements are added to the drawing depends largely on the child's development, her interest in the world, how much initiative she has. Some children show recurring themes such as the family dog, a shovel in the hand, a swing hanging from the tree. Other figures may join the person; sometimes a whole family appears. Details around the house, such as paths, driveways, parking lots, and cars are other possible additions.

"Person, House, Tree" drawings: What they can tell us

Audrey McAllen began her initial work with children who had learning difficulties. After a time of study she decided to use the "Person, House, Tree" drawings as a tool and support for understanding the child. She found, to her

astonishment, that students as old as eleven years were producing drawings with houses floating on the page. Trees had spindly branches or wide heavy trunks, with a ball shape for the foliage. She gradually became aware that these drawings could give the teacher an objective view of the physical structure and growth of the child.

Rudolf Steiner's philosophy

McAllen's work and research is based largely on Rudolf Steiner's view of the human being. His philosophy holds the view that the human being is fourfold, with a physical body, a life force, a soul force, and an ego. The physical body, along with the three other forces, develops as the child grows from birth to adulthood as each gains a foothold at different stages of the child's development.

The exercises

McAllen devised a movement sequence of exercises to be carried out before beginning the drawing. The process of jumping, clapping, and counting takes about two minutes. The sequence was designed to bring the whole body into movement, to "connect the body to all spatial dimensions, to challenge the will, to deepen the breathing, and enliven the circulation." (McAllen, *Reading Children's Drawings*) The resulting drawings contain the archetype of the human structure and form of the body as the child experiences it. The mediator of this imprinting is the jumping-induced deepening of breathing that activates the cerebral spinal fluid. McAllen recognized the objectivity of drawings after her students had done the movement and counting sequence, and later discovered that neurological research bore out her theory.

Three archetypes

McAllen saw the three archetypes of Person, House, and Tree as fundamental indicators of the overall picture of the child's body geography, spatial orientation, and sidedness development. She writes that the details belonging to the House, such as the windows, door, chimney, and path, show body geography that the soul has built up during the first seven years of the child's life. The Person gives the idea of the growth of the soul powers in building up the body, which should be ready for learning activities after the change of teeth. The Tree is described as "the lifeline," the picture of the breathing system and the nervous system.

Drawings as a tool

As a remedial specialist, McAllen used drawings as a tool to help her understand children who had learning difficulties. She makes a clear distinction between the child's school readiness as indicated by the structural development completion of the physical body and its constitutional aspects and that of the realm of the psychological. She emphasizes that the psychological aspect, as indicated at times by the use of colors, should be left to the class teacher.

The class teacher's role

For the classroom teacher, all the children's drawings can be a valuable tool for understanding where they are in their structural/physical development, as well as the state of their souls.

Each child has her own story to tell, and each child's story is unique. Children may have social difficulties yet be otherwise extremely capable. Children may have challenges in the classroom relating to their temperament or shyness, and yet be free and easy on the playground.

Children may have older siblings who have an effect on them that causes them to act in certain ways, either in the classroom or on the playground. Some children have extraordinary family circumstances or are adopted from different cultures. Some children may not have had all the opportunities to develop their physical bodies in their early childhood years. They may not have had the necessary stimulation for movement or the fostering and nurturing of emotional attachments and bonds so crucial to their well-being. No child is like another, and drawings truly reflect this in a wonderful way.

The children have much to tell their teachers, and drawings are an easily accessible tool for personal understanding and support of the child.

What the drawings of a seven-year-old can tell us and what to look for

Drawings can show that the child has completed the birth-to-seven development or if one or the other stage has not yet been completed. Drawings can show lack of spatial orientation. Certain elements can be missing, such as a house, a tree, or a person. Drawings can also show the figure as undeveloped, as in drawings done by three- and four-year-olds. There are many aspects of the elements in a drawing that can be viewed and studied.

The Person

Spatial orientation

Spatial orientation is how the child experiences and relates to the space around her: the front, the back, sides, above, and below. Are the elements in the drawing on the ground or are they floating in the air? Is there a sky above and an earth below?

Person-body geography

Children draw human beings parallel to their own development. It takes up to the seventh year for body geography to establish, when children become aware and can point to their various body parts. The human being should at this time have all the body parts present: head, neck, trunk, arms and hands, legs and feet. Children may draw persons without feet or hands, a figure without a waist and neck. The arms may protrude from the middle chest area, instead of protruding from the shoulders. Moreover, a person can be drawn as a stick figure, showing no thickness to the body.

The drawing of the archetypal human being indicates how the child feels in her own body and whether the process of development of body geography awareness has been completed. If some of the body parts are missing, or the limbs are drawn in an uneven or stilted way, McAllen suggests that "there may be some hidden structural compression to the natural function of the nervous system, affecting coordination and other bodily skills. This may lead to lack of integration of the vestibular system (sense of balance) and or proprioception (sense of movement)."

Birth history

McAllen recommends asking about the birth history of the child: the details of the birth itself, how the child cried, and whether there was any inexplicable crying during the first months of life. If the child has a complicated birth history, McAllen suggests seeking help in the form of cranio-sacral osteopathy to rule out and treat any possible misalignment of cranial bones and spinal structure.

Reasons for distortions

There are also other reasons for distortions in figure drawings, such as accidents in the early years or sudden, unexpected falls or banging of the head. The child's history from birth to school age can be helpful information as part of the analysis of children's drawings.

The House

The house has several aspects that are a very important part of assessing how the child feels in her body. The base square represents the physical-earthly body of the child, and the triangle as a roof on the top of the square is the soul-spiritual aspect. The windows represent the soul looking out toward the world. The crossings over the windows indicate the child is protected from the world. The door indicates a way in and out of the body, especially when there is a doorknob. The chimney signifies the will forces at work in the body.

Questions to ask are: Does the house have windows, how many are there, what shape are they and do they have crosses or curtains? Is there a chimney on the roof and how is it situated on the roof? What is the shape of the roof? Is the house "archetypal," consisting of a rectangle or square with a triangle roof that is separated from the square by a line?

The Tree

The tree indicates the breathing/feeling aspect of the child's stage of development. Aspects to look for are the height of the tree; the proportion between the trunk and the branches; and the roots, branches, and leaves. Analysis of trees can indicate asthma or congestion or other respiratory problems, the nature of the child's soul, and the nerve sense activity. Both breathing and sensing connect us to the world around us. "The tree of life is in us, but upside down: It is pictured in our trachea, bronchi, and lungs." In early child development, the fir tree is a favorite theme.

Colors

From years of observing children, McAllen found that the colors they choose in their drawings call attention to aspects of their soul life. She relates how certain soul conditions can be challenging, such as the egoistic qualities of greed and jealousy, or needs arising from family situations and circumstances. Sometimes there may be a need for medical help or artistic therapy.

The "Person, House, Tree" drawings over the eight school years

The "Person, House, Tree" drawing can be assigned at the beginning, middle, or end of the year or at all three times. The movement exercises that precede the assignments are easy enough to include in the early years when the students naturally imitate the teacher. However, from about fourth grade on, the exercises need explanation to increasingly maturing students, and a few jumping jack movements before the drawing may have to suffice.

The drawings can be completed in a 45-minute lesson time, though some children always need more time.

Observations and the teacher's research

There is much for teachers to observe in the drawings that will help them understand the children in front of them, and it will be especially interesting if the drawings are assigned each year as the children develop. To gain an insight into their soul life and their imagination is a real asset to the teacher. Most of all, it is a joy to have the possibility to look into their world and to try to understand their unique personalities and temperaments.

Recurring themes

A recurring theme may be a child sitting up in a tree, even in later years. Another recurring theme may be that of flowers bathed in sunlight with fruit on the branches of the trees, beginning in first grade and repeated all through the grades.

Other recurring themes are action, such as playing with a ball or working in the yard. In general children begin to depict movement in the figure only in the later grades, mostly beginning around fourth grade. Until then, the figures are mostly seen from the front and a few from the side.

It is possible after some years to begin to identify each student's style and to try to ascertain their temperaments as revealed through their drawing.

The temperaments

It is fascinating to observe children's temperaments and then to see whether or not this correlates to what they express in their drawings. At times it can be surprising. The most melancholic child can create the sunniest drawings!

In her book, *The Temperaments and the Arts*, Magda Lissau writes that the different temperaments can reveal themselves through their language of form, color, and intensity in the hatching stroke used in slant-line drawings. "Cholerics will tend to press down too hard on the paper and make large strokes and bold colors, and shapes will arise. Melancholics will tend to make small strokes, use dark colors, work slowly, and have difficulties in covering the whole paper evenly. Sanguines will work haphazardly. Phlegmatics will work beautifully but have difficulties in letting

Children's drawings

forms actually consolidate. Consequently, this is a technique eminently suitable for the healthy balancing of extreme temperament tendencies."

Helmut Eller has also written a book about *The Four Temperaments,* and of particular interest is the chapter on how they were revealed in a geography study in grade five. Students in the class created drawings of the Hallig Islands in the North Sea during a threatening storm surge. Eller presented four separate drawings in full color, and described in detail how each reflected the temperament of the student.

The melancholic temperament

The first drawing, by a melancholic boy, shows a well thought-out design with sharp, linear definition and fixed geometric forms. The sea is crystalline and looks like a mountain range, earthy and heavy. The houses are well-lit and tended, with three chimneys to make them cozy. The house is high up and protected with a heavy door and small curtained windows. A sun shimmers in the background. "But the house is supposed to be in danger, my teacher said so!" He adds a single breaking wave that looks like a curling lock of hair. "Hopefully nothing will happen to my house."

The phlegmatic temperament

The phlegmatic boy set to work with calm staying power and rhythmic evenness. He began at the base of the page with curved wave after wave of rhythmic repetitions. He suddenly remembered the islands, almost too late in the process. His first red building hardly fitted on a soft green island, and he repeated the house motif on other islands but each became smaller than the last. Brown doors were placed over the red siding with open windows. The background was evenly applied and looks shining in evening redness, with the sun on the horizon mirrored in the sea. The sky is restful.

The choleric temperament

The island took up two thirds of the paper. The choleric girl drew a dominant, red, stodgy house with a large, heavy red roof that sits on a powerful, heavy green island. She drew the sea with towering

waves, seething in all directions. The breakers gnaw at the house, followed by an intense blue drawn over the green. The sky is blue with black clouds, drawn with intense vertical strokes. "The lightning is missing!" Yellow zigzags were added over the blue and look green! They were then quickly covered with red.

The sanguine temperament

There are all kinds of features to discover in this drawing by a sanguine boy, thought-out in a lively, bubbly manner. He drew the green island first with yellow and brown lovingly mixed in, leaving a place for putting in a reservoir for rainwater.

He drew the main house with many details, including a small roof with stonework, a gigantic chimney, two colorful doors, and large windows. The waves are in two tones of blue and come in many forms: flat, semicircular, spiral, jagged, weaving, and round. The background shows several detailed ships, one of which is struck by lightning.

REFERENCES AND FURTHER READING:

Auer, Elizabeth. (2015). *Learning to see the world through Drawing*, Chatham, NY: Waldorf Publications.

Coles, Robert. (1992). *Their eyes meeting the world*. Boston: Houghton Mifflin Company.

Eller, Helmut. (2009). "A way to recognize children's temperaments," in *Curriculum materials for classroom teachers in the Waldorf school*, a compendium, Verlag Freies Geistesleben.

_____. (2017). *The Four Temperaments: Suggestions for Pedagogy*. Chatham, NY: Waldorf Publications.

Fein, Sylvia. (1993). *First drawings: Genesis of visual thinking*. Martinez, CA: Exelrod Press.

Kellogg, Rhoda. (1969). *Analyzing children's art*. Mountain View, CA: Mayfield Publishing Company.

Krenz, Armin. (2012). "The secret of children's drawings," in *Waldorf Journal Project #18*, Chatham, NY: Waldorf Publications.

Lissau, Magda. (2003). *Temperaments and the arts*. Chatham, NY: Waldorf Publications.

Lowenfield, Victor and W. Lambert Britain. (1964). *Creative and mental growth*, New York: MacMillan Co.

Malchioldi, Cathy. (1998). *Understanding children's drawings*. New York: Guilford Press.

McAllen, Audrey. (1974). *Extra lesson*. Stourbridge, UK: Robinswood Press.

_____. (2004). *Reading children's drawings: The person, house and tree motifs*. Fair Oaks, CA: Rudolf Steiner College Press.

Strauss, Michaela. (1988). *Understanding children's drawings*. Forest Row, UK: Rudolf Steiner Press.

Math
Introducing it the right way

Colleen O'Connors

Mathematics as such is alien to no man at any age. It arises in human nature; the operations of mathematics are not foreign to human faculty in the way letters are foreign in a succeeding civilization. But it is exceedingly important that the child should be introduced to arithmetic and mathematics in the right way. And what this is can really only be decided by one who is enabled to overlook the whole of human life from a certain spiritual standpoint. — Rudolf Steiner

Have you ever asked yourself what is the difference between a raindrop and a snowflake? The specific weight of both is roughly the same, that is, the same amount of water is in each. Though a raindrop may vary in shape, it never acquires the perfectly unique symmetry of a snowflake. What is the mathematics behind these phenomena?

Strange question? Both counting raindrops and calculating the probability of each snowflake's truly being unique fall clearly within the realm of mathematics. The activity of counting raindrops, one most often summed up by the experience of getting wet, differs tangibly from experiencing the beauty of a snowflake. The thought patterns required to recognize the rules of form that govern the radial symmetry of a snowflake differ markedly from those needed to perform probability calculations pertaining to its uniqueness. Probability calculations demand an intellectual rigor that not everyone will master; yet we are confronted with the results of those calculations when we pay our car insurance bills every month. Exposure to a specific subject area does not automatically translate into mastery thereof (nor require it), but it will precipitate a dusting of understanding, which can transform the landscape of the mind. It doesn't take much snow to brighten the drab winter landscape, and we all experience awe in the geometric perfection of a snowflake.

The progression from counting raindrops and experiencing the beauty of a snowflake to thinking through a probability calculation corresponds to the progression through the mathematics curriculum in a Waldorf school. Internalizing skills through immersion, discovering the beauty of mathematical and geometric patterns, and schooling problem-solving thought processes represent the age-appropriate activation of a child's willing, feeling, and thinking life. For the Waldorf class teacher nurturing this development spans eight years or more. It is very easy to become absorbed in the daily/weekly/block-wise delivery of mathematical activities and to lose sight of how the threefold nature of the child is served by the meaning-filled world of mathematics.

As always, the prerequisite for continuing student success is the continuing education of the teacher. Every class teacher needs to take a hard look in the mirror and ask her- or himself, "What is my relationship to mathematics?" In a lecture titled, "Origin and Goal of the Human Being," Rudolf Steiner stated, "Mathematics is nothing else than an internal experience. You can nowhere learn externally what mathematics is. There is no mathematical theorem which would not have resulted from self-knowledge, the self-knowledge of the mind in time and space."

Waldorf education is an education of relationship, and, in essence, mathematics is the most direct expression of the truths of relationship, eventually transcending earthly applications to represent higher orders of relationship. The awe which a heartfelt recognition and acknowledgment of that fact can inspire is the best place from which to teach math.

Counting raindrops – getting wet

Most children, upon entering first grade, will already be "counting" beings. The world of natural numbers (which, mathematically speaking, does not include zero) has surrounded them from birth. Within a first grader's numerical exposure lies the child's realities of "May I have another cookie?" or "He has three marbles and I have only two," as well as the parental quantities of "We're leaving in ten minutes," or "I want you to finish half your peas." The first two statements express a unity of will, feeling, and thought, whereas the second two are intellectual, abstract statements that carry little or no meaning for the child, even though he or she may imitate and use the language.

I remember the first time my daughter ran her own bath; she was in kindergarten or first grade. She came to me to ask how much water she should let in. I told her to fill the tub about one third full. She nodded, walked away, came back a few minutes later and asked, "How much is a third?" At that moment I woke up to her predicament. Joining her in the bathroom, I asked her how much she thought was a third. Ultimately she filled the tub with

roughly the right amount of water (very likely out of habit or experience), but she was visibly anxious the whole time. The measure of one-third was nowhere to be seen, neither along the rim of the tub, nor along the rim of my daughter's mind. It will be the class teacher's task to find the images that the child can experience in the outer world AND imagine in his or her inner world. The perpetual potential of anxiety induced by not having an inner image to match against the outer world should be (and can be!) avoided at all costs.

Allow the children in the class to build their own number relationships from the beginning. This is what Rudolf Steiner meant when he recommended teaching from the whole to the parts. The whole has both a quality and a quantity. In first grade both of these aspects of the numbers from 1–12 should be introduced and practiced. Circle activities such as the song "One for the Golden Sun" by Peter Oram, and some of the wonderful verses in Dorothy Harrer's book, *Math Lessons for Elementary Grades*, are a wonderful way to develop a child's sense of number. These provide effectively the foundation for the images of the numbers that the child captures in his or her lesson book.

Once children have anchored their feelings for the qualities of three or seven, they are ready to create and recognize the relationships between the individual numbers. These relationships will also be experienced in circle activities, especially those that fall under the general heading of rhythmic counting. Rhythmic counting lays the foundation for the multiplication tables. Again, numerous verses have been created to enhance this learning; but from my experience, it is not necessary to put a lot of words around the numbers. Let them stand free in their own glory! Anyone who has witnessed the sheer joy first graders experience in counting knows that the experience needs little enhancement. Counting by twos: clapping in back on the odd numbers, in front on the even ones; speaking the odd ones quietly, the even numbers loudly; adding stepping and stomping accordingly—these are just a few examples of a experiential build-up of the relationship of, as well as the child's relationship to, the twos.

Throughout the early grades, these kinds of activities should be consistently repeated. An imaginative teacher will easily find ways to vary the task and heighten the challenge. Depending on how may children are in the class (remember the value of having observers, both for them and for the observed!), various sequences of motion, corresponding to the number assigned to each of the children in the class, can result in a wonderful visual and audible choreography of number relationships. Corresponding images can be developed for the children to copy into their lesson books. Skipping rope is another whole-body experience of rhythmic counting that can morph into rhythmic practice of the times tables. "Skip to My Lou" is a well-known folk tune, which readily lends itself to, "Two is one times two, four is two times two, six is three times two, skip to my twos, my darling. Skip, skip, skip to my twos,..."

Do not underestimate the therapeutic value of these kinds of activities. Individuals may have or may lack a natural affinity for math, but it is a rare child who truly lacks the capacity to develop a sense of number. The word *affinity* expresses a quality of relationship, and relationships can be cultivated, nurtured, and developed.

Soon (but not too soon) after quality of number and rhythmic counting have been introduced, practiced, and internalized, the four operations will be introduced in rapid succession. If the teacher can truly experience these operations as further dimensions of the relationships between numbers, then the children in the class will too. Much has been written about stories introducing the operations (math gnomes, for instance).

I felt strongly that I wanted to create a story that emphasized both the symbolic image of the operational sign, and the relationship between the operations. I received inspiration from the book, *World of Numbers*, from the Waldorf homeschooling series Live Education. The story I told my first grade class introduced Mul de Plier, with her crossed sticks from the Tree of Life; Div Ider, with his sword and the pieces of stone he first cut in half; Minus the Miner, with his crowbar and who gave away whatever he mined; and Addy the Baker, who always had one more hot cross bun to offer. Each of them came to their sign through a plausible development in the story, but more importantly, Mul, a princess, whose parents had been kidnapped by the jealous ruler of a neighboring kingdom, was on a quest to find and free them. Problem solving was introduced from the very beginning, and the happy end came when all of the characters (all of the operations) utilized their relationships with each other, and by working together freed the king and queen. Mathematics is an expression of higher truth. The images we find to teach math must be true too.

Allowing the children to build their own number relationships, and moving from the whole to the parts now means

10 = ?

Using manipulatives (counting gems, beans, acorns, smooth pebbles)—children should be encouraged to creatively find as many number relationships as possible within the quantity of a given number, for example 10:

10 = 9 + 1, 10 = 8 + 2, 10 = 7 + 3, etc., but also:

10 = 11 − 1, 10 = 12 − 2, 10 = 13 − 3, etc., and

10 = 5 x 2, 10 = 2 x 5, or

10 = 20 ÷ 2, 10 = 30 ÷ 3, etc.

The activity of child-created numerical relationships, together with the activity of translating them into the symbols and capturing them on a page or a small slate, cannot be repeated too often in grades one and two, and for the child struggling with developing her or his affinity toward numbers, even longer than that. With variations and allowances for the individually differentiated levels of challenge, building numerical relationships should be practiced EVERY DAY.

The teacher can also prompt the class to find number relationships to solve a problem. For example, "I have nine and I want to get to three. How might I do that?" Allowing from the start that there are multiple answers, indeed the possibility of multiple steps to get to the answer, will greatly reduce any potential anxiety among the children in the class. Number sequencing and estimating can easily be built into this practice. "If I have 23 and want to get to 19, will I add or give away?" "If I have 23 and want to get to 44, how many 10s will I have to add?"

When teaching math, weigh your words well. Out of my original operations story, Minus the Miner, gave away the jewels he had mined everyday. For the next few years, subtraction was a giving, and not a taking away. This may seem to be insignificant, but in keeping with the demands of truth, think it through. If I have 7 and I take 3 away, I still have 7 but in two separate parts, 3 and 4. But if I have 7 and I give away 3, I no longer have 7, but only 4. It was out of this gesture of giving away and sharing, that I successfully introduced division and fractions. The groundwork had been laid.

Similarly, using homemade, large-format, laminated flashcards, which had a math expression on one side and a single number on the other, we used the following words to play this math game in circle.

If 7 + 3 was on the side of the card facing the child, the child said, "I have 7! Who has three more?" Now the child in the circle with the single number 10 on the other side of her card was called upon to recognize that fact and answer, "I do! I have 10. 10 is 3 more than 7." On the other side of her card was 10 − 5. So she then continued, "I have 10. Who has 5 less?" The child with the new answer replies, "I do! I have 5. 5 is 5 less than 10." These cards can be used during free play time, by individual children, or in small groups. The difficulty level of the cards can be increased as the class progresses. What is important is the language used! Spoken language is one of the main vehicles for learning in the early grades, even in math. If the child can speak it, she or he is on the way to mastering it.

Though I have emphasized developing number sense and number relationships as ways to foster a child's affinity to the number world, it is crucial that all teachers of math know that there is a medical condition, known as dyscalculia. It is a brain-based condition that makes it hard to make sense of numbers and math concepts. (Morin 2016) A child can have various degrees and qualities of this condition, but its most prominent aspect is the child's inability to develop a sense of number and its relationship to the order of the numerical world. For example, a child in my class was unable to establish an accurate sense of the sequence of the number line. When asked (in third grade) which number was smaller, 39 or 45, the child looked lost and most often answered 45, as 5 is less than 9. Allowing for not uncommon developmental delays, a class teacher, while continuing to astutely observe the child in question, can and should allow a first or second grader time to develop, but by third grade (or earlier depending on the severity of the condition) signs of potential dyscalculia will be obvious. It is imperative that a class teacher communicate with the child's parents regularly, honestly, and from the first inklings of such a condition. It is in conversation with the parents, with other teachers, and with educational support colleagues that the best course of action can be decided. The condition is not as well-known as dyslexia, and is known by other names (mathematics learning disorder, or mathematics disorder, or even math dyslexia), but recent studies suggest that it may be almost as common. For these children, the methods suggested in this chapter will be more imperative than for the rest of the class, but they will very likely not be enough.

In the middle grades (grades 4–6), I often posted on the blackboard, just under the schedule for the day, the day's "mice." The name came from a fifth grade teacher in Switzerland who practiced this with her class daily. I adopted it, though I never learned why she called it that. The "mice" were four numbers, for example 3, 7, 63, 42. The goal was to get as close to zero as possible, using all four numbers:

$3 \times 7 = 21, 63 - 21 = 42, 42 - 42 = 0$

Beginning with comparatively easy examples, say, using numbers which clearly had a relationship to each other, I moved on to progressively less related numbers, exercising the students' skill to place them in relationship with one another, for example 25, 6, 8, 72:

$72 - 8 = 64, 64 - 6^2 = 28, 28 - 25 = 3$, or $(6 \times 8) - (72 - 25) = 1$.

Obviously, the last example requires an understanding of the order of operations. It also reveals how these early activities can grow with the children's skill sets, lending a familiarity of mood with which to practice new skills that otherwise might be intimidating. Students might even discover a new way of placing the numbers in relationship to each other. Then they (and not you) can go on to teach their discovery to the rest of the class! The students in my class (at least most of them) eagerly awaited the new numbers each day, and it became their habit to arrive in the morning and get to work to find the most ideal relationship between the numbers. I alternated between having children read their solution pathways out loud, having a student come to the board and write it out for all to see, or having another student come to the board and write out what the inventor dictated. This game intrigued the students because of its riddle-like quality. It enticed even the weakest students, because there was no wrong answer. This short but daily reoccurring challenge did not tax the students, but it was effective because there was "nothing else than their internal experience" that would lead the students to their answer.

Measurement in grade three and all the purposeful activities that go along with learning it, can serve to build a solid bridge between counting (amount) and moving from the whole to the parts and from the parts back to the whole. If you ask the children in your class to measure the length of the school corridor, one of them will soon recognize that the linoleum tiles in it are 12" x 12", which is one foot; so counting the tiles will result in the length of the hallway, plus any inches for partial tiles. It is crucial that the teacher not gloat over or give away the obviousness of this fact, but that she or he lets the children discover these relationships. Indeed, measurement represents an early form of patterning to which I will refer later in this chapter. Weight, time, length, volume, and last, but certainly not least, money are all earthly quantities that allow a child going through the nine-year change to redefine and account for his or her relationship to the world with which he or she is no longer one. Cups, pints, quarts, and gallons are wonderfully concrete names of very familiar objects, which imply the doubling or halving of an amount without the math. Monetary units provide early exposure and practice of the decimal fractions, which will be formally taught in grades 4 and 5.

Division and its half-sibling, fractions (pun intended), hold a special position within the realm of math. If mathematics typically induces feelings of antipathy rather than empathy, then division and fractions usually induce even greater feelings of antipathy, most often due to uncertainty. In my initial operations story, dear Div Ider, was a bit of a hapless soul, who had to learn to wield his sword well so that things came out even. Working with manipulatives, the children can experience the reality that 21 cannot be divided evenly into 4 or 5 piles, but that one will remain. But what does the word "even" mean? If dividing is equated with sharing, then the antipathetic gesture of reducing a whole to a collection of parts is overcome by the empathetic desire to be generous and just. This feeling is alive in children and it can carry them willingly into this tricky field of mathematics.

On the eve of our first fractions block in fourth grade, I posed the following problem to the class. "I have 5 apples on my desk (I did), and there are 16 of you in the class. How will I ever be able to share these five apples evenly between you? Tomorrow I want you to tell me how I am going to do this." The solution pathways that arrived with

the children next morning were original and clever. Thought processes were made visible, as well as the corresponding number relationships.

Some students cut all the apples into 16 pieces and then shared evenly. Some realized that four apples could be cut into fourths, resulting in 16 equal pieces, and therefore only one apple needed to be cut into sixteenths. Some cut the apples into eighths, sharing two 8s with everyone, before cutting the remaining 8 slices in half (cross-wise, which is easier for your average fourth grader!) and then distributing the missing sixteenth. The philosophical among my students were very concerned about inaccuracies due to the inherent inequalities of apples. Their proposition: weigh the slices and make adjustments if necessary! Still, my favorite solution came from my weakest and least dexterous student. This child also chose to cut four apples into 4 pieces each, sharing each quarter apple among the 16 students, but to give the remaining whole apple to the teacher! Mathematics can provide a strong moral compass!

Conventional counting never truly disappears as a skill and activity (counting stitches on the knitting needle, counting change), though this foundation for further math skill development grows ever less visible as calculations and problem solving challenge the middle grades children. It not only becomes less visible, but counting and the child's relationship to the number world need to be internalized by the middle grades for a child to continue to be successful in math. A class teacher will choose to gently wean the "finger-counters" away from these perpetually present manipulatives and prompt them to do the math in their heads. (Those children who resist this weaning, who still ask for the abacus or the counting gems, need to be considered as potentially having dyscalculia.) They will need to be coached more exactly in how to group numbers than the students who easily internalize their math. As early as fourth grade, persistent finger-counters can be given additional math drills of basic computations. They should be instructed to use their fingers and their voices when doing the drills at home. Once they have the answers, they should read the examples with the answers out loud again without the tactile stimulation of their fingers. In a third and final repetition, parents or a sibling should read the examples back to the child who is expected to give the answer. Needless to say, a drill sheet should not have more than 10 computations on it if it is to be repeated three times. Small amounts practiced daily will support the internalization by uniting the outer experience more and more with the inner concept. Often these children will learn to hear their own voice saying the answer, rather than seeing the answer as most math learners do.

The math curriculum in grade eight revisits counting in connection with the learning and practicing of different number bases. Most eighth graders gain a tremendous appreciation for the unconscious quality of practiced patterns, which allows them to immediately comprehend a multi-digit number, when confronted with a multi-digit binary number, for example 1000101. Class conversations touch on the thought habits, raising an age-appropriate consciousness of the inner imagery that allows them ready access to the math that they have learned, and that can easily lead them to see the number one million, one hundred one, rather than the number 69, when reading the digits above. How does one recognize an even or an odd number in binary? Another relationship, another pattern that students may discover!

Snowflakes

Snowflakes delight young and old with their endless renditions on the hexagonal pattern. The repetition of and variance in form obeys cosmic lawfulness. If I draw a free-hand circle, I immediately see (and am irritated by) its imperfection. Where does this perfect circle live to which I am comparing the one I drew? It lives within me as an image, unerring in its exactness. If you and I were to agree on its dimensions, your inner image of the circle would not differ significantly from mine. It is this objectification of the imagination, the rigorous schooling of the inner image that is both the source and the goal of mathematics. In a lecture on "The Path to Freedom and Love and Their Significance to World Events" (1920), Steiner stated,

If, as is very rarely the case today, we make sincere endeavors to develop unbiased thinking, it will be clear to us that the life of thought consists of mirror-pictures if we turn to thinking in its purest form—in mathematics. Mathematical thinking streams up entirely from our inner being, but it has a mirror-existence only. Through mathematics the makeup of external objects can, it is true, be analyzed and determined; but the mathematical thoughts in themselves are only thoughts, they exist merely as pictures. They have not been acquired from any outer reality.

Mathematics, at a grade school level, is rarely thought of as pictures. Yet, the snowflake is a picture, a beautiful picture, a beautiful, mathematical picture. Beauty is experienced directly in the feeling realm. We all experience a spontaneous affinity to beauty. If a Waldorf teacher can create an experience of the beauty of mathematics, he or she will counteract any intellectually-driven antipathies toward the subject. The experience of beauty may begin in first grade with discovering the quality of number. If the teacher truly experiences it, the children may also feel the beauty of the operations and their polarities.

As early as second grade, patterns and sequences allow the students first glimpses into a realm of mathematical beauty that is truly awe-inspiring. Moreover, this cosmic lawfulness can be very reassuring. Especially the students with learning differences that make it difficult for them to feel successful in the world of numbers, can still revel in and relax into the world of mathematical beauty.

Number circles are an early example of how numerical patterns can be translated into visible and beautiful forms. Marking the numbers 1–10 or 1–12 as even divisions of a free-hand circle, the students may experience delight in discovering the forms that appear as they diligently move through the sequences of the two-, three-, four-, five-times tables. Chords drawn through the center of the circle can be alternated with arcs drawn outside the circle, in order to make a visible world of form for the students.

Even a well-executed times table, a 10 x 10 chart, as a summary of the mental math the students have been practicing, will provide the framework necessary for the students to discover the patterns of repetition therein: the magic row of squares; the relative position to each other of the numbers which appear twice; the numbers which appear more than twice; the 9-row or column, in which the ones place decreases by one as the tens column increases by one; and so forth. Color-coding these discoveries results in a satisfying pattern of relationship. These kinds of activities will not only reveal number relationships, but also the relationships students have to space, structure, and form. *Do not confuse a student's challenges with constructing an attractive number circle or multiplication chart with her or his not being able to appreciate the beauty of the patterns.* On the contrary, these are the moments that the appropriate amount of assistance from the teacher or from a classmate would be vital, in order to create an image in which the pattern is recognizable and the beauty therein obvious.

In every subject, but especially in mathematics, a class teacher needs to consistently move from the activity (math games or verses during circle, working with manipulatives at desks, creating beautiful block book pages) to the reflection on the activity, to the review, and onto an understanding of what it represents. *This is perhaps the greatest oversight, the most readily missed opportunity to raise the essential to an age-appropriate level of consciousness.* The quicker students, who readily glean their own learning abstracts out of classroom activities, will not suffer if the teacher lacks diligence in this area; the slower, more concrete learners will.

Remedies

- Cultivate a habit of re-reading the block books. Can students articulate in their own words what an image on a page represents?
- Have students with learning challenges bring their block books to you at snack time and have them retrace a number circle with their fingers. Cover up with your hand or have them cover up with theirs one half of a math sentence and ask them to recreate it.
- At recess, outdoors, have individual students repeat a math circle activity one-on-one with you. The younger students will love this individual attention, which should not last more than a minute or two, because recess time is important.

Waldorf classrooms are full of activity, and therefore usually full of happy children. The progression from a happy child doing to the best of her or his ability what the teacher is asking, to developing that child's ability to perform that same task in an increasingly independent and reliable manner—that is learning. If a child does not have a strong affinity toward math, that is, has an underdeveloped relationship to the world of numbers, then nurturing the child's relationship to the teacher, the child's relationship to the beautiful patterns, and the child's relationship to practice and repetition becomes vital and therapeutic.

Ideally, the teacher will find true images for math concepts, whose patterns are not as readily obvious. My son's class teacher developed the image of a "factor-y," in order to introduce early on the idea and language of factors in an age-appropriate fashion. A beautiful board drawing during the occupations block in third grade depicted a factory that made numbers. Everything that was needed to make any number was on the first, that is, the prime, floor. Any number produced by using two (prime) numbers from the first floor was moved to the second floor. The product of three prime numbers (even if it was the same prime number used three times, for example, 2 x 2 x 2 = 8) was placed on the third floor. Given how important it is to understand prime factory-zation throughout a student's math life, this image not only truthfully introduced the correct vocabulary, but literally provided a structure of understanding that was practiced over many weeks, and referred to throughout the rest of the grades.

In grade seven, I developed a code based on prime factorization and challenged my students to crack it. My least enthusiastic math student desperately wanted to be the one to figure it out. After five days, I gave him a hint about the basis for the code. This student audibly groaned, but he didn't give up, and instead, he came to school on Monday elated. He had broken my code and was able to explain the simplicity of it to his classmates. (This was in the pre-Google era, so I was safe in assuming he had figured it out by himself!)

In *The Teaching of Arithmetic and the Waldorf School Plan*, Hermann von Baravalle introduces perfect, abundant, and deficient numbers. They are determined by "the so-called sum of the aliquot parts. This is the sum of all factors except the number itself." (Baravalle 1967, p.83) With perfect numbers this sum is equal to the number itself; with abundant numbers this sum is greater than the number itself; and with deficient numbers this sum is less than the number itself. Six is a perfect number, twelve is abundant, as is eighteen, whereas most numbers are deficient. Pairs of numbers can be amicable, larger cycles of numbers are sociable, and there are even practical numbers! This could provide a teachable moment in the strained social dynamics of a grade six class! Number relationships are not so different from human relationships. Or is it the other way around?

Math

In a world where a 12- or 13-year-old may feel that everything has been discovered already, and there are no real surprises left, she or he may be astonished to hear that only 48 perfect numbers are known to date; the largest is 257,885,160 × (257,885,161 − 1) with 34,850,340 digits. A number such as that will kindle warm feelings of awe in the coldest of mathematical hearts!

The beauty of repeated, yet expanded repetitions of structure and form can be discovered in mathematical series and sequences. The simple patterns, which I referred to earlier, are revisited when sixth graders learn the divisibility rules. They will also be introduced to triangle, square, and rectangle numbers. Pascal's triangle and the Fibonacci series, arithmetic and geometric progressions and their respective spirals, as well as the golden mean are integral parts of the middle school math curriculum. These concepts, awe-inspiring in their beauty, will accompany the students well into their high school algebra and geometry classes. If the class teacher has set the stage skillfully, the reappearance of these early friends will engender empathy and security in the years to come. Investigating the higher multiplication tables, a chapter in Hermann von Baravalle's book (pp.56–63), delightfully demonstrates the patterning to be found in the summing of digits, (the digit sum of 12 is 3, 1 + 2 = 3).

Revisiting prime numbers with Leonard Euler's (1701–1783) prime number generator, as explained in Bengt Ulin's book, *Finding the Path* (1991, pp.48–49), allows the middle school student to still play with numbers, and experience joy in the beauty of the truly innumerable relationships which can (and should!) be discovered. However, the more plodding math student can be equally rewarded for her methodical diligence by working with the Sieve of Eratosthenes. This will also make prime numbers visible, while reviewing once again the times tables. The student can decide how large to make her table. The class might even work over several days or weeks on a large format Sieve. If it remains hanging as a proud symbol of the collective math potential,

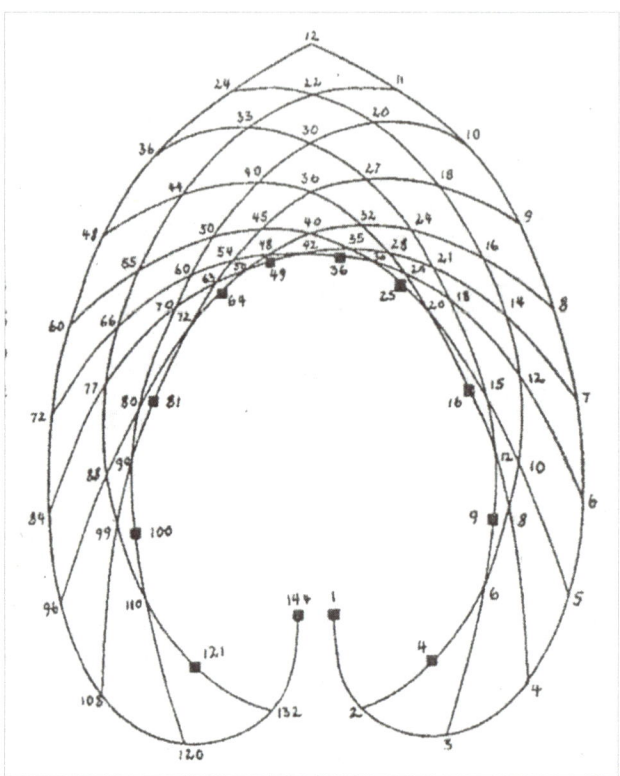

it will also serve as reference for those students who still require additional support!

Another brilliant example of numerical patterns and the beauty of the corresponding form can be found in a classic little piece, published in 1957, in *Education as an Art* by William Harrer. His limaçon of the multiplication tables 1–12 offers fascinating insights into the relationships of these tables to one another. He writes in his conclusion:

Working with the tables in the indicated manner is never drudgery. It is never dull. It offers ample opportunity for keeping the more quick, alert mathematicians in the class on their toes and at the same time keeps the slower ones constantly interested and alert.

These examples can serve as a vital antidote to the increasingly challenging quality of calculations and problem solving, which also accompany this age.

Familiarity with the existence of number patterns, sequences and series, can offer a solid bridge to beginning algebra. Identifying the unknown is perhaps the most common bridge, that is, 7 = 3 + (?), except now instead of a question mark, a letter is used, 7 = 3 + x. A more convincing example of the value of algebra is one that demonstrates its ability to state a generality, a rule, indeed a pattern. If the class teacher has nurtured a culture of mathematical riddling, through identifying and continuing number series, for example 2, 4, 3, 9, 8, 64, . . . the next number is? (Hint: one less than 64), then this pattern can now be expressed as a rule, beginning with x = 2, x2, x2 − 1, and not simply exemplified ad infinitum. My class loved using their newly found algebra skills in this way.

The Goethean phenomenological approach to studying the natural world guides class teachers and their students through the Waldorf science curriculum. Observational skills can and should be as rigorously honed in math classes. Feeling enchanted by rhythmic repetition and the beauty of form, exerting the will required for accurate and sustained observation, and exercising the thought forces necessary to re-cognize the inherent laws and patterns represent the best possible pathway for stimulating the mathematical interests and capacities of children and young people, and their teachers as well!

Probability of uniqueness

To immediately dispel any anxieties about having to teach probability as a class teacher, please be reassured that it is a ninth grade math block, usually called Permutations and Combinations. Yet the title of this section serves to place the focal point on the burning issue of calculations and the unique, right answer. This is the ultimate source, in my experience, of most math anxiety, fear, sense of inadequacy, insecurity, and distaste—the fact that the answer might be wrong! In the very early grades students may feel anxious when they do not (yet) know the answer because most students, especially the very young ones, will want to please their teachers by fulfilling their expectations. Not knowing an answer is a disappointment. It is not until after the nine-year change, when a child becomes more self-aware, that the anxiety will also spring from fear of giving the wrong answer.

Both results originate from a child's not knowing how to get to an answer, preferably the right one. The more emphasis a class teacher can place on the process, using the pathway of inquiry and discovery, the more confidence the whole class will have in beginning to do the work, and the less they will anguish over what their answer will be. In more advanced high-school level math, partial credit is granted precisely because primarily the thought pathways are being evaluated, and only secondarily the exact answer!

Paying attention to the language you use when correcting a child can again be key. If a child does a problem on the board and makes a mistake, the teacher can ask the rest of the class with genuine interest, can anyone explain how the child found this solution? Hearing one's own thoughts spoken out loud by someone else, especially by a peer, can help unite the inner image with the outer workings. Instead of all-too-quickly showing the child, or having a classmate show the child, what he did wrong, the teacher could ask the child if he now sees a different solution pathway. If the child has a healthy self-esteem, this can continue to be done in front of the class, as a class-wide exploration. It is wonderful if such a learning climate can be cultivated among a group of students. However, if the child is self-conscious, the rethinking can be done at the teacher's desk or with the teacher's help at the child's own desk.

In the first section of this chapter, I emphasized the inherent truth in math, and how important it is for a teacher to choose language that does justice to it. Continuing with this conviction, I suggest searching for solutions and not answers from the very beginning. This, too, may seem to be mere semantics, but the word "solution" implies dissolving a combination of two or more entities into a physical or chemical unity. The tension of being separate, the tension of separate beings is overcome and something new is created. It is an act, a generative process—problem solving, a de-cision. Of course, asking the students to practice and to learn their math facts, as Jamie York suggests, involves memorizing the right answers, but so did learning the multiplication tables by heart. This sort of calculation falls decidedly in the realm of developing confidence in number relationships.

This is especially true within the daily practice of mental math. Here students are led into the various strategies that allow them to successfully calculate sums, products, differences, and quotients in their heads. These are not at all the same thought processes used to do written math. When adding 19 to 44, students should recognize that 19's relationship to 20 is less one, so in adding 20 to 44 to attain 64, and then reducing by one, they quickly find the solution sum of 63. This requires practicing thought pathways regularly, and with the clear intention of improving speed and accuracy. York's website, www.jamieyorkpress.com, offers math practice worksheets beginning in grade three. I used them with success. It was part of the class' morning routine. Initially untimed, I introduced the time element toward the end of grade four, allowing five minutes at the beginning of grade five for sixty calculations. By January of grade five, I reduced the time to four, and then later to three minutes. Two months into grade six a boy finished before I, the teacher, did. He was ecstatic! Soon several others joined him in the ranks of being quicker than the teacher. I rapidly needed to make double-sided copies so that the quickest students had enough calculations to keep them busy for the full three minutes.

It was in grade six that I also introduced consequences for those who did not complete 60 calculations in three minutes or who got more than 3 wrong. They needed to complete and/or correct their speed sheets for homework. This usually happened during the school day, but it did require the students to review their weakest examples. (I had coached the class in how to take a speed-accuracy test; the incompletes were scattered throughout the sixty examples, as they did not allow themselves to get stuck.)

This process may appear ideally suited to cultivate competitiveness and stress, but that was not the case. I had a special egg timer with a 3-minute, 4-minute, and 5-minute sand glass in the same frame. Students could look up and see the time, and I announced when 3, 4, and 5 minutes were up. It was clearly an individual striving to improve one's own speed and accuracy, and it did not pit students against each other. Improvement was continuous among all the students. The class kept all their sheets in a special binder, and each quarter we used them to practice calculating the class median, mean, and middle, before recycling them all. The overall progress of the class was statistically documented.

Why spend time (it wasn't much each day, but it was every day for four years!) and energy on speed and accuracy? It is well known that children who do not acquire enough fluency in their decoding while reading, lose sight (literally) of the overall context and meaning of the story. A child needs to have a practiced habit of decoding in order to comprehend a text. It is no different in math. Many of the challenges grade school and high school students face in mathematics are due to a lack of speed and accuracy in basic calculations. I presently teach Algebra 2 to high school students. I quickly discovered that if I removed the time element from quizzes, midterms, and finals, my weak students would produce solid results. This often meant continuing proctoring during the lunch hour, after school, or during study hall. It also confirmed for me the long-term results of inadequate fluency in basic calculations. There will be students who upon entering their third seven-year cycle should be allowed to refer to a multiplication table. The rare student who truly cannot attain sufficient math fluency, who may even have a diagnosed dyscalculia, should not be held back from benefiting from the richness of logic and thought in the math curriculum of the upper grades due to anxieties surrounding basic calculations. But prior to a child's celebrating a fourteenth or fifteenth birthday, a class teacher should have done everything possible to support that child's achieving the best possible level of math fluency.

I would like to say a word about students who might join your classroom in the middle grades and who have not enjoyed the enthusiastic and joy-filled math foundation that the rest of the class did. My experience has been that most of them will be quite solid in written addition and subtraction computations, even of quite large numbers. Depending on their grade level, the multiplication tables will also be well practiced. Division may still be shaky. They may have random knowledge of areas of math that the Waldorf curriculum will not deal with until later, decimals for example. Most likely, however, they will not have discovered math for themselves, but will have been fed it. Drill and routine will have established fixed habits with little understanding and, more disconcertingly, without having connected the outer doings with inner concept images. Only this allows for malleability and growth of thought processes.

Written calculations and genuine problem solving are of an entirely different nature, though obviously fluency of calculation plays a pertinent part here as well. In grade one, math sentences are written horizontally, as language sentences are. As demonstrated above, the whole (the future solution) is given, and the child may pair the appropriate parts with the appropriate operation. In grade two, this order can be reversed. I introduced the chemical equation symbol first, $\leftrightarrow$, emphasizing that this math sentence is a two-way street. We are allowed to drive in either direction, or even around the world. My second graders had great fun reading equations forward and backward, or from any starting point. This can be a therapeutic measure for students who find subtraction and division challenging. Instead of reading $14 = 21 - ?$, I taught my student to feel free to begin with the question mark and ask what plus 14 will equal 21. Similarly $48 \div 6 = ?$, could be read what times 6 will equal 48. This may appear to be avoiding a weakness and catering to strength, but are there other possible explanations why a student might feel less comfortable with subtraction and division? What is the child's temperament? How old is the child, not just age-wise, but developmentally? Is the child still at home in the empathetic stream of the whole, of synthesis? Does the antipathetic stream of the parts, of analysis, still feel strange to the child? Feelings and math seem contraindicative, and yet there is hardly a grade school subject that evokes such strong sentiments. The class teacher should observe the children in the class closely, take their feelings seriously, and through reflection and working with the night, find ways to allow the child to feel good while doing math.

The operations are paired in polarities, and the more comfortable a student becomes with this relationship, the freer he or she will move about in the world of numbers. In reviewing the operations in grade two, along with the two-way street, I introduced the travel lane and the passing lane. When the students added, they were in the travel lane. If they multiplied, they were in the passing lane. I took the time for students to write out many versions of

$3 + 3 + 3 + 3 + 3 + 3 + 3 = 21$

and then

$7 \times 3 = 21.$

Similarly

$21 - 3 - 3 - 3 - 3 - 3 - 3 - 3 = 0.$

Therefore,

$21 \div 3 = 7.$

Often in these early years, not enough time is taken to make these relationships repeatedly visible. Remember, "mathematical thoughts in themselves are only thoughts, they exist merely as pictures. They have not been acquired from any outer reality." It is the duty of the class teacher to make these inner pictures visible for all the students. Many first and second graders are learning to see clearly with their inner eye. Their etheric, formative forces are only slowly freeing themselves from the child's physical body. Think about the care that is given to recall of the story from yesterday, the beauty and exactness of the board drawing or morning lesson book drawing! Is the same quality of attention to presentation, recall, and representation being given to math content? Does the class teacher see these inner images clearly and beautifully her- or himself? For only then will the true and enlivened games, activities, and images come! A first or second grader who can easily access these inner images will still happily represent them on the page. This will not be boring, but rather an exciting affirmation of the correctness of her or his inner life. This is the moral power of math.

Vertical written math follows the introduction and practice of place value, and the necessary techniques of borrowing and carrying. Here, too, the truth of the outer images brought to illuminate the inner concept is vital. We had gardened at the end of grade one, and therefore were gathering seeds from our annuals in the fall of grade two. We spread the seeds we had gathered onto a large colored sheet of paper and commenced counting. With a class full of voices counting simultaneously, child after child lost their place and had to begin again. Right when the frustration level began to rise, I noticed that there were children who were grouping seeds together, typically in groups of ten. I took up this example as a revolutionary idea, and we quickly set up a seed bank. (Of course, I had prepared this all in advance, but it appeared impromptu for the children in the class.) We had the bagger and the banker and many counters. The counters brought 10 seeds to the bagger, who placed them in a small wax paper seed envelope and placed them in a narrow little file box. When the box had 10 envelopes in it, it was filed in the bank. This kept us busy for easily half of a morning lesson, and in the end we had to open a warehouse, because we had more than 1000 seeds, and only 10 trays fit into the drawer of the bank. (Snapdragons and marigolds make numerous seeds.) When the last seed was counted, we used our categories to easily total our seeds. 10 filing boxes were in the storehouse, 2 filing boxes were in the bank, 5 full envelopes were on the bagger's table, and the last counter still had three seeds. Below is what I wrote on the blackboard. We read the math out loud, "1000 plus 200 is 1200. 1200 plus 50 is 1250. 1250 plus 3 is 1253," and that is where we left it till the next day.

Storehouse:	10 x 10 x 10 =	1000
Bank:	2 x 10 x 10 =	200
Bagger:	5 x 10 =	50
Counter:	3 =	3
Total:		1253

The next morning's recall revealed that the number was engraved in most of the children's minds. I wrote it very large on the board, and asked which digit represented which station. The stations had been set up in increasing powers of ten in front of the board the day before, so the order was clear:

Storehouse   Bank   Bagger   Counter.

I then led the students slowly through the scenarios of the day before, by re-setting up the stations with the seeds and containers. "What happened when the counter brought 10 seeds?" "How many envelopes were then on the bagger's table?" "How many seeds were left with the counter?" The answers are, of course, one and none. In this meticulous fashion we reviewed what happened with each station shift. It is very important to do this slowly and meticulously. The students ALL need to be absolutely sure what the zeros express. The term "place-holders" is meaningless in this context, and therefore meaningless to your average second grader. Once we had that down, I placed various amounts at the various stations and asked the students to tell me how many seeds there were. At a glance the quicker students called out the digits in the correct order, some of them even able to say the number correctly. The slower students were put to work to write out the math—how many seeds on the counting table, how many envelopes on the bagging table (x 10), how many seeds on the bank table (x 100), and so forth—to check the answers of the others. This was repeated several times, and written out in its entirety on the board each time, before I left the bagging table empty. With 3 files in the bank and 8 seeds with the counter, how many seeds are there?

I am belaboring this point because the first lesson in anything is crucial. Taking the time to bring these ideas alive through truthful outer images will help anchor the concepts as inner imagery in each student's being.

Multi-digit calculations—whether addition, subtraction, multiplication, or division—are repetitive, spatial, organizational, sequential, pragmatic, methodical, even rhythmical activities. Many students, especially after the nine-year change, will fall quickly into the reassuring beauty of these algorithms, but certain students will continue to struggle with focusing their inner imagery into enough clarity to guide them accurately through these multi-step processes. Difficulties can also arise with students who have attention/distraction issues, and especially those with spatial-orientation challenges. It can be very therapeutic for these students, and beneficial for all, to avoid the shortcuts that hide what is really happening during multi-digit calculations. Jamie York treats the danger of these misrepresentations and the correct image fully in his resource book, *Making Math Meaningful,* for grades one through five. Here are two examples:

$$\begin{array}{r} 235 \\ \times\,126 \\ \hline 1410 \\ 470 \\ \underline{235} \\ 29610 \end{array}$$

The above calculation is most often accompanied by the following monologue:
6 times 5 is 30, write the 0, carry the 3.
6 times 3 is 18, plus 3 is 21, write the 1, carry the 2.
6 times 2 is 12, plus 2 is 14, write the 14, and so forth.

```
235 = 200 + 30 + 5
126 = 100 + 20 + 6
6 x 5  =    30  | 20 x 5  =   100  | 100 x 5  =    500
6 x 30 =   180  | 20 x 30 =   600  | 100 x 30 =   3000
6 x 200 =1200   | 20 x 200 = 4000  | 100 x 200 = 20000
          1410           + 4700            + 23500
        = 29610
```

This calculation, obviously to be done first with a single-digit multiplier, reveals what is really happening, and reinforces the place value work that was so carefully introduced in grade two. Again we avoid the terminology "place-holder-zero," because the zeros represent the actual value of the significant digits seen. Similar to the introduction of the word "factor" in the number factory, the term "significant digits" may be introduced in this context. They are seen because of their significance! This will greatly aid the students in readily understanding later concepts such as decimal numbers, rounding, and scientific notation.

Similarly in division, the simple repetitive rhythm of "divide, multiply, subtract, bring down" will be enough to guide some students through the calculation, but spatially challenged and distractible students will need to understand, in order to be able to see the sense in holding the spatial order of a long division, or in order to find their place again when their attention has strayed. For example:

$$\begin{array}{r} 300 + 40 + 6 = \mathbf{346} \\ 14 \overline{)\,4844} \\ \underline{4200} \\ 644 \\ \underline{560} \\ 84 \\ \underline{84} \\ 0 \end{array}$$

The obvious visibility of the truth in this calculation makes sense and greatly aids spatially- and attention-challenged students to follow through the task successfully. This strategy can be dropped when individually appropriate for each student as his or her security grows. It can also be reassigned if the teacher sees an increase in mistakes or sloppiness creeping in again after a time. Child development is not a linear function! Going back in order to continue to move successfully forward is a legitimate and highly recommended teaching tool!

In continuing through the middle grades curriculum, the class teacher can continually review material already taught by integrating it into the creation of genuine practical problems that need to be solved. For example, combining practicing fractions and reviewing measurement could result in the following tasks. Nine inches is what fraction of a foot? A foot is what fraction of a yard? A cup is what fraction of a gallon? Or practicing decimals, while reviewing monies, might result in asking what decimal fraction of a dollar is a dime? A penny? These appear to be very simple, but it is exactly this connection of a new thought process with a concrete and familiar entity that will convince students they are getting it. My daughter was taught to play violin initially by ear. Not by playing songs she did not know, but by playing (for nearly three years!) songs she knew well. When the subtle corrections necessary to play in tune had become habit, then she moved on to less familiar pieces. This is an excellent strategy in math as well. Confidence is built through affirmation. Praise from the teacher is a wonderful thing, but if a child can recognize her or his own success, thanks to the teacher's skill in creating skill-level-appropriate practice, then the affirmation comes from the material itself. This approach is very effective for the middle school child.

The practical problems and the mental math can grow into multiple-step calculations, involving various operations. For example, Maria had a pound and a half of chocolate. The recipe for the cake she was making required 4 ounces of chocolate, but she needed to double the recipe. What fraction of the original amount of chocolate did Maria use to bake the two cakes? Or reviewing time, John needs 25 minutes to get ready for school in the morning. If he needs to be at school at 8:30 a.m. and the bus takes ¾ of an hour to get to school from John's house, when is the latest time John can get up? Not unlike the pedagogical stories of the earlier grades, a practical problem like this can bring objective attention to an area, with which a particular student in the class may be struggling.

Along the same lines, mental math examples should now be chain calculations:

$47 - 8 \div 13 \times 15 + 5 = ?$

The difficulty level of mental math can be highly individualized in verbal math games, such as Around the World, an all-time favorite of my class. One student stands behind the chair of another student sitting. The teacher states the math problems verbally. The first student to give the correct answer may travel further to stand behind the chair of the next student. The slower student sits or remains seated. Though I never set it, the goal for the class quickly became to travel around the world, that is, to get through the entire class and back to your starting place without being dethroned. My part in the continued popularity of this game was to provide the correct level of difficulty of calculation.

In introducing, but also when continuing practice of fractions and decimals, logical step-wise progressions will also help nurture a sense of security and ability in the class, especially when connecting these two related forms of expression. Beginning with the transition from identifying the remainder of a division problem to writing it as a fraction,

$$\frac{\text{remainder}}{\text{divisor}}$$

students can be lead through a series of thoughts that serve to meaningfully connect skill sets they already have. Fifteen minutes is what fraction of an hour? 15/60. Reduce by dividing both the numerator and denominator by 15 = ¼. We call ¼ a quarter, so a quarter of an hour is fifteen minutes long. But a quarter is also a coin! A quarter is what fraction of a dollar? 25/100. Reduce by dividing both the numerator and denominator by 25 = ¼. Could we write 25/100 another way? 0.25. So, dear students, what is the decimal fraction for 15/60? Whenever possible, search for and make these kinds of examples visible to your students!

The middle grades child is an enormously practical being. Prior to the twelve-year change, when the ratio of breaths to heartbeats approaches that of an adult, the child wants to feel empowered to figure out the world. Math practice should build on this as much as possible. Word problems will not be anxiety-ridden if they are the rule rather than the exception. In grade six, the so-called business math block, builds a crowning experience to showcase the wonderful math capabilities that the students have developed so far. One of the main goals of the material introduced in this block is for the students to be able to translate fluently and accurately from percents to decimals, to decimal fractions, to common fractions. For example,

$20\% = 0.20 = 20/100 = 1/5.$

It can be very instructional, when a student then remarks that 0.20 = 0.2, which means that 20/100 = 2/10 = 1/5. Students are often exhilarated when they realize that they are developing this kind of "x-ray vision." It is absolutely a "super-power" that should be encouraged as the students move up the grades.

The concepts of proportion, ratio, and scale are some of the last mathematical concepts introduced, prior to the students' moving into algebra. The appropriateness of introducing this material after the twelve-year change is self-evident and provides a wonderful example of the genius of the Waldorf curriculum. Though simply another take on division, and therefore on the "relation"-ship of numbers to each other or to the whole out of which they sprang, ratios and proportions are some of the most practical math skills your students will learn (and continue to use throughout their lives!). Scale, which allows for integrating the artistic element into the math lesson, separate from geometry, can also provide an objective viewing point of relative size, importance, and priority. These are all executive functioning skills that will not be fully developed in young people until well after they graduate from high school. Yet, in this pubertal phase, Waldorf students are given skill sets, which can provide both perspective (another grade seven topic) and direction in the young persons' lives. Even the simple concept of comparing apples to apples and oranges to oranges when setting up a ratio calculation has far-reaching implications.

Prior to introducing foundational algebra concepts, often called pre-algebra, negative numbers are introduced. This is another classic stumbling block for math students, and not only those who have typically stumbled right along. Here again, the class teacher's choice of both imagery and vocabulary can make all the difference for the class' understanding. The typical grade seven student of today will be very aware of the existence of negative numbers; temperature and grade six bookkeeping both offer examples. Unfortunately, knowing that they exist does in no way automatically translate into understanding how to calculate with them. There are many potential sources of confusion. The primary one is that the negative sign and the minus sign are the same sign! This is truly confusing, and a grade seven math teacher should recognize this, articulate it from the start to the class, and ask for ideas about how to tell the two different signs apart. Color-coding, the introduction of parentheses, and writing out the actual words were all ideas my class suggested. Pairing this with truthful imagery, a class teacher can review the bookkeeping experience and the words *balance*, *withdrawal* and *deposit*. As long as no more money is withdrawn than is deposited, there is a positive balance on the books. If more money is withdrawn than deposited, there is a negative balance. Here it becomes vital that the teacher refer to the sign similarity problem, clearly identifying deposit (+) and withdrawal (–) as the operations of adding and subtracting (or in this case, perhaps better still is the word *removing*) as different from identifying a positive balance with a plus sign and a negative balance with a negative sign. The first two are actions, verbs; the second two are adjectives describing the state of balance, a noun. These images and terminology allow us to pose the question—after a thorough elaboration of the more readily understood ideas of creating a negative balance or remedying a negative balance by depositing a sum greater than the missing amount—What happens if we remove a debt? How would we write that, dear class, as an equation? Allow the class to push through to seeing the only solution as subtracting a negative number. For example, if after an initial balance of $25 had been reduced by $37, for an interim negative balance of -$12, how much debt must be removed to attain a positive balance of $10? The students will already be familiar with the equation: $-12 + 22 = 10$, but now they are challenged to express the same result this way: $-12 - (-22) = 10$.

The thermometer, perhaps the most familiar provider of negative values, can prove trickier for the student than bookkeeping, unless the teacher is particularly careful in her or his word choice. The reality of adding warmth is equivalent to the first equation above, but the idea of removing cold is not real for a seventh grader, especially not one struggling with this concept.

In my research I have encountered objections to the use of the number line in helping students to understand negative numbers, based on the fact that the number line is in fact a pure abstraction.

Though it exists as little as the line of the equator on the face of the earth, my experience has cautioned me not to throw out this tool all too carelessly. As quoted at the beginning of this chapter, "Mathematics is nothing else than an internal experience." It is not easy as a teacher to know what outer image will most likely match or inspire the internal experience of the student. I have successfully used the image of the number line, in connection with movement, to remedy persistent negative number confusion in the following way. Drawing a large, color-coded (negative side one color, positive side a different color, meeting at a big white 0) number line with chalk on the classroom floor, I asked the student to stand, for example, at positive 2, facing in the direction of increasing positive numbers.

I then asked the student to move to positive 5, counting the steps as she went. I wrote 2 + 3 = 5 on the board. We agreed that facing in the positive direction represented a positive number, and that moving forward represented adding. I then asked the student without turning around to retrace her steps back to positive 2. I wrote on the board 5 – 3 = 2. We then agreed that moving backward represented subtraction.

I wrote the following on the board 2 – 5 = ?, and asked the student to walk it. Still facing toward the positive side of the line, the student walked backward five steps to end at negative 3. We did several more examples that utilized only these two options, always facing toward the positive and walking forward or backward, capturing the activity in a math sentence on the board. I also moved along the line, and asked the student to capture what I did as a math equation on the board. When the student appeared secure in this, I asked her to step back on the number line at positive 2 and to face the negative side. We agreed that facing the negative side of the number line represented a negative number. I then wrote 2 + negative 5 = ? on the board. This was a moment of great hesitation. I reviewed with the student that walking forward was adding. The student walked forward 5 steps to get to negative 3. I then asked the student if she remembered how else we had gotten from positive 2 to negative 3. Again several repetitions of adding (moving forward) a negative number (facing negative) were practiced and written down, both by the student and myself. Finally, I, on the number line at negative 3, facing toward the negative numbers, walked backward five steps to get to positive 2. I asked the student to write on the board what I had just done: (-3) – (-5) = +2. Repeating this most challenging form with the student as the mover and as the scribe concluded this extra lesson. This procedure has taken more time to write down than it did to do, but I have cured many a persistent negative number confusions with this 20-minute, after school, one-on-one session with a student, including that of my own son, once he agreed to do the "stupid" exercise with his mother at home.

Another middle school math theme is exponents and square roots. As mentioned earlier in this chapter, square numbers were discovered early on in the multiplication table. They were the magic numbers building the diagonal of the square. 1 x 1 = 1, 2 x 2 = 4, 3 x 3 = 9, etc. Revisiting my image of the travel and passing lanes, I told the class that by using powers they could travel even faster than they could with multiplication in the passing lane. Counting the number of numerals (use your words carefully!) gave the class the value of the exponent. 3 x 3 = 3^2 = 9, 3 x 3 x 3 = 3^3 = 27, etc. If the idea of inverse operations (new word, old relationship) was well anchored in the early grades, then it feels quite natural for the students that there must be a reverse operation for raising a number to a power, namely bringing it back to its roots.

This image of traveling speed also holds true for the order of operations; the most impatient is (usually) given attention first! On another note, during an evaluation, I heard a skilled storyteller teacher weave a tale to a math-tired grade seven class, lulling them into the comfort of the early grades. At almost the exact moment that the final student had completely relaxed into the moment, this teacher concluded with the punch line, "Please Excuse My Dear Aunt Sally." I am sure that those students will never forget that acronym for the order of operations!

As mentioned earlier, I introduced algebra as the language that allows the rules, the generalities of mathematics to be expressed. By introducing algebra in this way the students were invited to learn this language. For example by quickly and simply reviewing 5 + 4 = 9, and following the example of my code, I suggested substituting letters for the numbers. Since all three numbers are different, three different letters must be used, a + b = c. I then asked the students if this statement was always true; that is, if a number is added to a non-same number, will the result always be a third non-same number? This is a genuine thought process, as simple as it is. By asking it as a question, and not presenting it as a fact, the students are invited to think it through. There are always those wonderful students who are determined to prove you wrong. From the truth in this simple expression, the class teacher can progress to the other properties of equality and the field properties of real numbers (not all at once!) as a succession of thought development.

Along these lines runs the illuminating method of teaching how to multiply two binomial parenthetical expressions, as developed by Arnold Bernhard, a math teacher for many years at the Rudolf Steiner School in Basel, Switzerland. Building seamlessly on the vertical multiplication and long division examples already given, Bernhard suggests the following:

12 x 13 = (10 + 2)(10 + 3) = 100 + 30 + 20 + 6 = 156.

Later this may come to be known as "foiling." At least my students, even in high school, have always turned the mnemonic acronym FOIL (first, outside, inside, last) into a verb. Setting further examples on the board,

22 x 23 = (20 + 2)(20 + 3) = 400 + 60 + 40 + 6 =   506
32 x 33 = (30 + 2)(30 + 3) = 900 + 90 + 60 + 6 = 1056
42 x 43 = (40 + 2)(40 + 3) =1600 +120+ 80 + 6 = 1806

stimulates the students to discover a certain pattern. Sound familiar? Now the challenge is to express the pattern as a rule using their newly found algebraic language. The first product is always a square number; the second is the 30s tables; the third the 20s tables; and fourth is always the number 6. Looking at the factors, the only one that is the same is the tens value in both parentheses. Once this is discovered, the class can move hesitantly to the following expression:

(a + 2)(a + 3) = a^2 + 3a + 2a + 6, or a^2 + 5a + 6.

This is much more significant than pulling the algebraic rabbit out of the hat. It uses algebraic language to express an observed regularity, while acknowledging familiar number relations as a rule that can be generalized using letters instead of numerals.

The binomial theorems can now be developed in the same way, using two identical factors,

23 x 23 = (20 + 3)(20 + 3) = 400 + 60 + 60 + 9 =   529
33 x 33 = (30 + 3)(30 + 3) = 900 + 90 + 90 + 9 =   1089

A class will now quickly catch on to the new pattern and how it may be written.

(a + b)(a + b) = a^2 + ab + ab + b^2, or a^2 + 2ab + b^2.

The rules for factoring can be discovered using similar examples. (Bernhard 1991, pp.13–24)

My experience is that the students own the results of class discoveries much more than when the information is explained to them. The additional time that it takes to develop the students' thinking in this way will be more than made up for in the long term by a level of assurance paired with true understanding that will carry the students confidently and accurately into the demands of their high school mathematics curriculum.

As a middle school math teacher (class teacher or subject support teacher), you will be confronted with the question: Can Waldorf eighth grade students complete the public school Algebra I curriculum? Without additional time and energy spent outside of the regular algebra blocks and math skill classes, the answer is "no." The second question remains: Is this a good use of the students' time and energies? Here the answer is not as clear, and may be different for individual students in their specific constellations. However, if math has been introduced and taught with the level of consciousness, enthusiasm, and care illustrated in this chapter, teachers and parents alike need not fear for the further development of their children's mathematical ingenuity.

Students who have successively, and in age-appropriate manner, been introduced to activities, images, and thought processes that unite to mutually support each other—in short, students who have been introduced to math the right way will approach all further math (and not only math) learning with the same sense of wonder, joy, and curiosity, with the same unity of being that they feel when catching a unique snowflake on their tongue.

BIBLIOGRAPHY

Baravalle, Hermann von. (1967). *The teaching of arithmetic and the Waldorf school plan*. Englewood, NJ: Waldorf School Monographs.

Bernhard, Arnold. (1991). *Algebra für die siebte und achte Klasse an Waldorfschulen.* Stuttgart: Verlag Freies Geistesleben.

Bishof, B. (1998). *World of numbers*. Aptos, CA: Live Education!

Harrer, Dorothy. (1985). *Math lessons for elementary grades*. Chatham, NY: Waldorf Publications.

Harrer, William. (1957). "Multiplication tables can be interesting," in the Winter issue of the bulletin *Education as an art*. New York: Rudolf Steiner School Association.

Jarman, Ron. (1998). *Teaching mathematics in Rudolf Steiner schools for classes 1-8*. Stroud, UK: Hawthorn Press.

Morin, Amanda. (2014–16). *Understanding dyscalculia*. UNDERSTOOD.ORG USA LLC.

Oram, Peter. (1997). *One for the golden sun*. Cardigan, Wales: Starborn Books.

Rawson, Martyn and Richter, Tobias. (2001). *The educational tasks and content of the Steiner Waldorf curriculum*. Forest Row, UK: Steiner Schools Fellowship Publications.

Steiner, Rudolf. (1922). *Origin and goal of the human being.* http://wn.rsarchive.org/Lectures/

_____. (1920). *The path to freedom and love and their significance in world events.* http://wn.rsarchive.org/Lectures/

_____. (1921). *Paths to knowledge of higher worlds* (GA 79). http://wn.rsarchive.org/Lectures/

_____. (1922). *Spiritual ground of education.* http://wn.rsarchive.org/Lectures/

Ulin, Bengt. (1991). *Finding the path*. Wilton, NH: The Association of Waldorf Schools of North America

York, Jamie. (2003). *Making math meaningful*. Denver, CO: Whole Spirit Press.

Executive or higher-level function
One aspect of understanding day-to-day thinking

Mary Jo Oresti

The human future will be defined by our children's minds and the nature and quality of their presence on the earth. We need minds capable of creating and inventing new solutions to the world's increasing complex problems.
— Stephanie Pace-Marshall

Our day-to-day thinking is a manifestation of our cohesive integration and how well we have developed a vessel that reflects and welcomes the world of thought. This is a dance between spirit, soul, and body. Every day we are in situations that call upon us to be steady and thoughtful and to have flexible, organized thinking. This state of mind is often called *executive function*, a set of mental processes that helps us connect past experience with present action.

The work of influential researchers such as Michael Posner, Joaquin Fuster, their colleagues in the 1980s, and later Trevor Robbins, Bob Knight, Don Stuss, and others laid much of the groundwork for recent research into executive functions. For example, Posner proposed that there is a separate executive branch of the attentional system, which is responsible for focusing attention on selected aspects of the environment.

When hearing the words executive function, most people think of the following behaviors:

- planning and organizing ability
- managing time
- problem solving
- ability to control actions in order to reach a goal
- managing emotional reactions
- cognitive flexibility
- paying attention to and remembering details

This list of capacities could be simply classified into two basic areas: organization and regulation.

When executive function is active, there is an accompanying internal sense of time, space, and priority. How much time do I estimate for a project? What steps are needed? What is the big picture and the supporting details?

However, all these thoughts would only live in the head if regulation did not occur. To accomplish a task, we need the ability to act, to be steadfast, and also, when necessary, to wait or inhibit any possible destructive actions that would diminish our intentions. If we consider how Rudolf Steiner referred to the threefold human being, then we understand that, while thinking appears to dominate, willing and feeling also play their roles when speaking about executive function.

Regulation

First of all, let's direct our attention to the aspect of regulation. When viewed from the perspective of Waldorf education, we are directed to the different aspects of the will. In *Foundations of Human Experience,* Rudolf Steiner addresses the will. A strong will can be visible and active when we observe a grade school child completing a craft project or a young child in the early childhood classroom vigorously building. We help this quality when we comment on a child's efforts, not the final product.[1]

Executive or higher-level function

The will has another side. It is also at work when inhibiting an action or refraining from being distracted. We see this daily when children do not allow distractions to pull them away from their main lesson book work or to remain relatively still while waiting in line.

Many children in our classrooms demonstrate inner restlessness that will present the challenge of establishing the impulse control needed for higher functioning and require both an examination of the classroom environment and often a case-by-case exploration as to the cause of the restlessness.

The third player here, the feeling life, can also determine how successful we are with accomplishing tasks, as we learn that mistakes are not the first sign of failure but rather a step in learning.

Inhibitory control is necessary for overriding stimulus-driven behavioral responses. One example of practicing this type of concentration is a game that can be played in second grade, a version of the song, "Head, Shoulders, Knees, and Toes." First, stand in front of the children and together sing the song and do the actions. Now, ask the children to continue to do the same motions and sing. While they are doing the described motions, the teacher sings the song but does different movements. For instance, instead of touching your head for the first movement, touch your elbows or your mouth. Keep doing this throughout the song, substituting the usual movements with inventive ones. It is a lot of fun and not only builds inhibition of sensory stimuli necessary for better executive function but also creates a novel situation, so unlike the expected. Even games such as "Swing the Statue" and "Mother, May I?" demonstrate the wisdom of controlling actions.

Organization

The other aspect of executive function involves the ability to organize, prioritize, respond to both novel and familiar tasks, and exercise flexible, pictorial thinking.

The frontal lobe, thought of as the location for higher functioning, contains four areas of function. Researchers have found a link between good academic performance and a greater density of neurons in the frontal lobe. This is well explained in *Smart Moves* by Carla Hannaford. External stimuli are accepted from the body via the brain stem and the limbic system so that new experiences can be understood in light of past experiences.[2]

These capacities are dependent on an overall maturity. Many Waldorf researchers have examined how we develop the ego as the organizing principle in the human being. We find, just as in the mainstream, that the ego does not develop strongly without, on one hand, nurturing of the senses, especially the foundation senses: movement, balance, touch, and life; and, on the other hand, encouraging the child to explore new situations which strengthen the developmental path from "tummy time" to inner speech and complicated cross-lateral movements. These areas of senses and movement are beautifully described in *Being Human* by Dr. Karl König.[3] Exercises to develop these capacities can be found in *Exercise Manuals 1 and 2* from healingeducation.org.[4]

When one or more of the senses or the stages of development are hindered (for instance, if a child has a compromised balance system), the more conscious areas and functions control the body. Then these higher levels of functioning are not fully available for learning. Working memory problems are usually evident in a child with balance issues. Another precursor to abstract thinking is inner speech, which melds cognition and regulation. If it is not fully developed, self-monitoring and pictorial thinking become lessened.

Life stages and higher functioning

Of course the young child is always practicing how to solve problems. So is the pre-adolescent. However, there is a change in the adolescent, who has a spurt of attention and memory capacities at around age 15 and can begin to exhibit the more classically defined executive function. The adult from age 20 to 29 is at his or her peak and hopefully has accomplished inhibitory control to make full use of the physical myelination in the pre-frontal cortex. Although memory can decline, cognitive flexibility can remain vibrant until age 70.

Mainstream contributions

The term *executive function* has often been localized to the pre-frontal cortex; however, more research is now showing that other areas of the conscious and unconscious self are as important. The frontal lobes have multiple connections to cortical, subcortical, and brainstem sites. The basis of higher-level cognitive functions such as inhibition, flexibility of thinking, problem solving, planning, impulse control, concept formation, abstract thinking, and creativity often arise from much simpler, lower-level forms of cognition and behavior. Thus, the concept of executive function must be broad enough to include anatomical structures that represent a diverse and diffuse portion of the central nervous system.[5]

Current research shows that executive function develops over time and can continue and improve through our whole life, especially with physical exercise. It can also be diminished through stress, sadness, sleep deprivation, loneliness, and lack of physical fitness.

Rhythmic, meaningful, and repetitive actions also strengthen an emerging executive function. Early signs that an emerging organizing principle is being addressed can be seen already in early childhood when the little ones put their shoes in orderly pairs in the hallway. Our activity produces neurological pathways and bridges so that, when we dive into another project, we carry the lessons we learned from previous projects.

Let us remember that these behaviors listed under executive function are not sourced from the brain but rather registered by the organ of the brain. Like a thermometer which registers warmth, our brain registers and reflects the activity, mood, and health of the whole body.

Some examples from the school setting and higher functioning

The highest levels of operations and how we navigate through the maze of life are dependent on the frequent practice and strengthening of the physical capacities of our human form.

Audrey McAllen, a pioneer in helping children remove hindrances to learning, referred to the development of the human archetype as "anchoring the ego into the physical body." She crafted a whole body of exercises in movement, drawing, and painting aimed at helping the human being live into the human archetype or, in alternative phrasing, the spirit germ.[6]

We can learn cognitive principles from specific movement tasks. Rudolf Steiner refers frequently to the awareness of body geography, for example, as a means toward becoming "wise and prudent,"[7] and for combining ideas.[8]

In the study of gender learning and higher functioning, recent research has shown that girls, who tend to like individual expression in spinning, cartwheels and so forth, learn through language and express themselves well with language. Boys, who tend to like strong physical contact, develop their cognitive skills and the forebrain through rough and tumble play. Brain scans show this development occurring over time. To read more on this, go to movementforchildhood.com, a website from Jeff Tunkey. (see "Boys and Girls in Movement")

We can provide all the children, and especially our struggling children, with aids to bring structure to their lives. The National Center for Learning Disabilities has a list of "How to Manage Executive Function Problems," and there are many aids for organizing available now.

Conclusion

We all bring new impulses as well as our own individual contributions and quirks. The shift now seems to be the challenge for each of us to go even beyond the body/mind connection and realize that these two are, in fact, one. Helping our children find their path in life by mining for the gems in Waldorf education is our joyful task.

ENDNOTES

1. Steiner, Rudolf. (1996). *Foundations of human experience.* Great Barrington, MA: SteinerBooks.
2. Hannaford, Carla. (2007). *Smart moves: Why learning is not all in your head*, second edition, Salt Lake City: Great River Books.
3. König, Karl and Glöckler, Michaela. (1989). *Being human: Diagnosis in curative education.* Great Barrington, MA: SteinerBooks.
4. Association for a Healing Education. *Resource Teacher's Developmental Exercise Manual*, volumes 1 and 2.
5. Alvarez, J.A. and Emory, E. "Executive function and the frontal lobes: a meta-analytic review." *Neuropsychology Review,* March 2006, 16(1), 17-42.
6. McAllen, Audrey. (1991). *The extra lesson: Exercises in movement, drawing and painting to help children with difficulties*, fifth edition. Fair Oaks, CA: Rudolf Steiner College Press.
7. Steiner, Rudolf. (1995). *The kingdom of childhood: Introductory talks on Waldorf education* (GA 311). Great Barrington, MA: SteinerBooks.
8. Steiner, Rudolf. *A modern art of education* (GA 307). Great Barrington, MA: SteinerBooks.

Incarnational disrhythmia

Hypermotoric and inattentive challenges, cumulative stress reaction, sensory overwhelm issues, non-verbal disorders, oppositional defiance

Kim John Payne and Bonnie River

Getting "behind the label" of commonly diagnosed child and teen social, emotional, and behavioral challenges is taking on more and more importance for both the classroom teacher and the care professional. Of course, every child is whole and what you see laid out in this chapter is designed to better equip us to be helpers in removing obstacles to a child's full soul/spirit potential. The children who often need our extra support and are coming in to themselves are doing so in a way that is not typical and can be out of step with usual developmental milestones. That is why we use the term "Incarnational Disrhythmia." Given the help they need, these students will be fine, but their incarnation has its own ebb and flow. Our task is to do what we can to open up the stream through which their sense of place in the world and within themselves can better flow.

What we have laid out in these sections can help organize our thoughts and help us develop doable and depth-full approaches rather than feeling like we are being hit by an unrealistic tsunami of well-meaning but formulaic strategies.

How to use the guides

Most importantly, keep it simple and doable. Henry David Thoreau, inspired by Ralph Waldo Emerson's call to simplicity wrote an impassioned response. In a letter to Emerson he wrote of the need to "Simplify! Simplify!!" Emerson wrote back, "Dear David, Just one 'Simplify' would have sufficed." So, when you read through these pages a particular child will likely come to mind. Look for which of the descriptions in the "What Do I See?" of the four layers (physical, life forces, relational, self) seems to stand out. Now consider each of the "What Can I Do?" suggestions. Choose just one or two, and select the one that seems like it would be the most achievable and sustainable by you. There may be other ideas that seem like they would help more, but if they feel like it would be overreaching, give them a pass and perhaps circle back to them in a couple of weeks. From a quiet feeling of success, over time, you can increase what you are bringing to the child in a way that feels natural. Let the parents of the child or teen and your colleagues know your plan. Its simplicity can inspire others. In this way they gain good clarity of your support process and may even join you in their own way. It is so good hear the question, "Great, what can I do to help?" and to feel a circle gathering around the child.

In this way you are helping the child in need, but you are avoiding that troubling dynamic of diverting too much focus away from the rest of the children in the class. After all, keeping the four layers of the whole class healthy and moving along is probably what the individual child you are thinking about, needs as much as anything. No matter how good an idea sounds in the following pages, the children or teens need you to use strategies that seem natural to you so they hear your voice and intent. In this way they can move safely and easily into the small but increasingly beautiful learning space you open up each day.

Incarnational disrhythmia

The Hypermotoric Child

Physical Body

What do I see?
- Has problems remaining seated
- Fidgets with hands or feet or squirms in seat
- Displays compulsive movements such as tics, clearing throat, etc.
- Appears "on the go" and "driven by a motor"
- Displays overshooting, impulsive movements

What can I do?
- Increase physical prompting of student (e.g., hand on shoulder or back).
- The student could be given permission, by signaling, to get up and leave the classroom for an "aerobic break."
- Consider shortening main lesson rhythmic time and building in a movement time half way through the lesson.
- If appropriate, give the child physical compression such as with gentle firmness squeeze or rub her arms and shoulders. This can be turned into a game. If this is not possible, consider a very heavy woolen blanket wrapped around the child during which she can have a quiet reading time.

Life, Habit / Etheric Body

What do I see?
- Has organization difficulties and loses things
- Has problems in transitions
- Displays odd habits or compulsive behaviors

What can I do?
- Set timers or other visual reminders for transitions and seat work.
- Post all schedules and refer to them with the class. With younger students, use a pictorial schedule depicting the daily routine.
- Require the use of a three-ring binder or notebook and subject dividers (starting in fourth or fifth grade at the latest).
- Assist with the prioritization of activities and workload.
- Reduce the clutter and unnecessary visual overload in the classroom (brooms in corners, open shelving and student cubbies, counter clutter). Pay special attention to the chalk board and front of the classroom.

Senses, Relationship / Astral Body

What do I see?
- Argues or fights with peers or adults
- Has difficulty awaiting turn
- Uses inappropriate language or gestures in non-combative situations
- Cannot sustain planned rhythmic movements, as in circle activities

What can I do?
- Use private signals and cues that have been pre-arranged with the student to help focus attention.
- Design instruction for frequent opportunities to interact with peers.
- Assign special responsibilities to the student in the presence of the peer group so others observe the student in a positive light.
- Hold regular class meetings with carefully set up and monitored, age-appropriate communication skills.
- Play games that involve fast movement together with coming to a complete standstill. For example any one of the games that involve running and then having to stand as still as a statue. There are any number of good stalking games that involve moments of stillness (tension) and running (release) in a controlled and conscious way.

- Play listening games. For example "…listen to a noise far, far away, now a little closer, now in the room, now as close to you as possible." For older children: "Now keeping hold of the very close noise can you hear the faraway sound at the same time?"
- The soliloquy strategy. Many children who have attention issues also can be overly defiant when directly confronted. Try this. Quietly, within the hearing of the child, talk out loud to yourself about your reactions and consequences you are considering if it continues. Remember you are not talking to them but about the situation. This gives both the teacher and the student a valuable pause before a potentially negative conflict.

Learning, Organizing / Ego

What do I see?

- Interrupts during instructions (i.e., asks for clarification or distracts while teacher is speaking)
- Blurts out answers before questions have been completed
- Needs significantly more supervision than other children
- Impulsive in interactions, does not self-monitor
- Fails to give close attention to details or makes careless mistakes in his/her work
- Self-directs or soothes through speech (e.g., speaks to herself out loud or in a mumble what it is she is doing or wants to do. Sometimes it can also take the form of incessant humming or unconscious singing.)

What can I do?

- Break down longer assignments into smaller, manageable increments, providing a lot of structure, monitoring, and follow through.
- Teach students how to self monitor on-task behavior, so that they are using class time effectively for getting work done.
- Frame the area of the board you want the children to pay attention to by having a curtain, veil, or shutter to cover unwanted board work.
- Teach internalizing speech and actions. For example, move from singing a well-known song to reducing the volume more and more until humming quieter and quieter until the song is being hummed "inside" without any noise at all. This can be helped by keeping a beat. If you reduce the volume of the beat to none at all this can become a funny game if they try to join in at a signal from you and see if you are synchronized.
- A similar process can be achieved in movement by reducing a consciously carried out gesture making it more and more subtle until the child is motionless doing it "inside."
- The Calling-Out Scale. If a child is a "serial blurter" tell him about a 3-2-1 system.

  Three: Wrong comment – wrong time
  Two: Right comment – wrong time
  One: Right comment – right time

  Each time the child makes a comment, without any fuss, ask them which of the three categories they thought their comment belonged to. Also give them your assessment. You can do this for an individual student or for the whole class.
- Together with the student, design a simple self-monitoring card using a key goal such as "I spoke out at the right moment in the right way today." The child is reminded in the morning of his Key Goal. At the end of the day a one-minute review takes place where he gives himself a score from 1 (always) to 5 (very seldom), followed by the teacher giving him a score. He aims to accrue no more than say 10–12 points in a week.

Inattentive Type

Physical Body

What do I see?
- Is sluggish or drowsy
- Uses odd or inappropriate seating posture
- Appears to be "pulled down by gravity" when seated or standing

What can I do?
- High protein, low carbohydrate diet with Omega-3 fatty acid supplement
- Consider shortening main lesson rhythmic time and building in a movement time half way through the lesson.
- Touch or physically cue certain students for their focus prior to giving directions
- If appropriate give the child physical compression, such as with gentle firmness, squeeze or rub her arms and shoulders. This can be turned into a game. If this is not possible consider a very heavy woolen blanket wrapped around the child during which she can have a quiet reading time.

Life, Habit / Etheric Body

What do I see?
- Drops or loses materials
- Appears tired or complains of being tired
- Forgetful in daily activities

What can I do?
- Post all schedules and refer to them with the class. Use a pictorial schedule depicting the daily routine.
- Require the use of a three-ring binder or notebook and subject dividers (starting in fourth or fifth grade at the latest).
- Provide assistance (another student or adult) to help them regularly sort through desks, backpacks, and notebooks.
- Provide preferential seating up front, within cueing distance of the teacher, and away from doors, windows, and high-traffic areas of the room, keeping visual and auditory stimulation to a minimum.
- Allow for natural consequences of not having materials (do not replace lost items with new ones).

Senses, Relationship / Astral Body

What do I see?
- Avoids direct eye contact
- Doesn't listen when spoken to directly
- Easily distracted

What can I do?
- Establish a cozy or concentration corner where a desk is veiled off from the rest of the class or an alternative desk or chair in the room (two-seat method). This is not a punishment area.
- Assign special responsibilities to the student in the presence of the peer group so others observe the student in a positive light.
- Hold regular class meetings with carefully set up and monitored, age-appropriate communication skills. Ask the student to be the "keeper of the speaking rule." Her job is to notice when anyone transgresses the pre-agreed guidelines for the meeting.
- Play games that involve fast movement together with coming to a complete standstill. For example any one of the games that involve running and then having to stand as still as a statue. There are any number of good stalking games that involve moments of stillness (tension) and running (release) in a controlled and conscious way.
- Play listening games. For example "...listen to a noise far, far away, now a little closer, now in the room, now as close to you as possible." For older children: "Now keeping hold of the very close noise can you hear the faraway sound at the same time?"
- The soliloquy strategy. Many children who have attention issues also can be overly defiant when directly confronted. Try this. Quietly, within the hearing of the child, talk out loud to yourself about your reactions to their defiant behavior

and what consequences you are considering if it continues. Remember you are not talking to them but about the situation. This gives both the teacher and the student a valuable pause before a potentially negative conflict.
- Play various noticing games. For example, the children form two concentric circles. The group on the inside turns to face a partner on the outside. They have to look very carefully at every detail about their partner. They then close their eyes while the partner on the outside changes something about their appearance, let's say puts a ring on a different finger. The inside circle now all open their eyes and have to find what it was their partner has changed.

Learning, Organizing / Ego

What do I see?
- Seems spacey or disoriented
- Uses distracting techniques to avoid being on task
- Doesn't follow through on instructions and fails to finish work
- Resists work requiring sustained will
- Avoids dislikes and is reluctant to engage in work that requires sustained mental effort

What can I do?
- Break down longer assignments into smaller, manageable increments, providing a lot of structure, monitoring, and follow through.
- Teach students to self-monitor on-task behavior/work completion; and to set individual short-term goals to self-monitor.
- Frame the area of the board you want the children to pay attention to by having a curtain, veil, or shutter to cover unwanted board work.
- Teach externalized speech and actions. For example, ask the child to sing a song well known to her "inside her head." Next ask her to hum it quietly gaining in volume until she is singing out loud.
- A similar process can be achieved in movement by increasing a consciously carried-out gesture making it more and more visible until the child is making the motion in a large demonstrative way.
- Together with the student, design a simple self-monitoring card using a key goal such as "I paid good attention today." The child is reminded in the morning of her Key Goal. The teacher meets for one minute at the end of every day and the student gives herself a mark from 1 through 5. The teacher then gives his score in response to the written question. 1=Always, 2=Almost Always, 3=Sometimes, 4=Not Often, 5=Hardly Ever. The student sets her cumulative weekly target score of say 8 points, as this would mean really good behavior. An unacceptable score of say 12 is also set and a consequence for such negative behavior is agreed. After a set number of weeks a new goal is chosen and the system repeats itself.

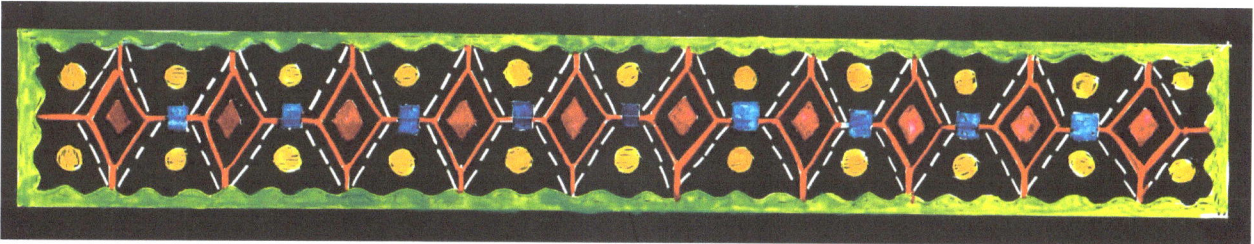

Cumulative Stress Reaction

Physical Body

What do I see?
Pictures of polarities
- He appears either disheveled or very neat.
- He is either awkward and hesitant in movements or very adept.
- He either stands tall and balanced or is slumped over and lax in form.
- Poor patterns of sleep reported: either restlessness and sleep-deprived or oversleeping and very difficult to wake up.
- Hypo- or under-aware of other children's space and hyper- over-aware of his own space
- Little awareness of proprioception. "…Where are my limbs in space and what are they doing?"

What can I do?
- Note, with a symbol on a calendar, the days when behavior is really bad; see if there is a pattern (often shows up on transition days of split household lifestyle). Bring this to the attention of other teachers or caregivers.
- Keep hygiene items in pouch for child and encourage their use for self-care and grooming.
- Use a lot of friendly, forewarned touch and movement to encourage relaxation. Avoid approaching him from behind or in a way that startles.
- Bach Flower Remedies could be considered: vervain for being high-strung and fixed, or beech for being stressed and critical. (Consult with your doctor first.)
- Warming foods such as oatmeal; also high protein.
- Warm clothing that can be tucked in and, if possible, woolen undergarments. Shoes that can be securely laced up
- Avoid situations of adrenalin arousal, increasing calming activities particularly at known points in the day of high complexity and stress.
- Teach him to notice his body tensions before he gets too tight.
- Teach him to take 10 deep cleansing breaths when he notices body tension.

Life, Habit / Vitality

What do I see?
- Listlessness, spaciness or hyper vigilance as seen in alertness to danger
- Large appetite, or small appetite (picky then indiscriminate)
- Need to use bathroom, drink, too often or not often enough
- Fixed routines, reacts habitually and/or chaotic habit life
- Startles at novelty and attends only to emotionally charged information

What can I do?
- Use gestures, close to the body and metaphoric, to focus student. For example, frame instructions by saying. "I am going to tell you to do three things. Number one (accompanied by gesture)." Or use the phrase, "Please look at me" or "Time to focus here."
- Allow her to use self-soothing actions (i.e., sitting on a cushion, holding a stone or crystal or stuffed animal…)
- Develop signals for drink and bathroom and anticipate her needs (be one step ahead, and subtle).
- Give previews of new situations. Foster and model delight in novelty.
- Predictability, predictability, predictability

Senses, Relationship Body

What do I see?
- He is vigilant but misses parts of the work; seems forgetful or sloppy.
- There seems to be a disconnect between the senses; seems to see but not hear.
- He is hypersensitive to touch but twists his own arm in a painful manner.
- He seems to crave something, like an attachment object, and without it, will display strange and out of proportion reactions to situations.

- Emotionally hair-triggered; very low tolerance for frustration
- Out of proportion explosion or implosion of anger/sullenness
- Low tolerance for others who he sees as different or "weird."
- Spreading the effects of negative events. Does not bracket/contain problems but lets them color everything even if many positive things have happened that day.
- He avoids spontaneous play and does not appreciate good humor. He scans others' laughter for possible threat.
- Formula: SSC + FP = ?
  High Social, Sensory Complexity
  + **Low** Form & Predictability
  = **Stress Response**

Do everything you can to create...
  Low Social Sensory Complexity
  + **High** Form and Predictability
  = **Safe Response**

What can I do?
- Develop a system with the student whereby you let the student know that he is "out the window." This alone helps him come back and focus on the task at hand.
- Forewarn the student that you are approaching, that something is going to happen, and use an even and soothing voice (the epitome of phlegma!).
- Keep visual and auditory input as much as possible on an even keel; forewarn and identify moments of chaos; tell student to watch you as these moments are not scary to you. (ha!)
- Invite him to try and see the world through different eyes, via stories, plays and creative projects.
- Appeal to his feeling life and introduce nuances of thought, feelings, and ethics.

- Listen to him with an open heart, calmly and patiently, without judgment.
- Tell stories and biographies of empathy and compassion.
- In socially complex situations such as playgrounds, increase form; even rehearse and later review, good, better, best response to usual trigger situations.

"I" / Learning and Organizing Body
What do I see?
- Confusion, frightened or blank expressions
- Withdrawal from the social milieu
- Rejects praise and consistently sees success as failure, an accident or not good enough
- Panics at deadlines, competition
- Low tolerance for new learning
- Cannot scan-read, multi-track, or maintain creative connection with material being learned
- Inability to make decisions and/or judgments, or inappropriate judgments
- Perseveres upon an action, or category of actions or content of thinking, as in scary or violent scenes.

What can I do?
- When appropriate, identify the persistent thoughts or behaviors and use direct and "quiet aside" language as in "forget the scene," similar to R. Steiner's approach with obsessive-compulsive disordered children.
- Bring the child into the social situation by assuring your presence.
- Work with healing-pedagogical stories.
- Increase structured cooperative learning strategies.
- Reduce any perceived competitive activities or give him a set role in the activity.

Sensory Overwhelm Issues

Physical Body

What do I see?
- Appears tight, rigid and hyper-vigilant in moments of high social input, particularly in the shoulders and abdomen
- Disturbances in activity level, floppy muscle tone and lack of motor coordination
- Random, goofy movements
- Very sensitive to being touched
- Very sensitive to "scratchy" clothing
- Banging into objects and other people
- Falling on the floor at seemingly random moments. However, looking closer, this usually occurs in moments of high sensory stimulation.
- Appears to go through exaggerated tension and release patterns where she is tight and tense, followed by being floppy and loose
- The life sense of well-being is affected, so the child feels she has to push back hard against a world that she feels is overwhelming her. This leads her to puff herself up and generally harden her face, trunk, and limbs or the opposite, getting floppy.

What can I do?
- Use a lot of friendly, forewarned firm touch and movement to encourage relaxation.
- Notice when she is tensing up or about to get floppy and give her a small movement task to do that relieves the tension without the usual explosion of movement or behavior.
- Excuse her, every hour or two and let her go to the swings and swing for a few minutes. When she returns, do some deep touch. For example, you may "polish her up" by rubbing her briskly or wrap her in a blanket, pretend she is a burrito, and roll her on the floor for a few moments. Or play "car wash" where the child crawls between your feet while you are standing, pretending you are the mechanism of a car wash.
- If things are improving, teach her to notice in her body which muscles tense up or get floppy when she is becoming frustrated. Develop a secret signal that she can give you to ask for permission to get up and move or to signal that she needs your help to work through a problem before it gets out of hand.
- Have the child sit on either a one-legged stool or a vestibular (wobble) cushion.
- Make a large lap-sized bean bag. If it's possible warm it up in a low heated oven and place it on her lap when you see early warning signs.
- Allow a child time to gather her thoughts. She will usually need more than typical processing time.
- Avoid chain-linked requests. Break your requests down into single directions.
- Bach Flower Remedies could be considered: vervain for being highly strung and fixed, or beech for being stressed and critical. (Consult a doctor first.)
- Consider allowing her to chew gum but only when she is feeling overwhelmed.
- Understand that her falling on the floor and bumping into things are attempts to secure herself in space.
- A Sensory Integration evaluation is very important.

Life, Habit

What do I see?
- He fails to learn from experience.
- He becomes easily upset when patterns or rules are changed.
- The Adult as a Part of the Self-Stimulating Loop: The high stimulation input, low-sensory absorption can be seen as the beginning of an addictive cycle. During stress arousal situations, hormones such as adrenaline, cortisol, and prolactin, are released. These "hormone hits" can become a sought-after effect whereby children will unconsciously provoke strong responses in order to achieve what has become a normal sensation that the survival instinct triggers. As adults we can become unwitting suppliers to this negative social/behavioral habit.
- Recovery from an outburst can take a much longer than typical time.

What can I do?

- Transparency: Children who have SI issues are often oppositional. They can go through times when they are nervous, stressed, and anxious. They are in a state of moderate or hyper-arousal for long periods of time. This leads them to choose between fight, flight, or freeze, with fight being most often used but the others applying as well. Predictability, rhythm and transparency of process are vital if the child is to relax, trust and feel safe enough to begin to allow other points of view into her life. Examine the aspects of life that could be simplified, made more rhythmical and predictable.
- He is often drawn to new people out of his well-developed intellectual curiosity, and although this is fine, it can quickly lead him to over stimulation. Therefore it is important to balance this by drawing him back to more predicable patterns and rhythms.
- Spend time being outdoors and connecting with nature every day.
- During transitions keep him close, give him a directed well-liked task (e.g., be the keeper of the jump rope), or draw him aside into a neutral sensory place and bring him back in once the other children have settled down.
- Avoid using the same area for different functions. For example eating in the play area or playing in the bedroom.

Senses, Relationship

What do I see?

- He may be over- or under-sensitive to sensory input.
- He will often be prone to unpredictable emotional reactivity, "hair triggers."
- He may show speech and language problems.
- He may seek revenge when angered.
- He can easily be targeted by peers and seen as annoying.
- He can often seek to emulate the behaviors of his least successful peers.
- He has a logic that revolves around denial of responsibility.

- He does not transition well; he can become confused, and can have quick flares of moods.
- He sees himself as often being singled out or picked on. It is not that he doesn't pick up social cues, for he may pick up way too much, leading to sensory overload. The paradox of this tendency is that he actually processes very little of the information. Think of a funnel with a very large opening but a tiny tube or spout, where lots comes in at the top but very little actually gets through. Because of this the child is led to high stimulation and high-risk situations.
- He will escalate arguments, seemingly unaware that he may be in a public place.

What can I do?

- Preview hot-spot social situations that are likely to result in the child/teen feeling overwhelmed and defiant. Rehearse "good," "better" and "best" response.
- Bracketing: Make a one-minute list at the end of every day of good and bad things. Help the child/teen see that the day did not consist of only bad and threatening things.

- Isolate him to avoid peer reinforcement and embarrassment: It is important not to speak to a child in a potentially escalating situation in front of others. This will only increase the sensory overwhelm and resulting fight or flight reaction. If the child or adolescent will not come with you to another room then ask the other children to please leave.
- Speak to his peers and coach them in how to best accommodate and deescalate.
- Allow him stay close to you. The loving presence of a trusted, reliable adult helps provide him with a "north star" by which he can navigate confusing sensory and social situations.
- Animal care on a regular rhythmical basis.
- Make a simple cozy corner tent out of heavy blankets and put a bean bag chair in it. This is good to use when he is showing early warning signs, but it is of particular use when he is very defensive or in a tantrum.
- Avoid talking, raised voices, or reasoning when he is in a tantrum. This may well prolong it. A soft soothing voice or even quietly singing will help.
- As soon as he gets over his tantrum, help him into a well-liked practical task.
- Defer evaluating with him until the next day when the strategies will feel less threatening.
- Make sure he has a safe, low-sensory-impact environment at break times. This will prevent a lot of problems from arising during less structured times.
- Recognize that a loud voice, unfocused play, decreased eye contact, falling are warning signs.

Learning, Organizing

What do I see?
- She will often have a very well-developed sense of intellectual curiosity.
- Poor self regulation
- She attempts to answer most questions with "I don't know."
- She will argue recklessly almost every point as if it is a life or death situation.

What can I do?
- Project work that provides opportunities for her highly developed research capacities helps create safety and challenge. It also helps her peers see her strengths.
- Stories that rehearse potentially stressful situations are helpful.
- Don't interrupt play that is going well, but stay close so that if the situation becomes confusing, you can help. However avoid "saving" him, but better help him problem-solve.
- You cannot win an argument with a child who has oppositional tendencies. Simply put, a child that is oppositional can become reckless, even outrageous while you have to be the responsible parent or teacher. If you abandon this role in the name of "showing her that you too can be powerful or insulting" then you abdicate your authority. Either way you lose.
- Processing/Sequencing: Seeing the sequence of events as they are objectively played out is not at all easy for a defiant child who is so often in a stress reaction pattern. Because she will tend to miss some key aspects in the buildup that led to a difficult situation, she can feel unjustly blamed. Look for the points that escalated the situation. Where could the people involved have "got off the escalator"? What could have been some different choices? And something that is often enjoyed, what could you have done that would have made it even worse? As the parent, teacher, and child become more practiced at this, the child can often begin to see the sequence of events more clearly.
- Play the "thinking out loud" game: This is particularly useful for younger children where you (the adult) speak your thoughts out loud, within earshot but not directly to the child, about your concerns and maybe three or four other ways the child could act.
- Self Monitoring: For the over-nine-year-old... If she is receiving SI treatment and improvement is happening, meet with the child (and parents if possible) and identify one target improvement in behavior, such as, "I will do what the teacher

asks the first time I am asked..." This is written down on a card and kept by the teacher. The teacher meets for one minute at the end of every day and the student gives herself a mark from 1 through 5. The teacher then gives his score in response to the written question. 1=Always, 2=Almost Always, 3=Sometimes, 4=Not Often, 5=Hardly Ever. The student sets her cumulative weekly target score of say 8 points as this would mean really good behavior. An unacceptable score of say 12 is also set and a consequence for such negative behavior is agreed. After a set number of weeks a new goal is chosen and the system repeats itself.

REFERENCES

Ayres, A. Jean. (2005). *Sensory integration and the child*. 25th anniversary edition. Torrance, CA: Western Psychological Services.

Hanschu, B., as cited by C Healy. (2003). *Neurochemical responses and sensory strategies.*

Kranowitz, Carol. (1998). *The out of sync child*, New York: TarcherPerigree, Random House.

Smith, Karen. (1999). "The impossible child: A new treatment offers hope for the undiagnosable," *Psychotherapy Networker*, www.psychotherapynetworker.org/magazine/article/880/the-impossible-child

Zaidel, Eran. (2002). "The parallel brain: The cognitive neuroscience of the corpus callosum," *Issues in Clinical and Cognitive Neuropsychology*. Cambridge, MA: MIT Press.

Non-Verbal Learning Disorder

Physical / Bodily

What do I see?
- Often low flaccid muscle tone and spastic-like movements
- Muscles of the face often lack definition of expression leading to a flat affect, except times when the student is acting a part, as in a play; then, expressions appears be gifted and sharply discerned.
- The senses of balance and self-in-movement (vestibular and proprioceptive) are immature, leading to clumsy, awkward and disorganized movements.

What can I do?
- Touch the student on the shoulder as a signal to attend to the following two interventions.
- Use identifying words for feelings or nuance as you are making the gesture. It's like "read my lips" as you smile, you point to your lips and say, "This, means I feel happy or content."
- Use large signals, as in American Sign Language, to signify such nuances as, "This is a joke or a twist on words," "This is serious," and so forth.
- Provide many small, repeated, predictable activities to stretch, lower the head below the waist, and practice movements that involve listening for the number of movements, as in tapping hands against the floor in a rhythm.

Life, Habit / Vitality

What do I see?
- Student appears pale, flushes quickly, and seems to become breathless or dizzy at moments of high social input.
- Student does not transition well, becomes confused; can have quick flares of moods.
- Student does not seem to have a "sense for time"; phrases such as "in a flash" or "quick as a wink" are not signifiers of a length of time.

What can I do?
- Direct the student to get up and get a drink of water (as in directing them to "assume stage left") just before the class breaks into a transition.
- Help student develop coping skills, such as stepping back, sitting down, and listening to the words being spoken while diffusing the sight. "Look out a window and listen to the words…," and so forth.
- Provide a verbal list of the schedule, have the student put stars or some symbol either where the schedule is changed or where she needs to use a coping skill to make the transition. (Icons do not always work.) Keep the schedule visible for the student (as a sideboard or a photocopied schedule which the student can alter using color indicators for change or transition. Use a line to indicate length of time as a visual picture.)

Senses, Relationship Body

What do I see?
- The eye and the hand seem disconnected, and the student is "sloppy" in grapho-motor skills.
- Student does not appear to empathize or understand nuance of social cues; is literal and not figurative in concept building.
- Student seems very attentive, watching, but does not follow what is being directed He will describe a game but not enter it—or will enter, stand, and describe, revealing confusion.

What can I do?
- Provide a liner page, workbook formats, form drawings they may trace.
- Point out concrete objects which portray figurative speech to create a bridge to metaphor or analogies: "Look at the columns on the front of this building; they stand straight and tall. Now you stand like the columns. See, numbers like to stand up like this, too, and they make columns… ." Look for straight lines and curved over and over again, to verbally describe movements in the world.
- Write out the rules of the game. Move figures about on a page or board as you talk the rules. Use the phrases "stop," "turn to the left," etc. Do not assume that a gesture is read appropriately.

"I" / Learning and Organizing Body

What do I see?
- Student can read, but doesn't have certain skills of story predicting or judgment of right or wrong actions taken by characters. Operational reading skills linked to pictures (for example, how to follow picture-based furniture assembly instructions) are better than narrative reading.
- Skills taught as lessons of "moral laws" or metaphors for human interactions (for example, the interaction of personified characters depicting the relationship of the number processes or the actions of the parts of speech) are often not processed and retained. The information was not concrete and they, consequently, missed the point.
- Use of temporal language indicators is often misinterpreted. Causative phrases such as "If you do this, then you will need to do…." Can become confusing.

What can I do?
- Discuss the nature of the reading ahead of time. Make the predicting statements more concrete. Ask the student, what words tell you that something may, or is going to happen? With younger students, use homophonemes such as in the Amelia Bedelia books and make the choice of what they are saying, concrete.
- Try to take the NLD students aside and tell them the link behind the metaphor and the law. For example, say, "When I say fractions are for sharing, I mean this…," and ask them to give you half of something. Then say how you feel because you enjoyed the sharing as it was fair or vice versa.
- Make causative phrases concrete. For example, "If I run through a stop sign, there will be a consequence, or a price to pay. I did not obey a law and I did something that is wrong. Numbers need to obey laws too, or they will do something wrong… ."

Opposition & Defiance

IDENTIFICATION & STRATEGIES

All children and teenagers challenge boundaries. It is a healthy way in which they further define their individuality and their place in the world by meeting loving, conscious boundaries and resistance. Key questions are: What is normal and what is not? In general the line is crossed when a child seems driven to defeat the adult at all costs. He will be relentless in attempting to prove adults wrong and try to defeat any attempt to exercise authority over him by greatly exaggerating any perceived weakness in the adult.

Here are some typical behaviors or attitudes that are oppositional.

Oppositional children or teenagers...

1. Live in a fantasy land in which they are able to defeat all adults.
2. Look at every situation as a win-lose proposition which they always win
3. Fail to learn from experience
4. Feel you must be fair to me regardless of how I treat you
5. Seek revenge when angered
6. Need to feel tough and hide their vulnerabilities
7. Believe that if they ignore you long enough you'll run out of moves
8. Believe themselves to be the equal of their parents and teachers
9. Can often seek to emulate the behaviors of their least successful peers
10. Attempt to answer most questions with "I don't know"
11. Have logic that revolves around denial of responsibility

In more extreme circumstances this problem is known as Opposition Defiance Disorder (ODD) and is described as a pattern of negativistic, hostile, and defiant behavior during which four or more of the following are often present. The time frames given below are approximate. The child or teen ...
(Has occurred at all during the last three months)
1. Is spiteful and vindictive
2. Blames others for his or her mistakes or misbehavior

(Occurs at least twice a week)
3. Is touchy or easily annoyed by others
4. Loses temper
5. Argues with adults
6. Actively defies or refuses to comply with adults' requests or rule

(Occurs at least four times per week)
7. Is angry and resentful
8. Deliberately annoys people

THINGS TO KNOW

Structure & Discipline

Consider flexible structure and discipline that subtly expand when things are going well and contract when things are not. This is particularly effective in working with oppositional tendencies. In terms of consistency if the child comments "... but last week I was allowed to...," then a simple and meaningful response is, "Yes, but last week we were enjoying ourselves and you were behaving very well. Now you are not." In *The Soul of Discipline* three distinct gestures are detailed: the Governor (close holding), the Gardener (moderate holding) and the Guide (close holding) (Payne 2016).

Transparency

Children who are oppositional are often nervous, stressed, and anxious. They are in a state of moderate or hyper-arousal for long periods of time. This leads them to choose between fight, flight, or freeze, with fight being most often used, but the others applying as well. Predictability, rhythm, and transparency of process are vital if the child is to relax, trust, and feel safe enough to begin to allow other points of view into her life. Examine the aspects of life that could be simplified, made more rhythmical and predictable.

Hyper-vigilance

Children who are very oppositional amplify many aspects of life, therefore seeing them as threatening. They often see themselves as being singled out or picked on. It is not that they don't pick up social cues; many pick up way too much, leading to sensory overload. The paradox of this tendency is that they actually process very little of the information. Think of it as a funnel with a very large opening but a tiny tube or spout, where lots comes in at the top but very little actually gets through. Because of this the child is led to high stimulation and high-risk situations in order to obtain what in reality is a small amount of integrated information. Another way to look at it is to think of someone eating processed food. They need to eat quite a lot of it in order to obtain even a small amount of nutrients the body needs.

The Adult as a Part of the Self-Stimulating Loop

The high-stimulation input, low-sensory-absorption can be seen as the beginning of an addictive cycle. During stress arousal situations hormones such as adrenaline, cortisol, and prolactin are released. These "hormone hits" can become a sought-after effect whereby children will unconsciously provoke strong responses in order to achieve what has become a normal sensation that the survival instinct triggers. As adults we can become unwitting suppliers to this negative social/behavioral habit. This usually happens when the child pushes us beyond what we can take and we go into our own fight-flight-freeze response. This is a primitive survival reaction, which, as mentioned, the child is already experiencing, then is fed further. We enter into a loop that can go on over long periods of time. You could see it as the children self-medicating. However, the effect is strongly anti-social and destructive.

Parents & Teachers Cannot Be Held Hostage

Often children who are defiant will threaten to do harm to property or to themselves if they do not get their way. In these situations it is important to take their threat seriously. Tell them you will call the appropriate authority or trained professional to help them if they go forward with their threat. This helps break the hostage syndrome, while ensuring the safety and accountability of the child. In essence it is a reality check.

Anger as Familiar Ground

Children and teenagers who are habitually defiant will often provoke adults into anger. They do this because other emotional responses are unfamiliar, even scary for them. One of the simplest yet most effective strategies employed is to answer every increasingly frustrated question with "I don't know." Two strategies are helpful: first, humor that has no trace of anger and, if that fails, deferment such as, "We are not going to talk about this right now because it will not get us anywhere other than a bad place where you will end up even more frustrated," or "We are not going to talk about this now as we will end up appearing weak or silly rather than responsible and strong," or even, "I am going to assume that if you say 'I don't know,' you mean 'maybe.'"

Allowing the Child to Be Miserable.

Breaking the cycle of provocation usually involves you as a parent or teacher giving yourself permission to allow the child to be miserable. For a teacher it usually involves open conversations with one's colleagues or administration but in particular with the parents. For example, if a child is habitually provocative and defiant, let her know that, sadly, you will withdraw every single privilege she has that is within your control, such as car or bus rides to places she wants to go, play dates, trips, new clothes, pocket money, or recess privileges. If the child says that she will do even more bad things, then thank her for giving you the opportunity to practice these things that you need to do but don't really want to do.

Insulate Them to Avoid Peer Reinforcement and Embarrassment

It is important not to speak to a child in a potentially escalating situation in front of others. If the child or adolescent will not come with you to another room then ask the other children to please leave. Children and teens that are oppositional often have strong leadership capacity and a sense of pride that easily leads to embarrassment and defiance if publicly challenged.

Give Clear Messages about Negative Behaviors and Their Costs

From a simple reinforcement perspective, it is good for any negative behaviors to cost more than they are worth. These costs are best explained in advance when possible.

You Cannot Beat an Oppositional Child/Teen in an Argument

Simply put, a teen that is oppositional can become reckless, even outrageous, while you have to be the responsible parent or teacher. If you abandon this role in the name of "showing her that you too can be powerful or insulting," then you abdicate your authority. Either way you lose.

Defer and Deflect

Don't try to "have it out" with a teen in an oppositional outburst. Let him know that the matter will be taken further but at a time of your choosing.

What Impact Is This Behavior Having on His Life?

Unless a child or teen can see that his behavior is negatively affecting his life, why should he change? Although he may not admit as much, he may well listen as you run through some of the negative results of his behavior.

Offer Replacement Behaviors and Thoughts

As a step along the way, encourage the child or teen to be behaviorally "bilingual." They can be more open with their opinions when with their friends, but when they are with adults, they will significantly benefit from being restrained. "I understand, but that's not one of your choices." Children struggling with defiance need help to know what is within their range of choices and what is not.

Admire Their Attempts to Be Strong

Oppositional children or teens view themselves as fighting for their rights. The main mistake they make is to see boundaries as contravening their rights. By looking beyond their words and appreciating the fact that they can stand up for themselves, you can show that you are someone who may understand.

Processing / Sequencing

Seeing the sequence of events as they are objectively played out is not at all easy for a defiant child who is so often in a stress reaction pattern. Because they tend to miss some key aspects in the buildup that led to a difficult situation they can feel unjustly blamed. A few things to consider...

1. Listen carefully to their perception and have them sketch out a cartoon-like sequence of well-spaced boxes as they describe the situation. If they do not want to draw then do it yourself. Even simple stick figures will do.
2. In the spaces between the boxes add you own pictures using a different color. If she disputes your view agree to disagree if necessary. If she seems open to going further you might try...
3. Look for the points that escalated the situation. Where could the people involved have "got off the escalator"? What could have been some different choices? And something that is often enjoyed, what could you have done that would have made it even worse?

As the parent, teacher, and child become more practiced at this, the child can often begin to see the sequence of events more clearly.

Set Clear and Firm Non-Conflicting Goals

Ensure that the goals are understood. If asked, give a straightforward and brief explanation, not justifications for what you are asking. A good explanation usually contains...

- ~ The effect this behavior will have on others
- ~ The consequences if directions are not followed
- ~ One or two replacement behaviors or other choices that will help her be more successful

Play the "Thinking Out Loud" Game

This is particularly useful for younger children where you (the adult) speak your thoughts out loud, within earshot but not directly to the child, about your concerns and maybe three or four other ways the child could act.

In trying to talk to a child who is regularly defiant here are ten key points to communications:

1. It's not really possible to defeat all adults.
2. It's good to be optimistic. But use your optimism to plan how to win a game or do your work, not how to prove people are wrong.
3. If you fail to learn from experience, you'll go on getting into trouble.
4. Don't expect others to treat you fairly unless you treat them fairly. You are not the sole judge of fairness. Everybody has an opinion.
5. Revenge is not always the best option. Lots of people believe this but visit a prison and ask the prisoners if they feel this worked.
6. It's a mistake to believe nice people are weak. Ask a martial arts teacher.
7. When you use the tiniest flaw in what someone is saying to prove they are wrong, you only leave the impression that you are unwilling to consider others' opinions.
8. Few people believe children and adults are equal. They share the rights not to be harmed, but otherwise children need to get more experience in order to run their own lives and have it work out.
9. People who remain ignorant of their impact on others are doomed to live in a world in which they feel picked on.
10. If you believe parents and teachers will run out of moves, and if you ignore their attempts to use logic and reason, you are wrong. By ignoring them you invite them to use more drastic solutions.

WHEN TALKING FAILS

Some of the suggestions that are about to be made may seem behaviorist in their emphasis. However, this style of consequences for actions is simple and direct. It allows a child or teen to not get caught in complexity and to get fairly instant feedback for their behavior. These children tend to disassociate from their actions. By instituting systems like these, you lead the child or teen back to seeing what actions are acceptable and not. These are not the only approaches, but they are very helpful early steps in a situation that needs changing.

WARNING SYSTEMS

One-Two-Three System

An age-old way of warning:
One = Please stop; that was unacceptable.
Two = You are continuing to be out of line.
Three = Now there will be a consequence.

Red-Yellow-Green Light

Take a piece of paper. Fold it in three and tape the ends forming a three-dimensional triangle. Color each side either red, yellow, or green. Place the paper somewhere discreet yet clearly visible.
Green = Well done, appropriate.
Yellow = Not good, inappropriate; proceed with caution.
Red = Unacceptable; you have gone too far and will now have a consequence.

WHEN WARNINGS FAIL

Action-Oriented Interventions

Remember that most oppositional children or teens feel that if they ignore you for long enough, you will run out of moves and give up. So finding yourself having to engage, intervention is not at all uncommon.

GOALS AND ACHIEVEMENTS

Developing Perspective-Taking and Self-Monitoring

Children or teens who regularly are involved in behavioral difficulties often lack the ability to see things from different points of view. These children also need help to be able to see their own actions objectively without feeling that the adults are picking on them. A Goals and Achievements agreement is a simple daily way to develop these skills.

Who is it for?

These agreements have primarily been used for children who tease and bully. It is to help them know when they have crossed the line and when they have done well. However these agreements can also be effective for children who are targeted or for bystanders who support either the child bullying or perhaps the child being picked on.

How does it work? There are three steps.

ONE: The teacher and, if possible, the counselor meet with the parents to outline the process. It's important that the parents see that this is not blaming their child but instead designed to catch the child being good and help the child reflect when he has not done well.

TWO: The teacher, counselor, and parents meet with the child and listen to the child's perspective of what the problem may be. A positive statement is worked out, describing what the child will try to do to improve the situation. For example, if the child is central in a clique that is excluding others in the class, the sentence may be, "My goal is to consider the rest of the class and the teacher and to find the right time to speak up if I feel that something is not fair." This statement is written down on the Goals and Achievements Card. The card is explained to the child. The "How to score," "Where to write the scores" and "How to add my scores" is explained. It is an extremely simple process that children understand right away.

THREE: At the end of each day the teacher meets with the student; the scores are added up and compared to her target score. A very brief discussion is held about why the score is better or worse than the target. A plan is made to either "keep the good work going" or "how to do better tomorrow." A mark is made for that day on the graph provided on the back of the card.

Do we do this for every lesson through the day?

This depends on the nature of the problem and the commitment of the faculty. Some teachers feel that they will apply this only during morning lessons, recesses, and other times in the day when they can keep an eye on things. Other teachers will want to extend this to all lessons throughout the day, as they feel they have the support of the subject teachers and because often the problem often comes up in these times. What has proven important is to make sure that recess and after-school times are included, as these are sometimes the most socially challenging.

How does the card move from lesson to lesson?

The easiest way is for the child to carry it with him. It's best kept in a plastic sleeve. At the end of the lesson the child marks in his score and then gives it to the teacher. In order not to draw attention to this process, it is better if the child is last to leave the class. If the child starts to lose focus and forgets to give the card to the teacher, then he has 24 hours to find the teacher and get the card filled in. If it's not done by this time, a score of 4 is put in the box. If this is too much for the child to manage, then simplify the system so that the card is used only in the class teacher lessons. Once the child is in the habit of giving in the card at the end of the lesson, the system can be extended to include the whole day.

How long should we use this system?

At least one month. After the initial period you might have a break where you assess if the situation has improved so much that another round of using the card is not needed. What is common is that while the behavior may have improved in most areas, some times of the day remain problematic. The card can be reinstated targeting this time. If another round of using the card is needed, it is good if possible to shift the focus of the goal. For example, Samantha is now doing better, but she still struggles to accept other people's points of view. So her new goal might be, "I will do my best to try to listen when people say things I don't agree with and understand that they see things differently than I do."

For what age of children and teens is this appropriate?

Self-monitoring is woven into the fabric of a child's knowing who he is, who he is not, and who someone else is. This is the foundation of empathy and moral development. This slowly emerging quality of "I am" can be seen from the earliest years but comes more into focus only after the eighth or ninth year. This is when a system such as this can be implemented. Prior to this age, the gesture of goal setting and measurement can still be done, but it relies more heavily on the adult setting simple goals and sensitively reviewing them. With younger children the review is best done in the moment, such as, "I see that Jonathan shared those blocks so nicely with Sam."

Doesn't this wake up the child too early?

A child who doesn't know where her space ends and another child's begins is often already overly awake, nervous, and anxious. This has the effect of taking the child into "fight or flight," and sometimes "flock," in that she may create cliques to gain protection. Because the gesture of social and behavioral Inclusion, including Goals and Achievements agreements, is "no blame," a safe container is created that allows for the possibility of a child being able to be a part of changing her actions rather than fighting or retreating from suggestions of adults and classmates.

Isn't this behavior modification?

The system of affecting a child's behavior using reward and punishment has limited effectiveness, as it relies on the extrinsic judgments of adults. Rather than strengthening a child's ability to self-monitor, it can weaken it. While using the Goals and Achievements process still provides the reality check of the adult's observation, it calls first on the child to reflect on his behavior, therefore exercising the "muscles" of perspective-taking and empathy.

Why might this not work?

- Introducing too much too soon. Start small. You might be able to handle this for recess and the classes you personally teach.
- Lack of supervision and observation. Stay close. Make sure your judgments are based on real observations; otherwise the child senses a lack of authenticity and feel unfairly judged.
- Lack of conviction. Commitment is essential in this process. Initially this needs to come from the teacher and hopefully the parents. Once committed, insist that the agreements are kept. For example, the card must be checked briefly at the end of each day. It's the child's ticket to getting out of the classroom.
- Too busy, too many calls on your time. Isn't it so often the case that when one is drowning the life buoy floating nearby seems like another obstacle. After a set-up meeting of about 30 minutes, this system takes about two to three minutes a day and it's usually pleasant. If we really look at how much time we spend in semi-urgent, disciplinary mode with the child, it is often much more.

INDIVIDUAL TRANSITION AND PLAYGROUND PLAN

Supporting a student during the times of the day and subject areas that are problematic is very important not only for the children involved in the oppositional tension, but also for the rest of the class. This support is based on the principle of reducing Sensory and Social Complexity (SSC) and increasing Form and Predictability (FP).

NEGATIVE OUTCOME:

SSC + ↑   FP = ↓   STRESS REACTION

POSITIVE OUTCOME:

SSC + ↓   FP = ↑   SAFE REACTION

These are two ways to anticipate and reduce the possibility of a stress reaction.

Transition Support

This is a simple-to-implement plan that involves...

1. Meet with the student you know has a tough time transitioning and explore the times of the day that are hard for him. Times like going to lockers or cubbies, bathroom or drink breaks, moving from class to class are common problematic times. Involving the student in this way gives him a feeling of warmth and inclusion.
2. Ask the student for his ideas about how the transition could be made easier, less busy and less likely to lead to problems.
3. Add your own ideas and then give an overview of the plan. Be as grounded and specific as

possible. Work out when to start and how the plan will work practically for you and the student. Make it simple to remember and doable.

A good plan usually involves one or more of the following strategies…
- *Keeping Close.* The teacher staying within two to five feet of the student during the transition.
- *Alternative Task.* An alternative quiet and focused task being given to the student during the transition. Something that is enjoyable and helpful.
- *Altering the Timing.* The student making the transition either before or after the larger group.
- *Transition Buddy.* This involves one or two students who cope very well with transitions being asked to be transition buddies. They can provide a kind of cloak for a student in need of support. This has an advantage of being subtle, still fun, and yet models what is needed to navigate a transition. This works well for bathroom visits which can be a real trouble spot.
- *Preview.* Most importantly, the key to a transition plan is briefly previewing the transition and the student's plan before any movement takes place. This need not be a long, drawn-out chat, but just a few words or even a pre-arranged signal.
- *Celebrate.* Be sure to catch the student at being good when things go well and compliment him.

Playground Support

This plan is based on giving the right amount of space and autonomy to a student so she can be supported and coached to navigate recess and feel successful, rather than "always getting into trouble." While the area a child has to play in is limited, it increases the support.

Why Is Playground Support Needed?

Fringe Dwellers. Traditionally students who tend to need the most support during recess are just the ones who move around the periphery of the playground or recess spaces and receive the least support and interaction with the playground supervisors.

Getting Out Their Energy. Letting children run freely at recess is a great thing… if they can cope with it. Sometimes in the name of "getting their energy out," the student who has problems with self-monitoring in the first place gets more and more out of control and wild.

The Badlands. Many children who might be less assertive or concerned about their safety during recess tend to avoid going out into the "badlands, where there be dragons." They tend to cluster near the areas most frequented by the supervisors or close to the school building and doorways. The problem with feeling that the playground is a place to survive rather than to enjoy is that their understandable concerns can become escalated into daily anxieties. Also, the whole idea of the playground being a place to "run around," may be true for only a minority of the fringe-dwelling, socially less able kids.

The Control – Rejection Cycle. Most experienced teachers would tell us that children who struggle with social issues on the playground are drawn to games that they feel they can control. These are often situations involving children who play in more of a low key or cooperative way that does not seem to have one dominant player. The child can see this as a leaderless game and move into a role that the other players do not like or want. Controversy ensues, and the game either dissolves or the child is rejected. This pattern repeats itself as the child drifts from one game or play situation to another and can result in the child's feeling intense and broad-based rejection.

The Outside In Playground

The solution to this dynamic is simple: Bring the kids in from the edges of the playground into the center where they can get informal coaching and support to play in a healthy way. This opens up the playground for the majority of children to repopulate the playground because now it is safe to do so. By doing this, a subtle but huge shift takes place in the playground culture. Here is a well-tried and tested way to support children who need help to play in a helpful and safe way.

CHECK IN AND PLAN

Moderate Supervision (Check in-and-Go)

This is a simple system where a child reports to the duty or class teacher at the beginning of every recess and lets the teacher know where she will be playing. It needs to be one specific game or area, and the child may not leave that area without checking back in. The teacher may see that what the child is suggesting is fine or perhaps that it needs some adapting. Now the teacher does not have to follow the child all over the playground mediating in each social controversy that arises, as she may play only in the designated area agreed upon. It also means that the child can get the support and coaching she needs to have a happier recess.

1. Meet with the child in need of support and let her know or remind her about the check-in process.
2. Listen to the child's plan about where she will be playing.
3. Very briefly speak to the child about any potential problems she might encounter and what her plan will be to work them out.
4. Tell the child that this is the only place she may play and that, if she wishes to change games or places, she must check back in.
5. Make a point of visiting that area often and supporting the child if needed. Added support can be given by assigning a couple of older students to act as "Game Helpers." This kind of student citizenship is a wonderful thing to cultivate and further creates a healthy and safe playground.

It is important that the child know that he or she will be doing this check-in before every recess until the play is going well. It should be at least for a week and can last as long as three to four weeks. One or two days on this plan are not usually enough to shift old ingrained habits.

Problems involving shared times and spaces need a shared response.

This simple plan can be one of the single most effective ways to support a healthy playground culture. Countless numbers of teachers have been very surprised at the positive changes at recess. However, the level of success of this plan will be in direct relationship to the involvement of all adults in the school, particularly playground supervisors. It requires broad "buy-in" and coordination from the playground supervisors and teachers. Although our schools are for academic achievement, they also stand for social learning, and the playground is just as much a learning environment as a classroom.

Close Supervision (Check in-and-Stay)

If improvements in the student's behavior during recess and transitions from implementing the Moderate Plan, we now consider the Close Supervision Plan. The aim here is not to punish but to bring the needed increase in form and decrease in complexity that may be continuing to trigger the difficulty.

We have come from *Moderate.* Check in-and-Go

NEGATIVE OUTCOME:

SSC + ↑   FP = ↓   STRESS REACTION

POSITIVE OUTCOME:

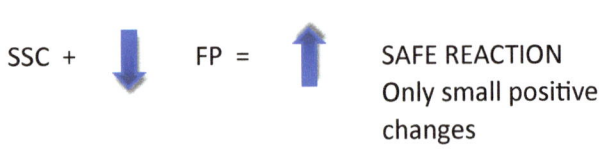

SSC + ↓   FP = ↑   SAFE REACTION
Only small positive changes

We want to create via: *Close.* Check in-and-Stay

NEGATIVE OUTCOME:

SSC + ↑   FP = ↓   STRESS REACTION

POSITIVE OUTCOME:

SSC + ↓   FP = ↑   SAFE REACTION

Process

The process of developing the plan is similar to the previous Moderate Plan, but now there is an emphasis on working out why certain areas of the building and playground and times of the day remain a problem.

Playground

Now the child is informed that his play area will be restricted to a clearly designated place. This space is usually a small area that is easily supervised, but it is important to have activities that are of interest for the student that happen in the area. The child must report to the duty teacher and be reminded of his Recess Goal before being allowed to begin recess. He is then directed to the designated play area.

Transitions

In a similar way, the child is now given a significantly more directed way to move through transitions. He must check in with the teacher and be reminded of his Transition Goal before making the transition. The teacher will hold the child back until there is a calmer moment in the traffic flow to make the transition and not allow the child out of sight. If the Transition Goal is not met, the child will be asked to redo the transition in that moment, or, if this would only inflame the situation, the child may be told that he will practice the transition in a quiet moment later in the day.

Support

It is often very helpful to involve older student helpers in the close supervision area of the playground. They do not need to over-focus and embarrass the child, but they can help with games in general and model good social problem-solving behavior.

Time Frame

The Close Supervision Plan stays in place until there has been a noticeable shift in behavior and then the child goes back on the Moderate (Check in-and-Go) Plan.

Level System

Be clear about what the usual rules are at the beginning. This is a system that is not meant to be applied briefly, but used over at least a month. Levels can go down only for a day. The level the child or teen begins with each day is a "new page." Review with him at the end of the day. If his behavior has been OK, then he starts the next day on level three, two if it was borderline, one if it was highly oppositional.

    Level Three. All privileges are normal.
    Level Two. Privileges are cut in half, or even
        two-thirds, usually in a time sense.
    Level One. All privileges are withdrawn.
    If that doesn't work…

Pay-As-You-Go

This is a short-term intense intervention used for only two to three days at a time. It requires a lot of work from the adult. The day starts with the equivalent of level one: no privileges are allowed. For every half hour of acceptable behavior, a half hour of level three (full privileges) is given. If any oppositional behavior occurs, the clock goes back to zero and the half hour of no privileges begins again.

Children and teens who are oppositional are often bright, creative, and inventive, and this is to be admired and valued. Although you might not agree with many things they do, let them know that there are many things about them that you would never wish to change. When they present themselves in such a negative manner, often these attributes are submerged or manifest in the extreme. They fight the world with such vigor because they feel they will be overwhelmed if they do not. Therefore it is essential to let them know that they are valued and what they say and do, if expressed in appropriate ways, will be listened to. Above all they need to feel they can effect their environment in more ways than simply saying "no." Working toward achieving this, the children or teens will come to experience a broader range of response and a feeling of trust in the school and family in which they live.

This overview of oppositional children and teenagers is designed as a beginning point, in that it focuses on boundary-setting and intervention. Does this not intensify the feeling that they have to fight a crushing adult world? No; if these guidelines are followed in a consistent, transparent, and fair way, they can lead to feelings of being met and of security; the children and teens will experience that they do not have to fight for survival in an out-of-control world.

REFERENCES

Barkley, Russell. (1997). *Defiant children*, second edition. New York: Guilford Press.

Forehand, Rex and Long, Nicholas. (1996). *Parenting the strong-willed child*. Chicago: NTC Publishing Group.

Köhler, Henning. (2000). *Working with anxious, nervous and depressed children*. Chatham, NY: Waldorf Publications.

Koplewicz, Harold. (1997). *It's nobody's fault: New hope and help for difficult children and their parents*. New York: Random House.

Riley, Douglas. (1997). *The defiant child: A parent's guide to oppositional defiant disorder.* Lanham: MD, Rowman & Littlefield, Taylor Trade Publishing.

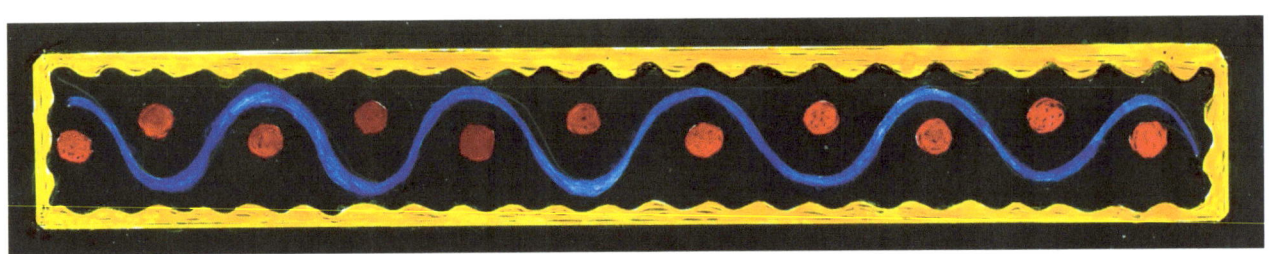

Imagination and memory
Rich or poor?

Arthur Auer

We must help children develop mental imaging (Vorstellen), feeling and willing." – Rudolf Steiner

A main task
Developing the capacity of mental imaging in children and ourselves as teachers

In 1919 Steiner presented teachers with a main task: "We must help children develop *Vorstellen*, mental imaging (often translated one-sidedly visually as 'mental picturing'), feeling and willing." In Waldorf education there is considerable emphasis on developing mental imaging, imag-ining, and imagination in children and teachers alike. "Teachers, imbue yourselves with the capacity of imagination (*Phantasiefähigkeit*)."[1]

In a later course, he identified six constitutional types of children of which two, a polarity, are called: "Imagination-poor" (*Phantasiearme*) and "imagination-rich" (*Phantasiereiche*). He pointed out that there are "all possible intermediate stages" between the two extremes.[2]

Stressing how important and valuable it is to observe and work with the capacity of imagination in children, Steiner advised teachers to pay particular attention to the related aspect of memory ability. "You notice [the two types] less through the actual unfolding of imagination (*Phantasie*) than through the development of memory (*Gedächtnis*). Memory is closely related to the activity of imagination."

According to Steiner, imagination-poor children "quickly forget the images (*Bilder*) of what they have experienced or heard, [and] cannot hold onto them; the images disappear easily…"

For imagination-rich children, "the images not only remain but acquire an independent power of their own; they keep coming up again and again, involuntarily, and cannot be controlled…Memory causes the images to surface in a changed form. Most frequently, however, the images surface unchanged as reminiscences so that the children become captives of what they have experienced." Such children are rich in images but also rich in a distracting and unhealthy pattern of imagining, mental imaging, and remembering. Would a better description and translation be "imagination-rich-captive"?

After characterizing the two types, Steiner gave seed-idea examples of ways to help children with these strong tendencies. Teachers are meant to creatively develop and expand these suggested activities.

Steiner's indications for imagination-poor children
(those who "do not easily bring up memory-images")

- Encourage these children to observe more during reading.
- Place greater emphasis on listening to what has been narrated.
- Do eurythmy consonant exercises with the arms and standing still.
- Consonants engender and call up mental images.
- Encourage imagination-poor children to play musical instruments.

Imagination and memory

- A wonderfully harmonizing effect can be produced... through the dual experiences of listening to music (instrumental) and making music. ...We can alternate one half playing and the other half listening
- Listening to music exerts a healing, therapeutic influence on what the head is supposed to do for the organism.

Steiner's indications for imagination-rich children
(those who are "liable to be bothered and tormented by their memory-images")

- Give greater consideration to consciously practicing coming-into-movement, for example, in writing.
- Cultivate painting. [Wet watercolor is moving, flowing.]
- Bring the whole body into motion through running and walking.
- Do frequent eurythmy exercises with vowels.
- Vocalization of vowels has a calming effect on rising mental images.
- Involve these children in singing.
- A wonderfully harmonizing effect can be produced... through the dual experiences of listening to music and making music. ...We can alternate one half singing and the other half listening.
- Singing has a healing influence upon what the body is supposed to do for the head.
- Listening to music exerts a healing, therapeutic influence on what the head is supposed to do for the organism.

The essence of all of Steiner's recommendations is, in his expression, to have them quite consciously "come-into-movement (*In-Bewegung-Kommen*)" to loosen fixed images that involuntarily keep surfacing and interfering with a healthy stream of mentally processing the world.

Insights
from Dr. Michaela Glöckler

In 1989, Pine Hill Waldorf School's doctor Tom Cowan and I attended the first groundbreaking International Kolisko Conference of Waldorf teachers and physicians and heard Dr. Michaela Glöckler's seminal lecture on the six constitutional types.[3] Here are some of her key points relating to imagination-rich and imagination-poor children:

> The human "I" lives in remembering and forgetting. There are people who are tormented by the fact that they cannot forget, and others who suffer because they can't remember. In both cases of suffering, they are deeply affected (*betroffen*) in the central core of their being, in their "I."
>
> Steiner indicates that in children who have an imbalance in either direction (imagination-poor or -rich), we are dealing with "a disturbance in the metamorphosis of the growth forces."

It is important to prepare young people for a developmental process which will enable growth forces, as they are released from the body, to be released in such a way that they can be taken up by the "I," and remembering and forgetting can be dealt with in as conscious a manner as possible. This capacity cannot develop if we merely let ourselves be carried along by the daily flow of events. We have to regularly practice... gaining an overview of what we have experienced, then consciously forgetting it again. This is an exercise of the will. Rudolf Steiner wants to draw our attention to the preparation for such possibilities when he describes imagination-rich and imagination-poor children.

With [these two types of children], our attention is focused on the content of consciousness—how the "I" deals with what the astral body brings to consciousness, what lives in sleeping and waking, what is present in the "I" as remembering and forgetting.

Remembering... is the awakening of an integrated group of mental images (Vorstellungskomplex). *Forgetting ...is the going to sleep of an integrated group of mental images.*
– Rudolf Steiner, *Foundations of Human Experience,* lecture 7 (p.133)

Dr. Glöckler went on to develop some of Steiner's indications in more detail and with practical examples:

On imagination-rich-captive

[The imaginative-rich child] is in a situation in which more growth forces have been freed up [for imaging] than the "I" can freely cope with. If the teacher has said something that is important to the imagination-rich child, it may be taken in by him, who then continues to think about it to the end of the lesson and is thus no longer open to anything else during that time... Instead of ...integration, we have manifestations of isolation and fixation. [The child]...has the tendency to have compulsive thoughts (*Zwangsgedanken*),...is unable to forget, and to let go of ideas and images."

Take subjects where "getting into motion" can be consciously practiced. Through [physical] movement [running, writing], something will start moving in the mind. Writing ... in a flowing hand allows thoughts to move, flow and get unstuck.

Singing can be of real help... for the whole body is permeated with vibrations of [one's] own activity, allowing the life of mental images (*Vorstellungsleben*) to flow freely again, without obstruction.

[In eurythmy] move with the whole body in threefold walking, in skipping, and in running. The vowel sounds have a special effect on these children, for the vowels live in the bloodstream and form the organs. When the children practice them while doing threefold walking... they have a calming effect on the mental images (*Vorstellungen*) arising too intrusively from the organism. They stimulate the growth forces to develop the organs, and anchor the forces there, so that they cannot so easily be freed up. In his *Curative Eurythmy Course* (CW315) (1981), Steiner describes how the vowels stimulate self-becoming (*Verselbstung*), the consolidation of the development of forms.

On imagination-poor

What a teacher presents does indeed reach the child, but lands deep in the body.

Help an imagination-poor child to learn to make use of his senses. For through the activity of the senses, his thought life can be firmed up into ideas and images which can be recalled.

On these points, she provides examples:
Have the children watch while someone is painting, or observe carefully or listen attentively.

[In] instrumental music, precise listening is required. Steiner encourages having the children sing and play instrumental music in the same lesson, so that making music and listening to music can alternate. In this way, the children have a hygienic effect on each other, even though imagination-rich children are supposed to make music and the imagination-poor to listen.

For [such children] it is good to practice consonants, mostly while standing. Consonants help to dissolve fixed forms, to counteract deformations—they "de-self" (*entselbsten*). They have the effect of loosening up the spiritual forces (*Geistige*) from the metabolic/limb system. They bring the organs into a situation such that rigid forms are loosened up, allowing them to get accustomed to new possibilities of form and to change in a healthier direction, with the growth forces more easily freed up for thinking.

Dr. Glöckler relates an account of a high school student who sat for hours every afternoon trying to do his homework. He had great difficulty remembering what had been covered in the lesson that morning. In drama rehearsals, standing and doing consonants over an extended period unleashed his ability to complete his main lesson book.

An educator has to observe life more deeply, if she is to be able to appropriately and fruitfully meet the needs of the growing child.
— Rudolf Steiner, *Practical Advice to Teachers*, Lecture 6

Teachers and anthroposophic doctors have taken Steiner's and Glöckler's indications further and added descriptive language and expressions for symptoms:

Imagination-rich children are dealing with an overproduction of untransformed images and thought processes that become too body-bound. The "I" cannot bring the thoughts under control. Such children have difficulty forgetting events, especially those connected to trauma, and can be fearful. They can't get rid of thoughts that press themselves too strongly into the organism. In school such children may fix on one image midstream in a story and can't move along to subsequent ones. They also cannot easily attend to details. The digestive process is too strong; the middle system needs to be strengthened and activated by exercises that improve the breathing process.

The indications and insights above are guiding thoughts and seed-ideas for class teachers to explore, try out, and inventively modify when they identify children who need help. They also set teachers on the path to discovering new activities. Furthermore, Steiner's discussion of extreme cases opens up a whole research area that is applicable and of benefit to the whole class:

- How developed are the capacities of imagination and memory of individual children and teachers?
- How do we observe the unfolding of these capacities?
- How can we strengthen in a healthy, balanced way these related capacities in our students and in ourselves?

Activities

Observe how children are re-*membering* and inwardly *imag*-ining

Observe the body language of a student engaged (or not) in listening and attending to a story: Are the eyes opened wider? Is the jaw dropped? and so on. When a story or scene grips a child, a teacher may see her suddenly sit up and lean forward as warm interest stirs the blood that in turn actually takes hold of muscles and posture.

In lesson recall/review/discussion the next day, notice how vigorously (or poorly) individual students speak to elements of a story/presentation. This can be a strong indication of the strength or weakness of the children's mental imaging engagement with the new material. The quality of voice and expression and body language may tell us the extent to which they are inwardly reliving the event. Do they particularly describe visual aspects, colors, actions, warm/cold or rough/smooth, scents, and so forth?

How do the children draw or paint images and how absorbed are they in the process? How do they inventively and energetically work on projects individually or in groups, e.g., making a diorama?

How absorbed do they become in reading books, and are they able to enthusiastically share plots? Do they lose themselves in a world of imagination? Do they recount what they read in a lively way?

How do the children play at recess? Do they engage in imaginative play and act out roles? How do they build forts and sandbox forms in the play areas? How do they model images in clay (kinesthetic imagination)?

Watch for those who easily catch onto melodies and harmonies and can improvise (musical/auditory imagination).

Some children have a way with words that is not necessarily intellectual or attached to visual pictures but is poetic. Words are inspired into and through them and take wing (word imagination).

Ways to build memory and strengthen mental imaging in children

Project feelings of enthusiasm and high interest-forces toward imagination-poor children. A teacher's astral body works on a child's etheric body, the sculpting force for image-formation and the repository of memory. (pedagogical law) Feelings are naturally attached to images and images to feelings. "We accompany feeling content with... mental image content (*Vorstellungsinhalt*),"[4] or as neuroscientist Dimasio has found: "It is feeling that accompanies the making of any kind of image—visual, auditory, tactile, visceral—within our organisms. The feeling marks those images as ours..."[5]

Know and be into your subject material so that students are drawn into an imagination space between you and them, as opposed to reaching out and loudly grabbing their attention as do storytellers on television.

In class presentations and activities, find exciting ways to strongly catch the attention of memory-poor individuals and involve them in special, active ways. For example, ask a child to come up and help with the steps of a demonstration. The next day call on her to describe what she helped do and ask about its significance.

Dramatize stories and descriptions daily to stimulate students to imagine and experience a variety of scenarios. For example, Steiner suggested that we tell fairy tales so that they "evoke a kind of silent thrilled awe (within limits, not sensationally) and in a way that evokes pleasure and sorrows that continue to echo...."[6] He also recommended that, in the telling, we "chisel our consonants," the alphabet sounds that most call up in imagery the form structure of things around us.

Use a variety of multisensory imagery to create vivid "ah-ha" or "wow" moments and experiences—not only visual (with colors) and auditory images but also actions (kinesthetic), warm/cold or rough/smooth qualities, scents, tastes, discomfort/well-being; sense of space/place and time; sense of other beings, and so forth. In animal studies, for example, stimulate fourth graders not only to visualize or picture the account of a shimmering octopus, but also to feel its slimy skin (touch) in the cool salty water (temperature and taste) and the roughness of rocks (touch) around it (sensory for imagination-poor).

Encourage imagination-poor children to engage fully and carefully in the sensory, hands-on procedures of all the arts: making their own main lesson books, shaping forms and applying colors in painting and drawing, direct tactile shaping of clay images in modeling (not using tools), systematic use of tools in transforming wood in woodworking, spatial movement and balance in eurythmy and gymnastics, imaginative gesture-oriented acting in drama, and so forth.

Have memory-poor children particularly in mind when you conduct the next day's review and have them regularly recall. The Waldorf practice of repetition and focusing on the same subject for weeks.

Strengthen memory forces. Strengthen your own imagination and memory. (see "Imbue Yourself with the Power of Imagination")

Focus on modeling, the balancer: Mind sculptures and hand sculptures

We mold images with our minds. We mold images with our hands. As neurologist Frank Wilson asks in his book, *The Hand*, who is to say where the brain ends and the hand begins?[7] In correspondence with him, he made me aware of the management consultancy of John Ward who has business people kinesthetically model in clay new ideas for their company's future—new business models!

The hands come into motion and explore and think forms. The primal activity of image-modeling externalizes and makes visible in physical matter what the "I" as mental sculptor does in shaping the mind sculptures we variously call concepts, ideas, mental pictures, and so forth. Hand sculptures work back and become mind-sculptures and vice versa.

Modeling images in clay is an excellent balancer for all children, including the healthily-imaginative, the imagination-rich-compulsive as well as the not-so-imaginative and imagination-memory-poor.

For the Imaginative-rich child, modeling takes hold of the source of an overabundance of metabolic forces shooting into repetitive, unhealthily-captivating imaging. Using metabolic-limb activity (the hands/arms), it stimulates and expends metabolic blood energy in a moving process of physically shaping images. It literally brings images into simultaneous physiological and mental circulation so that a child is able to become unstuck and can move on. Furthermore, the hands are not just part of what Steiner calls the metabolic-limb system. By virtue of their rhythmical shaping movement and their sphere of activity by the chest, they raise the activity up toward the interconnected middle, rhythmical heart/breathing system, the true human balancer. Steiner remarkably calls the hands the etheric eyes of the rhythmical system.[8]

When a child is modeling, breathing and circulation change and are harmonized—two important functions reaching up into head-brain-nerve system and its imaging function.

There are people who exclaim, "Oh [in modeling] you need so much imagination!" But the opposite is true; you get ideas in the process of working which you never had before. Powers of imagination are activated and unfold by themselves. The soft, formless clay is a willing helper in your effort."
– Michael Martin, educator and artist

For imagination-memory-poor children, modeling also reaches down deeply into the sleeping area of the metabolic growth forces into which "images disappear easily." Steiner also refers to imagination-poor children as being "more phlegmatic (*phlegmatischer*) in bringing their images back up."[9] Modeling is therefore very suitable for phlegmatic children, whose temperament and watery consciousness are very strongly seated in their etheric bodies and metabolic systems. Modeling, as the quintessential etheric art, homeopathically meets and calls on the forces of their life sense. Energetic exertion naturally adds "fire" to their "water."

In working with the wonderful resistance of clay, all students must call up these same metabolic-will forces in an ether-laden blood stream into the moving muscles of their image-shaping hands. In the creation space between their two active hands, they behold thought and memory images coming to life in concrete, tangible reality. The modeling process strengthens a circulation of metabolic processes "below" into and with conscious cognitive formations "above." Steiner's ideal method for teachers in general is to first help fully educate the

action-limb-will of the young child, as well as part of the feeling-rhythmical system, so that the head-brain-nerve system wakes up and matures naturally. This happens without the typical premature emphasis on filling the child's head with memorized knowledge.

Class teacher and sculptural researcher Hella Loewe describes the working together of metabolic-will with the cognitive maturity in a boy in her class. For him all tasks challenging imagination were extremely difficult. There were only three subjects he really enjoyed in the first years of school: the movement game class, painting, and modeling with clay. Up into the fourth grade, this boy had the opportunity to regularly engage in modeling with his class once a week in the winter months. In the following years this boy made good progress in his physical body and in soul and spirit. He was able to complete his high school education and graduate after twelve years. In summary we can say this child could not take hold of his cognitive faculties for a long time, a difficulty certainly related to the grave weakness in his metabolic processes.[10]

As a class teacher, Hella Loewe strongly experienced the therapeutic effect of modeling on this boy and many other children over the years and challenges educators and therapists to explore further its harmonizing, healing value, particularly for metabolic weaknesses:

- Is it possible that the activity of the inner organs, for example, the intestinal peristaltic, is beneficially stimulated through clay modeling experiences?
- Is it possible that development and improvement in the metabolic-limb system might be brought about by rhythmically impulse pushing, groping, and forming movements of the modeling process?[11]

From Loewe's descriptions, one can immediately detect how modeling works strongly on the four lower metabolic-will senses and helps bring about a healthy metamorphosis of the metabolic growth forces involved into the region of the four higher cognitive senses. Modeling, above all, is an activity of the etheric body and its seat in the life sense metamorphoses into the sense of thought. The movement sense transforms into the language sense; the balance/spatial sense, into listening skills; and the touch sense, into a social sense of interaction with other students. Body-based versatility and dexterity become the foundation for mental capacities and academic work.

Harvard professor of psychiatry John Ratey puts it, "Mounting evidence shows that movement is crucial to every other brain function, including memory, emotion, language, and learning ... our higher brain functions have evolved from movement and still depend on it."[12]

Steiner expressed it similarly: "The movements of the fingers are to a great extent the teachers of the elasticity of our thinking."[13]

The children

Further case examples from class teaching

Children when very young tend to be more imaginative and even eidetic, with photographic memories. They then tend to lose the vividness of these capacities as they mature and left-brained word-based intellect increases. Steiner therefore recommends that educators become even more imaginative with teenagers so that they develop and retain both language and imaginal capacities for life.

Children can be abundant in imagination but not necessarily caught in a chronic pattern of unhealthily, overly rich-captive remembering. Imaginative ones can tend, however, to be more vulnerable to strong age-inappropriate imagery and experiences. I know of one imaginative Waldorf graduate who avoids scary or violent films because images can persist into and disturb a night's sleep (but usually not more). Here are some examples of observations of generally visually imaginative and very sensitive, impressionable children.

Steiner's emphasis on the polarity of extremes helps us understand the full spectrum of possibilities of imagination/memory capacities in children. Most children are found in the intermediate range in between the two poles. Here are some interesting examples of in-betweens.

Three healthily-Imaginative children (Imagination-abundant but not compulsive)

H. is a dreamy, round-cheeked sanguine/phlegmatic whose eyes are bright and attentive when listening to a story. She is shy in recall and never wants to speak up on her own, so I do not press her in the first three grades. What she is inwardly imaging pours out into her beautiful crayon drawings and paintings with strong colors and forms. I know H. is a child with a rich imagination. Images from the classroom live out and persist healthily into her play out at recess and go home with her for a limited period.

J. is a stocky, red-headed choleric who listens to stories intensely. In first grade he was hesitant to speak up, and when he did, he retold parts of stories in a slow, halting way. I knew, however, from the way he listened that stories, particularly action ones, went deep into him. Then one day at the beginning of second grade, he raised his hand to recall "St George and the Dragon." He started retelling with a new energy and did not stop until he had retold the entire story on his own. The class listened in awe and surprise. J. was intensely active in his wax crayon drawings depicting story images. He pressed down hard with his wax crayons and applied strong, choleric colors, reflecting the vividness and dramatic action of his imaginings.

A.: Before I took on my second first grade, kindergarten teachers warned me that the new group had an unusual number of soft-speaking voices. I confirmed this during our first class attempts at recalls of stories. Many children were reticent to speak up, and when they did, it was hard to maintain a flow because they could not hear each other very well. Fortunately, in this group there was A. who was always eager to contribute. I allowed her to retell large chunks of stories. She became a trendsetter and model for other children whose voices grew stronger in the second half of first grade and then in second grade, we were definitely in a take-off stage. A. had an excellent auditory memory and could recount stories word for word; I could tell from her body language and the lively, animated way her eyes lit up in retelling a story that images were rolling through her mind in sequence as she emotionally relived the story. She was also very absorbed in drawing and painting vivid pictures.

A memory-poor child

Steiner refers to imagination-poor children "who are more phlegmatic (*phlegmatischer*) in bringing their images back up, who less strongly bring their images up."[14] While not specific to children with just that temperament, it does seem characteristic of it in my general experience.

S. is a chubby, pink-cheeked phlegmatic boy who is shy and never wants to speak up in class. When called on, he blushes and has difficulty in recalling what he has experienced in a lesson. His drawings are immature and not very expressive. However, I do not have the impression that things are going in one ear and out the other. Instead, lesson experiences are landing deep in his body. S. needs regular encouragement, but not extra educational support. Over the course of the early grades, he wakes up and becomes less sunk in himself as a regular course of the Waldorf curriculum and method have an effect: His hands and fingers move dexterously in regular modeling and on the recorder, he stomps strong rhythms on the floor, does weekly eurythmy, experiences repetitions of images and concepts, is regularly called on to contribute, and asked about what he has just read in reading groups. On a daily basis the artistic environment works on his senses and motor skills. S.'s father is a builder, and the strong sensory-practical world of his family helps S. to emerge as a more verbal, social, incarnated being.

A child captive of his own imaginative fictions

R. is a unhealthily imaginative child whose spontaneous imaginings interfere with his sense of truth and morality. He makes up stories and explanations to suit his advantage and to justify his behavior. He is captive and taken up in his own mental creations of the moment and does not realize that they have very little to do with the reality. R's imagination leads to kleptomania and stealing. When caught possessing a stolen article, he fabricates a story and believes it belongs to him. His mother is also unbalanced in her own way, defends him, and does nothing to help him control his troublesome fantasies. Before the faculty has enough time to help M. significantly, the family left the school. Steiner recommends pedagogical stories for kleptomania: Teachers "transplant [themselves] wholly into the particular case [they] are dealing with, and invent legends or tales in which things that are done by the child are shown to end in absurdity." Imagination homeopathically is to cure imagination!

The "electronic media machine-gunned" imaginative child: A cultural disorder

Imaginative children—and young children in general—are very vulnerable to having artificial light images electronically gunned into their brains and souls. Even if they are not unhealthily imaginative-compulsive, strong exposure to inappropriate electronic media imaging can make some of them so, as can other kinds of trauma. From my own experience and from the reports of other teachers, I have become familiar with many instances of children haunted by strong images that flash up and persist in their minds to the detriment of their full engagement in the real learning at hand. Effects can linger over days. How such experiences are

affecting them in their sleep processes one can only guess. In an attempt to purge themselves, such "possessed" children often compulsively disgorge the screen imagery to other children in a stream of verbal diarrhea. They are trying to excrete the artificially injected detritus out of their system. Typically conscientious parents of the children less exposed to such influences complain about the effects of "media-polluted children" in the Waldorf classroom. Working with individual families and in class meetings is the only cure for cutting down on unnecessary exposure. A most relevant classic on the mental effects of screen image watching is the study, *Four Arguments for the Elimination of Television* by Jerry Mander. For a homeopathic cure, watch https://www.youtube.com/watch?v=m3NBEurnIqY and a dozen or so related video presentations.

Imagination and memory supplement and depend on each other

In a profound article (which every teacher should study), Norwegian educator Jørgen Smit characterizes the elusive nature of imagination:

> A systematic, scientific description of imagining is already a self-contradiction. It can be compared to a pressed flower or a butterfly on a pin. For imagining is not so systematically conscious. It is not well-defined and ordered.

Its core is the overflowing life, the primal forest of surprises, and the wide-eyed wonder over unimaginably great realities, the warm enthusiasm and joy over becoming one with things. When imagination has been productive, we can look back upon it and discover some inherent order. We look back by remembering our observations.[15]

He also describes the "scale of ...forces of remembering and imagining" mixed in different types of personalities. He points out that these two opposite forces "supplement each other, much as inhaling and exhaling," one as an "organ of the past" and the other, "of the future." This becomes a valuable insight for teachers who aim at rhythmically balanced, breathing lessons of alternating contraction and expansion.

We always use imagination to help in remembering. Imagination helps both make our memories and recall our memories. Most importantly, imagining helps us fill the holes in our memory, for the memories must be whole if we are to hold onto them well. We color and form all of our memories with the power of our imagination...The power of imagination is like an emerging stream of blood that keeps alive our ability to remember. Without imagination, our memories die. And our imagination would be helpless without the ability to remember.... Without our memory's ability to hold continuity, the uncontrolled activities of imagining would be lost in bottomless chaos.[16]

Smit goes on to show how teachers can help students "to enliven imagination so that it grows and develops into 'exact imagining'"rather than random fantasizing and dreaming:

Every school day should have both of these elements: summarizing, clarifying exercises in remembering, during which the previous day's products are ordered, digested and understood; and a new effort, experiencing something new and foreign, always with the power of imagining.[17]

The importance of healthy feeling for healthy learning, imagination, and memory

Teachers and parents would do well to continually keep in mind that feeling is the carrier of a child's memories and imaginings.

It is our life of feelings—with its joys, pains, pleasures, displeasures, tensions, and relaxations—that is the actual vehicle for the enduring quality of ideas and mental images (*Vorstellungen*) that we can recall at a later stage. Our mental images change into stirrings of feeling, and it is these stirrings of feeling that we later perceive and that enable us then to remember.[18]

In the language of today's neuroscience, Antonio Dimasio describes how every image that occurs in us is accompanied by a reaction of emotion, even if subconscious.[19] That feeling then becomes the mechanism for the image to be recalled.

Waldorf educator Claus-Peter Röh takes the idea of the feeling life as a "vehicle" for memory further and describes how it is due to our astral or emotional body interacting with our etheric body:

Conscious memory arises to the extent to which the astral body, as the vehicle of consciousness, can newly experience, sense and read the imprints of the ether body. ...In the complex process of memory formation the first thing that happens is that the outer experience is imprinted in the etheric of the organs. The astral body's rich world of feeling that newly "senses and reads" the vivid impressions then becomes the actual vehicle of memory.[20]

A healthy process of remembering depends on healthy feeling experiences during the learning process. These impressions go deeply into multiple organs of the body, not just the brain. Dry, deadening memorization (unfeeling) is not real learning and undermines health over time.

Since the affective life of the child is so important for learning, Rudolf Steiner gave a great deal of practical advice on how to enhance memory and imagination (in addition to the advice at the beginning of this article): "Memory [of students] will be greatly strengthened if we put feeling into our words, if we teach with warmth, if we spice our lessons, allowing children to experience corresponding emotions, if we make them smile or feel sad, if we endeavor to go beyond the merely intellectual aspects to the life of feeling."[21]

To bring feeling into our words, we teachers not only have to have a connection to our students, but also an inner connection to our subject and know it by heart (not using notes in presenting). To do this, we need to have not only memorized but also penetrated a given topic with our own warm imagination permeated by warm interest—its images, questions, higher meanings, value for our children's soul development, and so forth.

Our relationship to the students and the subjects finally translates into the musicality and tone of our voice, the carrier of feeling.

ENDNOTES

1. R. Steiner. (1996). Lecture 2 of *Foundations of human experience* (*The study of man*).
2. R. Steiner. (1996). *Education for adolescents*. Lecture 4, June 15, 1921, Great Barrington, MA: SteinerBooks, pp.65–66.
3. Teachers would do well to study her full lecture published in *Developmental insights,* David Mitchell, ed., Chatham, NY: Waldorf Publications, 1997, pp.45–49.
4. R. Steiner, *Practical advice to teachers*, Lecture 2.
5. A. Dimasio. (1999). *The feeling of what happens*. New York: Harcourt.
6. R. Steiner. (2000). *Practical advice,* Lecture 1, p.15.
7. F.R. Wilson. (1999). *The Hand: How its use shapes the brain, language, and human culture,* New York: Knopf Doubleday.
8. R. Steiner. *Anthroposophie als Kosmosophie 2* (GA 208). 10/28/21, p.78.
9. Op. cit., Steiner, *Education for adolescents*, p.67.
10. H. Loewe. (2006). *Basic sculptural modeling*. Chatham, NY: Waldorf Publications, pp.92–93.
11. Ibid., p.93.
12. J. Ratey. (2002). *A user's guide to the brain*. New York: Vintage Books, p.148.
13. R. Steiner. (2001). *Mystery of the universe*, Lecture 9, p.121.
14. Op. cit., Steiner, *Education for adolescents*.
15. J. Smit. "Remembering and Imagining," *Research bulletin*, Autumn/Winter 2015, Vol. XX, Nr. 2, p.50.
16. Ibid., p.49.
17. Ibid., p.50.
18. R. Steiner. (1996). *Education for adolescents*, Lecture 1, June 12, 1921, p.18.
19. Op. cit., Dimasio, p.58.
20. C. Peter-Röh, "Anthroposophical aspects of memory formation," *Pedagogical section journal*, 2014 No.54, pp.12–13.
21. Op. cit., Steiner, *Education for adolescents*.

REFERENCES

Dimasio, A. (1999). *The feeling of what happens*. New York: Harcourt.

Loewe, H. (2006). *Basic sculptural modeling*. Chatham, NY: Waldorf Publications.

Mander, J. *Four arguments for the elimination of television*: https://www.youtube.com/watch?v=m3NBEurnIqY

Mitchell, D., ed. (1997). *Developmental insights*. Chatham, NY: Waldorf Publications.

Ratey, J. (2002). *A user's guide to the brain*. New York: Vintage Books.

Röh, C-P. (2014). "Anthroposophical aspects of memory formation," *Pedagogical Section Journal*, No. 54. Dornach, Switzerland.

Smit, Jørgen. "Remembering and imagining," *Research bulletin*, Autumn/Winter 2015, Vol. XX, No.2, pp.47-51. Wilton, NH: Research Institute for Waldorf Education.

Steiner, R. (1996). *Education for adolescents*. Great Barrington, MA: Anthroposophic Press.

⸺⸺. (1996). *Foundations of human experience*. Great Barrington, MA: Anthroposophic Press.

⸺⸺. (2001). *Mystery of the universe*. Forest Row, UK: Rudolf Steiner Press.

Ward, John. on kinesthetic clay modeling http://manyminds.com/

Sleep on it
The most important activity of the Waldorf school day

Arthur Auer

Morning is wiser than evening.
– Russian proverb

Sleep is such a regular and familiar activity that we can easily overlook its powerful presence and influence. When we examine it, however, sleep strikes us as mysterious. Picture us changing into special nightclothes. It is dark outside and we lie down on specially padded platforms. Many of us face heavenward with eyelids shut. In horizontal positions such as this, we spend roughly a third of every day—more when we are young or old, perhaps less in between—unconscious. Our breathing is altered, and we pass through rhythmic periods of rapid eye movement. The realm of sleep sits like an enormous, mostly unnoticed elephant in the room of our lives. It has a huge impact on everything we do in our waking hours. In Waldorf schools, which have taken sleep into account since their inception, sleep is more than just resting for the next day; it is a matrix of all learning and teaching.

Sleeping on it

At the heart of Waldorf school methods is the practice of "sleep learning," pursued by both teachers and students. In the evening, as a regular part of preparing the next day's lessons, teachers review their experiences of each of their students and how the lessons went that day. They then carry these reflections and their lesson preparation into sleep—they "sleep on them"—along with all sorts of questions and aspirations for doing well the next day.

Students also conduct reviews, but theirs occur—consciously, at least—during the day. As an integral part of every morning lesson, they recall and review, and may even discuss the previous day's lesson before proceeding to a new topic. Their experience of new material and activity and their anticipation of the next day's subject—stimulated by some words from the teacher—then follow them into sleep that night. They sleep on their impressions. The cycle begins anew the next morning, as they recapitulate and reawaken various aspects in conversation and in the creative activity of their cooperative learning communities.

A daily rhythm that includes recall, review, and discussion is not just a key feature of a Waldorf school method of teaching and learning. It is, in my mind, the most important event in a school day. Recall and review also constitute the most challenging parts of a lesson to orchestrate, sustain, and transform artistically, especially as students grow older.

Sleep learning as a powerful force in building intelligence

Modern sleep learning research received a real impetus in the early 1950s when Eugene Aserinsky, then a graduate student in physiology, electronically monitored his sleeping eight-year-old son, Armond. One night he detected percolating wave patterns, rapid eye movements (REM), and a neural state of alertness even though the boy was still sleeping. Aserinsky's subsequent findings and paper in the journal *Science* set off decades of research on what he called REM sleep (associated with Rapid Eye Movement), the arena in which dreams appear to occur. This mysterious state of "awake sleeping," with slow wave deep sleep (SWS), has been found to be a font of inspiration and inner development.

In spite of all the studies exploring how we sleep, scientists still have to admit half a century later that we do not really know why we sleep. New technologies, such as brain scans, MRIs, and EEGs, and ever more ingenious psycho-physiological experiments, nevertheless have brought this research into an exciting new phase and, perhaps, a new threshold of discovery. In the first eight years of the 21st century, a cascade of studies has been converging to build a remarkable picture of how sleep enhances learning. Numerous articles summarize findings with such themes as "Sleeping brain, learning brain," "Intellect thrives on sleep," "Practice with sleep makes perfect," and so on.

For a long time it was thought that sleep primarily enhanced "procedural memory," which allows us to do repetitive things such as knit or play the violin or keep a checkbook. Recent focus on the more elusive area of "declarative" or "informational" memory of such things as facts, vocabulary, and dates indicates that this second kind of memory is also aided by sleep and is similarly preprocessed through the part of the brain called the hippocampus. "Sleep after learning aids [declarative] memory recall," as one study expressed it.[1] The hippocampus is the part of the brain associated with short-term memories. The neocortex tunes in to the hippocampus's process and is associated with capacities to judge which short-term memories are useful for long-term memory, skills, capacities, and conscious thought.

Added to this growing picture of sleep-enhanced memory are studies on the highly unusual manner in which the hippocampus and neocortex process memories. Investigations show that these parts of the brain apparently replay memory data over and over again, recapitulating them in backward order.[2]

Several other studies have found that sleep enhances learning not just by providing more mental energy for memory, which makes obvious sense, but more significantly by giving the brain the "down time" to mysteriously sort out and consolidate the disparate memory data of a day's impressions and even to reconfigure them into bigger pictures. A state of sleep seems to be particularly favorable for brain plasticity, that is, for flexible reshaping of experiences. The new mental combinations that result are then utilized not only in more effective memory, but also in achieving spurts and breakthroughs in learning on the day after a night's processing—or even after naps, as well. In one study, for example, researchers posed mathematical problems in which hidden rules and shortcuts could be discovered. The research team concluded that "sleep inspires insight":

> Insight denotes a mental restructuring that leads to a sudden gain of explicit knowledge allowing qualitatively changed behavior. Anecdotal reports on scientific discovery suggest that pivotal insights can be gained through sleep. Sleep consolidates recent memories and, concomitantly, could allow insight by changing their representational structure. [In our study] we show a facilitating role of sleep in a process of insight. ...More than twice as many subjects gained insight into the hidden [mathematical] rule after sleep [than] after wakefulness, regardless of time of day. ...We conclude that sleep, by restructuring new memory representations, facilitates extraction of explicit knowledge and insightful behavior.[3]

Sleep thus enriches our minds and entails an activity that is creative, solves problems, and produces new mental syntheses of our inner and outer experiences.

Education as learning to sleep and to breathe properly

For more than two decades at the beginning of the 20th century, Rudolf Steiner carried out research on many different facets of sleep and found that this mysterious feature of human behavior is a key to education. The central goal of the method he created is to help children "learn to breathe and to sleep properly."[4] For Steiner, sleep is also a breathing—a "breathing out" of the soul at night and a "breathing in" of the soul each morning. The right educational practice can profoundly influence how children breathe on many levels— not just physically, but, more widely, with their senses and feelings and in their interactions with other human beings. Sleep can assist students as they grow older in learning how to more effectively process their daily experiences in sleep. For Steiner, proper rhythms in sleeping and breathing, and in a child's daily activities in general, are critical to healthy incarnation and development. Universal rhythms are nature's way of enabling the soul and spirit to gradually and organically grow into the life of the body, take hold of and fit into it. Education, above all, needs to have rhythm at its heart.

Of fundamental significance for learning, according to Steiner, is the ego's rhythm[5] from one waking day to the next, with the night's sleep in between. In this two-day rhythm he observed that what is experienced on the first day continues to vibrate in the soul at night. What is more, the soul goes over its experiences and "between falling asleep and waking, the human being actually experiences a kind of reversed repetition of what she or he carried out during the day."[6] This recapitulation, he found, has a balancing (*ausgleichend*) effect and helps in the digestion, consolidation, and remolding of experiences into essential learning. Steiner's description of reversed recapitulation accords with recent studies

of hippocampal and neocortical replay in the brain. In addition to this reversed recollection, according to Steiner, our day's experiences undergo other complicated transformations in sleep.[7] The human soul, he claims, traverses "three states" of unconsciousness[8] in which it works at learning and at making earthly experiences its own (*aneignen*):

> [Experiences] are transformed [into ability and wisdom] by being taken in their immediate form into our sleep each night. ... There the experiences ... are changed into essences. ... If one wants to master or coordinate a series of experiences in a single sphere of activity, it is necessary to transform these experiences in periods of sleep. For example, a thing is best learned by heart by learning it, sleeping on it, learning it again, sleeping on it again.[9]

What is experienced during the day is reviewed, sorted, and prioritized with the most valuable and essential elements metamorphosed into long-term capacities. Above all, through the three stages of sleep, the soul regularly replenishes its three essential forces—willing, feeling, and thinking— with a counterpart of cosmic willing, feeling, and thinking forces that can be tapped only in sleep.

Every night on going to sleep our souls take with them something from daily life. …[T]he fruit of our experiences … is transformed during sleep in such a way that it becomes our abilities and capacities. [For example], all our earlier efforts to shape the letters have been transformed [in sleep] into the capacity to write. … Forces higher than those available in our conscious life become available during sleep; experiences are transformed into faculties and the soul becomes more and more mature. … We bring out of sleep much more than we brought into it through our conscious experiences. During the day we use up forces by participating in what is going on around us. In the evening we feel fatigue because these forces are exhausted, and during sleep they are replenished. [Sleep] is therefore the source of innumerable forces we need for waking life. … [T]he [universal] forces which have streamed into [the soul] the whole night long … [are akin] to its own three inherent forces: Will … Feeling … Thinking.[10]

Sleep is the great shaper of experiences into learned capacities and the great harmonizer of thinking, feeling, and willing into a human balance. Taking this state of unconsciousness into account and working with it constitutes the heart of Steiner's method and curriculum. Children, according to Steiner, only gradually learn to bring a day's experiences effectively into sleep and then fruitfully back into waking life.

However, there is something else [besides breathing] that children cannot yet properly do, and we must address this in order to create harmony between two parts of the human being, between the temporal body and the spirit-soul. The other thing children cannot yet properly do at the beginning of their earthly existence … is to complete the transition between sleeping and waking in a way appropriate to human beings. At a superficial level we can, of course, say that children sleep quite well. They sleep much more than older people do. They even sleep into life. However, the child is not yet capable of the inner basis of sleeping and waking. Children experience all kinds of things in the physical plane. They use their limbs, they eat, drink and breathe. However, because they experience so much in the physical plane—what they see and hear, and what they do with their arms and legs— when they go from waking to sleeping, they cannot take everything they have experienced physically into the spiritual world, process it there, and then bring the results of this work back to the physical plane.

Children's sleep differs from the sleep of an adult. Normally, adults process their waking experiences during sleep. Children cannot yet carry their waking experiences into sleep. Thus, in sleep they settle into the general universal order without taking their physical experience into the universal order. Through proper education, we must bring children to the point that they can carry their experiences in the physical plane into what the soul-spirit does during sleep. As teachers, we cannot give children anything from the higher worlds. What human beings receive from the higher worlds comes to them during sleep. All we can do is use the time children spend in the physical plane to help them gradually become able to take what we do with them into the spiritual world. Then, what they carry in can flow back into the physical world as strength, strength they can bring from the spiritual world to become real human beings in physical existence.[11]

Up to school age, children's consciousness is relatively dreamy or sleepy and is still in a paradise-like unity with the world. Waking blends into sleep in a kind of natural continuum. Around the first dentition, children generally develop a new memory capacity that generates less dreamy mental images and begins to form and differentiate a deepening inner soul space. Around the ages of 9 or 10, this growing inner world reaches a point at which children feel acutely separate from the world. They see things more graphically and critically, and their mental pictures acquire sharper contours.

Because they are able to experience themselves as increasingly separate from the world during the day, they are increasingly able in sleep to differentiate and sort out the more vivid aftereffects of daytime experiences. This process is intensified by the fact that their soul body, though not emancipated until around age 14, is gestating and gradually forming basic powers of feeling and discernment that will ripen into the capacity for judgment in high school and adulthood. The incarnating soul body and ego play a growing role in sleep in sorting out, evaluating, and judging impressions of the day. This is reflected in brain development in that the hippocampus processes immediate experiences that the maturing neocortex then helps the soul to form into capacities of the human spirit.

> When a young child sleeps, its soul and spiritual members leave the physical sheaths, just as happens to a grownup person, and they reenter the body during the moment of waking. But in the case of the child there is as yet no great difference between the conscious experiences in the waking state and the unconscious experiences during sleep. Under normal conditions, that is, if no reminiscences of what happened during the day enter the child's world of sleep—and this hardly happens in childhood—the child's life of sleep moves about in spheres lying far beyond the earthly realm. It is from these higher worlds that the active forces are drawn which, during the waking state, work from the brain downward into the child's entire organism. During the second dentition, certain soul and spiritual forces in the child are released from working entirely in the organic sphere. They begin to assume an independent soul and spiritual character. Between the change of teeth and puberty, the child develops a freer thinking, feeling, and willing than was the case previously. No longer is it only an imitator, but through its natural feeling for authority, it develops the degree of consciousness necessary for it to make contact with the world. ... As a consequence, more and more experiences from the child's waking state will enter his (or her) soul and spiritual life also during sleep. And to the same extent to which earthly experiences enter his (or her) sleeping state, replacing those of the spiritual world, is the possibility given to us teachers to reach the child between the change of teeth and puberty through our educational endeavors.[12]

Pedagogical advice

Steiner gives helpful advice in several lectures on how to reach children in this gradual sleep learning process as it evolves from elementary through high school. The first step for teachers is simply to imbue themselves with an ever-expanding awareness of the significance of sleep: "A true teacher is concerned not only with the waking life but also with what takes place during sleep."[13]

> Further: The effectiveness of teaching comes from the thoughts the teacher has had during the entire time of his or her existence and brings into the classroom. A teacher concerned with developing human beings affects the

students quite differently from a teacher who never thinks about such ... thoughts ... as the cosmic meaning of the breathing process and its transformation through education, or the cosmic meaning of the rhythm between sleeping and waking.[14]

Second, with the mysteries of sleep in mind, teachers can benefit from engaging in continual observation, research, and practice that take the effects of teaching and sleep into account. Above all, according to Steiner, they need to notice how what they bring to the children on one day plays into the children's consciousness and seeks expression and engagement the next day.

> Let us assume ... that the children are listening to a story you tell them, or that they are looking at a picture you drew for them on the blackboard, or that they are looking at a diagram of an experiment, or that they are listening to a piece of music you play for them. ... [W]hat you are inserting into the children in a roundabout way through the physical [body]—be it through the eyes, the ears, or the comprehending intellect—everything that is thus placed into the children very soon assumes a quite different form of life. The children go home, they go to bed, they go to sleep. ... What you did with the children ... continues [outside their life and physical bodies and] in the soul body and the ego [which have lifted off into] a quite different environment. They experience something that can be experienced only during sleep, and everything you taught the children participates in the experience. The effects of the lesson that remain in the soul body and ego are part of the experience during sleep. ... The children will present to you on the following morning the results of what they experienced between falling asleep and waking.
>
> ... Everything that has been impressed on them continues during sleep to vibrate in them. Ego and soul body actually repeat—in the more intricate and spiritualized way peculiar to their nature—what they experienced. ... They repeat all of it. And what they thus experience during sleep, this the children take with them to school on the following day. The children incorporate the experience into their life and physical bodies, and we have to reckon with that. Considered in totality, the human being presents an extraordinarily complicated structure for us to come to terms with in our lessons.[15]

Having to reckon with and accomplish a positive influence on this day-to-day process becomes a teacher's primary intuitive quest. On the one hand, how are we to engage children in wholesome activities so that these experiences "vibrate" to good effect in sleep? On the other hand, how, on subsequent days, are we to "draw out" the insight and fruits of this consolidation and transformation to the benefit of each child? The effects of artistic activity are particularly illumined by Steiner's example of how eurythmy affects sleep:

> Let us consider a child who is doing eurythmy. The physical body is in movement, and the movements of the physical are transferred to the life body. ... [T]he activities of the physical and life bodies are impressed on [the astral body and ego]. Soul body and ego then separate during sleep and connect the impressions to spiritual forces that are quite different. On the following morning, soul body and ego return the impressions to the life and physical bodies. We can then see a remarkable harmony between that which was received from the spiritual world during sleep and what the life and physical bodies experienced during eurythmy. The effect shows itself in the way the sleep experiences adjust to what was prepared and carried out on the previous day. It is only in this complementing of the physical nature and life by the spiritual that we can see the special healing element of eurythmy. Indeed, spiritual substantiality is brought to the human being upon awakening in the morning after a day including eurythmy.[16]

Steiner describes the effects of geometry and form drawing similarly:

Geometry [including form drawing] … harmonizes with every part of the human being. … By virtue of its own inherent vibrational forces [our body of formative life forces] … has ever the tendency to bring to perfection and elaborate what has been brought to it. … During sleep [it] continues supersensibly to [vibrate and] calculate, continues all that it has received from arithmetic [geometry and form drawing]. … For example, we draw some figure on the blackboard … and indicate the beginning of a symmetrical line. Then we try to make the child realize that the figure is not complete and by every possible means to get the child to complete it out of himself. In this way we activate an inner active urge. … The child will wake in a life body—and a physical body also—inwardly and organically stirred into activity. He will be full of life and vitality. A true teacher is concerned not only with the waking life but also with what takes place during sleep. In this connection it is important to understand certain things that happen to us all now and again. For instance, we may have pondered over some problem in the evening without finding a solution. In the morning we have solved the problem. Why? Because the life body, the body of formative forces, has continued its independent activity during the night. In many respects waking life is not a perfecting, but a "disturbing" process. … What is to be striven for … is to assist the continued activity of the etheric body during sleep.[17]

Through form drawing, a child performs a process that her life body then continues to perform to greater perfection in sleep. Her life forces are challenged and healthily invigorated in a creative fashion. Here is another example from singing and making music:

When we let a child sing, the essential activity is that of the life body. The astral body must strongly adapt to this activity and [then take] it into the spiritual world. The soul body returns, and what it brings back again expresses itself in effective healing forces. We may say that in eurythmy we have a force that mainly affects the health of the child's physical body, while in singing a force expresses itself that mainly affects the child's mechanism of movement and, through movements, then again the health of the physical body. … [The children] take [the singing experience] into the spiritual world during sleep. On the following day we let them listen to music—we let them listen to rather than make music. What was done on the previous day is then consolidated in the listening to music—an extraordinary healing process. You can see that under ideal conditions —that is, a curriculum structured to adapt to the conditions of life—we can affect the children's health in an extraordinary way.[18]

Here, Steiner gives specific pedagogical advice on how to add a daytime counterpart to carry further sleep's consolidation of the experience of singing and music. He recommends that making music on one day be complemented by listening to music on the next. Performance experience comes first and then sensory discernment and reflection come next. This principle of reversal or inversion of outer action to inner experience can be applied to other activities as well.

Steiner gives further indications on how to reckon with the transformative effects of sleep on other subjects. In physics, for example, he advises that a teacher sequence two days of lessons so that a teenager's life processes are taken into account. He recommends that the teacher first make an experiment so engaging that

> the whole of the human being is occupied [and] is asked to make an effort. ... I then draw the children's attention away from the instruments I experimented with and repeat the various stages. Here I am appealing to their memory of the direct experience. During such a review or recapitulation—without the presence of the apparati, purely in the mind—the rhythmic system is especially enlivened. After having engrossed the whole of the human being, I now appeal to the rhythmic system, and to the head system, because the head naturally participates during recapitulation. The lesson can then be concluded ....dismiss the children. They go to bed and sleep. What I activated in the whole of their being, then in their rhythmic system, now during sleep continues to live in their limbs when soul body and ego are outside the physical body.
>
> Let us now regard what remains lying on the bed, what allows the content of the lesson to keep on working. Everything that has developed in the rhythmic system and the whole of the human being now streams upward into the head. Pictures of these experiences now form themselves in the head. And it is these pictures that the children find on waking up and going to school.
>
> ... When the children arrive at school on the following morning they have, without knowing it, pictures of the previous day's experiments in their heads, as well as pictures of what—in as imaginative a way as possible—I repeated, recapitulated after the experiment. ... And I shall now reflect on yesterday's lesson in a contemplative way. Yesterday I experimented, and in reviewing the experiment I then appealed to the children's imagination. In today's lesson I add the contemplative element. In doing so, I not only meet the pictures in the children's heads, but also help to bring the pictures into their consciousness.
>
> ... On the [second] day, we discuss the previous experiment, contemplate it, reflect on it. The children are to learn the inherent laws. The cognitive element, thinking, is now employed. ... If I were to immediately start with a new experiment, without first nourishing them with the cognitive, contemplative element, I would again occupy the whole of their being, and the effort they would have to make would stir up these pictures; I would create chaos in their heads. No, above all, what I must do first is consolidate what wishes to be there, provide nourishment. These sequences are important; they adapt to, are in tune with the life processes.[19]

By having students briefly recapitulate the experiment in their imaginations on the first day, a teacher helps students start a process of mental picturing and consolidation that will rhythmically and emotionally affect what happens in their sleep. According to Steiner, a student's experience of an experiment streams up at night from limbs and heart, from the whole body, into picture-forming in the head. The next morning, the teacher builds on the mental consolidation and metamorphoses of the night. Students bring their evolving mental pictures to consciousness in a review or discussion and take hold of them cognitively in words. New insights arise as students engage in contemplation of what they have experienced. They practice discernment in thinking and come to their own judgments and concepts. By coming back in this way to the same subject they have slept on, they anchor new knowledge and new capacities in their souls more firmly and organically. The progression here is from whole-body experience and action, through rhythm and repetition, to contemplation and concept development—from limbs to heart to head.

Such a sequence during the day mirrors aspects of what transpires in sleep itself—recapitulation, memory consolidation, and insight and concept formation. It has its reflection in the organic progression in the brain of the raw memory of experience being processed first in the hippocampus and then subjected to the faculty of judgment and conscious thinking focused in the neocortex. This meaningful sequence is nourishing to the mind and soul and avoids "creating chaos in [students'] heads." Before going on to a new experiment and experience, the soul wants to digest and come to terms with what it has been mulling over. A rhythm of action, contemplation, and new action is in keeping with life processes and vibrates healthily in the soul in sleep. This rhythmic learning and teaching, breathing and sleeping, is salutogenic, that is, health-producing. Steiner applied this salutogenic sequence also to the teaching of history.

> I give the children the mere facts that occur in space and time. The[ir] whole being is again addressed just as during a [physics] experiment, because the children are called upon to make for themselves a mental picture of space. We should see to it that they do this, that they see what we tell them, in their minds. They should also have a mental picture of the corresponding time. When I have brought this about, I shall try to add details about the people and events, not in a narrative way, but merely by characterization. I now describe and draw the children's attention to what they heard in the first part of the lesson. In the first part, I occupied their whole being; in the second, it is the rhythmic part of their being that must make an effort. I then dismiss them. When they return on the following day, they again have the spiritual photographs of the previous day's lesson in their heads. I connect today's lesson with them by a reflective, contemplative approach, for example, a discussion on whether Alcibiades or Mithridates was a decent or an immoral person. I shall allow the three parts of the threefold human being [willing, feeling, thinking] to interact, to harmonize.[20]

For Steiner, taking sleep and life processes into account goes beyond good school practice. It is key to enabling what is truly human to incarnate in each child through the balancing of thinking, feeling, and will. Working with sleep is critical to the healthy birth of human beings as free, creative individuals who are capable of independent thinking, heartfelt judgment, and morally responsible action:

> The examples I have given you will illustrate the path our teaching must take if it is to connect to life conditions, to life impulses, in a healthy way. We cannot be satisfied simply with mediating facts. ... We must see the human being in his or her totality, as a being who is also extremely active during sleep. ... [I]f we ignore the fact that the content of our lessons continues into sleep, develops further during sleep, we will have the quite definite effect of making the human being into a robot, an automaton. We could, indeed, venture to say that today's education is in many respects an education not toward humanness but toward the most obvious type of human automaton—namely, the bureaucrat. Our children are trained to become bureaucrats. Such people are no longer really human. They are fixed, they have an existence, they are finished. The human being is lost, is concealed behind the label. We have an appointment with an officer, be it a clerk or barrister, and it matters little who the actual person behind the label is.[21]

Lest we be overwhelmed by all the research, Steiner pointed out that the details of the sleep process are incredibly complicated and that a teacher cannot possibly know all that is transpiring, nor needs to, in order to teach and work fruitfully with the rhythms of sleep. Discoveries in neuroscience and other fields can confirm what teachers do out of pedagogical insight and instinct, but they cannot teach us how to teach. We can best do that through meditation and sleeping on how best to serve the children in our care. In addition to who we are ourselves as teachers and developing human beings, it is our deeper meditative efforts that make our method and curriculum work.

ENDNOTES

1. S. Gais and Lucas Born. (2006). *Sleep after learning aids memory recall*. www.learnmem.org/cgi/reprint/13/3/259.pdf. See also: N. Axmacher and others. (2007). "The role of sleep in declarative memory consolidation: Direct evidence by intracranial EEG," www.cercor.oxfordjournals.org/cgi/content/abstract/18/3/500.
2. See www.nytimes.com/2006/12/18/science/18memory.html. See also: D.J. & M. Wilson. (2007). "Coordinated memory replay in the visual cortex and hippocampus during sleep," *Nature Neuroscience* 10, pp.100–107, and www.nature.com/neuro/journal/v10/n1/suppinfo/nn1825_S1.html.
3. Wagner, Gais, Haider, Verleger and Born. (2006). *Sleep inspires insight* (2006), see www.nature.com/nature/journal/v427/n6972/abs/nature02223.html.
4. R. Steiner, *Foundations of human experience.* (1996). Great Barrington, MA: Anthroposophic Press. pp.40–44.
5. See M. Kranich (1992, p.23). Waldorf teachers work with four main rhythms: Waking up each day is an "ego rhythm," as is the "sun rhythm" of Waldorf school main lessons that happen day after day. The weekly rhythm of such subjects as painting and modeling can be experienced as a "soul rhythm," the monthly rhythm of block unit studies is a "life body" rhythm, and the annual rhythm of seasons and festivals is a "physical body rhythm."
6. R. Steiner, *Geistige Zusammenhänge in der Gestaltung des menschlichen Organismus*, CW 218, p.272, cited in S. Leber, 1996, pp.85–86.
7. Trying to gain insights into and a comprehensive overview of the sleep process was, for Steiner, "some of the hardest scientific investigations of the spirit." See *Esoterische Betrachtungen karmischer Zusammenhänge*, CW 236, p.258. Cited in Leber (1996, p.87).
8. Stefan Leber correlates Steiner's three conditions of sleep, as well as imagination, inspiration, and intuition, with the stages of sleep investigated by researchers today (REM, SWS, etc.). *Der Schlaf und seine Bedeutung: Geisteswissenschaftliche Dimensionen des Un- und Überbewussten (Sleep and its meaning: Dimensions of un- and superconsciousness in the light of a science of the spirit)*. (1996). Freies Geistesleben. This study is an excellent source of most, if not all, of Steiner's findings on sleep in the light of modern research.
9. R. Steiner. (1983). *Metamorphoses of the soul*, p.59.
10. Steiner was ahead of his time in recognizing "multiple intelligences." In addition to thinking or head intelligence, he investigated heart or emotional intelligence, and will-developed or limb-based, hands-on intelligence. The Waldorf school method strives to balance and harmonize these three intelligences.
11. Op. cit., Steiner, *The foundations of human experience*, pp.41–42.
12. R. Steiner. (1986). *Soul economy and Waldorf education*, pp.223–224.
13. R. Steiner. (1972). *A modern art of education*, p.156.
14. Op. cit., Steiner, *The foundations of human experience*, p.43.
15. Steiner (1996). *Education for adolescents*, Great Barrington, MA: SteinerBooks, pp.46–48.
16. Ibid., p.48.
17. Op. cit., Steiner, *A modern art of education*, pp.154–157. In sleep the life body continues to vibrate with the experiences of a child's less-than-perfect efforts at what could be called "challenge drawings." It is stimulated to repeat, perfect, and harmonize them in a more ideal form in another dimension and thus exercise and strengthen its powers, powers that are also the basis of memory and health. Interestingly, as Robert Stickold, of Harvard Medical School, points out, "You learn things in pieces and then sleep smoothes them out." Steiner speaks of the "evening-out (*ausgleichende*)" effects of sleep. See http://www.revolutionhealth.com/conditions/sleep/sleep-basics/sleep-health/memory.
18. Op. cit., Steiner, *Education for adolescents*, pp.48–49.
19. Ibid., pp.50–51.
20. Ibid., pp.52–53.
21. Ibid., pp.57–58.

REFERENCES

Kranich, M. (1992). *Die Bedeutung des Rhythmus in der Erziehung (The meaning of rhythm in education)*, Stuttgart: Verlag Freies Geistesleben.

Leber, S. (1992). *Der Rhythmus von Schlafen und Wachen*, untranslated *(The rhythm of sleep and waking)*, Stuttgart: Freies Geistesleben.

_____. (1996). *Der Schlaf und seine Bedeutung: Geisteswissenschaftliche Dimensionen des Un- und Überbewussten*, untranslated *(Sleep and its meaning: Dimensions of un- and superconsciousness in the *light of a science of the spirit)*, Stuttgart: Freies Geistesleben.

Loebell, P. (1995). "Der schlaf als aufgabe der Waldorf-pädagogik," *Lehrerrundbrief* 53, Bund der Freien Waldorfschulen.

McAllen, A. (1986). *Sleep: An unobserved element in education*. Stroud, UK: Hawthorn Press.

Steiner, R. (1997). *Cosmosophy*, Vol. 2, Australia: Completion Press.

_____. (1996). *Education for adolescents*, CW 302, Great Barrington, MA: Anthroposophic Press.

_____. (1976). *Esoterische Betrachtungen karmischer Zusammenhänge*, CW 236, Switzerland: Verlag Steiner Nachlassverwaltung.

_____. (1996). *The foundations of human experience*, CW 293, Great Barrington, MA: Anthroposophic Press.

_____. (1976). *Geistige Zusammenhänge in der Gestaltung des menschlichen Organismus*, CW 218, Switzerland: Verlag Steiner Nachlassverwaltung.

_____. (1973). *Geisteswissenschaftliche Menschenkunde*, CW 107, Lecture 12/21/1908, Dornach, Switzerland.

_____. (1983). *Metamorphoses of the soul*, Vol. 2, CW589. Forest Row, UK: Rudolf Steiner Press.

_____. (1972). *A modern art of education*, CW307. Forest Row, UK: Rudolf Steiner Press.

_____. (1997). *An outline of esoteric science*, CW 13, Great Barrington, MA: Anthroposophic Press.

_____. (1986). *Soul economy and Waldorf education*, CW303, Great Barrington, MA: Anthroposophic Press.

Therapies
Music, art, eurythmy, and Spacial Dynamics

Juliane Weeks, Karine Munk-Finser, Barbara Sim and Jane Swain

Music therapy
By Juliane Weeks

Music is food from heaven for the soul. Children blossom forth in their whole being when their souls are warmed and strengthened by music.
— H.W. Holzapfel, MD

A growing number of children today show characteristics of heightened sensitivity, which manifest as anxiety, restlessness, inability to concentrate, and increasing challenges in the social realm. Music therapy can be of invaluable help when imbalances of the soul, behavioral symptoms referred to as ADHD, and developmental challenges are to be met.

The foundation for the work with music as a healing art is the view that each human being is a being of body, soul, and spirit. The elements melody, rhythm, and harmony are musical expressions of our microcosmic nature. In the therapeutic setting, these elements are used to support the growing child on his unique journey and help him reconnect with the healing sources deep within his own being.

Working with the rhythmic element enlivens the will and calls up the ego to be present and direct its impulses with stronger determination and purpose.

Working in the realm of melody supports the healthy integration of thoughts, ideas, and imagination, by opening pathways to express musically what lives in soul and mind. Specific keys, intervals, and modes may be applied depending on the need and developmental stage of the child.

The realm of harmony addresses the realm of breathing. Contraction and expansion exercises on stringed instruments such as the lyres serve to find a greater balance between these two gestures that define our relationship to the world around us.

Our voice is the most precious instrument we have. Working with the voice is an important part of the therapeutic work as it expresses in an essential way who and how we are.

Thus each of these elements, applied and combined according to the individual needs of the child, can offer support on the deepest level. Through a musical "fine-tuning," which actively involves the child, a greater sense of harmony can be achieved. By cultivating a deeper capacity to listen, children can regain access to the sources within themselves which, given the stimulating environment children are exposed to today, can easily get lost.

Therapies

Music therapy is offered in concentrated sessions over a course of several weeks or months. Each music therapy block has a unique design. For the child, it may resemble a journey into a magic land where instruments of all kinds, many of them unfamiliar, awaken his or her curiosity. Children are gently led to encounter and make friends with the music of the stars, which they know deep within their soul; or they might find themselves in playful tone conversation and other musical interactions without the use of words. They may engage in creative accompaniments to a story or image that can offer guidance at this time in their lives. New ways of listening, singing together, and movement can enliven the sense of self by supporting a healthy sensory-motor integration.

Each music session begins with a moment of quiet listening to the clear, warming tones of the lyre. For a restless child, movement and gestures at the beginning of a session may facilitate the transition into a quiet mode where the child can experience an inner peacefulness and feel a readiness to engage musically. An opening song, little verse, or rhythmic games can help an anxious child to feel more at ease in body and soul.

Simple streaming movements on the kinder lyre, maybe as part of a story or song, will be calming and harmonizing for one child, while working with rhythms and movement may be the focus when working with an older child who shows symptoms of ADHD. The therapeutic plan and process is different for each child. Many teachers as well as parents have noted positive changes in their children's behavior following the music sessions. It is this sense of wholeness that music gives to us.

Art therapy
By Karine Munk-Finser

Color is soul. It is the soul of the entire universe and you participate in this soul when you experience color. – Rudolf Steiner

There once lived a sun-colored butterfly that fluttered among the spring flowers. It had been a long journey for her to finally enjoy these flowers!

For the longest time she had lived in a quiet place, but she was different then. Now she had filled herself with all the beauty of heaven on earth, and she had spread her wings and leapt off the tallest plants with great joy. Everything seemed to go her way, and there were so many other butterflies to share the gardens with. And so her life was quite wonderful for a long time.

One day a terrible thing happened: A dark cloud covered the sun and a strong wind blew wildly for many days. Without sun, the flowers began to wither. Then the rains came pouring down and all the pretty colors faded. The butterflies scattered, and this butterfly fled to a cave where it found the darkest corner as far away from the doorway as possible.

This first part of a story could offer a good sense of what the inner landscape of a child who has suffered some degree of trauma may look like. It could manifest as sadness, stomach ache, anxiety, grief, depression, obsessive-compulsive disorder, or other outer expression, all sharing in common an inner inflexibility or a chronic situation that needs immediate attention. A class teacher may feel that a child is hard to reach, that he or she is enigmatic, unhappy, and that the curriculum becomes ineffective in meeting his or her needs. The child is not present and available for learning and class participation: The teacher can't see the child fully and needs support. The child may need one-on-one time with a trained painting therapist who may help the child, and support the class teacher. Parents also need to be involved, and sometimes an anthroposophic doctor is necessary to help a child come through a difficult period in his or her life.

The painting therapist is trained in the laws of light, darkness, and color and in the corresponding lawfulness in the soul landscape, in the individual color gestures. Just as a homeopath knows his herbs, the painting therapist lives into the color landscape of the child and, through initial paintings, can objectively read the color gestures. A color journey is decided upon that will help the child strengthen and build resilience while addressing the child's innate capacities for self-healing. In a period of seven to twelve weeks, this non-verbal therapy accompanies the child on a weekly basis.

It is the full attentive approach, together with knowledge of the developmental unfolding of the child and the color gestures of the soul, that can help the child regain her sense of wholeness.

The painting therapist is devoted to finding that unscathed place where the child is still completely well, and "make it larger," bring it to full artistic expression, while helping the child trust her strength anew.

I have found that if I let the child paint her story, while the colors are given just as a homeopath hands out her remedies, the child may discover her own beauty anew. Every child's journey is individual, yet the lawfulness of the colors that support the telling of the story helps to embrace the child where she is perhaps struggling, then to transform stuck places into more health-giving movement to overcome a hindrance, and finally into discovering a healing motif. The process will support the child's well-being and healing.

Process

Preparation comes before any work, and when the child enters the room, the painting therapist is ready. I like to invite the child to look at some beautiful, colorful postcards, and a special card is chosen for the session, put before us on some pretty silk next to a vase with flowers. Some children want the same card throughout all the sessions, and others like to choose different ones. This little ritual helps us enter the painting session together.

In the example of the blue-gestured child mentioned above, who was stuck in "a cave, far away from the light," the child's first diagnostic paintings will reveal his soul state directly. In this first session, the painting therapist offers the child a beautiful array of twelve colors and may also look at his drawings, other paintings, and writing to help in objectively reading his soul gesture, or the inner soul landscape the child is living in.

The first painting may be accompanied by asking the child: Can you paint a sunrise? It is always a discovery to see which of the twelve colors the child will choose, where she sets the first paint on the clear moistened paper, and how the story of pigment, water, and paper flow together into a tender, new beginning and welcome her to breathe out her story. In this painted story, where all is possible, the child is safely guided by the painting therapist so that consciously chosen colors or color combinations become the helpers on the way to resolving the challenges that undoubtedly will become visible in gestures and in the story the child will express. These stories children tell are profoundly moving, and whether the painting therapist is working with a child who has stomach aches, or a child who has recently lost a parent, or a child who has developed anxieties after a divorce or major changes in the family, or someone who is beginning to have compulsive thoughts maybe accompanied by sudden tics, it is always an honor to be allowed into these story color worlds.

The journey begins with the sunrise, and then the gentle embracing stage in the second session. You can't suddenly give the withdrawn child a lot of red: It would be scalding! This may mean that if the child is sad or grieved, stuck on the blue side, the darker blues will be offered in the second session, after the free sunrise painting. The child will "breathe out" the dark blues but before the session is over will be offered lighter blues. Magenta may enter and bless the painting, offering comforting lilacs. The painting therapist can begin with one or two colors, listen and observe, and as the sessions progress, add what seems right so that light and warmth are gently invited into the paintings. It is important that the child always leaves the painting session with a lighter heart, or with some new inner movement introduced in the session. The child will first paint, then tell the story of the painting, and the painting therapist keeps all the words in her little book. It is a good habit to read the whole story and then invite the new part, after painting.

There once was a sunrise. It was hiding behind the clouds. A great mountain was hugging a lake, and there was a forest right next to the water. A lion lived there all by himself. He was a lion but he had no roar, and so he had decided to go look for his roar. He was a lonely lion but he had hope.

The above is a story spoken by a nine-year-old after painting his first painting of a sunrise behind clouds, a large mountain that reaches into the sky, and trees by the water. Somewhere behind the

trees a still invisible lion is hiding, shy and hopeful. The colors are beautiful: the child is excited to have so many colors. He is trying all the pink and magenta colors and then covers them all up with the mountain. The trees are all in a line, and look alike, and there is a clear blue lake in front, in the lower part of the painting.

Over the next few weeks, the child comes to these painting sessions with a smile on his face, eager to tell, eager to paint. He paints with more energy now, accepting the limited palette that is offered. I give the child the colors of blue and green and magenta soon after the first session. These colors plus the gold for the lion will be our helpers for a while. Soon, we have both blue and red. It is important that we reach a comfortable relationship with the reds since the child was "so blue" to begin with. It is important, in this case, to approach the reds with some caution before fully embracing them.

In the fourth or fifth session there is nearly always a crisis in the story.

The lion could not find his way in the forest, and there was no friend around. He sat down close to a cave in the rocks and was very sad. He was afraid that he would never find his way. It was dark and the night was very long. He was alone.

It is important never to leave the child with such grim feelings without giving him some comfort, and so here I added:

A star above his head shone down upon him, and little by little the lion knew he was not alone. His heart began to remember all that he loved, all that he longed for, and he could hear a song he had forgotten.

Together we open up the dark sky and the child places a golden star above the lion's head. I remove a little color around the lion, and the child paints in the gold. Since this particular child is very musical, it's important that there's a song the lion remembers. Both story, color, and eventual healing motif need to help the child feel embraced first, then moved slightly, then moved a bit more, until the colors that are the most helpful are approached, the story culminates, and a final image in the last session, emerges.

The lion arrived at the end of the cave. A warm light was everywhere and there lay the ruby, shining and ready for him to pick up by its strong rope. He put it around his neck and ran back outside into the sunshine. He climbed up on the green hill, and was surrounded by all the friends he had found on the journey. They were waiting for him. He opened his mouth, the red ruby on his chest, and he roared. He roared so loudly that all the animals cheered! He was happy and he was home. The End.

It is worthwhile to note that the cave became a green hill, and this is one of the ways the painting therapist can guide the story even though it is the

child's own story. After all, a hill is a cave turned inside out! Healing elements are thus offered, and the child feels completely safe and trusts the painting therapist. The child has been given complete attention and his feelings have been fully expressed while he is safely held in the therapist's consciousness. The challenge in the story is overcome, feelings have been felt, but never while alone.

Aims and wishes

One of the goals of these special, supportive sessions is to help make the child more present and happy. The "blue" child is turned toward the past and can't readily enjoy all that's happening. It is the hope that such sessions will have strengthened the child to a point where he will feel much more able to participate in the regular classes again with his class teachers and other teachers.

Other considerations

I have shared an example of a blue-gestured child, but I could have just as well shared a child who was a bit lost in the chaotic reds! Then the journey would be quite different, and it would be a wish that the child's will-forces be given guidance and more direction toward more form, toward some of the more reflective and tenderly shaping blues.

It is also true that some children bounce back and forth between the blues and the reds, since the soul will seek wholeness, and if the pendulum is

swinging too far out, it will undoubtedly swing too far in as well. Finally there are children who struggle more in "the middle." The painting therapist has to have insight into all these soul gestures and into all the nuances of the colors. Most important of all, the painting therapist has to be fully devoted to the well-being and thriving of the children who come into her care and actively "live" within the colors as if they were their best friends, so that they can call upon them at any time to bring new life, new hope, and health-giving beauty.

Therapeutic eurythmy
By Barbara Sim

Rudolf Steiner tells us that all healing is based on the principle of bringing into harmony what is not harmonious within the human being, be it physical, emotional or spiritual. Eurythmy means "harmonious rhythm," and the gestures are the revelation of the divine spiritual movements within the human being, which Rudolf Steiner developed out of his spiritual scientific insights. Thus, through eurythmy the individual is united with the forces out of which he or she is developing.

When the human organism tends in the direction of imbalance and leads to illness, eurythmy used therapeutically awakens the will to heal and can affect a profound change. Because therapeutic eurythmy is an active therapy, it allows one to take part consciously (will) in the process of becoming more balanced and to achieve true healing, not merely a cessation of symptoms. To look at imbalance or illness more positively, it is a unique possibility for transformation within the individual. The challenge is to restore the balance by tackling the root causes, not just the symptoms. The result is that we grow and develop as individuals as we go through the healing process.

In addition to those exercises which originate out of sound and gesture, therapeutic eurythmy encompasses coordination and concentration exercises, rhythmical exercises, spatial orientation exercises, as well as exercises with copper rods and balls and work with the elements of tone.

Eurythmy is truly alchemical in the sense that it is able to bring about transformative forces within the human being.

Practical implications

Some of the applications of therapeutic eurythmy as an adjunct or independent therapy include: nervous disorders, stress, headaches, mental and emotional disorders, sensory integration, developmental disorders, learning disabilities, digestive disorders, structural growth problems, allergies, weight control, thyroid imbalances, asthma and respiratory problems, eczema and skin problems, insomnia, high blood pressure, anorexia, lime disease, scoliosis, and cancer.

The process of therapeutic eurythmy normally takes place on a one-to-one basis, and a very important aspect of the therapy is the relationship developed between the therapist and recipient.

Depending on availability and funds in a school, therapeutic eurythmy can be requested for a student by the teachers, the parents, or the care group. The request is discussed with the members of the care group and the class teacher, and, depending on the nature of the request, possibly the child's physician. A consent form is then sent

to the parents for permission for the therapeutic eurythmist to work with their child, ideally twice a week for a half-hour session, within a cycle lasting six to seven weeks.

For children in the younger grades (K–4), it is preferable to arrange these sessions to be first thing in the morning during attendance and the rhythmical section of the main lesson. For the upper grades, the time of the session would be discussed with the class and subject teachers. After a space of time, the request for therapeutic eurythmy can be repeated, and a second cycle of sessions can take place.

The process of therapeutic eurythmy is movement, and movement is a joy to children. The sessions are filled with exercises that allow the child or adult to take part consciously, with the will, in the process of becoming balanced and achieve true healing.

Therapeutic aspects of Spacial Dynamics
By Jane Swain

We aren't normally conscious of space, but it's there—between us, within us, and around us. Largely unrecognized and unexplored, it is truly one of the world's untapped natural resources. Jaimen McMillan has dedicated his life to unlocking the mysteries of space for his fellow human beings. In 1985 he founded Spacial Dynamics®, an important application in the therapeutic domain. It offers tremendous insights and help for physical, social, emotional, and cognitive issues to people of all ages.

Our bodies are spaces, and beyond our bodies are also spaces. We each live in these spaces in our own unique ways, as a kind of spatial signature, and this impacts our thinking, our feeling, and our doing. Just as it is possible to change our handwriting, it is also possible to change our spatial signature, and this can profoundly affect our lives.

What actually happens is that the space moves first, and then the body follows. The spatial gesture essentially blazes the trail and carves out a pathway into which the body is drawn; the body has no choice but to follow. The therapist works with archetypal spatial configurations and streams that are most conducive to health and freedom of body and soul. Children are invited by the therapist to move into these spatial streams, and to gradually make them their own. This happens through hands-on practices by the therapist, through imitation, and through exercises, activities, and games. Therapists must have fine-tuned their own spatial gestures in order to offer models worthy of imitation. The younger the child, the more important is the spatial configuration of the adult.

Therapists must also understand the spatial developmental sequence in order to meet the child. Spatially, newborns are actually more around themselves than in themselves. Gradually through the working of predetermined and universal spatial patterns that surround the physical bodies of infants, they come more into their own, that is, they come inside the spaces of their physical bodies. Over time the predetermined and more primitive spatial patterns are transformed into spatial streams, which allow them to come back out through their bodies in order to meet what's in the spaces of the world in more fluid, coordinated, and sophisticated ways. Essentially this is the spatial description of the long and glorious process of integration of the primitive reflexes.

Just as the early printing of grade school children looks alike and then progresses to cursive writing that can become markedly individualized, so do the stereotypical reflexive movements transform into unique movement expressions of individualities. Unfortunately, in today's world this transformative process often goes awry. Spacial Dynamics offers a unique means of remedying this situation because it recognizes and addresses the underlying spatial contributions to reflexive movements and behaviors.

There are spatial configurations to basic human conditions, and understanding these can provide the therapist with a pathway to progress. For example, children with impulsivity usually have an imbalance in the front/back plane of space, that

is, they are too far ahead of themselves. Typically, when running through the jump rope, these children will run through faster than is necessary and will have difficulty stopping. Some will run through, even before the rope is turned.

Learning to change an aspect of oneself (one's tempo) in relationship to something outside of oneself (the rope and the other jumpers) can have crossover effects in other arenas where it is beneficial to hold back, such as keeping an open mind without jumping to conclusions and holding one's tongue in a challenging social encounter.

There are many other conditions where Spacial Dynamics offers insight and help, including tactile and auditory sensitivities, clumsiness, disturbances in the sense of life, poor balance, midline orientation and crossing midline issues, autism, asthma, OCD, aggression, social clumsiness, nonverbal learning disorders, attention issues, and hyperactivity. Slow-motion Spacial Dynamics exercises and hands-on techniques help to weave that which is "at loose ends" toward an integrated whole.

Therapists must hone their movements and moment-to-moment spatial observation skills. This provides an objective means of evaluating how the child is responding to your intervention, and whether you need to change what you are doing. The intervention is not a predetermined recipe to be imposed upon the child, but rather an invitational interaction between therapist and child.

Therapists must also understand the physical, soul, and spiritual requirements of movement activities and games in order to select developmentally appropriate ones. For example, hand clapping, string games and bean bag games can meet the younger grade schooler for midline orientation and crossing midline, whereas the older student would be more attuned to tinikling (dance with bamboo poles), ball games, and circus activities such as juggling, balancing, and acrobatics. A spatial approach to these activities assures that the child is learning more than that skill; what is learned is a new spatial relationship that will carry over to other aspects of a child's life.

The therapeutic activities and practices of Spacial Dynamics described in this article offer a means by which children can take the next step in their spatial development and thereby enable other aspects of their lives to positively unfold.

Extra support with music
Singing and recorder

David Gable

Perceiving Pitch

"But I'm tone-deaf!" How often have we heard this protestation from individuals—children and adults alike—who experience challenges with group singing? Perhaps they have arrived at this conclusion themselves, or perhaps (and more likely), they have been told by someone else that they are tone-deaf. In my experience, however, true tone deafness is a much rarer phenomenon than most people believe. There are, to be sure, varying degrees of pitch sensitivity, some people experiencing more difficulty with tonal differentiation that others, but, in all my years of working with and teaching music, I have encountered only one individual whom I might categorize as "tone-deaf." In most cases, it is more a matter of belief. A person who believes him- or herself to be tone-deaf will give up on any attempt to discern pitch. It is a classic self-fulfilling prophecy.

It can be difficult to break through this kind of mistaken belief, particularly when a third party, perhaps a teacher or parent, or perhaps even a hearing specialist, has made the diagnosis. There are, however, some simple activities that can help dissuade a person from the notion of tone deafness.

Take a large glass jug or bottle. An old-fashioned milk bottle or cider jug will do quite nicely. Place it beneath a faucet. Then tell the person professing to be tone-deaf to close his or her eyes and put a hand on the faucet handle. Instruct the person to turn the water off just before the jug overflows. Then turn the water on. The gurgling sound of water pouring into the jug will remain quite steady for a while. Then, as the water level reaches the narrower neck of the jug, the pitch will rapidly go up. The effect is quite dramatic.

Most people are able to do this, if not on the first try, then certainly on the second or third. For some, the revelation that they are not tone-deaf is so profound that they may want to do the activity over and over. The discovery has opened a door into a whole new experience of tone.

There are other activities that can help break down the misperception of tone deafness. You may have observed that when cupped hands are clapped together, the resulting tone is deeper and more resonant that when flat hands are clapped. Clapping cupped hands at waist level, then gradually raising and flattening the hands so that the pitch rises as the hands move upward, can visually reinforce auditory perception. Lowering the hands

while gradually returning them to a cupped shape completes the exercise, which can be repeated several times in a row in a very short period of time. This activity, by the way, is also an excellent tool for associating pitch with a position on the staff. Higher, brighter tones are positioned higher on the staff than the deeper tones.

In a similar way, sliding the voice from low to high and back again, especially when reinforced by the raising and lowering of hands, can not only help break through the misperception of tone deafness, but also help the singer identify how different tones feel in the larynx. When I have a student who is struggling to match pitch, I have him or her simply hum a tone at a comfortable pitch. Then, following the movement of my hand, the student slides his or her voice up or down until the correct pitch is attained. Reiterating the correct pitch and sensing how it feels, as opposed to how it sounds, goes a long way toward the goal of singing in tune.

Another exercise, particularly helpful for those who either have difficulty controlling vocal pitch or are shy about singing, is to match tones with musical instruments. In the classroom this is likely to be the recorder, but in fact any pitched instrument can be used. The teacher plays a simple note pattern from a position where the student cannot see the fingering, and the student tries to replicate the pattern. Initially I like to begin with G (the "top hand" note) and use exclusively the notes G, A, and B in different groupings, but as the student becomes more adept and develops more confidence, I extend to other tones and longer patterns. As with the aforementioned exercises, students are often surprised by their ability to duplicate note patterns.

Or course, playing the tune on an instrument while children sing is an old standby method of helping them sing in tune. I have found that the ideal instrument for this purpose is the violin, both because its lower to middle range completely encompasses the children's comfortable singing range, and also because its string timbre is very like the sound of the human voice. For me, being a performing violinist in my other life, this has been a good tool, but that is not the case for most classroom teachers. The recorder is often the instrument of choice, and most children can readily sing in tune an octave below a soprano recorder (the pitch of which is an octave higher than written). However, children who experience challenges with pitch differentiation frequently mistake timbre (tone color) for pitch, and when asked to sing with a soprano recorder may force their voices unnaturally high in a futile attempt to imitate the brightness of the instrument. The child's natural register is mostly encompassed by the alto recorder and entirely by the tenor, but many teachers hesitate to use these instruments with younger children out of concern that they may be too incarnating. I do not believe this needs to be a cause of worry. The tones of alto and tenor recorders, while deeper than those of the brilliant soprano, are mellow and soothing, and as mentioned earlier, they are in the correct octave for young singers. Also, were we to attempt to shield children from low timbres, we would have to recommend that fathers not speak to or sing with their children, that children never hear the sound of a cello, never put their ear to the side of a purring cat.

I would like to say more on the idea of feeling, rather than hearing pitch when singing. Although my background is as a performing musician, I do not have what is often referred to as "perfect pitch," that is, the ability to identify random pitches or sing a specific pitch without any frame of reference. Yet, when I sing with my classes I am consistently able to begin a song on the same pitch without needing to refer to a recorder, pitch pipe, or chime. This is because after I have sung the song enough times, it is my body, rather than my ear, that recognizes how it feels to sing the correct pitch. You might compare it to being able to write your name with your eyes closed. It is the kinesthetic memory, not the ear, which identifies the tone. I have found that this is true of children as well. In fact, it was my observations of children singing that led me to this discovery in the first place. To cite a specific example, I was once rehearsing my middle school chorus when I inadvertently gave them an E rather than the D to which they were accustomed as a preparatory pitch. To my amazement, nearly the entire group began singing in the usual key. They were singing "by feel" rather than by ear.

Of course, I do not necessarily recommend beginning songs without a pitch reference. Rather, this observation actually serves to underscore the importance of always singing a song starting on the same pitch if we are to develop a good sense of pitch in our students. If using an instrument or pitch pipe allows the teacher to accomplish this, by all means it should be used.

Rhythm

Another common truism among struggling musicians is, "I'm not good at music because I'm not good at math. I can't count." While there is no doubt that developing one's sense of rhythm can greatly benefit one's mathematical acuity (I, myself, am a good example, having survived fourth grade arithmetic by translating multiplication tables and fractions into rhythmic patterns), there is absolutely no reason to believe that being mathematically challenged must necessarily impede one's musicality. While mathematics can be reduced to purely abstract concepts, rhythm must be understood not in the head, but rather with the body. For this reason, children's initial experiences of rhythm should be through musical and motor activity rather than notation.

In lecture 6 of *The Inner Nature of Music and the Experience of Tone*, Rudolf Steiner indicates that only after about the age of 10 should children's attention be drawn to the rhythmic element in music. By this I do not believe that he means we should use arhythmic music prior to age 10, but rather that we should not turn rhythm into an intellectual exercise. A child's whole being is inherently rhythmic. From the faster rhythms of circulation and respiration to the broader rhythms of waking and sleeping, we all live steeped in rhythm. Before age 10, however, we want the child to experience both these biorhythms and musical rhythms as part of an organic process rather than as abstractions.

Rhythm is the musical expression of the will, and the best way to develop rhythmic sensitivity in children is through activity of the will. Jumping rope, skipping, swinging, and other rhythmic gross motor activities (the standard fare of Waldorf elementary students) gives children an inner understanding of rhythm upon which a cognitive understanding can later be built. These or similar activities, rather than any attempt to teach rhythmic understanding by way of musical notation, is the best approach to take when helping a child with an undeveloped sense of rhythm.

From large bodily movements one progresses to smaller, more detailed rhythmic activities. Walking with a rhythmic step and clapping the hands in sync with the feet is a good next step. Clapping the hands twice to every step, then in alternation with the steps, can follow.

Simple duple meters and rhythms (un-syncopated quarter and eighth notes in two-four or four-four time) are the best for remedial purposes, as they reflect the body's rhythms in a way that triple meter (three-four time) and triplet rhythms do not. These fundamental rhythms can progress toward more varied rhythmic patterns clapped in time with the steady stepping of the feet. I find it best to have the feet provide the continuous pulse, and have the hands create the rhythmic patterns that are overlaid upon that pulse.

Only when the child has developed an inner sense of rhythm does it become productive to deal with rhythmic notation.

Reading music

There are two main elements to reading music, and these are the two musical elements discussed above: pitch and rhythm. While these are sometimes lumped together in the general category of reading music, they are conceptually quite different and involve different thought processes.

The musical staff is essentially a graph. High notes are positioned higher, low notes lower. Notes that are too high or low to be written within the five lines of the staff are written with extra lines called ledger lines. (I like to compare these to an extension ladder when teaching children about pitch notation.) This means that every pitch has a characteristic visual appearance when written on the staff. Just as one can look at a thermometer and see whether the temperature is hot, cold, or moderate, one can glance at a staff and see whether the pitch is higher, lower, or in the middle.

The earliest examples of written music in the West do not have staves. Symbols called *neumes* were used to show the general shape of a melody rather than its specific pitches. During the 10th century, a musician known as Guido of Arezzo devised a system using four lines that allowed for the representation of specific pitches. Since then, staves of four, five, and six lines have been used, the five-line staff being the standard today, though Gregorian chant is still often written on a staff of four lines, and the general idea of note position following the shape of the melody has persisted. Keeping this in mind is very helpful in learning to read notes.

A proficient sight-reader does not think the names of the notes when singing or playing. Rather, he or she follows the shape of the line. Each interval, in addition to having a characteristic sound, also has a characteristic appearance. A second (step or half step) moves from a line to the next space or from a space to the next line. A third moves from space to space or line to line. A fifth skips a line or space. Learning to recognize the visual appearance of notes on the staff and of intervals between notes is much more important than learning the names of notes. This is not to say that learning note names is not useful. It is, but mostly for the purpose of enabling us to communicate with each other about the music.

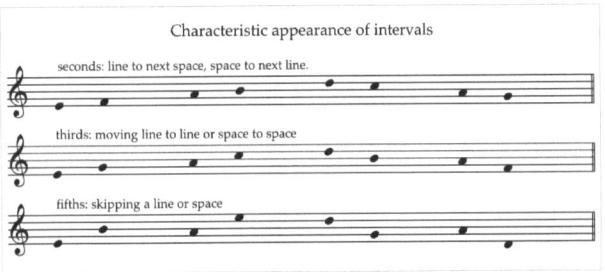

I have found that the best method for teaching students to read pitch is to have them learn a tune initially by demonstration, then follow the music with the eyes while playing or singing. The hands and larynx do not recognize pitches by name, but by feel. Hands "think" spatially. To the hands of a person playing a soprano recorder, a note on the second line (G) does not indicate a pitch so much as a setting of the fingers of the left hand. For a violinist, the same note indicates a place to be stopped on the D string. To a singer, it indicates a tone that feels a particular way when sung. Unfortunately, the most common way of teaching pitch notation is to focus on learning the names of notes rather than building a connection between the eye and the hand or larynx.

Rhythm notation, by contrast, is a more symbolic way of writing. There is no particular reason why a round shape with no stem should indicate four beats, no particular reason why a dot placed after a note should indicate extending the note's value by half. It is simply a matter of convention. There is a measure of logic, of course, to the addition of flags or beams when indicating increasingly short beat subdivisions, but even this is convention. We could just as well draw horizontal lines on the staff to indicate note duration. The conventional method, however, has the advantage of being very systematic. If one is able to comprehend divisions and proportions, one is able to comprehend rhythm notation. Observing that beams group notes into beats is key to mastering the reading of rhythms.

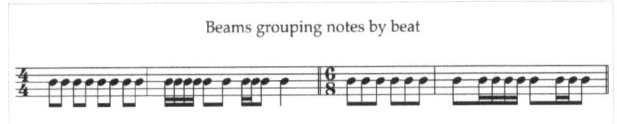

Although rhythm notation is independent of spatial proportions (imagine how inconvenient it would be if it were necessary for every whole note to take as much horizontal space as sixteen sixteenth notes!), I find that positioning notes relative to their durations is extremely helpful for students learning to read rhythm. When I write a rhythmic pattern for reading practice, I make sure that one quarter note occupies approximately the same horizontal space as two eighth notes or four sixteenth notes.

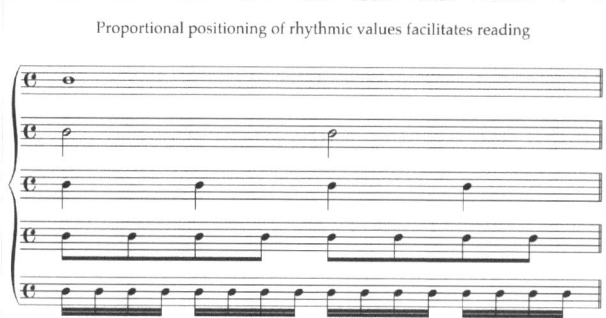

Proportional positioning of rhythmic values facilitates reading

A question that often comes up is, What is the best time to teach reading music. My response is that there is no single time. Reading music requires multiple thought processes, and some elements of notation are more readily grasped by children at an earlier age than are others.

As noted above, our method of notating rhythm has no direct relationship to the length of notes. It is a fairly abstract notion. It is also, as is rhythm itself, an exercise in proportions. For these reasons, I feel it is most appropriate to introduce rhythm notation in fourth grade, the year in which fractions are introduced. There need be no concern that students might be confused if notation is presented prior to fractions. In fact, since beat subdivisions are customarily beamed together in one-beat groupings, music notation provides a visual aid to the understanding of equivalent fractions. Two eighth notes are equivalent to a quarter note, and so forth. The fact that we refer to them with fraction-like names is also not a problem. It is very easy to see that eighth notes are so called because eight of them will take the same amount of time as a whole note.

One concept that can become confusing is the time or meter signature. Often these are explained as if they were fractions, and "three-four time" is sometimes referred to as "three-quarter time." This is not correct. A time signature, though it looks like a fraction, does not identify part and whole the way a fraction does, but rather indicates how many beats are in a measure and what type of note is used to express a single beat. Thus, "three-four time" indicates that each measure has three beats and a quarter note receives one beat. Also, unlike fractions, "three-four" is not the same as "six-eight." In the former, a measure might include three pairs of eighth notes (or the equivalent), but in the latter there are two beats, each of which may be comprised of three eighth notes.

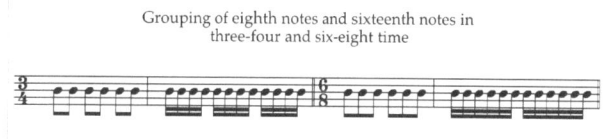

Grouping of eighth notes and sixteenth notes in three-four and six-eight time

The notation of pitch is basically pictorial, with the rise and fall of note heads indicating the rise and fall of pitch. The staff is easily likened to a ladder, and possible pictorial images abound. Children intuitively recognize that when a teacher's hands go up and down when the class sings, their voices should follow. The hand clapping activity described earlier is another way in which high and low pitch can readily be connected to staff positions. For that matter, the very fact that we use the words "high" and "low" suggests a natural connection between what we hear and what we see on the staff. Because of these factors, it is quite reasonable to introduce the staff and pitch notation earlier than rhythm notation. I have found that by third grade nearly all students are able to grasp the general idea. I do not, by the way, promote the approach taken in some method books of writing notes without a staff and with the note name written within the note head. As indicated earlier, it is not the letter name of the note that is most important; rather, the essential point is what the note's position on the staff tells the musician to do with hands or voice.

It is obvious that one cannot introduce pitch notation in isolation. I see no problem, however, with third graders seeing music with rhythmic indications. In response to their questions, I simply reply that the variations in the notes tell us how long they are to sound, and that we will learn more about that later. It is like allowing kindergartners to see words in print without attempting to teach them to read. It becomes a mystery to be revealed at a future date.

Recorders

The effect of instrumental music on children is quite different from the effect of singing. Vocal music tends to excarnate, to lift their consciousness out of their physical bodies and into the astral, the arena of pure feeling. Playing an instrument, while still working in the astral, has a more grounding effect. I believe this is due to the engagement of the limbs and the need (even for string players) to coordinate hands and breathing. Playing a musical instrument engages and helps integrate the astral and etheric with the physical body. I believe that it is essential for children, especially as they enter the middle school years, to be involved in both singing and playing, if not daily, then at least on a regular basis each week. This is also true for children with sensory-motor challenges and children who join a class "midstream." These children, though, may need extra support in order to feel successful.

There are five elements of recorder playing that frequently cause difficulty for students. These are the embouchure (mouth position), posture, fingering, breathing, and tonguing. The first thing a teacher must do is identify which of these is creating the problem.

The correct embouchure for the recorder has the tip of the mouthpiece resting on the lower lip. The mouthpiece does not enter the mouth, but many children, especially those with sensory integration difficulties, will insert it deeply. This causes problems with tonguing and breathing, and must be addressed first. I tell students to let the tip of the mouthpiece rest on their lip, then to bring the upper lip to the mouthpiece as though sipping water through a straw. For some children it is necessary to practice finding the correct embouchure. In the early learning stages, I remind children of it every time we play. Once the embouchure is established, other matters may be addressed.

Correct posture is as important to playing the recorder (or any instrument) as it is to performing eurythmy or dance. It is, however, difficult to convey in writing because many details vary according to the size and proportions of the hands, arms, and torso. Therefore, I will not attempt do so here. That said, there are certain aspects of posture that I have found create difficulties for more than a few students, and these warrant mention. One is the position of the instrument itself. There should be a straight line from ear lobe to mouthpiece to bell. Many students look down, as if trying to see their fingers. This creates poor breathing posture. (By the way, reading music lying flat on a desktop also lends to this problem. I strongly encourage the use of music stands.) The solution, however, is not necessarily to address posture directly. If the student is looking down because of fingering uncertainty, the best approach may be to sensitize the fingers so that he or she can play by touch. Have the student hold the instrument in playing position, but not blow into the mouthpiece. Starting with the top index finger and thumb, place the fingers on their respective tone holes and try to feel the entire circumference of the hole. It may help the student to do this with eyes closed. Take the fingers away to see if the outline of the hole is visible on the pad of the fingertip. If only a crescent is visible, the finger is not completely covering the hole. Proceed in similar fashion down the hand.

After this exercise, have the student play a B (top index finger and thumb). While playing, gently rock the finger so that the hole opens along the edge. Do the same with the thumb. Have the student listen to the way the tone and pitch change. Once the finger is securely covering the entire hole, the tone becomes clear and the pitch is true. As with the silent exercise, proceed down the hand to A, G, low E, and low D.

Many students develop poor fingering habits simply because they are trying too hard. Some, for example, lift the fingers very high. If the fingers are lifted too far from the holes, it is harder to place them accurately and in synchronization with each other. The fingers should stay fairly close to the instrument, being lifted and set gently. Others press the fingers too tightly into the tone holes. White knuckles and deep tone hole impressions on the fingertips are evidence of this problem. Imagining that the instrument is coated in fine gold dust, which will be rubbed off if gripped too tightly, can help a student lighten the fingers satisfactorily. The problem of overworking is exacerbated if the student is moved too soon into larger instruments with wider spacing between tone holes. Before a student takes up alto and tenor, the teacher must ensure that she or he can reach the lowest tone holes without straining.

Breathing, too, is impacted by too much effort. I sometimes see students breathing between all the notes. They quickly become fatigued and even light-headed. It should come as no surprise if they come to dislike playing the recorder. Other students try to breathe too deeply, lifting the shoulders and gasping for air. This actually inhibits deeper breathing, as it constricts the lungs. Proper breathing is done through the mouth, by raising the upper lip from the mouthpiece. Breaths are taken at musically appropriate points in the phrase, not whenever we happen to run out of air. With a little practice, even younger children can learn to breathe easily and deeply enough to take in enough air to play several beats without taking another breath.

Students should be taught to play with full air, but not to over-blow. Over-blowing obviously causes the instrument to shriek most unpleasantly. Under-blowing, though, is just as problematic. It results not only in meager tone, but also in flat and wavering pitch. Sadly, when cautious children play, they under-blow in hopes of not standing out. When they hear the unsatisfying tone that results, they become even more cautious, and the problem becomes self-perpetuating.

Proper breathing is also assisted by tonguing. In tonguing, we touch the tip of the tongue to the roof of the mouth just behind the teeth. The student should take care that the tongue does not contact the end of the mouthpiece. Proper tonguing stops the air momentarily, preventing the disintegration of tone and flattening of pitch that occurs when the air is stopped from the lungs. The action of the tongue is the same as saying "tah-tah-taht" or "dah-dah-dahd." I find it is quite helpful to have children sing the tune with the tonguing syllables. This allows them to practice the technique without the distraction of fingerings.

Many students find certain fingerings, like F natural and B flat, to be difficult. This is because they require the lifting of fingers in the middle of the hand while the outer fingers are held down. "Half-hole" fingerings such as C sharp and E flat are also difficult. These challenges result largely from fine motor issues, and some of the best remedies are built into the children's regular program: knitting and clay modeling, for example. However, some children need more fine motor activity to sufficiently develop the finger independence required to play the recorder.

Have the student sit with arms resting on the top of a desk. The angle of the upper arms should be about the same as when playing the recorder,

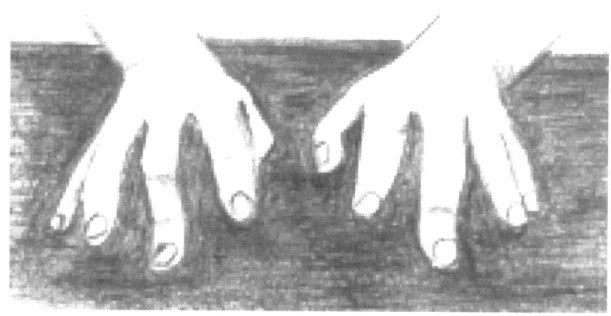

relaxed and not extending outward. The fingers are relaxed and allowed to curl naturally, not held flat against the top of the desk. I refer to the fingers by number. Thumb is simply "thumb," but the others are as follows: index fingers are "1," middle fingers are "2," ring fingers are "3," and pinkies are "4." Have the student gently and rhythmically raise and lower fingers in various groupings. Start with raising each finger independently while the others remain relaxed on the desk top, one hand at a time. Follow this by lifting the same finger on both hands. Then move on to neighboring pairs (T - 1; 1 - 2; 2- 3; and 3 - 4) on single hands and neighboring pairs on both hands. Move them simultaneously and in alternation. Lifting odd-numbered fingers together and even-numbered fingers together is more difficult, and lifting odd and even pairs in alternation is most difficult (for this consider the thumb to be part of the even group, so that the combinations are T - 2; 1 - 3; 2 - 4). Throughout the exercise, it is vitally important that the hands stay relaxed. If anything begins to hurt or feel strained, stop. This activity, when practiced systematically and rhythmically, helps the student develop the finger independence needed to play the awkward notes successfully.

Patience

As Waldorf teachers, we tend to take pride in our students' aesthetic accomplishments. Their beautiful artwork adorns classroom walls, their drama and music resound in our assembly halls. It can be frustrating, to say the least, to have a student whose sense of pitch or rhythm mars an otherwise exquisite performance, and we certainly want to help such children develop their musicality more fully. However, our motivation should not be for the quality of the performance, but rather for the benefit that musical activity has for that student. By no means should a student with musical challenges be asked to sit out or be relegated to always playing a drum (though the latter is an excellent fallback option for the student with a broken arm!). Neither should a student be pulled from music classes to receive remediation in academic areas. Nor should children be required to take private music lessons in order to participate in the school's instrumental music program. Music is an inclusive art. When we make music together, we meet each other on a higher plane. We transcend our day-to-day idiosyncrasies and differences in the pursuit of the art. We learn to listen to each other, to harmonize, and to resolve dissonance. When an individual child does not perform up to the standard of his or her peers, we may seek to help, but not to exclude. We must work patiently for improvement, but not for perfection. If our assembly presentation is less than ideal, it is no crisis. They may not sound like the Vienna Boys' Choir or the National Youth Orchestra, but that is no matter. It is the engagement, the activity, and the collaboration with peers that are important. A colleague recently commented on a performance by my middle school orchestra saying, "It may have been a little ragged—any middle school orchestra is—but they were playing their hearts out." To that I would add this thought: When they play their hearts out, their hearts meet, and when their hearts come back home, they are larger than before.

Speaking and listening
A teacher's greatest tools

Robyn Hewetson

"Not only as your councillor do I come, but as your physician; with words as medicinal as true."
— From *A Winter's Tale*

So says Paulina, possibly Shakespeare's greatest character, in one of his last plays, *The Winter's Tale*. She speaks these words to King Leontes, who is eaten up with his own jealousy and unable to see the truth, to give him a chance to hear the truth to which he is so obviously blind. Herein lies something very important; often when we recognize our profession or path in life, we name it our calling. Both these things speak to our need to be able to hear well.

The importance of being heard

After 40 years of working on the art of speech formation, as given by Rudolf Steiner since 1919 and brought to me by Maisie Jones at the London School of Speech Formation, I have realized that all the work done to bring speech into form and flow, to be filled with life and art, is all for the sake of the listener—to be heard. In today's world where there is so much electronic communication and so many courses available, so many languages and forms of communication coming toward us in so many forms, it is ever more important to all of us to be heard. Why is it that so often we do not feel we are heard? Teachers, parents, partners, leaders, and many others often feel that what they are saying falls on deaf ears. On the other hand, to be heard—to be understood and to be responded to—is a blessing that often leads to healing. In Goethe's fairy tale, the Green Snake asks, famously, of the Gold King: "What is more precious than Gold?" The King replies, "Light." The Green Snake then asks, "What is more refreshing than Light?" "Conversation," rejoins the King simply. This is something so many of us have discovered in our lives: To speak to someone who listens well and then responds to us from their own hearts, in such a way that we find our own voice and are more able to express our true thoughts and concerns, is often the way to finding our true path in life, to solving our soul issues and to discovering new enthusiasms and answers in life. Why is this so rare?

Models for speaking

It is because today our daily speaking is often so void of life and color. We are surrounded by noise. So often even young children hear mechanical voices everywhere—telling us to put our seatbelts on, to turn off our cell phones, to cross the street and so on. Many new toys speak to children, but with the most deadening and lifeless voices. These toys are often built to repeat and repeat foolish and pointless phrases. For so many children, these voices and the recordings on television and so on are the models for speaking that they follow. It is small wonder then that they speak without their breath in sharp, high, and dead voices. Their words are often without depth or color to them. And the children become very poor listeners.

Speaking and listening

Speech lessons for teachers

When the Steiner schools were begun in 1919, Rudolf Steiner, with the aid of Marie Steiner, gave to the teachers all the speech exercises. He hoped that all teachers in Waldorf schools would take speech lessons from a trained teacher of speech formation every week of their teaching lives. Why was this so? Certainly it was not so they would speak correctly, or in a manner approved by certain sections of society. But the Steiner schools were developed primarily to develop the children's imaginations, to develop their capacity to bring a response to what they heard spoken or presented, to bring their own individual picture-forming imaginations to bear on it and see that which they heard spoken. What an amazing gift this is. Anyone who has told a story to young children, and who knows it has been told well, can tell you that, as they look at the children in front of them, something very remarkable happens. You see the children become very still, and although they are looking directly at you, they no longer "see" you; their pupils are enlarge, and their eyes seem to look right through you. When the story ends, you may hear the children sigh deeply, seemingly return to themselves, and then a moment later say, "Again." These children have been so inspired by the storyteller's voice that they have been able to see the world the story speaks of and to fill it with their own color and creatures and events. Why did Steiner want teachers to take lessons in the art of speech formation? So they could develop in themselves a stronger access to the powers of inspiration. This is the most essential faculty for a teacher to have to awaken the imaginations of the children in the class.

The healing power of speech

The story is often told that, when the first school had been going for some months, Steiner came, as he often did, to visit. When he saw that so many children had colds, he exclaimed, "If these children had speech formation lessons every day, they would never get colds." The work of speech in our schools is to help our children be well. I call my own speech business "WellSpoken" because of this.

The image behind our word *well* is of a hole in the ground, often lined with stone, which is a source of fresh, clean water. However, part of this image is that without a means to bring the water to the surface, the well is not usable to us. This well-ness which we speak of in so many ways today is often an image of this very activity, of being able to reach down into the source (or sauce!) of life and to bring it to the surface. This is what the art of speech

formation teaches us and what we must bring to the children in our kindergartens and our classes—this never-failing method of reaching into the power of inspiration.

So often we say, "You do that so well!" "Are you well?" "I want to be able to do it well," and so on. I am sure all these phrases are reminding us that we have to reach deep to find this source of strength and light and life.

Standing and speaking

Steiner tells us early in his educational lectures that children do not speak until they stand. For all parents or people dealing with very young children, this is a momentous time to watch and see what happens to them. From the beginning, children make sounds and noises; they gurgle and sigh, squeal and cry. The laugh of a very young baby is one of the most beautiful sounds on earth. The "Nga, Nga, Nga!" crying of a very upset baby is one that no parent ignores. Funnily enough, this very sound is often the beginning of words in the Maori language of New Zealand, where I now live. Formed at the back of the throat, it is often expressive of anger—and is very strong.

The first words

But actual spoken words that contain meaning do not come until the child stands. And not only do they have to stand, but to be load-bearing. When that moment comes, and it is powerful to watch, often the hand comes up too, and the first word is spoken. When my oldest daughter spoke for the first time, we had recently returned to Forest Row in Sussex and staying at Yenneden, the house of a dear friend by the edge of Tablehurst Farm at Emerson College. Every day I would take her out in her stroller to see the cows. Her first word was *cow*. "Cow, Mummy, Cow!" she said, hundreds of times a day. The joy was evident, and her meaning was clear. Those large, peaceful creatures had spoken to her, and she wanted to tell everyone about them. My son, born in New Hampshire, was lighter and more nimble and got to his feet earlier. When he said his first word, he was always in motion,

with his right hand pointing straight out into the world. "See! See!" he told everyone. My daughter is now a farmer and raises beef cattle, and is daily surrounded by cows that she breeds to have healthy calves. My son is a movie editor—always looking for the right point of view and the right angle. Isn't that interesting!

From beneath the soles of our feet

Steiner tells us that the capacity to speak comes from beneath our feet, that we get the sounds from the stars. We call the bottom of our feet the *sole*. And it is only when the child firmly grips the earth and comes into uprightness that the sounds of speech come forth into the world, always in their own utterly individual and unique voice.

Steiner also tells us that there is no more creative thing a human being can do than speak one syllable. One syllable that contains at least one consonant and one vowel combines the outer forming, shaping power of the world through the consonants and the individual experiencing soul of the speaker in the vowel. For instance in my daughter's first word, "cow," we have the consonant C shaped at the back of the throat on the soft palate, that meeting place of the back of the tongue and the flexible but thick and blunt soft palate at the back of our mouths; this is where the will sounds are made. These sounds, which include C, K, G, Ng, and H—all speak of action, of kindness, of capabilities, clarity, exactness, and so on. This is the sound of Sagittarius. The vowel sound *ow* or *au* is a Sun sound. So, this little girl in Forest Row, speaking her first word, was combining Sun forces and those of the Archer to speak her first word. My son used S—the sound of Scorpio (or the Eagle, as some suppose) and the EE from Mercury.

The breath

Thought of this way, those first words can speak to us of the worlds from which our children come, and perhaps of the paths they are taking up. Considering this thought at all can give us pause to think: The capacity to speak comes from beneath our feet, and we bring the sounds of speech from the fixed stars and the planets to the earth on the sound of our own voice and with our breath. Most modern people now speak very fast. Reading and computing have made us very clever, and even little children speak very quickly, often without breath, and a great deal with no regard at all to the sounds that make up our words.

The fifth limb

Often when I have a new group of teachers in a class, I ask them, "How many limbs do we have?" Often they tell me, "Four." By this, they mean, of course, left hand, right hand, left foot, right foot. But this is not complete. We have five limbs! The bottom jaw is a limb. Anyone who has studied super-sensible physiology (as I had the great good fortune to do with Dr. Mees at Emerson College in 1973) will learn that the lower jaw is almost a transformed leg on each side, meeting in the middle. Our lower jaw is a vital limb. It is responsible for all that we are able to take into our bodies in the form of nourishment, from the first suckling of the infant to the more laborious chewing of stronger food later in life. This amazing limb is also responsible for our being able to speak. The musculature of speech is the most refined in our bodies.

Our most individual part

This fifth limb helps us form the star—the five-pointed star we often use to describe the human being. It also indicates to us that both our eating and our speaking are deeds. Isn't it interesting that the very place where we put our meals and take our drinks is also the very place where we express our thoughts and form our questions and statements to the world. What does it mean that this organ of taste—and the beginning of the destruction of our food in order to ingest it and begin the process of selection and elimination which is our digestion and life-giving source—is also the place where we form the sounds and shapes of the words which are home to our thoughts and the seat of our voice; the most individual part of us? This mouth has lips, tongue, teeth, hard and soft palate, and very many refined muscles which help us both to chew and swallow, to form the consonants, and to place the vowels of all our words, no matter how many languages we speak.

Developing the organ

Surely if this is so, we need to develop the sensitivity of this organ to tasting the food we eat and the words we say. How many times we hear phrases such as "how sweetly she said that," or "such bitter words," or "salty thoughts." This organ of speech is very sensitive, perhaps one of the most sensitive places in our body. Sensing our words and the forming and placing of consonants and vowels brings us to a far greater awareness of our own

words and thoughts, which leads down a very long road to better hearing, listening, and understanding of others.

The journey of teaching clear speaking in the classroom begins with stance. Standing straight, with feet gripping the earth in an active but firm stance, brings strength into the voice, uprightness into the thinking, consciousness to what we are saying, and access from beneath our feet for the forces of speaking. Further, we can notice that, while our eyes are looking forward, our ears are reaching back and up as if they are listening for help from the stars. This puts us in the right place to begin speaking.

Morning verses

Often in our schools teachers will begin the day with a verse. The thoughts, given in the verses spoken to the children for them to learn to say, are far-reaching thoughts.

Verse for Lower Grades
The Sun, with loving light
Makes bright for me each day.
The soul with spirit power
Gives strength unto my limbs.
In sunlight shining clear
I reverence, O God (Creator Being)
The strength of human kind
That You, so graciously
Have planted in my soul,
That I, with all my might
May love to work and learn.
From you comes light and strength,
To You rise love and thanks.

Verse for Upper School
I look into the world i
In which the sun is shining,
In which the stars are sparkling
Where stones in stillness lie;
Where living plants are growing,
Where animals live in feelings
Where man within his soul
Gives dwelling to the spirit.

I look into the soul
That lives within my being.
The World Creator weaves
In sunlight and in soul light
In world spaces there without,
In soul depths here within.
To you, Creator Spirit,
I turn my heart to ask
That blessing and pure strength
For learning and for work
May ever grow within me.

What mighty words these are. The third sentence in the verse for the lower classes is long and complex. It is quite a journey to move through it and to hold the thought clearly in our own minds. Why is this a part of our curriculum—and why do we do it? Speaking is a deed. It is as much a deed as carving a bowl or baking bread. When we speak, we bring our thoughts into the powers of sound, and on the flow of our breath, we send them out into the world. Once spoken, words form part of our destiny. By speaking such powerful and healthy words with our classes, we are beginning the day by doing something that integrates the children. By standing freely and firmly on the earth, and speaking with our own voices, but joining with the voices of our classmates and teacher, we are bringing clear thoughts into the room where we will learn and work for the day. These thoughts, as we bring them through us and onto our breath full of sound, come through us and give us a chance to reunite with them afresh, finding ever new aspects of them and reminding us of things that matter. Often after a verse with my classes, I would share some of the thoughts that would come to me, helping them to see that their thoughts and responses are important too.

Forming the sounds

Learning to form the sounds of the consonants clearly and using the forming, shaping impetus of the consonants to actually shape and move the vowels out of us and into the room, is a very healthful activity. Sending our well-made words out of us into the room to be heard by others can make us feel alive, present, active, healthy, and joyful.

These words can remind us of our truer intentions and help us to shape the way we will react to the day. Speaking well is absolutely the best step on the way to thinking well.

In the kindergarten years we are often told that "play is work." And in the school years, "plays are work." Speaking and forming thoughts clothed in words is work and is a deed for the world. Teaching children to speak well, to form the sounds of their words carefully and artistically works back on their own well-being.

The cornerstone of memory

Speaking fun words, clever words, rhyming words, and rhythms in these early morning times before the other classes can bring humor, life, light, laughter, joy, sadness, empathy, balance, uprightness, courage, and more into our lives. Choosing the right rhythms and rhymes for each year and for each child is an important part of the class teacher work. Rhythm and rhyme are the cornerstones of human memory. And for true learning that will last a lifetime, memory must be engaged. In today's world one of the most dreaded illnesses is that of memory loss. So many people now lose their memories long before they die. When this happens, fear and anxiety become daily companions. Often for these people, the poems and stories they learned in early childhood are the things that remain longest in their memory. One could even surmise that the teaching of great poems and literature to our children for them to learn by heart could be a means of increasing their courage for life!

Learning poetry by heart

Helping our children to have happy, healthy memories is part of the work of learning many poems, games, limericks, and speech exercises by heart. At first children do not even need to know they are doing speech exercises; these can be just games. But learning to speak together as a group and learning poems or phrases that are fun to say, that taste good, and that are demonstrated well are health-giving and awakening for all children.

Breath exercises

After standing and learning to stand well, with feet not too close together, with hands loose and lightly by their sides, and heads up and also lightly held, it is important for children to learn that their words can come through them into the room, and not just fall out of their mouths onto the floor in front of them. This is done with breath exercises. I often use a modified version of the breath exercise Rudolf Steiner gave to speech teachers.

Fierce Gales
How ling Streams
Fla shing Streaks
Light te ning Strikes
Thun der Rolls
Trees Up roo ted
Roofs Cleaved
Ha vocs Wrought
U pon the Heath

I have tried to write this exercise so you can see the initial consonant or blend for each syllable. I have taken some license with "light te ning" so that it can be a three-syllable word, as some lightning looks as it flashes across the sky. Practice saying these words one syllable at a time, using the initial consonant as if it were a train pulling the vowel out, as if it were the carriage being taken out of the tunnel. The consonant must be allowed to shape the vowel and to move it—so that the word comes out of your mouth on the breath on a spiral that descends from behind you and above you, moving forward in front of you and down toward the earth. The goal is to use up all your breath on each line. Many of the consonants at the end of the words, such as M and S, use up lots of breath. Done well, this exercise teaches you to use up all your breath until you are completely out of breath; this means you have to take a full new breath for the next line. All this takes time. And this time is well spent. The underlying principle of the breath exercise is that you speak only on the out-breath—sending your word and voice into the world as a well-prepared deed. Then, you close your mouth on the in-breath

and use this time to collect a new thought, to be prepared for the next thing you will say, and to be available for a new inspiration. Rudolf Steiner said to his teachers at their courses in preparation for class teaching:

The amount of inspiration available to you at any time is in direct relationship to the amount you have breathed out on the last words you spoke.

Learning to love your own voice

In older yoga practices, much attention was given to the in-breath. Steiner spoke of these exercises as the New Yoga, where all our attention was given to just giving all our breath away. Then, he says, without any work at all, you will be given back all the breath that is needed.

As this new breath is given to you, you may also be given a completely new idea or impulse to say something quite different from what you had planned, that is perfect for this moment in your class. This is the greatest gift from the gods: Inspiration. Inspiration relates to respiration!

But the main condition that most modern people are speaking with is no breath at all. Many people hold their breath while speaking. This makes them tired, grumpy, and lifeless; it prevents re-oxygenation of their blood, nourishment to their brain and limbs, and access at all to a new or inspired thought. Such teachers get sick of the sound of their own voices and fall asleep about what they are saying, and so do the pupils about what they are hearing. Bringing your voice into a deeper relationship to your own breath is the most enlivening thing you can do with your voice. Suddenly you will feel better, think of new things to do and say, enjoy the words, awaken to new life in yourself, and develop vigor and love for your work. In her book, *The Listening Ear,* Audrey McAllen gives an example of a lovely breath exercise for children.

> *Big Brown Bear*
> *Sleeps away the winter cold*
> *Deep down there.*
> *Where the snow lays Fold on Fold.*
> *When springtime comes to wake him*
> *From his wintry bed we'll shake him.*
> *Through the springtime woods he'll go*
> *To see the leaves and flowers grow.*
> *Where the bees will make their honey,*
> *Smooth and gold and sweet and runny.*

There are many collections of wonderful verses, poems, and sayings for class teachers to use to speak together with their classes. I always encourage my new teachers to begin with ones they love. Learn them and speak them, using the consonants to move the vowels out into the room on the outgoing flow of the breath.

Knowing the poem before teaching it

Learning verses and poems by heart before you teach them to the children is essential. Remember, if you are reading to the children, the main thing they learn is: "The teacher doesn't know it, so why should I learn it?" It is interesting that we say, in English, learning by heart. The rhythm and rhyme that are such essential memory builders are all heart faculties. Breathing and heartbeat rule such memorizing. Speaking in deep relation to our breathing and to our beating heart brings all our body into health and order. Sensory integration is a phrase much spoken about in schools today. Lively group speaking, working with the consonants to shape the vowels, and using the breath to fill out the sounds, all the while standing actively and using arms and hands to help the breath out into the room—all this is an activity which fully integrates the whole human being.

Choosing for the whole class or an individual

Children who have worked on speech exercises and poems and stories in this way will be deeper and more accurate listeners, more lively thinkers, better at digesting both their meals and new thoughts or concepts. Their powers of listening will develop and grow into better imaginations, empathy with others, and fellow feeling for the world. After breath exercises there are many articulation exercises that can be played with. Dorothy Harrer gave many for children, and in Maisie Jones' book, *Creative Speech,* you can find the first English translations of the exercises Steiner gave to the teachers; these also can be used. But from the many rich collections of poems and speaking games, you can choose lively poems and stories that include the sounds you think your class needs to work on. When making selections, you can choose for the whole class, their age, the main lesson material you are working on. You can also choose for one particular child in your class and have everyone work on the same thing. This often has truly magical powers to heal and to help children move through blocked places.

Verse by Rudolf Steiner on speech

> To one who understands the sense of speech
> The world unveils its image form.
> To one who listens to the soul of speech
> The world unfolds its true being.
> To one who lives in the spirit depths of speech
> The world gives freely Wisdom's strength.
> To one who lovingly can dwell on speech
> Speech will accord its inner might.
> So will I turn my heart and mind
> Toward the soul and spirit of words.
> In love for them I will then feel myself
> Complete and whole.

Another breath exercise that can also be done with children is working on the different realms of speech in the mouth. At first you take no breath at all, but say "S," making it sound as if a tire has a puncture and all the air is going out. Keep saying it as long as you can. Then, on the next line you say "S F," making each sound last as long as you can and using your whole breath. Then "S F M." Then "L S F M." Then "K L S F M." The complete exercise goes like this:

S	teeth
SF	teeth, top teeth & lower lip
SFM	teeth, top teeth & lower lip, both lips
LSFM	add tongue and hard palate
KLSFM	add soft palate
LSFM	then work backwards until
SFM	you
SF	are
S	back to just teeth

Consonantal conversations

This can be done daily as part of your morning routine, playing with making the sounds last as long as possible, but saying the whole line each time on one breath. Sometimes you can ask the children to have consonantal conversations. Put them in pairs. The first person chooses a consonant, perhaps M. The second person chooses one, RRRRR. Then ask them to have a conversation using only their sound. This can be fun, and they will use more breath and more nuance and play with the sound. Lots of different things can be said with the same sound.

Sounds from the fixed stars—consonants

The sounds themselves are our teachers. It is only a matter of knowing how to engage their help. If we have once understood this, then that will mean that the several parts of our organism of throat and mouth have been received as pupils into the world of sounds. The sounds are verily the Gods from whom we are to learn how to form our speaking.
– Rudolf Steiner

Constellation	Image/Quality	Sounds
Capricorn	The Goat	L
Taurus	The Bull	R
Scorpio	The Scorpion	S
Sagittarius	The Archer	K G
Cancer	The Crab	F
Gemini	The Twins	H

Aquarius	The Water Bearer	M
Leo	The Lion	T D
Pisces	The Fishes	N
Virgo	The Virgin	B P
Aries	The Ram	V F
Libra	The Scales	Tz

Sounds from the planets – the vowels

Sunday	Sun	au
Monday	Moon	ei
Tuesday	Mars	ae
Wednesday	Mercury	ee
Thursday	Jupiter	o
Friday	Venus	ah
Saturday	Saturn	oo

Taking lessons from a eurythmist or a teacher of speech formation can help teachers to become more familiar with the sounds and their formation. Then they can "prescribe" poems for their class with more precision, choosing sounds which can help the children at certain times, or strengthen aspects of them.

The elements of speech

Another way of considering the sounds of speech is to explore the elements within the sounds of speech. These include Fire, Water, Air and Earth—and within earth sounds there are those that have a more metal sound, or resonance.

Blown sounds	Fire	W Wh F V S Z Sh Y H
Vibrating sounds	Air	Wr Rrrrr
Flowing sounds	Water	L
Impact sounds	Earth	B P D T J CH G K
	Metal	M N NG

Much has been written about the rhythms themselves and how they often reflect the temperaments.

Sanguines	^^—^^—^—	Anapest, Iamb
Choleric	—^^—	Choriambus
Phlegmatics	—^—^^	Trochee and Dactyl
Melancholics	^—^	Amphibrach

All these ways of exploring the sounds and tasting them can help the teacher with writing poems for the children, for helping children to learn to speak poems, with telling stories, and later writing and directing plays.

Report or birthday verses

Much can be done once you understand all these relationships. Choosing a poem for a child in your class that has the primary rhythm in it for their temperament and which changes into its opposite at the end can be very therapeutic.

Heinz Müller offers a process for class teachers on how to write report verses for the children in their classes in his book, *Report Verses in Rudolf Steiner's Art of Education* (translated by Jesse Darnell). These verses, when written by their own teacher, often have the most far-reaching results. The method for choosing the rhythms, which you think express where the child is now, and then moving into a new rhythm, which will help them to grow and find balance, is the beginning. Then choose the consonants, which will help the child form the speech and themselves. Lastly come up with the images for the poem. Any teacher who takes time to write especially for one child or for their class works untold healing powers. These words and images have far more impact on the children than even the excellent poems from works of great literature.

Speech exercises

It is good to begin the day with poems, games, and small verses that provide exercises in forming certain sounds. You do not need to draw the children's attention to these sounds, but demonstrate good speaking yourself, emphasize the sounds clearly, and let them do the work.

B   *Blossoms beautiful and bright*
        Bursting into bloom
        Bees and butterflies in flight
        By the banks of broom

D *The day is dark*
And dank and dreary
Dank and dreary
Drives the rain.

Notice all the words ending in *d*. Helping the children to sound the *n* and let it lengthen as it indeed wants to, and then to finish the word with the *d*, can give them a wonderful experience of how the word itself teaches you how to think. The word *land*, as in when a plane comes in to *lannnnnnd*, can give a vivid picture of the plane landing, taxiing to the gate, and finally stopping.

F *The farmer flings the fruitful seed*
Afar, upon the furrowed field

There are many sources of such exercises, and all are good to work with. I have included the names of many excellent books in my reference list.

The realms of the speech instrument

Our speech instrument is made up of three very clear realms.

The Lips: **W WH M B P**

Made at the front of the mouth with both lips, the WH is a very different sound from W; it is blown and makes a huge difference when it is said fully as in *Why What Where*.

In many languages the sounds of M B P are used in the names of our primary family connections: Mama Baby Papa. This shows the sounds all speak to us of warmth and memory and feeling. This region of our speech instrument indicates FEELING.

The Hard Palate: **N D T L Rrrrr**

The tip of the tongue presses against the hard palate. These sounds almost require us to draw our lips back out of the way. The absolute clarity of these sounds brings definition, objectivity, facts and truth into our speech. This is the realm of THINKING.

The Soft Palate: **Ng G K H**

The back of the speech instrument is formed where the soft palate and the back of the tongue meet. These sounds are the WILLING sounds and speak to us of action, strength, and competence.

Doing exercises which isolate these sounds and help children to find them in fullness and with their breath can bring new worlds into the poems and words they are speaking. They will bring depth, movement, flow, and form into your stories and indeed into your classroom instructions if you work on them for yourself.

Exercises to correct unformed speech

The sound of the letter *R* can have three different placements;

Hard Palate	as in *right* (rrrrr)
Lips	as in *wrong*
Soft Palate	as in *loch* (can be rolled too)

Today many children cannot roll their *R*s. Since this is the only vibrating or mobile sound left in the English language, Steiner encouraged us to help them do it.

Exercise to roll *R*:

Stand and say clearly	D T D T D T D T
Speed it up	DT DT DT DT DT
Then say	B T B T B T B T
Speed that up	BT BT BT BT BT BT
Mix them up	DT BT DT BT DT

Go as quickly as you can. This can help children find mobility in the tip of their tongue and can lead to being able to trill this sound.

Stuttering

Stuttering is a common problem for many of our children. Much has been written about this, and if you have a therapeutic speech teacher to call on, this is a good time to use her.

But in class you can also play games combining speaking and throwing a bean bag; the object is to time the overhand throw from above the head with the launching of the initial sound of the word. The partner catches and repeats throwing it back. This combination of movement, speaking, and a full outbreath can help to distract the stutter and release the voice. Many stutterers do not do so when singing, so bringing movement and breath into the voice can help.

The twelve senses and auditory processing

Early in the last century, Steiner gave his description of the twelve senses. Today most of these have been recognized in neurology and have even been given very specific names. They are arranged in three groups:

The Lower Senses: The senses of touch, life, movement, and balance.
The Middle Senses: The senses of smell, taste, sight, and warmth (which often does not mature until around age 12)
The Higher Senses: The senses of hearing, word, thought, and ego

The higher senses

In speaking, while we use many of the senses, it is the higher senses that are called into play—and which are so needed in our time. Any work a class teacher does to teach poems, speeches from plays, games, riddles, and later whole plays and drama, is helping to build these hugely important senses for our times. Let us explore them a little.

Hearing

It is a miracle that we hear at all. The ear is fully formed by four and half months in utero. So the child can hear from inside the womb. Many have even called the ear "The Architect of the Soul" because the ear not only governs what we hear, but is also responsible for our being able to pull ourselves into uprightness, and to be able to balance. Every parent knows that a child who gets a high fever, or an ear infection, can also get dizzy or lose her balance. This is when the inner ear is affected.

Not only does the inner ear help us find our uprightness, it is also responsible for our sense of laterality, our sense of where our limbs are in space. Dancers, movers, athletes, jugglers, and playing children all have a strong sense of where their hands and feet are and can coordinate them. In our speaking classes we often move our feet and our hands in time with our speaking to work with this much-needed synchronicity. This is where sensory integration is helped and does much for the child's journey in gaining full mastery of the physical body.

The inner ear, the cochlea, is a spiral that takes the sounds we hear deep inside us. The substance of that tubing appears in only one other place in the human body, in the gut. This tells us a great deal about our sense of hearing. We need time to digest what we hear!

In today's schools we often hear of children diagnosed with auditory processing challenges. Might this not have a great deal to do with the way the people speak around them? The speech, the lack of formation of the sounds of the words, the deadening sound of the voices, the lack of breath—won't this discourage a child from listening?

The ear longs for breath and to hear a story told in bite-sized pieces. A child who hears a line of a story or an instruction on the breath of the speaker, who is given one line at a time for her to digest while the speaker stops speaking and reaches for the next part of his message, is being given time to work with the very construction of her own inner ear. She needs time to take in what she has heard, for it to travel deep inside the inner ear where it can be almost magically transformed into understanding and comprehension. But for this she needs time!

There are people who are very clever at what they are talking about and can speak very quickly, using words they know very well, and relate at the speed of light. But their listeners may struggle to transform into understanding or even grasp the thoughts!

Gaining the sense of the word

The higher senses include the fundamental sense of hearing, being able to hear sounds from the world outside. Then there is the sense of word itself. This is our amazing ability to recognize that sounds are words and that there is a meaning or an intention to them. Anyone who has traveled where he does not speak the language can relate to this. He can still be perfectly certain whether a sound is just a noise or actually meaningful words.

The sense of thought

Beyond this and through this is the sense of thought. It is vital in all classroom situations to be able to speak the words of your thought or instruction in such a way that the children not only hear you and hear the words, but are given time to grasp the thought contained in them.

Anyone who considers the work of our digestive system can be given great insight into the demands of the sense of thought. When we eat, we take something into our mouths which may have appeal, may taste wonderful and have great textures, but then we crush it up, move it around in our mouths, feel it, taste it, and begin the process of selecting what we like and what we do not. At this point we can even take it out of our mouths! Then we swallow. And that food goes on a long journey of being utterly destroyed before we complete our process of selecting what we will keep and what we will eliminate.

The ear needs time to do the same process: to take in as fully as possible the words of the thought, to have time to move them around and deeper into our realm of hearing, and to go through the same selection process of taking in what we choose and eliminating what we don't.

If the speaker is working hard with her own breath and forming the sounds with care, the listener does not even notice the gaps when she breathes in because, in the silence, the listener can do the largest work, the initial digesting of what has been said.

This is monumental work. You can all remember a time in your life when someone gave you a completely new thought and you had to rearrange many of your long-held thoughts to accommodate it.

Auditory processing

This takes time! Today's children need time! Integration is the work of time. Processing takes time. Auditory processing is a phrase telling us that our children need, first of all, well-made, and well-chosen words with clear and imaginative thoughts within them; then they need ways to process what they hear. Some will need to move, some will need to draw, some will need to speak about it. But they need time to process it. So say something they will want to process and remember!

The sense of ego

The highest sense, one filled with mystery, is the sense of ego. A huge faculty, this speaks of our ability to hear who someone is from the sound of the voice. And we have the ability to remember a person's voice for a lifetime. Those people who matter to us, who have influenced us deeply, whom we love—their voices matter. We can go years without speaking to a dear friend, but even on a busy street, if we hear his voice, we will spin around and call out his name. We can remember voices for the whole of our lives. This is one of the most compelling reasons for us as teachers and parents to work on our own voices, to make them worth remembering. We all know that there are people whose voices we love to hear. And yet there are those for which we even say, "If I just hear her voice, I feel sick!" This speaks to the reality of the digestion of sound: If that sound is indigestible, it can make us sick.

Be a model for the children

In my lessons and courses, my deepest and last message to teachers and parents is: "Your voice matters! Work on it, learn to use it well. It is the source of great power and magic. Make certain the magic is healing!"

All our classrooms have spelling lists on the board, but few stop to consider the deeper meaning of "spelling." It is about magic. All words are spells. The power comes from the stars themselves that lighten our dark nights. The power to speak comes from our own human-ness and our uprightness. The words come through us as our most human deed and offering. And the sound of our voice is as unique as we are.

Being models for children, being those who take care of our voices, who strive to master the world of sound and the power of words to express thoughts that are true and which can heal and motivate and last—this is a way to bring our voices into the memories and even the destiny of those we teach.

REFERENCES

Bauer, A. (1989). *Healing sounds: Fundamentals of chirophonetics*. Barbara Baldwin, trans. Fair Oaks, CA: Rudolf Steiner College Press.

Kennedy, D. (2011). *The Waldorf book of poetry: Discover the power of imagination*. Living Arts Books.

Masters, B. (1980). *Meteor showers and us: Poems for speaking aloud in School and Home*. London: Temple Lodge Press.

McAllen, A.E. (1990). *The listening ear, The development of speech as a creative influence in education*. Stroud, UK: Hawthorn Press.

Muller, H. (2013). *Report verses in Rudolf Steiner's art of education: Healing forces in words and their rhythms*. Jesse Darrell, trans. Edinburgh: Floris Books, and Forest Row, UK: Steiner Schools Fellowship Publications.

Schwartz, E. (1990). *Seeing hearing learning, The interplay of eye and ear in Waldorf education*. Fair Oaks, CA: Rudolf Steiner College Publications.

Steiner, R. (1995). *The genius of language: Observations for teachers* given to the faculty of the Waldorf School in Stuttgart, Germany, Dec. 26, 1919–Jan. 3, 1920. Gertrude Deutsch and Ruth Pusch, trans.. Great Barrington, MA: Anthroposophic Press.

Steiner, R. and von Sivers, M. (1999). *Creative speech: The formative creative process of the spoken word*, a selection of lectures, exercises and articles. Winifred Budgett, Nancy Hymmel, and Maisie Jones, trans. Forest Row, UK: Rudolf Steiner Press.

Thomas, H. (1987). *A journey through time in verse and rhyme: Collected poems*. Edinburgh: Floris Books.

Von Heider, M. (1981). *And then take hands*. Millbrae, CA: Celestial Arts.

_____. (1984). *Come unto these yellow sands*. Forest Row, UK: Steiner Schools Fellowship Publications.

_____. (1996). *Looking forward: Games, rhymes and exercises to help children develop their learning abilities*. Stroud, UK: Hawthorn Press.

Drama
Does Perseus have to hold Andromeda's hand?

Dennis Demanett

Man is a complete human being only as long as he plays, and he plays only as long as he is a complete human being. – Friedrich Schiller

The uses of drama through the grades

The natural activity of the child is to play, to pretend, to invent worlds and enter them with intensity and a sense of purpose that we might often associate with the adult at work. The function of drama or "play-acting" in education is perhaps best understood as an aid to help the teacher recognize this natural impulse in children, and develop it in such a way as to deepen inborn gifts, overcome possible weaknesses, and clear obstacles that may otherwise never be noticed. These somewhat lofty tasks unfold in the class teacher years through a curriculum rich with possibilities for making pedagogical content come to life through dramatic arts with speech, music, movement, color, and a host of other appropriate activities.

While class plays have become a much-loved tradition in most Waldorf schools worldwide, Rudolf Steiner neither wrote nor said very much, if anything, about them. Yet, we can note the multiple admonishments Rudolf Steiner made to the teachers to strive to bring true artistry to the task of educating children, and from this, assume that through the dramatic arts we have an opportunity, indeed a responsibility, to practice some of the most important principles at the heart of this education. The evolution of a class play involves work on speech, singing, instrumental music, movement, visual arts, and most importantly, the reliance on using imaginative characterization rather than definition. Furthermore, the ranges of capacities we can develop in class plays are not merely useful for the life of the plays themselves. Natural gifts that unfold in a fifth grade play, for example, may truly manifest fully only at age 30 or 40 in the person's life. Indeed, for me, the joy of working on plays with children of all ages is often eclipsed by my conversations with these "children" as adults when they can recall being involved in plays as among the most shining memories of their Waldorf education, yes, even when Perseus did undeniably have to hold Andromeda's hand! A recent conversation with one of the several Perseus-portrayers I have directed over the years was enlightening. This young man, now a 33-year-old independent filmmaker and actor, told me that being Perseus in that fifth grade play made him realize, if only in looking back on that 10-year-old experience, that he possessed something within himself that could overcome any hardship. He was not carrying Medusa's head in his hip pocket, but he was grateful to have a deeper sense of his own courage partly because of that childhood experience.

Before we explore the possibilities of capacities we can develop with children, behind the scenes as it were, we will make a quick overview of plays as I have used them over the past 40 years I have spent as a class teacher.

Survey of drama in grades 1–8

First Grade: The plays were not much more than what we did in circle time each day. There were no individual speaking parts, and singing carried most of the stories. We used minimal costumes, a few props, and the audience, parents, siblings, perhaps kindergartners and second graders, gathered forming an outer circle to witness the play. Themes included fairy tales, nature, and seasonal/festival celebrations. Examples: *The Lonely Pine Tree* at Advent, *The Water of Life* at Easter

Second Grade: The children performed the plays in the classroom, or perhaps outdoors using nature as the backdrop. Individual speaking parts were kept to a minimum, one or two lines perhaps, while the story was conveyed through singing and choral speaking. We used simple costumes and a few props. The audience consisted of parents, siblings, perhaps our grade one, grade three, and kindergarten neighbors. Themes: *The King of Ireland's Son* (*The Winning of Fedelma*), St Frances, St Bridget, *Ly Chee and the Dragon*, *Nkosnati and the Dragon* (these last two at Michaelmas, performed for the whole school, together with the sixth grade).

Third Grade: I moved the plays into bigger spaces, but not yet to a stage in a larger hall or auditorium. Individuals now took up more substantial speaking parts, though music, singing, and choral speech moved the story. Costumes consisted of simple tunics and veils in strong colors, as we brought in eurythmy and folk dancing. All the children remained on the stage during the performance, as in the Oberufer *Shepherd's Play*. From this grade onward, we invited the other classes in the school to be our audience. Themes included: The Creation Story, David and Goliath, and Moses.

Fourth Grade: For the first time, we staged the play, using lights and more costumes. Individual parts emerged as we practiced, although music and choral speech still helped to carry the play. Again, the children remained onstage throughout, on benches at the back or sides. Themes arose from Norse myths and local geography, and included: *The Treasures of the Gods, The Theft of Thor's Hammer*, and *The Death of Baldur the Beautiful*.

Fifth Grade: I added to the staging in fifth grade, with sets the children helped to design and paint, shadow plays with puppets made by students, and other "stage tricks" such as waving water and storms. Costumes became more detailed, not so general, suitable to the play's contents. We used a little stage makeup starting in this grade. Choral speaking and music, now with students playing instruments, help to carry the story. In some classes, students began to help write the plays. Themes included: Perseus and Andromeda, Rama and Sita, and United States geography.

Sixth Grade: For the first time, students began to "act," to take on roles that were often a stretch for them. I added staging, props, costumes, always with help (if not leadership), from the students themselves. We sometimes performed our plays as part of the festival celebrations at school in this grade. Themes arose from history lessons as well as age-appropriate contemporary stories. Examples of themes I used: *Waiting for Papa*, a play that introduced the Advent garden to the school, *Holly and Ivy* (a musical based on the story by Rumer Goden), *Julius Caesar,* and *The Wedding of King Arthur* performed at May Day to introduce the May Pole dancing to the whole school.

Seventh Grade: I continued to work on staging with input from the children, often using eurythmy when the eurythmy teacher was available to help. Together we built sets, wrote dialogue and music, and spoke more about the importance of mood, use of voice, and developing a character. We performed for the whole school, and, I have to admit that, in all five seventh grades I have taught, I ended up doing a biographical play, *Joan of Arc,* which evolved over the years, becoming a full-blown musical with dance and eurythmy.

Eighth Grade: This is the year with multiple possibilities for choices of plays and ways of performing them. Most important was to involve the students in the selection of the play and to find a means of using the many talents that will have emerged by this time. In the five eighth grades I have taught, my classes performed *As You Like It* (two of the classes), *The Wizard of Oz*, *The Curious Savage,* and most recently a cabaret/whodunit.

Against the backdrop of this brief survey, we will investigate experiences of the possible clearing of obstacles, overcoming weaknesses, and enhancing of inherent gifts that can occur while working on drama in the classroom.

Removal of obstacles

A tin goblet-shaped vase, painted a muted, metallic gold and a few fake jewels strategically glued on around its circumference, becomes a suitable receptacle for the Water of Life in a first grade circle play. Not a drop must be spilled as the precious fluid, warm and almost at the brim of the goblet, is carried from child to child. Twenty-five first graders silently, with devotion, deliver the water to the prince, a classmate who can now break the spell that enchanted his sister, the sleeping princess, a girl earnestly reposing on a silk-draped desk, arms crossed over her heart, and eyes closed. With the deepest seriousness and pure reverence, the boy places his finger in the sacred water and touches the girl's forehead gently. She smiles, open her eyes, awakens! The children burst into singing: "Early one morning, just as the sun was rising ..."

A few days earlier, three of the grade one boys grudgingly joined the play, reluctant to put on an

imaginary crown, or worse, scornful of the very idea of imagining what is not physically present, to pull something from a source within. These children had basically "cut their teeth" on facts, piles of information, something that tends to obliterate the once natural capacity of wanting to pretend, to play. Yet, even these dear, wizened children can be freed from the factual prison house. Drama, in the form of our Water of Life play, invited them to put aside their disbelief, and in the end, these boys not only carried the water with reverence and joy, but also asked that we do the play again and again.

This example speaks to one of the most pervasive obstacles I have seen in recent years, which is not attention deficit or learning differences, but a plethora of disconnected bits of information, a swarm of factoids drowning emerging minds in random "truths" unconnected to meaning, devoid of soul nourishment. These children, intellectually bright, curious, and often academically capable, lack the capacity for wonder, for experiencing the thrill of discovery through their own efforts. As an educator, I feel one has to teach these youngsters to imagine, to play, and if we can achieve this, then the obstacle disappears, and an innate ability awakens, the capacity to form inner pictures, crucial to the task of placing these dear ones on a path toward freedom.

In one of my second grade classes, I recall a little boy who was suffering terribly from his parents' divorce, throwing a huge obstacle on this sensitive child's path. Emmet was much loved in the group, a boy always chosen as a partner, a child with a generous, if sad little heart. This boy emerged in our circle play of *The Winning of Fedelma* as an obvious choice to be the King of Ireland's Son. Sorrows and aloofness seemed to melt away as he took up this role, which involved slaying his beloved, using her bones as a ladder to get the Ring of Life from the bottom of a well, and then, putting Fedelma back together and reviving her with the ring! The course of the story truly echoed the process in Emmet's life, as he literally had to rebuild his shattered world and find the way to travel onward. As I write now, this young man is on the route to becoming an educator himself, teaching young children in an Asian country, and often looking back in gratitude for the support he received through Waldorf education.

Apart from class plays and circle work in the early grades, the use of puppets is an effective method for allowing imagination to survive, if not flourish, in the children. I consider puppetry an important form of drama, especially appropriate if the teacher needs to bring an important social message to the class and can use puppets in the same we employ the pedagogical or curative story. For example, in one of my first grade classes, we had a beloved squirrel puppet named Nuthatch, who often regaled the class with his adventures, his experience of changing seasons, his visits to the crows in the tops of the great oaks on campus, and so on. One day, it came to my attention that some of the children had been throwing rocks at recess, and even in games class. When the children came in to the classroom from their recess, Nuthatch was sitting on my desk, quite alone. I had put a large band-aid on his head. Of course, the children wanted to know what had happened! One of the girls even asked, "Oh dear, did he get hit by a rock?" Well, Nuthatch related that indeed a rock had struck him on the noggin, and he was sure it could not have been any child in our class or our school. Nonetheless, three of the students, with big eyes, admitted that they had been throwing rocks, but they hoped that they did not hit Nuthatch. The conversation continued and it was duly noted that it could be dangerous to throw rocks on the playground. At least for that year, to my knowledge, not another child in the class threw another rock on our playground!

Of course, the obstacles in front of children in our time can manifest in all realms, including physical health. I once had a little girl in my class, who at the end of the fifth grade year was discovered to have a large brain tumor. She loved our class plays, and had happily portrayed one of the gray sisters in our Perseus play and did it with a Cockney accent and many inventive gestures and expressions. When I visited her in hospital, I told her that I was looking forward to our sixth grade play, and thinking about what it might be. She perked up at the thought, and her mom told me she often spoke about the coming sixth grade play through the course of her illness. Members of our school community met every morning during this time, forming a meditative and protective circle of light around this child. Doctors were astonished when they operated to discover that the tumor was nearly diminished "of its own accord," and the little girl would not only survive, but regain all her faculties. So, in sixth grade I had chosen to do a musical play, *Holly and Ivy*, and invited this child to be Ivy, an orphan who runs away at Christmas time, seeking for a home. Although the girl was Jewish, she happily played this part in a Christmas story, through the unfolding of rehearsals and the performances, surprising all of us with her gift for singing and entering her character with a sense of the miracle of her own life reflecting the miracle that lies at the core of the play. I can assure you that at the moment Ivy discovered her "mother" in the play, there was not a dry eye in the house.

In another class, another time, we were at work on the seventh grade play, *Joan of Arc*. I would cast three girls as Joan: Joan, the Girl; Joan, the Warrior, and Joan on Trial. I found it easy to cast the first two, but the third one, the most challenging, eluded me as well as the class for a few days. Then I thought of Melissa. She was a quiet girl in class, and found learning poems or songs to be a great burden. I remembered first grade, when I often simply had to hold her hand through the lessons to keep her calm, walking up and down the room with her tagging along. She was a nervous girl, nails usually bitten to the quick, and she cried easily, usually at odds with one or the other girls in the class. She had never had a big part in the plays. But this seemed to be Melissa's moment, and when I talked to her about taking on this role, her face shone, her eyes moistened and her radiant "yes" convinced me, even before one rehearsal, that this was the right choice. Every rehearsal was a steppingstone for her, and Melissa learned her lines overnight, ready to enter the part with an earnestness one might not even get from an adult taking this role. She was far too quiet at first, nervous, and somewhat wooden. But she listened to me and to her classmates, and in two weeks, amazed us all in the dress rehearsal. From the moment she stepped onto the stage in our first evening performance in her black velvet tunic to face the judges, Melissa was transformed, speaking with clarity and volume so that even the old lady in the back of the auditorium who had forgotten her hearing aid could not only hear her, but respond to the emotion in her heart-felt words. The obstacles for the three days of performances, at least, were gone. Years later, now a fashion designer, Melissa contacted me to express her gratitude. "Being Joan of Arc was the best thing that happened to me in grade school," she said. "But I also liked the class trips!"

Sylvester was a boy in one of my classes who found school to be a wonderful social experience during the first three years, but hardly a place where actual learning could take place. Our school doctor suggested that he was endowed with too many sympathy forces, and we needed to develop antipathy in him—an interesting obstacle indeed. By the end of third grade, this child, with the dawning self-awareness of the nine-year change, noted that he was not yet reading, that his math was a problem for him, and he felt sad and stupid, in his own words. The combination of a summer vacation, a diligent, non-judgmental mother, and the Waldorf curriculum came to the rescue! Sylvester was motivated, as he awakened to his own obstacles, to do work himself, to force himself to focus, to practice, to make headway in the academic work that had thus far eluded him. Norse mythology was a wonder to him, and his writing, spelling, and artwork improved through the course of the fourth grade year. He took on the role of Thor in the class play and wore his mother out, throwing imaginary hammers around the house, "practicing for my part, Mum," being the excuse. But it was the fifth grade play a year later that really helped the stronger, more confident Sylvester emerge. He did play Perseus, and it was his question, since the girl playing Andromeda was his fifth grade heartthrob, that gives this piece its title. He learned his lines quickly, helped with every aspect of the play, including working to make a Medusa puppet to use in the shadow sequence, and offered advice daily, wanted or not, to all the other fifth graders. Oh, he never did lose that sympathetic/social side, but he gained just enough antipathy to hold his own in our lessons and to shine in our productions. By eighth grade, he was able to take the role of Orlando in *As You Like It*, particularly striking and lovely, as he was a full foot shorter than our dear Rosalind. But, that is another story…

Conquering weaknesses

The story of the girl who played Rosalind in the very production just mentioned is relevant to the process of conquering weaknesses, especially when we would never have seen these issues if not for working on a play. Irena came to the class in the middle of fifth grade, arriving after the Christmas break under sad, unique circumstances. I had met Irena and her parents at our school Christmas Fair in December. Her father had taken me aside, begging me please to accept his daughter in my class. It is so important that she come to your school, he stated. Over the Christmas holiday, this man died suddenly, and his previous words seemed like something of an edict, prophetic and important for me to understand. Irena was bereft of a much-loved father, and we had to do something. "Help me, Hierarchies," I remember intoning on a daily basis.

Irena seemed strong in many ways, bursting with energy, emotional, easily in tears over almost any swing in emotion, happy or sad. She walked across the room and the playground with a powerful stride, looked everyone unsmilingly in the eye, and called bluffs whenever she sensed them. These attributes did not win immediate friendships, but her sense of humor and wacky jokes and ability to use accents and voices impressed her new classmates. So it seemed natural that, when we came to putting on the class play, she could have a part that would call on these gifts. Cast as one of the gray sisters in Perseus and Andromeda, she had us all in stitches as she used the lines and her own ad libs to turn these three who shared an eyeball and a tooth, into master clowns. It was her idea to use a tennis ball as the eyeball prop, so that it bounced when dropped on the stage.

Now, imagine my shock, when on the day of the first performance, I find Irena behind the stage, sobbing, gasping for breath, telling me she could not go on. "I just can't. I will faint if I go out there. Call Mum, she's got to take me home." Here, the one girl she had befriended, a little New Zealander named Angelika, came to something of a rescue. "I can do the part for you," she assured Irena. "I know the lines." I suggested that we could do that, but then put my hands on Irena's shoulders gently and said something about how we had all enjoyed what she had done to make the gray sisters so funny, and she never would have to actually look out at the audience. I was sure this was just drivel to her, but she stood up and started to put on her costume. "Can you smear up my face with black make up?" she pleaded. "I do not want to be recognized." So we did, and still subdued, she crept onto stage and admirably performed the part, though not with the gusto she had mustered at rehearsals. By the third performance, she was in top form, but afterward she came to me and said, "Stage fright, that's what it is. I still have it, but you better not keep me from being in plays in the future, all right?" How could I dare anything of the kind?

Indeed, Irena played the part of an old apple-seller in our sixth grade Advent play about a family waiting for the return of a traveling parent, poignant for her, as it did bring up memories of her own father. In seventh grade, she was one of Joan of Arc's judges, stern and awful, a surprise to most of us, but no shock at all to her mother, who told me, "Irena is going to be a really difficult teenager, you wait and see."

Well, what we did see, a few weeks after this play was a shocking medical diagnosis for this 13-year-old girl. Irena had cancer and would need to have her uterus removed. How on earth does anyone deal with such a blow? Our way of dealing with it at school was to treat Irena as normal, once she was back in class, at the beginning of grade eight. She insisted she could do all the work, did not want any special attention, and got down to the job of being the difficult teenager her mother had seen coming. But the old weakness was still there. On a hiking trip to a nearby youth hostel, she wanted to walk with me and confessed quietly that she was really scared that once she left school she would not be able to do anything. "I really want to be an actress," she said, "but I can never do that. I would die every time I went on a stage. I think I will end up an old maid living with my mum," she moaned. "Hell on earth," she muttered.

Fast forward to casting our eighth grade play, *As You Like It*. Well, dear Irena was the only girl in the class who wanted to tackle the part of Rosalind, but refused, unless we double-cast. Angelika to the rescue again, agreed to be Rosalind's understudy, although she really wanted to be Touchstone, the Fool. Knowing this, Irena talked her rival in the class, Patricia, into being the other Rosalind. So those two girls played Rosalind in alternate performances, though Sylvester happily played Orlando to each. We nursed Irena through the whole ordeal, reassuring her before each show, calming her with herb tea and scented candles backstage.

Now, the most interesting part of this story comes years later. Irena did go to drama school, graduated with the promise of a career on stage, but decided in the end to move to Paris and run a travel agency. Chutzpah she never lost, but stage fright we only temporarily overcame!

Liam stuttered when he came to first grade. Self-conscious and large for his age, he was reluctant to join in movement activities and refused to speak verses or rhymes. Yet he learned songs easily and sang with a clear, tuneful voice without uttering many of the words, and settled quietly in the classroom only when listening to fairy tales. He soon became engaged by the circle-plays we did in grade one, that is, he listened intently, attempted to move with the class, and continued to sing the melodies, not the words, of our songs. He especially seemed to love the part of our Michaelmas circle called "Searching for a Sword," which involved repetitive rhymes as we knocked on the doors of the Metal Gnomes, and only after asking for a sword from Copper, Silver, and Gold, did we come to the Iron Gnome, who of course, had the sword. I realized we had a breakthrough when Liam, who had never spoken the rhymes in circle time, could be heard through the door, one morning before school, organizing his classmates, and lining up outside, into speaking, singing, and acting out the sword search! "Knock, knock, knock, Mr. Gnome! Are you home? Can you be? Do you have a sword for me?" I am sure you can well imagine my joy and surprise when I peeped out the window and beheld this spectacle on the porch outside the door!

From then on, Liam participated in (I would daresay, even led) the circle activities once he learned them. Speech exercises and rhymes, usually humorous ones, helped with the stutter, and plenty of repeated poems and songs strengthened his pronunciation and enunciation. He went on through the years to take part with confidence in class plays. I remember especially his eighth grade project public speech on how to use stop-action filming of beeswax characters, to create a venue for teaching children about the dangers of drug usage. The speech was clear, confident, devoid of any issues, a real crowd-pleaser.

Fourth grade Norse mythology plays offer such a perfect range of characters for children in this phase of development, newly burdened with the thought of their own mortality, while marveling at the notion that they are the one and only one of themselves, that nobody else is who you are, and you are not anyone but yourself! It is a lot to take in, and then here comes the parade: lofty, wise but flawed Odin; raging, funny, good-hearted Thor; sassy, lovely Freya; clever, but eventually darkly evil Loki; and dear, lovable Baldur. While doing our play about the theft of Thor's hammer, we were asked to perform at the school's annual Winter Fair, and the children were thrilled at the invitation, excited and willing to do it on a Saturday. Tickets would be sold, and the proceeds would go to the school. What could be better? Then, on the morning this performance was scheduled, I got a phone call: One of the main characters, the Giant Thrym, was down with a fever and a terrible chest cold.

However, the show must go on, right? What to do, but call one of the other children in the class, Zach, a fellow who was a reliable, if phlegmatic young man, dependable, but never too interested in bigger parts in the plays. He was still in bed when I called, but his mom brought the phone to him. I explained the situation. He thought he knew the lines; he had paid attention in the rehearsals. But he would need to think about it. After about 45 minutes, I got the call back. He would do it, but could he please practice the lines with me before? I agreed. Of course, this becomes the classic "a star is born" story, because young Zach stormed through the part, surprising all of us, including an audience who did not even know the children!

By the way, we had sold out the performance, and a sad queue of people was hoping we would do our play again. I asked this class if they were willing, and Zach, the new Thrym, led the chorus of "YES! WE WILL!" We did it again, of course, but not without remembering to send good thoughts to the poor sick Thrym at home. That boy got to be King Arthur in our grade six play, and did not need to be replaced... As for Zach, he never again was quite satisfied to play a part of the chorus.

Deepening newly discovered gifts

Often the removal of an obstacle can lead to the discovery of a new gift, while overcoming a weakness can also lead to transformation of something previously not obvious or even present. Most of my examples do overlap into all three

realms of possibility, but this illustration has to do with a whole class discovering new gifts, and deepening them through the process of putting on a class play.

It is normal procedure in Waldorf schools to study one's home country in the geography lessons of grade five. In a previous class, I started the main lesson block with a story about a Mississippi riverboat captain and his grandson. We then branched out to various regions of the country—contrasting life on a Louisiana bayou with the experience of living by a lake on a dairy in northern Wisconsin, then looking at ranch and farm life in the Midwest and Great Plains, deserts of the West, and Appalachian, New England, and Big City life in the eastern regions of the country. This picture evolved into our class play when our story got back to the riverboat captain. Seems he was entered in a riverboat race from Cairo to New Orleans, when the great boat got stuck in a muddy sandbar and would have to wait for a surge in the river to move it on. What to do with all the people on board, while they waited was the captain's problem. Then he had an idea: Since people in the boat came from all over the country—couldn't they form groups, work together and then present a little show, a skit with music and all, to the others, and then he, the captain, would chose the best one! This became the framework of the fifth grade play, with the title "Stuck in the Mud."

The class, divided into five groups: East, West, South, North, and Central had to research their areas of the country further, write dialog, find music, and make it fit together in the framework already mentioned. The children charged into this play as they had never done before. They owned it while they developed their stories, found music (with teacher help), and worked up the blocking, movement, and overall presentation of their sections of the play. There were five children in each group, plus a captain and a first mate to keep order. Our set was a beautiful rendition of a riverboat called "The Delta Princess," and the props were the travelers' suitcases, but that was it. Each group managed to teach something about their part of the country without being pedantic, and, of course, they wanted to be funny.

The greatest achievement, in my view, was the way in which the youngsters worked together, collaborating in writing their skits, sharing the load, making music together, and finding costumes that suited the characters they had created. After a few days work, the stories became tall tales, which allowed for many interesting developments of plot and characterization… The Southern group used their brass instruments and entertained their fellow passengers with competing tall tales about an alligator that swallowed a saxophone and stopped roaring about the bayou, but now played "Sweet Georgia Brown," when he opened his jaws, along with a proud peach orchard owner from Georgia and a pepper farmer from Alabama. This group brought a rousing interpretation of "Jambalaya," the song by Bobby Gentry, "Louisiana Man," and a finale that had the whole cast, and some of the audience marching around to "When the Saints." Our East Coast group got out their fiddles and played an Appalachian folk tune, while one of the characters, Johnny Appleseed, did a little dance. One of the East Coast folk, a taciturn Vermonter, ended up really being a ghost! Paul Bunyan who was also on the boat, was portrayed, with a fifth grade sense of irony, by the shortest child in the class. This Northern set talked a lot about dairies and cheese, as well as ice fishing and a terrible mishap where a pickup truck sank in the lake. The Midwestern family had twin girls named Omaha and Chicago and delivered their entire skit in a Kansas/Oklahoma style vernacular. The Western crew managed a surreal meeting of a surfer dude, a desert gold prospector, a dithery but kindhearted woman named Ari Zona, a mythical cowgirl named Tex, and sweet woman from Oregon who worked at the Shakespeare festival. The captain, in the end, did not pick a winner, declaring them all winners— since the boat had picked up the surge, raced on down the river, and won the race. They ended the performance with a rousing version of "This Land Is Your Land."

Newly discovered gifts in this process included writing, speaking, playing a new kind of music—the fiddlers had played only classical music before this— working with regional accents, and collaborating as a method of learning. For example, they decided to collaborate with all the singing, joining to support each other so that no one group of five had to sing on its own. "It is so much better when we all sing, more rousing, right?" a fifth grader noted during one of our many meetings in which we discussed the whole play together. It was a turning point for this class, especially in the realm of writing and working together to achieve a greater result than any on their own could have managed.

The first graders in our school, at the time of this fifth grade play, were encouraged to send thank you notes, with illustrations, to the fifth graders. This exercise was telling indeed, as the pictures the first graders drew illustrated the stories they experienced, including detailed drawings of the tales told. One child drew the alligator that had swallowed a saxophone, in the process of the deed, and of course, we had no alligator on our set! This process of working on a play, even if never produced for an audience, continued to serve us through the years that followed. Our African geography block, in grade eight, for example, culminated in a series of skits based on African folklore, employing music and drumming from the regions studied. We performed for each other and parents who were able to attend.

In many ways, all that we do with the children throughout the years involves a series of discoveries, gifts unfolding, perhaps when we least expect them. Recognizing these gifts is part of our task, then deepening them so the children can make use of them, keeping them for further development. I think of a boy in second grade, not so very interested in doing a class play unless he could be the main character. "I want to be the King of Ireland's Son," Ben announced. Gently, I had to let him know that children saying, "I want," is not generally how we decide who will play a part. "Okay," he said, "Then I want to be the Enchanter of the Black Backlands." It was clear that this might take awhile to sink in.

Ben played a bird in the second grade play, but by third grade still had not quite understood. "I want to be Goliath in the play. I can do it!" He was cast as an archangel, bestowing gifts on David before his birth. Ben listened to pedagogical stories, sometimes meant just for him about how we treat other people, perhaps not always putting ourselves first. He especially liked the story I told the class near the beginning of fourth grade from my own childhood, when I, as a fourth grader, so longed to be chosen to play Peter Rabbit in an all-school musical, even lobbying the music teacher in charge, haranguing her as she crossed the playground to get to her car. I also knew that my best friend, Billy Hamm, wanted to be Peter. I knew he would be better at it, and then one day, I told the teacher how good he would be. She smiled at me and nodded. In a few days, she chose Billy to be the part, and then, to my surprise, handed me the role of Farmer McGregor!

Ben asked me to sing the Farmer McGregor's song for the class, and I did. Shortly after that, on a class hike in the forest, someone ran past Ben and stomped in a puddle, splashing him with muddy water. This other boy, Francis, Ben's best friend at the time, laughed and sneered, deliberately stomping a second time in the puddle. Ben stomped back, and then pushed his friend into the water. Both boys ended up, if not in tears, red-faced and ready to continue the battle. I stopped them, had them walk with me, and when we got back to our classroom, I sat them down for a little conversation. I told them more about my best friend Billy, and how we sometimes fought. Mostly, we got along, and being in that play together certainly helped us. I also told them that, suddenly in fifth grade, Billy moved away to another state, and I never, ever heard from him again. The boys gave each other significant looks when I said that. I was thinking of the upcoming play we would be doing, *The Theft of Thor's Hammer*, and I wondered if either of these boys would benefit from this story.

Both Francis and Ben loved the tale when I told it, and both of them cheered, along with most of the class, when I announced that this story would be our play. Ben asked to speak to me at recess a day or two after the announcement. "I think Francis would really be a good Thor," he said. "And I am pretty sure that Laura would be so good at Sif or Freya. It is just an idea," he added. This was the gift, hidden for a time, in this boy. I guess I would call it empathy. He sincerely wished for his friend to be Thor in the play, unlike in my little story when I had hoped the teacher would see how much I really wanted the part, enough to suggest someone else, and hoping that would impress her. Fortunately, Ben must have taken something else from the story, or he discovered something in himself, a social gift, awareness of others, perhaps warmth toward his peers that began to unfold from fourth grade onward. Neither of these boys played Thor that year, but Ben was Thrym and relished being what he called "The Bad Guy." He never again asked to be any part in the plays, always seeming grateful to take the role offered: the Nasty Owl in *Holly and Ivy*, Joan's father in *Joan of Arc*, and Jacques in *As You Like It*, the cynic who delivers, "All the world's a stage."

What emerged in this young man, at least partly because of his process in dealing with the plays, was truly his regard for his fellow human beings. The class chose him to be president of the eighth grade year, and asked him to speak at our graduation. He was interested and patient with all his classmates and with other people he would meet, regardless of their age or position in life. He studied environmental education in college, trekked across dangerous areas of the world including Patagonia, and then ended up going into investment and financial development. He told me he was once in a coffee shop in a major American city, chatting with friends and others sitting around. The owner of the shop came over and listened to him, watched him carefully. Then she asked, "Did you go to a Waldorf school?" He smiled, and said, "Yes, how did you know that?" Her answer: "The way you are with people."

Drama as a healing force: A last example

It is clear to me in looking back over the many experiences that I have had working with children on plays, that something of major importance tends to happen in the fourth grade year. It is a time when destiny often shows itself, a life-direction comes into awareness, often not quite recognized except in retrospect, from an adult point of view. It can also be a time when life deals a child such a blow that it will echo through his or her entire life.

Rupert came to my class toward the end of grade three, a radiantly beautiful child but, clearly from his demeanor, one of the saddest human beings I had ever beheld. In the month before he came to our school, Rupert's father had committed suicide. Not only that, but he had phoned the child just before he died, telling Rupert that he should never love anyone as he loved his father. I was a beginning teacher, so I turned to colleagues and to my mentor for help. Jesse Darrel, one of the early teachers of Michael Hall School in England, was my mentor, and he gave me sympathy and sage advice. He suggested I work with stories, using them as "reverse-dreams," that I could offer images that would enter the child's sleep, where the meanings of the stories could achieve a reality I should not try to approach directly. Stories about fathers supporting and helping their children, Jesse suggested, perhaps Native American stories. These tales proved to pique the interest of Rupert, as did the visual artwork we did. He plunged into creating beautiful main lesson books, lovely paintings, splendid form drawings.

Though Rupert played with the other children, often wildly and with plenty of yelling and shouting, he seldom spoke in class. He stared into space when we recited or sang, and his speech was quite slurred, with no force or volume, when he chose to participate in class.

His mother assured me that he was happy in the class, that he loved the stories, but it was truly difficult to see that. I would at times find him alone on the playground, but he would only shrug and run off to play when I tried to approach him.

Then, in fourth grade, as would happen so many times in my experience, the Norse myths arrived as a healing force. Rupert loved the stories from the creation onward. We had a Swedish student teacher in our class then, and she taught the children to say the words with the correct accent. Rupert relished the Swedish way of saying Ginnungagap, Muspelheim, Niflheim, and so on. More and more animated in the listening and retelling of the myths, Rupert said he was looking forward to the class play when I mentioned we would be doing one. I was not sure which story we would take for the play, but I finished telling the course of the myths before deciding. Watching Rupert listening to the penultimate *Death of Baldur* tale, I knew what it had to be, and that this child would very likely play the role of Baldur.

I did not tell the children which parts they would have as we began to practice the play, working first in choral speech, and taking turns being different characters. But it was clear to me, and to all his classmates, that Rupert was the natural choice for Baldur. He was amazingly unself-conscious in the rehearsals, enjoying the scene where the Gods and Goddesses throw things at him showing that nothing can hurt Baldur. As he lay down on the floor in the death scene and then the funeral scene, he was still, peaceful, one could say, radiant. We staged the funeral quite dramatically. The children sang the sad round, "Ah, Poor Bird," while goddesses, using a translucent purple silk cloth, covered the reposing body of Baldur. In solemn procession, as the song continued, the gods and goddesses filed past him, dropping red roses on the body. In the performance, we used real roses, so the room was fragrant with them as the play reached its climax. Finally, Baldur rose on the darkened stage, saying the final lines of the play, "I shall return, I shall return."

The play was over, and after putting away the costumes, clearing the classroom of scripts, props, and so on, I decided to take the class on a walk in the forest just next to the school. We wandered along together, and I let the children run ahead to the Sticklebirch Clearing where they often played tag. They were all running and shouting along the path when I suddenly felt a hand in mine. It was not one of the usual hands that grabbed mine, so I glanced down to see who had taken my hand so firmly, but so quietly. It was Rupert, who as far as I could remember, had never taken my hand before. "I have been thinking," he said softly. When a child says this, I am always ready to listen, all ears. "Tell me," I encouraged him. "I was thinking that our lives are like a day. When we wake up in the morning: that is like being born. Then we go out to school or something, and that is like going on with our life. When it starts to get dark, the end of the day that is like the end of our life. We go sleep, or we die, and get ready to wake up for a new life. It is the time when our father calls us home." He looked up at me for confirmation, but I had to look away for a moment, to wipe the tears, and I managed to utter, "Yes, Rupert, I think you are right." "Yeah," he said and ran off to join his classmates in their game of tag.

I cannot say that the burden young Rupert bore left him as a result of that class play, but I do know that this, as well as number of other events and people, placed him on a healthy life path. He is working as an artist, now a father himself of two children.

It seems in the end, the greatest gift our work on plays can give children has to be related to our striving to work with living images, to allow thinking to develop in a direction that is not burdened with set or fixed ideas, but rather will continue to grow with the individual human beings on through their lives. Playing Joan of Arc, the Tin Man, Baldur the Beautiful can be of lasting importance only once the experience becomes a memory, a seed in the soul, which will grow, blossom, and bear fruit again and again. The child who learned to solve the problem of her too-quiet speech or his miss-timed sword thrust will take this learning to other situations, will have a better chance to meet life with flexibility, humor, and good will to those around.

Note: The names of the children in my stories have been changed to protect the innocent.

REFERENCES

Moffat, P.S. (1967). *21 plays for children*. Edinburgh: Rudolf Steiner School Trust Ltd.

Pittis, A.M. (1996). *Pedagogical theatre*. Chatham, NY: Waldorf Publications.

Steiner, R. (2007). *Education, teaching, and practical life*, Mado Spiegler, trans. Chatham, NY: Waldorf Publications.

_____. (1981). *The renewal of education*. Fourteen lectures given to Swiss teachers in Basel, April 20–May 11, 1920, Roland Everett, trans. Forest Row, UK: Steiner Schools Fellowship Publications.

_____. (1995). *The spirit of the Waldorf school*. Lectures surrounding the sounding of the First Waldorf School Stuttgart, 1919, Robert E. Lathe and Nancy Parsons, trans. Great Barrington, MA: SteinerBooks.

_____. (1947). *The spiritual ground of education*. Nine lectures given at Manchester College, Oxford, August 16–25, 1922, Daphne Harwood, trans. Great Barrington, MA: SteinerBooks.

_____. (1966). *The study of man*. Fourteen lectures given in Stuttgart, Germany, August 21–September 5, 1919, Daphne Harwood and Helen Fox, trans. Revised for this edition by A.C. Harwood. Forest Row, UK: Rudolf Steiner Press.

Imbue yourself with the power of imagination

Arthur Auer

Ways for teachers and adults to strengthen the capacities of imagination and memory in the service of children

To help students from an early age to remain good imagers and image-thinkers, and at the same time become very good word-thinkers, teachers themselves need to rediscover and increase their own childlike powers of imagining, memorizing, and sensory freshness. These capacities enable educators to fathom more deeply:

- who the children are as individuals and as a group.
- what they need to experience.
- when to orchestrate subjects/activities optimally at particular ages.
- how to bring a given subject imaginatively, inventively and experientially.

Know thy children and thy subject by heart

Children naturally resonate with high interest forces that genuinely radiate from their teachers. They sense how a subject is living in their instructors and manifesting in enthusiastic teaching. The following are a few ways to develop and strengthen mental imaging in yourself. Select and try whichever ones suit you and practice over a sustained period of time of your choosing. The time can vary widely from person to person, from days, weeks, months, and sometimes years.

Remember and imagine a striking person, event, and/or scene. Pick one that is as vivid as possible but not of a traumatic nature.

Practice very attentive observation of the same object each day over an extended time. Directly afterward, close your eyes and bring to mind a memory image of it; this can be visual, auditory,

kinesthetic, tactile, smell, taste, warmth—any one or a combination of any number of these. If you cannot visually imagine an object at first, don't worry; the impression is there but lurking in your unseen subconscious. Inwardly sense whatever other aspects of the impressions the object has made on you. Possible subjects: houseplant/flower, tree, body of water, landscape feature, cat/dog, face; you choose something.

Exercise individual sensory memory images:
- With eyes closed, feel the shape of an object (touch-movement) and remember it after it is out of sight—and out of reach! Mentally feel its warmth and remember it.
- With eyes closed, move your outstretched arm/hand in a circle and then remember the feeling of the motion (kinesthetic memory).

Practice image-making arts and mentally re-view, re-hear, re-move, or re-touch what you created: a painting, a musical composition, a dance movement, a clay figure, and so forth.

Experiment with bringing to mind images from all twelve senses. Try not to have visual images interfere or dominate. Call up one at a time non-visual feeling memory images of:
- joy/pain/discomfort (life sense)
- movement
- a strong smell, taste
- pure warmth/pure cold
- a sound (of a bell or a person's voice)

Re-member:
- a person's face, body contours, how she dressed, walked.
- the image of a triangle, circle, spiral, sphere, cube.
- multisensory landscape experiences: hiking up a mountain or through forests, paddling on a river, plunging into a lake, walking barefoot on a sandy shore, taking in an expanse of ocean or forest or grasslands.
- sunrises/sunsets, sun in a blue sky, rainbow, clouds in a storm, lightning, the front of your house, going in your front door, the Eiffel Tower, a Greek temple.

Visualize a growing plant from seed to root to shoot, seed leaves, stem, spiral unfolding of leaves, bud, sepals, calyx, pistil, anthers, fruit, seeds. Mentally touch a leaf, sense its life, appreciate the overall form, visualize colors, smell fragrance, feel sun warmth on its petals, and so forth.

Re-member a child: her or his overall gestalt, face/gaze, gait and characteristic movements, tone of voice, handshake, handwriting, how he or she draws, and so forth. Class teachers can do this regularly as part of a compact nightly review: Imagine the face/look, some telling action from the day, other aspects. If you cannot recall one action, you will the next day!

Re-member a story: Read a story and imagine its images—characters, actions, sound, forms, colors, smells/tastes, temperatures, the appeal of different

Imbue yourself with the power of imagination

parts to different temperaments, and so forth. Put the text out of sight and re-imagine the story calling up the same sequence of inner images. Re-read the text and note what you left out. Repeat the process until you know the story by heart (at least one or two more times).

Create your own exercises, strategies, and schedules. Class teachers develop a variety of strategies to learn their stories every night and tell them the next day without notes. They gain the capacity to memorize them relatively quickly because they do this so frequently. (Telling stories from notes gives the children the message consciously or unconsciously that you do not really know your material: Why learn?!) Learning and living into folktales, myths, biographies, math and science processes immensely help adults regain their hidden powers of imagination over time, especially in the service of children, who draw them out of you.

Waldorf education enlightens the mind, warms the blood, and moves the whole body. Current neuroscience is discovering that the brain is not a compartmentalized machine, but an amazing, living ecosystem in which every part is connected to and knows about the others. In Waldorf education, teachers work with the idea that this interconnectivity is due to a body of non-physical life forces permeating and interconnecting every cell and all cerebrospinal fluid. This etheric brain coincides with and interpenetrates the physical one. It is part of the etheric body of the whole human body which in turn is connected with the etheric forces of the universe in which thoughts reside and originate. The entire human organism is one of incredible intelligence and learning power and can be closely tuned in to the world around it.

Consequently, Waldorf education is a whole-body—and soul and spirit—education, not just a cerebrocentric, head-centered education. The physical brain is viewed as a mirror, a reflector of human action and not its executor.

Only looking at her image in his shield, Perseus cut off the head of dread, snake-haired Medusa. Blood poured into the earth and from it sprang Pegasus! Forthwith Athena, Goddess of Wisdom, tamed and presented the white-winged horse to the Nine Muses of arts and sciences—the gift of high-flying imagination! – Greek mythology

The real source of will behind brain and muscle functioning is the human individuality, the "I" which lives in the warmth and sun energy of the driving blood stream. Very recent research and early experiments suggest that, instead of being at the beck and call of nerve cells, blood can actually control them—a role reversal. Talking about blood directing the brain is odd in the context of the normal working brain. "Does the blood somehow make decisions for the brain?" asks neuroscientist Elizabeth Hillman of Columbia University.[1] Steiner points out that our increased brain power as humans is due not so much to having a larger brain but to the fact that our blood is able to nourish it so fully.

The ancient Greeks had the sense that Imagination rose up out of blood as a winged horse Pegasus—high flying imagination! In Waldorf education words, thoughts, and actions take wing. This educational approach activates the individual initiative, stirs the blood and a warm passion for learning.

People who think in pictures often doubt that others do not. People who lack imagery... are skeptical that anyone has it. Visualizers and verbalizers inhabit different worlds. A good imager, whose memory is a vivid multisensory collage, can raise his blood pressure by imagining that he is running an exciting race, or dilate the pupils of his eyes by imagining himself at the trail's end at dusk. The verbalizer can recall such scenes but only as non-sensory husks. No internal image can make his pulse race or his nostrils flare. – Robert Sommer[2]

Sommer refers to individuals as being visile, audile, and even motile imaginers, "better suited to … mentally performing a complicated dance step."

Researching further: Multisensory imagery and the different ways of learning

It can be valuable for teachers to become familiar with some of the fascinating studies that have been generated in recent years. There is an overwhelming amount of research—and debate!—about mental imagery, how the mind really works, and how findings may be applied to education. For example, child development researcher Linda Silverman, who coined the term "visual/spatial learner" in 1981, found that 45% of people use both visual/spatial thinking and thinking in words; 30% strongly use visual/spatial thinking; and only 25% think only in words. Of the 30%, even a smaller percentage are true picture-thinkers, using this mode of thinking to the exclusion of the others. (see sources for further study at the end of this article)

Image blindness

Many adults today are unable to produce visual mental images clearly or at all in their so-called mind's eye. In their waking life, many can only conjure up very shadowy, greyish, colorless images or think predominantly in words rather than in images. However, many of these same people can have, at times, colorful dreams at times. In contrast, children tend to think in lively, colorful images produced by their naturally stronger sensory experiences. The task of the teacher is to educate students so that their initial right-brained capacity for feeling-filled imaging is nourished regularly, strengthened, and preserved for a lifetime, while simultaneously fostering an equally strong left-brain word/language development. Whole-brain thinking is a valuable capacity for all sorts of occupations. Rigorous academics need not come at the expense of the imagination.

The current test-oriented emphasis on reading and math in an increasing number of schools focuses on a limited number of skills, mainly centered in the left side of the brain. This one-sided approach is literally "narrow-minded" because it educates only a small fraction and narrow sliver of a child's enormous mind, brain, and body potential and spectrum of capacities. It neglects the huge resources for learning of the imaging and feeling-motivational right side of the brain. We are thereby stunting, prematurely aging, and burning out our children and depriving them of their full childhood forces.

Neuroscientist Ian Robertson calls attention to the deeper cultural roots of this crisis, which have been building over the past century.

> Western societies have largely lost the ability to think in images rather than words.
>
> [M]odern neuroscience backs [this up]… [I]t is the nature of words that they tend to transform experiences into a rather bloodless code that can starve our brains of the rich images that wordless imagining can evoke. [W]ords trigger images as well as other word-thoughts. Yet most of us, most of the time… don't think in images enough.
>
> Language is the great achievement of evolution—an essential ingredient in what makes human beings unique on the planet. But there are costs to the way we have grown dependent on the spoken and written word. Imagery consists of the mental sights, sounds, smells, tastes, touch, and other bodily sensations that we can re-create with incredible vividness in that private, infinite universe within our skulls. The human brain is the most complex

object in the known universe, and it has the most incredible abilities, some which—like imagery—are underused. Imagery is important, but in Western culture, language is king. In school we steadily wrap our children's brains in the "cool web of language." It would be terrible if we didn't, but there is a cost to everything. By neglecting imagery we risk the withering of a whole set of quite remarkable mental capacities... Children think mostly in images before word-dominated school clouds their mind's eye.[3]

Robertson goes on to say what this one-sided intellectual emphasis means for adulthood and how art tries to be a cultural corrective:

Most of the time we [as adults] see, hear, feel, taste, and smell what our brains expect rather than the sensations themselves. Much modern ART tries to shock or surprise us out of these image-clouding mental habits into seeing more purely with the mind's eye, uncluttered by well worn categories and labels ... (p.4)

The older we get, the harder and harder [it becomes] to have an experience that's completely new...When you classify experiences like this, you begin to experience the class and not the event. In other words, your conscious experience becomes once removed from the immediate sensation... (p.12)

The brain's predilection for prediction and categorization is not confined to the visual sense. It also anticipates what we see, hear, feel, taste, and smell.... For much of our lives, we taste memories—what we expect—not the raw, fresh complexity of the sensations on our tongues. (p.18)

But the outside world can hijack our attention. It is ... at ... rare moments that we are closest to the unfettered, uncategorized seeing that we attribute to young children and to savants. (p.19)

Children cry or shout at the "wide glare" of the looming sky. (p.20)

In his book, Robertson presents corrective measures for adults who are aware of the staleness of compulsive mental habits and who want to regain a childlike freshness in their sensations and experiences—in addition to being shocked by modern art! "[You] can train your own mind by practicing imagery" and thereby connect more directly with the world, which includes not just the visual realm but also sounds, smells, tastes, touch, and other bodily sensations. He points out that we also have a mind's ear, a mind's nose, and so on. I daresay, so much of the brain is devoted to the hand that we also have a mind's hand.

Robertson focuses on the wordless imagery but also acknowledges all along that language can be a catalyst for imaging—in poetry and metaphor for example. One can use words artistically so that they "take wing" experientially and trigger emotionally moving pictures. And there are many meditational practices for adults to develop and restore inner visualization when the juices of imagination have dried up.

Galton's discovery

In 1880 Sir Francis Galton made a surprising discovery that sparked the imagery research and debate which followed in the next centuries:

To my astonishment... I found that the great majority of the men of science [in the Royal Society of London] ... protested that mental imagery was unknown to them. On the other hand, when I spoke to persons ... in general society, I found [that] many men and yet a larger number of women, and many boys and girls, declared that they habitually saw mental imagery ... perfectly distinct to them and full of color... Many persons, especially women and intelligent children, take pleasure in introspection ...

An over-readiness to perceive clear mental pictures is antagonistic to the acquirement of habits of highly generalized and abstract thought, and if the faculty... was ever possessed by men who think hard, it is very apt to be lost by disuse. However... the missing faculty seems to be replaced so serviceably by other modes of conception ... chiefly ... connected with the motor sense...

Men, who declare themselves entirely deficient in the power of seeing mental pictures, can nevertheless give life-like descriptions of what they have seen and can otherwise express themselves as if they were gifted with vivid visual imagination. They can also become painters of the rank of Royal Academicians.[4]

Galton pioneered an imagery questionnaire to back up his initial observations.

The interesting case of Oliver Sacks

In his book *The Mind's Eye*,[5] mind explorer Oliver Sacks, after surveying current research and many case studies of mental imagery in the sighted and in those blind from birth or blinded later in life, was still left with the mystery of how the imagery really works in the human mind. He uncovered an array of differing capacities, processing modes, and unaccountable anomalies and contradictions. Sacks himself as a sighted person, for example, admitted that he was one of those who was apparently visual-mental image-blind and posed the question:

> What, then, of people like me ... who cannot evoke any visual images voluntarily? One must infer ... that we have visual images that allow visual perception and recognition but are below the threshold of consciousness. (p.231)

Already early in life around age 14, Sacks became uncomfortably self-conscious of his deficiency. He learned that his mother, a surgeon and anatomist, was able to see and mentally move objects "in her mind as clearly and vividly as if she were looking at them." In comparison, he "felt bewildered, and very stupid. I could hardly see anything with my mind's eye—at most, faint, evanescent images over which I had no control." (p.221). He added to this example one of a surgeon, who like himself, could not conjure up conscious mental images and yet was capable of designing solar panels. His colleague's theory was that "there must be representations or models in the brain that get matched up with what I am seeing and doing. But they are not conscious. I cannot evoke them." (p.222)

But what might these other modes of conception be? Sacks thought that they may lie more deeply and mysteriously than we might think:

> When I talk to people, blind or sighted, or when I try to think of my own internal representations, I find myself uncertain whether words, symbols, and images of various types are primary tools of thought or whether there are forms of thought antecedent to all of these, forms of thought essentially amodal. Psychologists have sometimes spoken of "interlingua" or "mentalese,"... the brain's own language ... Vygotsky ... used to speak of "thinking in pure meanings." (p.226)
>
> There is increasing evidence for the extraordinarily rich interconnectedness and interactions of the sensory areas of the brain, and the difficulty, therefore, of saying that anything is purely visual or purely auditory, or purely anything. (p.238)

Sacks described particularly revealing case studies of the congenitally blind who "have rich and varied perceptual experiences, mediated by language and imagery of a nonvisual sort. Thus they may have a 'mind's ear' or a 'mind's nose.'" And how does one account for the fact that "Helen Keller's writing...startles one with its brilliantly visual quality." (p.239) He leaves the reader with this enigma.

ENDNOTES

1. Laura Sanders, "Head Rush," *Science News*, November 14, 2015, pp.22–25.
2. Robert Sommer is Professor of Psychology at UC Davis. *The mind's eye: Imagery in everyday life*, 1978, pp.1–2.
3. Ian Robertson, Professor of Psychology, Director of the Institute of Neuroscience at Trinity College, Dublin; previously at MRC Cognition and Brain Sciences Unit, Cambridge University, *Opening the mind's eye*, pp.2–3.
4. Sir Francis Galton, "Statistics of mental imagery," *Mind*, 5, pp.301–318, 1880.
5. Oliver Sacks. (2010). *The mind's eye*. New York: Knopf.

SOURCES FOR FURTHER STUDY

Auer, A. (2017). "The image problem." This article summarizes some of the debate by psychologists and neuroscientists about mental imagery in cognition and examines how mental imaging and imagination play a central role in Waldorf education.

Galton, F. (1880) "Statistics of mental imagery," *Mind*, 5, 301–318. http://psychclassics.yorku.ca/Galton/imagery.htm. Galton was creator of the first psychological test of mental imaging factors: (1) an image's brightness or dimness (illumination), (2) how sharply it is defined, (3) how distinct and natural is its coloring.

Kosslyn, S. et al. (2006). *The case for mental imagery*. Oxford: Oxford University Press.

Lacey, S. and Lawson, R., eds. (2013). *Multisensory imagery*, New York: Springer.

Maria J. Krabbe Foundation for Visual Thinking http://psychclassics.yorku.ca/Galton/imagery.htm

Marks, D. "Vividness of mental imagery questionnaire." http://socrates.berkeley.edu/~kihlstrm/MarksVVIQ.htm. This is a questionnaire format to assess the strength of a person's mental imaging that has stimulated many psychological studies.

Robertson, I. (2002). *Opening the mind's eye*. New York: St Martins.

_____ .(1999) *Mind sculpture*. London: Transworld.

Sacks, O. (2010). *The mind's eye*. New York: Knopf.

Sanders, L. (2015). "Head Rush," *Science news*.

Silverman, L. (2005). *Upside-down brilliance: The visual-spatial learner*. Denver, CO: Deleon Publishing.

Sommer, R. (1978) *The mind's eye*. New York: Delta.

Listen and you will hear
Meditation as a way of life

Patrice Maynard

A question had been bothering me for many weeks. Hoping to find an answer, I took a hike in an isolated and beautiful place in nature. No answer came. As I sat on a rock in frustration, it occurred to me that I really could not find the answer. This increased my despair, and the best word for what came over me was *surrender*. I just had to give up. Looking around at the bushes near me and up at the sky, I gave myself up to the world of answers I couldn't reach and asked for another force from around me to answer the question. As soon as I asked this, and surrendered, the bush nearest to me began to sing. There was a bird singing with clear might and energy. On and on the song filled the air and me with a direct answer of joy and response. I knew then the answer I needed.

Flush with gratitude and excitement, I decided I would watch to see the bird. After a long, long song, the bird stopped. As I watched carefully, it struck me that the bird would either sing again or move. If it moved, I wanted to see it. The silence remained and I waited, attentive, still shot through with exhilaration and relief at finding an answer and in such a glorious way. But I never saw the bird. After a very long wait, a bush eight yards away began to sing with the same song. The bird had moved without my seeing it move. Magic. I laughed out loud.

All around us there are invisible forces at work waiting for us to allow them to help us. People call these forces by many different names. Meditative practice helps develop the capacity we need to connect and receive the assistance available. It doesn't always happen in this way—it happens

in myriad ways—but with practice and inner concentration, the possibility is there.

Waldorf teachers build relationships with their students, knowing that it is through relationships that children comprehend beyond mere intellectual understanding and will understand more deeply into knowing things "by heart." We might call this "making it your own." This way the children not only understand but also apply the concepts out of themselves. The meditative practice of the Waldorf teacher builds this relationship strongly and is an effective remedial approach to support every child's learning.

Living a self-reflected life

Changing one's lifestyle to include daily rhythmical meditative work is one of the first efforts a Waldorf teacher must make to transform the inner self to become an authentic Waldorf teacher.

Observing ourselves as we accomplish each day takes inner discipline and commitment. The first demand of a teacher is to review every day before falling asleep. It could be said, "...without falling asleep." The practice recommended by Rudolf Steiner is to start with the present moment and then to move backward through the day in one's inner imagination until one arrives at the waking moment of the day. This prepares us for sleep and, as teachers, prepares us to work through the night in sleep on correcting those elements that need attention.

Teachers also benefit from reviewing each child in the class of children entrusted to them. One by one to visualize each child, especially if this can be done with a clear picture of every child in movement or in play, is especially informative. This is the goal. It is good if this can be done with the review of the day, but one way or another, each child needs to appear before the teacher's inner eye before sleeping.

This commitment of living a self-reflected life is primary to becoming a Waldorf teacher. The practice is to review without emotional engagement, as if we were watching ourselves in a movie or on stage, unable to interrupt, intervene, or re-live the experiences we watch. In the original lectures Rudolf Steiner gave to the first teachers of the first Waldorf School (*The Study of Man* in one translation or *Foundations of Human Experience* in another), he points out to the teachers that regret is a useless experience. Best is to recognize when we have erred and then to resolve how to avoid the same error or how to correct the error in the future.

Rudolf Steiner also gave preparatory exercises for strengthening our concentration so that we can do this daily review with rigor and without losing consciousness in sleep or endless distractions. The practice each day of review and visualizing the children is a strengthening effort and provides answers for us as we wake the next morning and during the day as we interact with the children we teach.

- Daily review of each day is a necessary practice for becoming a Waldorf teacher.
- Visualizing each child entrusted to one's care as a teacher before retiring for sleep at night is another necessary practice for Waldorf teachers.

Receive the child in reverence

The task of becoming a Waldorf teacher holds the opportunity for developing a meditative practice. Without it, teaching is a limited activity. With this as regular practice, vistas open. Because of the commitment to "receive the child in reverence," such reverence must be cultivated inwardly in the heart, soul, and mind of a Waldorf teacher to allow for a space to open in which the children can occupy us as teachers in a productive way.

The view of the human being held by Waldorf teachers is remarkably different from more mainstream points of view about children and childhood. Children come as messengers recently arrived from the spiritual world, from the cosmos. They come imbued with the "dew" from the stars. Just as morning dew allows us to see things otherwise invisible, such as spiders' webs or the tiny filaments inside of flowers, so children enable us to see into the spiritual world through their messages. Most parents have at least one story to tell of a message like this from a little one who states or observes something that fills up the heart that brims over with wonder that their child could be so wise. The wisdom in these cases is nothing we could have told the child or that the child could have learned from experiences here on earth.

This "dew gathering," let's call it, is part of the mystery of this first part of the Waldorf motto, "Receive the child in reverence." As teachers, observing children is the source of all information for decision-making in a Waldorf school. Even as teachers hold the positions they should of authority, this authority is granted to teachers only by the love from children who understand that they are recognized by their teachers as being important to the world, and acknowledged as bringers of truth.

Child observation

The first round of meditative consciousness comes from the teacher's observation of the child. The teacher must notice everything about the child. Noting the gesture of each child in the expression of movement is an important starting point. In picturing the child at the end of each day, the ways he or she moves provide rich help in finding insight into what the child's message or mission in life might be. Noticing characteristic gestures of each child may help in identifying the movements that might very well be compensating for some limitation not before seen. This helps the teacher in "solving the riddle of each child," as Christof Wiechert stated in his book, *Solving the Riddle of the Child: The Art of the Child Study.*

Not only is noticing the child's movements and gestures of importance to the teacher, but the teacher's innermost reactions to the child are also vital to observe. If a teacher experiences antipathy in reaction to a child, this is an indication that the child has come to this teacher to instruct in tolerance or in compassion. Antipathy is like a directional arrow for a teacher to know where the most important work lives in developing a relationship to each child and to the whole class. If a child is annoying, then the teacher has the chance to practice love beyond ordinary limits. It is, for example, to focus on some part of the child that is not annoying but very shapely or beautiful. Believe it or not, it is possible to find a way to love a child through pondering the mystery of form in one graceful part of the child.

Careful observation of the children also makes the review effort at the end of the day more fluid and quick to complete.

- Observing the children becomes, after a time, second nature to a teacher, and helps the teacher comprehend who each child is and what each might become as he or she grows.
- Observing the children aids in overcoming annoyance or antipathy.
- Observing the children provides references for calling the children to mind before sleep and rich substance for the review of the day.

Educate the child in love

This then gets to the second part of the Waldorf teachers' motto: "Educate the child in love." Love is a necessary part of the teaching practice in a Waldorf school. This does not mean maudlin, sentimental indulgence, but a rigorous and devoted attentiveness to who the children are. Through this teacherly love, children feel seen and appreciated. They feel safe and tended in the best of ways. This is the result of the observation of children described in the previous section. Without love, very little educating can happen on any deep or lasting level. With love, everything is possible.

Rudolf Steiner explained in his seminal work, *The Philosophy of Freedom*, that the folk saying "Love is blind" is the opposite of what is true: love makes us able to see things in another that cannot be seen by those who do not love. In other words, love is the beginning of a kind of clairvoyance that opens our inner eyes to the true nature of each child.

- Love makes the impossible possible.
- Love begins the process of clairvoyance.

Child study

Child study is a practice unique to Waldorf schools, like eurythmy and form drawing. Christof Wiechert's article on child study is an excellent introduction, as is David Mitchell's listing of the elements of presenting a child in a study, both included in this collection of essays.

The child study bears repeating here because it is such a key element in both the Waldorf school and the inner life of the teacher. It is a part of the meditative work that a teacher can use to assist in finding different paths to a relationship with any child. The admission on the part of a teacher that help is needed is a key element in the success of this approach. In this vulnerability, the faculty can build stronger relationships among themselves through the essential task of a Waldorf school: devotion to the children.

The humility needed to enter properly into the mood of the child study can soften rivalries in a circle of colleagues. New compassion can be born from understanding how challenging a life a child might have, and, in turn, how much a teacher must face in attempting to include a child in the class. In focusing intensively on a youngster, focus diminishes on internal collegial conflict. As with all artistic activity, new admiration can be engendered for one teacher from another, out of the dedication of that teacher's keen observation or astute diagnosis of an aspect of a child's constitution.

In describing why a child is being studied and what help the teacher is seeking, colleagues can understand the main lesson teacher's inner life and approach to a class of children. Some teachers who are loud and easily forthcoming, for example, giving an impression of impulsiveness, might have a chance to dispel negative impressions by representing the depth of insight living in the questions and the number of ingenious solutions tried on behalf of the child being studied.

Also, for teachers on a faculty who might have given up on the path of meditation, the child study affords an opportunity to awaken in all teachers the yearning, once again, to master the techniques of meditation. The reminder that child observation is at the heart of the work of Waldorf teachers and a key meditative practice can be healing for all involved.

Wiechert's description of the necessary mood for a successful child study is all-important. Out of a well-prepared child study often comes a deep feeling of awe at the magnitude of the young human being's gifts and challenges. The best results occur when this feeling of awe cannot be answered immediately. The mystery of the child rests in the silence that follows a thorough and comprehensive description of the child in question.

Wiechert points out that this time of "not knowing" is the most important time and must be protected, as this space of humility in the hearts and minds of teachers is the space into which the true "riddle of the child" can express itself. It is in this space that the most learning happens for the teachers.

Review of the process of the child study is also very helpful, both immediately following the child study and again in a few weeks to assess how the ideas considered were implemented for the child and if they had any effect.

There are many stories to illuminate the results teachers have experienced as a result of introducing a meditative practice or a careful child study:

One new teacher, struggling with a sixth grade special subjects class (that is, not the main lesson teacher) was asked in a faculty meeting if she pictured the children each night before sleep. The teacher had not heard of this before and resolved to try it. After the first night of the teacher's practicing this, the sixth grade class changed dramatically and behaved, suddenly, very well for the subject teacher.

Once, a challenging boy in fifth grade was studied, and all who taught him despaired because he never removed his hat in class and his very long hair hung down in his eyes. This hair and his hat interfered in a number of ways with the daily class activities. The teachers discussed possible reasons the boy needed these head coverings and shared with humor and compassion his stubborn insistence that his hair and his hat not be considered obstacles. The next day the boy entered class in the morning with a short haircut, and he took his hat off without prompting and did not wear it except to go outside.

These experiences of immediate results from meditative considerations of the child's whole being on the part of a teacher and then in union with a whole faculty are not typical, but they do happen. They point to the power in the art of child

observation and child study. They also point to the signals children give to us when we "get it right" on their behalf through careful consideration of all the clues about themselves they present in any given day.
- Child observation is a key element in learning how to teach a child and a class.
- Child observation leading to child study gathers the consciousness of a whole faculty to a particular child in a supportive way and can sometimes solve challenges or lead to solutions to those challenges.
- Child studies in faculty meeting are the "university" or "high school" where teachers learn about methods of teaching and ways to unite their hearts with the hearts of children to truly see the mysteries they come to offer.
- Teachers learn from the children and from each other in child studies.

The six basic exercises

Rudolf Steiner explained a path of preparation for developing strong meditative capacities. A practice to build the meditative "muscle" leads any meditant —not only teachers—to an authentic ground for clairvoyance and connection to unseen worlds.

Whole books have been written about these supplementary exercises, and they can be studied. It is best to actually practice them. Faculties in Waldorf schools sometimes use the books as a study in the weekly meetings and then discuss them and support each other in doing the exercises.

Rudolf Steiner pointed out that their sequence is important. The exercises are:

Control of Thought. This exercise gives a person practice in not allowing the mind to wander in endless associative thinking. The exercise is to pick an object such as a pin, a pencil, or a paper clip and think about it exclusively, allowing no thoughts to enter one's mind that have nothing to do with the object. Maintain this concentration on the object for five minutes. Do this exercise daily for 30 consecutive days. Choose the same object or a different object each day. Once this can be done for thirty days, take up exercise number two.

Control of Will. For this exercise choose an action to accomplish at the same time each day. It is best if it is an action you do not ordinarily do. Steiner himself recommended watering a plant. Some say it should not serve anything else, such as turning your ring around at noon each day. Accomplishing the task dutifully each day at the same time is the goal. This exercise, too, is to be done for 30 consecutive days. Once this is accomplished, the third exercise can be started.

Equanimity. Unlike the previous two exercises, this exercise must be practiced throughout a daily, busy life. This practice is to find balance in feelings, no matter what might occur. So navigating as precisely as possible between joy and sorrow, ecstasy and despair is the goal. When strong feelings rise up, maintaining composure is the point of the exercise. The practice is not to repress all feelings, but rather to effectively process these feelings in a state of inner quiet, and not become overwhelmed by the feelings. After 30 days of relative calm in reaction to strong feelings, exercise four can be started.

A Positive Attitude to Life. Looking for the good, the beautiful, the purposeful in all things, all events, all people, is the goal of this exercise. Avoiding criticism and, more importantly, the habit of criticism. To accept that all things have a reason for being and that all events are purposefully bringing a kind of wisdom to us from the future is the practice toward an inner habit of positivity. This is not a practice of denying that bad things occur. Rather, it is one of searching to find something positive in all events and people. When this can be done for 30 days consecutively, exercise five can be started.

Openness. This practice accepts all events, opinions, and points of view without immediate judgment or negative reaction. Rudolf Steiner listened so openly to the views of others that he could explain their points of view flawlessly. Some would even get angry with him when, in lectures, he might point out the possible error in a certain point of view. The originator of the point would be convinced while talking to Steiner that he agreed with their point of view, confusing openness with agreement. The goal of this exercise is complete receiving of the opinion or assessment without blocking, but with acceptance, listening, and a concentrated effort to comprehend the perspective of others. After 30 consecutive days of this practice, exercise number six follows.

Practicing all Five Preceding Exercises. Combine two, three, four, or all five of the exercises in varying forms until all of them become a harmonious way of being, perceiving, and reacting—this is the sixth exercise—until it becomes a habit of living with all of these working as a matter of course.

The ongoing practice of these exercises strengthens the capacity of any individual for a meditative practice and prepares an individual for perception into worlds that exist beyond the visible.

Remembering the departed

At the end of this road of life, once we pass through the portal of death, it is important to be remembered by those still living. The conscious remembering of the dead builds a bridge to the spiritual world and enables those who are deceased to keep the link of love alive with those still living.

To vividly picture one who has died allows feelings of love and gratitude to rise up in our hearts. Appreciation makes a connection of warmth between the living and the dead. That connection is a path across which help can come.

Those whom we love who have recently crossed the threshold understand our striving and can help from across the threshold to improve things. If a child in school is having difficulties, often a beloved grandfather, aunt, or cousin who has died can be pictured vividly and asked to help the child they loved in whatever difficulties they might be having.

It takes only moments of concentrated picturing to imaginatively connect to this support. This can sometimes make a great difference in how things continue for a child and for a teacher!

Powerlessness as a necessary step on the path to higher consciousness

There are moments every day in the life of a teacher when a feeling of helplessness may arise. Although a teacher must always appear to a class to know what the correct course of action will be, the teacher does not always know the correct course of action. If an extraordinary situation occurs, and examples abound—September 11, 2001; or a child falls and breaks an arm; or the weather turns unpredictable and the long awaited outing is rained-out; or an enormous jar of Prussian blue paint spills all over a child's desk and the floor—what is a teacher to do?

It seems that everyone not involved in the situation knows afterward what really should have been done, but the truth is that no one really knows in the moment what is exactly the right thing to do. Our mettle as human beings speaks in moments such as these, and often we fail. During a sudden eruption of a volcano years ago, like Pompeii, frozen in time, was a teacher who was caught by lava climbing out of the window in panic ahead of his students, while another teacher in the same school was found sitting in a circle on the floor with students around her. It is almost impossible to predict how we will react in the face of the unexpected or the frightening.

In the moment of uncertainty (What should I do? How shall I answer? Why did this happen?), we learn the most we can ever learn in life. In the quiet blank of a moment, a space is made for choices to rush in that we never expected, both good and questionable. To have in one's life a meditative practice is to find an element of trust in these times.

Some of the best moments in a teacher's life are preceded by utter chaos, a terrible mistake, or a bad reaction. Catching oneself on a mistaken path and turning it in a different direction in that moment can often wreak the most breathtaking and sun-filled solutions. Here's a story from the classroom to illuminate this:

Once getting ready for a new first grade, a teacher received a gift from a kindergarten teacher

of a moss garden that included a little gnome house and a darling, needle-felted gnome. In the center was an African violet. All summer long the violet bloomed and bloomed, and the teacher loved the violet and told the violet that the children would love it too.

Two weeks before school began, the violet stopped blooming, and the teacher was very annoyed at it and thought, "What's the use of blooming all summer in the first grade classroom when the children are not yet here?" The teacher tried persuading the violet to bloom, but to no avail.

School started and the first graders all loved the moss garden and the little gnome who lived in it.

This class was a particularly lively class with many strong individuals in it with many learning difficulties. One little boy had spent a year in a public school first grade. This was a very dreamy little boy, a beautiful child with blond curls and big blue eyes. For this story we will call him Finbar. The boy had proven useless in spelling in his previous school. The solution applied was to give the boy an extra spelling test each Friday. From that point forward Finbar ran a fever every Thursday night and could not attend school on Friday.

In his new first grade, Finbar continued to be a dreamy child, trying to decide whether he would participate or not. Sometimes he seemed present with his class and sometimes he seemed to be very far away in his thoughts.

Finbar had a habit of absent-mindedly swinging his rip-stop nylon lunchbox around by a very long shoulder strap. Several times he had unintentionally hurt children with this swinging juggernaut. Many conversations about not swinging the lunchbox had ensued.

At lunch hour a group of children needed to get on the bus to go home on time as the bus drivers would get angry and impatient if the class was late; so the playgroup teacher who stayed with the children who did not go home at lunch hour had to make it to class on time to allow the first grade teacher to take the home-bound children to the buses. It was a high-pressure time and on this day, the playgroup teacher was late and the teacher had to get a line of children out the door and to the buses promptly.

Far on the other side of the line of children who had the teacher pinned at the door, other classmates were getting their lunches in anticipation of the arrival of the playgroup teacher. At the far end of the classroom, Finbar came sauntering down the aisle with his lunchbox swinging a full, wide circle around himself. The teacher tried to get past the children waiting to leave, but she did not get to the boy soon enough. His whirling lunchbox caught the edge of the gnome's house and the whole moss garden toppled onto the floor upside down.

The whole class, in an uproar, shouted Finbar's name many times in anger. He stood staring at the ruined gnome house. The teacher climbed over the children in front of her to rush over to the boy. She quickly got down on hands and knees and began scooping up the parts of the moss garden, the soil, and gnome's house and asked Finbar to help her. The boy seemed unmoved by the results of his actions. He knelt down next to the teacher and vaguely tried to help gather up the spilled parts of the moss garden.

The teacher was stressed and angry. She had to swallow hard to avoid speaking in that state of mind and soul. As the teacher worked to remain quiet and to repair the garden, she was taken completely by surprise by a direct sensation, received from Finbar, which landed deep inside of her. The child's extreme remorse came from deep inside of him and

it hit the teacher like a physical wave. The teacher looked at the boy. His face seemed passive, yet he was flushed very red. Upon receiving the wave of remorse from somewhere inside the child, she was mightily ashamed for her anger at him.

The teacher then said in gentle tones, "I think the gnome needed a rearrangement of his yard!" The teacher and the boy kept working and, again, the teacher experienced another wave from inside the boy, this time of gratitude. Finbar then worked more actively.

The two put the moss garden back together and put it on the windowsill, the unblooming violet replanted and the gnome sitting happily in his house again. "It looks better. Don't you think?" the teacher asked the boy, still feeling ashamed of herself for her impatience and anger in light of this wave of remarkable remorse she received. Finbar smiled gratefully and nodded. The teacher asked him, "Did you learn something?" He answered almost inaudibly, "I shouldn't swing my lunchbox around." This entire incident took, perhaps, ten minutes.

The next morning was busy and the teacher gave no thought to the moss garden. But during circle time she happened to glance at the windowsill as she passed by it while doing an exercise with the class using hands and legs. The African violet had at least eight buds on it! In her excitement and shock, the teacher made a hasty trip around to the opposite side of the circle, without losing the rhythm of the exercise, until she arrived at the place where Finbar was doing the exercise. The teacher whispered, "When you go by, look at the moss garden." It was a long distance to the garden from where the boy was situated, and the teacher was convinced that he would forget by the time he got around to the moss garden.

Lo and behold! When Finbar arrived at the place near the gnome's garden, he did look. The teacher watched while continuing on with the class. The boy turned to look at the teacher and a slow smile of wonder and realization spread on the boy' face. He had seen the buds. The teacher smiled back at the boy. She beamed warmth of heart to him in great waves of appreciation; she could tell these were received.

The story is a fine example of a powerful transformation of the boy, the teacher, and the African violet. The substance that nourished this transformation included:

- the teacher's accepting her powerlessness without reacting in anger,
- her reviewing her day, examining difficult moments in the day objectively before sleep, without reliving them emotionally,
- and having a magical answer arise from this work on holding back the negative reactions, the power of the boy's remorse, and the likely work done the night before while teacher and child slept.

These were all answered with a response from the plant kingdom.

Trust is an important element that rises from a steady meditative practice. Even trusting the feeling of powerlessness, and trusting that unseen forces are always at work, that every human being has a higher self, a guardian angel, a fairy godmother, or a dæmon. Whatever we call it, this being or force is guiding our lives striving to cultivate:

- a calm and energetic trust that powerlessness will lead to resurrection;
- that we are never alone;
- and that the ever-present help of the whole universe is one fine element to help in developing confidence in ourselves as teachers.

When, in the face of catastrophes, large and small, or in the face of a feeling of being completely powerless, we remember that the space can be filled with our higher intentions, our love for the children we teach, and our confidence in life as purposeful, then remarkable learning almost always follows. In these spaces, tiny and enormous miracles have room to appear. Not always immediate, these miracles must be seen or perceived for them to have life and to influence events.

- Inner quiet aids perception.
- Regular practice aids consciousness.
- Remaining open to receive what cannot be perceived by ordinary senses allows for heightened awareness.

These are all elements that help in blank moments of not knowing what to do.

Prayer

There is a definite place for prayer in the meditative life of any teacher. Prayer must not be confused with meditation, nor is it a substitute for the meditative practices outlined here. However, there are times when it seems impossible to reach a student or the parents of a student, or a colleague, or one's own higher self. These moments of darkness are inevitable in a human path of life. At these times, it becomes important to remember that there are unseen beings hovering and waiting to help. The feeling of surrender described earlier is very conducive to prayer.

Adam Bittelston, one of the first priests in the Christian Community Church, wrote this prayer, called "the intercessory prayer." It illustrates a way to pray, especially when speaking directly to solve a problem isn't possible , for example, a teenager or a colleague who avoids contact.

Thou Angel, who keepest watch over the soul of (any name)
In sleeping and in waking and through the long ages of time,
May my thoughts, filled with hope, reach her (him) through thee.
May s/he be illumined by the fonts of wisdom that touch the inmost heart.
May s/he find peace by the fonts of love that bless the human being's work.
May s/he be strengthened by the fonts of will that bear us toward freedom.

The ever-present help

Rudolf Steiner instructed that the urgent need of our time is to reintroduce through the veil of materialistic thought the reality of the spiritual worlds as an ever-present source of interest and positivity. This source is not tied to any particular religion or dogma. Spiritual elements are simply part of practical life.

Think of love, inspiration, aspirations, imaginations, school spirit, compassion, and looking into the eyes of another as examples of spiritual experiences that need no religion to be identified and yet are powerful realities in our everyday lives.

To ensure that there is time in our days for meditative practice develops the inner capacities necessary to build strong connections to the realities of the spiritual world and to access the support from those worlds. This practice distinguishes Waldorf teachers.

The meditative practice of the teacher is a potent tool for remedial help with a child who is experiencing difficulties. The practice of daily meditation invisibly instructs the child in self-discipline and confidence that there are spiritual forces at work in our world that, with steady effort, can be called upon to help when the need arises. Children will imitate this confidence and this trust in the ever-present help we have available to us. The practice of meditation also visualizes the best in our world and in others and the correction of errors or problems. This visualization is in itself a powerful agent for transformation.

- Meditation creates worlds of opportunity for teachers.
- Meditation allows children to weave into everyday life the pictures they bring, the "dew" they sprinkle from heaven, into daily existence for teachers to gather ever so carefully.
- Meditation creates transformative potential that cannot be measured in ordinary material ways.
- Meditation offers relief for teachers to avoid thinking they are alone.
- Meditation builds realities that can expand exponentially, that can make plants bloom, and bushes sing.

Send the child forth in freedom

This is the last part of the motto for Waldorf education. The goals of Waldorf education are to help young human beings fulfill their destinies with able bodies, tempered feeling lives through daily artistic work, and capacities for clear thinking and sound moral judgment. When these can be accomplished, freedom is the result. The disciplined work of the teachers forges a clear path for the emerging human being to walk out into the world. And the path becomes the child's own as increasing independence rises from the youngster's urgent mission for life. The stages of development for a child include:

- imitation in younger years, of teachers who work to be worthy of imitation through disciplined effort,
- imagination in the middle years, stimulated by teachers' striving to carry children through the history of the world, traveling on the wings of imagination, and
- intuition in the upper grades, instructed by teachers leading students to trust their own inner voices with attentiveness and their own practiced intuition.

This is the ultimate goal of meditation as a pedagogical tool, as well as a tool for self-development—freedom. For the child, freedom from physical limitations, freedom from heavy emotional restrictions, and freedom from muddled thinking that might impair judgment. With the highest intentions of the youngster woven seamlessly into the child's physical and emotional self, and the "dew" of the child's unique individuality absorbed into everyday deeds, the burgeoning adult can then step into life with purpose, able to direct actions with confidence, clarity, and compassion. That's freedom!

Parent–student–teacher triangle
Night and day: Waldorf education in practice

Regine Bruehl-Shemroske

And when education is permeated by the night air, the future itself will learn to love the past in the lessons which the teacher gives. Then we will see that this will become a most wonderful karmic equilibrium.[1]   – Rudolf Steiner

Night

This is how my work begins. I meditate. Every evening and every morning, I picture peace, light, and love around each child and between us. I ponder questions. I remember and reflect on my observations. What are the children's gifts, strengths, struggles, their abilities and limitations? How can I envision the children's meeting these challenges and reaching their potential in the course of the day, week, month, and year? I envision the parents, filled with gratitude for the work that takes place with their children in the classroom, gratitude for me as we partner and collaborate on this journey through Waldorf education. In the process of the child's becoming, we need to work together. We are connected in what could be called sacred geometry, and I welcome the parents to join in this triangular relationship that includes the parents or guardians, the child, and the teacher.

As I meditate on the students and their parents, I invite a higher journey to unfold where higher self meets higher self, where renewal takes place for all involved: the parent, the student, and the teacher. However, there is a difference between working with the children and working with the parents. The parents are much more part of my daily work, while the children constitute the greater part of my night work. That may seem odd at first glance, considering the fact that I spend the majority of my day hours with the children and proportionally very little daytime with the parents. But in truth, the deeper my night work, the better prepared and more connected I am for my students. The students will in turn sleep on what transpires during the day, thereby digesting living, nurturing lessons during the night.

For the teacher, the relationship developed with the parents will be crucial for a successful educational journey. This relationship must be built on trust, since the parents release their children into the hands of a "relative stranger whose very role brings her in contact with the child's most intimate soul."[2] In *The Essential Conversation, What Parents and Teachers Can Learn from One Another*, Sara Lawrence-Lightfoot writes:

> The parents' child is the most important person in their lives, the one who arouses their deepest feelings and greatest vulnerabilities, the one who inspires their fiercest advocacy and protection. And it is the teachers—society's professional adults—who are the primary people with whom the parents must seek alliance and support in the crucial work of child rearing.

Our productive working together day in and day out is crucial for the parent's peace of mind. The relationship between parents and teachers is charged with a mandate that can be burdened with trepidations and expectations. In order to gain the parents' trust and to stand before the children with confidence, each constituent must learn to work well with the other.

Without incorporating night and day into my student and parent work, the fabric of the class community begins to weaken. Without my meditative work, the day is more likely to result in chaos, confusion, and mayhem. Without my conscious, self-conscious observation, and participation, a stream of which I am unaware can manifest. Through meditation, I become more flexible and confident in my work. The day forms and the night expands. During the day I do. At night I rethink (rewind). During the day I speak and listen. At night my senses are silenced. I breathe in and out, waking and sleeping in rhythmic returns. Consequently, a beautiful harmony works its magic during my day work, surrounding my interactions with parents and students.

My night work includes the spiritual, unseen world that is ever present to help. Over time, I have learned to invite the angelic world as mediators between the parents, and the students, and myself.

"That is wonderful," the youth said. Allow me to be your pupil and to learn from you."

"I cannot teach you anything," the old man replied. "Your soul is much richer than mine. But I can teach you who your teachers are."

"And who are my teachers?" the youth asked in surprise."

"The cosmos itself," the old man told him. "The only reason you met me was to recognize the poverty of the people of my century. You will enrich them. But look, a bluebell; observe it closely. Do you see its blue mantle? Protectively it is wrapped around a small yellow light within. This flower is an image of the soul. It, too, carries the light of the spirit within. It must never be extinguished. A blue mantle surrounds this light to prevent it from being extinguished. You also wore such a mantle before your mother conceived you. Keep it in your consciousness."[3]

This protection of the bluish light, the soul, makes up the collaborative task of the teacher and the parent.

A triangular relationship develops

The years from birth to seven, mark a close-knit bond between home and the family. As the child enters the first grade classroom, the parents entrust their child to our guidance. In turn, I invite the parents into this new relationship: "I don't teach your child alone; we collaborate. Your trust empowers me to draw forth what lies sleeping in your child's inner nature and helps build a bridge for new capacities."

With the loosening of the child's teeth, the hereditary forces undergo a kind of loosening as the hereditary physical forces and the developing soul-spiritual individuality begin to work on each other. In the school-age child, the soul-spiritual nature of the child begins to develop and emerge. In the space of that tension, teeth fall out. *Zahnlücke* or empty space, or the space between, represents potential growth of new life forces, the etheric, that are part of the shaping and sculpting head. Without words, the child says, "Thank you, dear parents, for bringing me this far! Now, I am casting off my baby teeth, and I am ready to become myself." The years seven to fourteen begin a journey wherein a new dynamic unfolds between parent-student-teacher.

With the change of teeth, a second birth emerges over the course of the child's education. The hereditary soul forces which have helped shape the physical body give way to a secondary being, the soul, nonphysical and invisible in nature. Parents and teachers become onlookers or un-lockers, witnesses and liberators, protectors and guides.

The torch that is passed from parent to teacher as the child leaves home and enters school is reflected in the light of the individual child. During this significant moment, I recognize that I am not the teacher of the child, but someone who has accepted a mandate to guide, protect, and guard the child's innate being. The child's nature, consisting of a physical body, a soul, and a spirit, takes gradual yet significant steps in separating somewhat from the influence of home, hearth, and parents before entering school.

The new caretakers

Rudolf Steiner asked the students of the first Waldorf School the question: "Do you love your teachers?" Perhaps Steiner was suggesting that, in order for education to bear fruits in the future, there must be love in the school. In the following poem, Erika Blete, a student at the first Waldorf School, reflected on the love she felt for her teacher, Ernst Lehrs.

> When I see your countenance
> Warmly bathed in your dear look,
> I sense the field of stars around you,
> And it is as if I see far back
> Somewhere, before I came here,
> The same image cast a spell on me.
> Wordless do I feel your being-development
> Kindred to my inmost soul
> The same footsteps I hear sound,
> The same star tone reminding me of home;
> But while I am still walking, you are bounding,
> What I would be, you are.[4]

The life of the Waldorf teacher follows an inner path strengthened through nightly preparation. With regard to this dynamic, Steiner gave us a potent picture during a lecture in 1915:

> You must not think that you are educating the child you see there in front of you. Neither must you imagine, as you stand there in your own body, that you really have anything to do with this physical child. But something in you and something in the child have intimately to do with one another.[5]

We learn that the students' past incarnations and our future incarnation are intimately intertwined and like passing ships or hands that hold for a moment's greeting, this karmic relationship takes shape. The teacher meets the result of the past incarnation not in the body, but in the abilities and limitations of the child who stands there. The teacher helps form the child for a future incarnation the way the seed forms in a flower, while stem, stamen, and blossom shape the flower. Such hidden life secrets the plants reveal in their eternal dying and becoming. The seed, a metaphor for new life, potential growth, and marvelous unfolding, begins its journey during the night, as does the actual growth of the plant.

Teachers are the new caretakers of what unfolds over the school years. Through night work I can meet the students anew each day. I wake up with an idea for teaching, a thought about a student, a word for a parent. Often I am refreshed and clearer due to this offering up of my intentions, plans, preparation, and questions into the night. The new day allows me to plan my work and work my plan, with confidence overcoming temperamental imbalances, student disciplinary issues, social interruptions, and fire drills! The class comes into form, like a pendulum beautifully balanced on the fulcrum called alertness. My lessons are centered and inspired; breathing takes place between home and school, night and day, past and present, present and future.

The importance of sleep

The gift of the night is a kind of imprinting. What takes place during sleep due to the preparation I have done manifests during the day as the fruits of my labor! Scientific research is not ignorant of the fact that the morning is wiser than the evening. In his essay "Sleeping on It," Arthur Auer confirms that "for a long time it was thought that sleep primarily enhances 'procedural memory,' which allows us to do repetitive things such as knit or play the violin or keep a checkbook. Recent focus on the more elusive area of 'declarative' or 'informational' memory concerning such things as facts, vocabulary, and dates is also aided by sleep and is similarly pre-processed through the part of the brain called the hippocampus."[6] Research confirms that "sleep after learning aids memory recall."[7]

The students are our textbooks from which we read the manual for life: the curriculum. It is that easy and that difficult—because how do we know how to read the textbook called the child? Look at how the students breathe; physically, yes, but also

soulfully, emotionally, intellectually, and practically. Look at the color of their cheeks as you tell a story or during circle as they memorize the times tables. The art of teaching means to create the flow of the lesson that helps the child to connect with the lessons. A lesson must not be too stimulating or too difficult. When it is just right, the child can go home inspired, content, and relaxed, resulting in sounder sleep and healthier soul breathing, and emerge better prepared for the next day.

We take each child's essential being into our meditative life during the night; in that way we sleep on our experiences of the day and shape, adjust and align our lesson plans accordingly for the next day. That is our nightly work.

> Every night on going to sleep, our souls take with them something from daily life. ...The fruit of our experiences ... is transformed during sleep in such a way that it becomes our abilities and capacities. [For example], all our earlier efforts to shape the letters have been transformed [in sleep] into the capacity to write. ... Forces higher than those available in our conscious life become available during sleep; experiences are transformed into faculties and the soul becomes more and more mature. ... We bring out of sleep much more than we brought into it through our conscious experiences. During the day we use up forces by participating in what is going on around us. In the evening we feel fatigue because these forces are exhausted, and during sleep they are replenished. ... [Sleep] is therefore the source of innumerable forces we need for waking life. ... [T]he [universal] forces which have streamed into [the soul] the whole night long ... [are akin] to its own three inherent forces: ... Will ... Feeling ... Thinking.[8]

We prepare lessons that are threefold, addressing: the nerve-sense system, the metabolic system, and the limb system in relation to one another. We teach to the intellectual, artistic, and rhythmical nature of the child. We work with the child's temperament. We stand in confidence in front of the class. We are their sun and continue the work of the hierarchies. We collaborate on the one hand with the parents and, on the other hand, with the spiritual world. We work with the children overnight and bring into the daily lesson anew what they need from us. While in ancient Egypt, a child would have had to leave the home of the parents for many years to enter an initiate's path, in today's world, the teacher invites the parents back into the educational process through close collaboration, comparing and sharing of values, and ... Love. This is key!

For children of the 21st century, learning is one of experience. Concepts may be acquired by the child, but pictures generated by imagination and "light," turn into a new substance, nourishment, or "grail food"[9] as Frans Lutters puts it in *An Exploration into the Destiny of the Waldorf School Movement*. What the student has learned the previous day is on its way to becoming new life forces. When this occurs, transubstantiation is taking place, a sun-inspired process that weaves between teacher and student in which, in Lutters' words, "the grail is invisibly present, and each feels herself to be a Parsifal who goes through a journey."[9] The power of the grail heals and rejuvenates.

I was inspired by Ruth Sidney Charney's book, *Teaching Children to Care,* when I wrote in one of my newsletters: "It is my hope that the work we have begun as a class can be taken up in earnest. As a class community, the students have been given the power to regulate themselves, to anticipate consequences, to give up immediate gratification by realizing long-term goals, make and carry out a plan, solve a problem, think of a good idea and act upon it, sift through alternatives, and make decisions."[10]

We live in an exciting time and constantly run the risk of incurring injury through intense sense impressions that may be difficult to process. Norse mythology depicts these diminishing life forces as birds gnawing away on Yggdrasil, the Tree of Life. The nightly dew (water in a transformed stage), restores the tree.

In Parsifal we find the archetypal human being of today: Out of his own spiritual yearning, he human being invites the help and rejuvenation of the spirit. The human being must first recognize his innate illness and the need for healing. Meditative efforts coupled with conscious and deliberate acts bring forth the questions we must ask each other as contemporary travelers.

My efforts inspire a breathing process in the child that interweaves home and school. My artistic practice also transforms at night. My research and preparation, such as memorization, imprint into the higher self or ego, astral, etheric, and physical. This rhythm continues the next day through a reverse process: physical, etheric, astral, and ego, and learning can take place in the student.

The pedagogical foundation for both student and teacher requires sleeping on the lessons. Meditation plays a pivotal role for teachers. I call teaching my night work as well as my day work.

Day

The parent-student-teacher triangle

My day begins with a morning meditation before I leave for school. Like the rainbow bridge to first grade, my morning meditation helps me transition from my night work to my day work with the children in the classroom and my connection with the parents.

The parent-student-teacher relationship provides us with a unique dynamic that holds a parent's trust, a student's love for learning, and a teacher's pedagogical insight. When the parent-student-teacher triangle works well, we encounter the strongest geometrical form, an equilateral triangle. It is stronger than a circle or a square in terms of constructional laws. Where all centers meet in one place, each side influences and balances the other equally. When all parties trust in the strength of a triangle, healthy education can flourish.

In an article by Nancy Blanning, "Discipline: Guiding Angel Style," she emphasizes the importance of building trust and cooperation as a foundation for school.

> Children have come to learn how to live life and are looking for guides and companions to help them find their way rightly in the world. They are truly tender little beings like the children lost in the woods of a fairy tale. They are not cerebral and logical. They will be logical later, but now they follow adult models and directions.[11]

The parents are collaborators in the process of educating their child. With the parents we reach toward the student and our work is to begin drawing forth from the child the wisdom that is in them. *Educare*, in Latin, means literally, "to draw forth."

In order to create a healthy parent-student-teacher triangle it is important to understand the role each plays and then work together out of respect, trust, and love. Like a windmill, each part influences the other in a balanced flow. Although

Parent–student–teacher triangle

we work together, the teacher is the ego at school, and the parents have that role at home. The students move between school and home feeling held by both their parents and their teacher.

The parents

Insights shared by parents who have watched over their child since the moment that child was born are wonderful and very helpful for the teacher. Parents can describe the child's early development, likes and dislikes, emotional ups and downs, home life, sleep patterns, the child's temperament, nutrition, rhythms, strengths, health, medical history, and challenges. This information will aid the teacher in understanding the child more fully.

An important aspect of a successful parent-student-teacher triangle relationship is the understanding the parents' hopes, dreams, and wishes for the child. There is so much that we as teachers can learn from the parents. By understanding the parents' vision for their child, we will be better prepared to work together.

A first bridge between home and school

Home visits provide us with invaluable information about the child and build that first foundation for all learning: a loving relationship between parent, child, and teacher. I prepare a small gift, a crocheted star, which at the right moment will be given to the child, usually as I tell a story:

Little Star felt herself seated at the edge of a forest ready to explore the world. Filled with enthusiasm, she yearned for the hills and to follow the paths that lay ahead far beyond the horizon. She closed her eyes and heard the familiar music of the stars. Suddenly, when awakened, she realized that she was all alone. Where were her brothers and her sisters? She set out on her journey to find them and listened each night to the familiar music of the stars that will guide her.

The child and I may be seated on the couch or in the child's room while I tell the story; the parents are sometimes nearby. The child listens attentively and receives the gift. I ask to see pictures of the child and her favorite toys. During the visit, I am asking myself, Who is this child? Does the child prefer reading to playing? Does she prefer playing indoors or outdoors? I observe the child's movements, speech. What are her interests? Does she make eye contact? What are her questions and how comfortable is she on this first day? I find that these home visits create places in my heart and in the family's heart that begin to grow. This is an important beginning or birth of the parent-student-teacher triangle. The child feels held between the parents and the teacher.

Class representatives as parents

As a new teacher, I ask colleagues and parents who might make good class representatives. I like to have six parents in roles that support the class: two as fundraisers and treasurers, two parent council representatives, and two class representatives. The class representatives will help me plan class trips, organize community gatherings (at least two a year), as well as an "Eat, Sweep, and Be Merry" classroom cleaning event before the school year. The class reps will help plan art projects (needle felting, pumpkin carving, puppet shows, lantern making, and so forth) and offer a hand with class plays. My parent helpers are invaluable in many ways. I have learned to listen to them carefully because they often see things and hear things in the class community that I may not.

The student: working with the temperaments

One of the most precious gifts we can give the students is to recognize and work with their given temperaments. Parents, too, love to learn about effective ways to help balance their child's temperament. Arising out of the constitution of the child, the temperament is a wonderful part of who the child is. Parents and teachers can help harmonize but should not change the temperaments.

In the classroom and at home, the melancholic child needs to feel empathy from his teachers and others. The sanguine child learns best when he loves the person teaching him. One could say in that way all children are sanguine by nature. They learn best when they love whoever is teaching them something. The choleric child learns best from people he respects, and the phlegmatic child is supported when the environment is comfortable.

As the student approaches adolescence, he can participate in the parent-student-teacher triangle. Meetings that involve the student will enhance his self-empowerment and strengthen the triangle.

The teacher

Like a conductor of an orchestra, teachers invite students and parents to create a harmonic whole, a symphony, which I call the class community. We listen and imagine the future while enjoying a diversity of instruments creating music.

Providing opportunities

Consciously or unconsciously, parents hunger to be part of the spiritual atmosphere inherent in our Waldorf schools. For example, the main lesson curriculum recapitulates stages of human development and cultural evolution. These are insights the teacher has gained through the study of anthroposophic literature and through being a student during Waldorf teacher training. Because parents are often excited by how the curriculum inspires their children, it is important that opportunities for parent education are offered by the teacher.

Waldorf education nourishes the parents as well as their children. Study groups, newsletters, and communication between school and home support a productive educational environment. Before each school year, I send out an August packet that contains a parent survey and a yearly overview with guidelines, dates, and developmental highlights. During the year, I offer monthly parent meetings and a three-week parent study. Parent studies build trust, foster respect, and inspire class community. Some of the books I've worked with in parent studies include:

Karl König, *Siblings*
Hermann Koepke, *Encountering the Self* and
    On the Threshold of Adolescence
Rudolf Steiner, *The Poetry and Meaning of Fairy
    Tales*
Marjorie Spock, *Fairy Worlds and Workers:
    A Natural History of Fairyland*
A.C. Harwood, *Recovery of Man in Childhood*

Working with the parents, I strive to make the sessions educational, but not from the top down. I am not teaching the parents; we are exploring topics together. The parents' stories and questions and insights are the true life of our studies. We share with our parents the threefold, multi-sensory curriculum that our children receive. The parents perceive that our knowledge of their children helps their development, awakens new capacities, and fosters growth. In these sessions, the parents can experience directly the enriched soil from which new capacities grow. Rudolf Steiner's verse, here freely translated, captures the essence of these meetings:

*May all who enter here bring love.
While here true knowledge shall we seek.
Upon leaving, let there be peace.*

Class Meetings

Here is an example of a class meeting:

Class Meeting Agenda
6:30–7:00 Social Mingling (refreshments)
7:00   Biographical Sharing
7:20   Child Development & Anecdotes
7:30   Artistic Experience (circle, form drawing…)
8:50   Curricular Topics (the main lesson book, adolescence, media, reading, math, science, the class social, our twelve senses…)
8:30   Announcements & Verse

Airing of Individual Concerns

A teacher must remain awake when things come up in class evenings. When concerns veer away from the agenda, great care must be taken to work with the issues that arise. No one should be given time to air a personal agenda during a meeting without its being an agenda item. It is important that meetings are not the place for individual concerns or complaints. These are best resolved during parent-teacher meetings or scheduled office hours.

Parents' concerns and worries are important, but they must also be dealt with in the right way, at the right time, and contained properly. The parents must trust that each child's needs will be appropriately addressed, but not necessarily in a class meeting. Parents need our guidance with regard to when and where to share their concerns. This must be done in a loving and caring manner. It is also crucial that a teacher is able to firmly but again lovingly create proper boundaries. Reinforce the fact that the proper platform or vessel will be found to work through the issues and concerns at hand, but that we cannot do it at this meeting. We will schedule another time.

As teachers we must be awake for the moments when parents are upset and are attempting to railroad the meeting into a place that can be potentially divisive if not handled in a timely manner. When issues come up, at times erupting like a volcano in the middle of a class meeting, this can actually provide an opportunity to redirect the question and to reinforce the importance of the parent-student-teacher triangle. Any personal complaint, with foresight, can be turned into a topic of interest, perhaps the basis for a study group.

I had an interview once with a parent who had a history of complaining about the school. The parent made a strange comment: "I would like to change the school culture by working through you." Her comment was a concern to me. When I met with the parent again, I felt that we could work together, and I was impressed with her child. However, things did not go well. I soon noticed other parents coming to me about the discontent from this new parent. Class meetings started to feel divisive. Everything was going well as far as the class, and her particular child especially, but I felt there was a whole layer of social anger and discontent in our class community that was building because of this particular parent.

Looking back, I see that my inexperience allowed the situation to escalate. I did not deal with it swiftly, so the problem soon became untenable. Even a mediator could not remedy the situation. The final result was that the family had to leave. This experience helped shape my belief in the parent-student-triangle and the need for the child to be in the center of the parent-teacher relationship. If this is not the most important reason for the parent, then the teacher must contemplate whether to accept that family into the class. One cannot be perfect in screening for possible future problems, so it is important that the teacher is vigilant in working with potential issues.

As the class teacher, one has a responsibility to all parts of the triangle. Parents and students need our confidence, guidance, and leadership. Teachers have to be willing to be kind, flexible, compassionate, humorous, and creative problem-solvers, and devoted to our multifaceted task as Waldorf educators, that is, our day and night work. If a parent is upset about another child, that must not be addressed in the large group. Individual triangles working well together create a beautiful crystal and a vibrant class community. Individual triangles in conflict will begin to erode the crystalline strength of the class.

When the triangle needs help

Problems can develop when the triangle is not balanced. The connections of the triangle need constant attention in order to remain strong and alive. The Waldorf school as a whole is a karmic meeting place where the ideals of threefoldness and parent-teacher collaboration become possible.

If a parent-student-teacher triangle is failing, it is usually due to an erosion of trust. Support may be needed in order to restore the health of the triangle by resolving the issue at hand. A lower school chairperson, a college member, an educational support teacher, or another parent may be brought in to help heal the triangle. Those who help must be vested in restoring the original strength of the parent-student-teacher triangle. If the trust has eroded, one must do everything possible to repair it. Bringing in a colleague or school director can be helpful, as long as the colleague does not become a permanent crutch or an alternative for the parent to vent without ever having to honestly work with the teacher in the triangle. Fewer outsiders intervening (less is more) is best when it comes to the parent-student-teacher relationship.

Drop-in office hours and parent-teacher conferences

Offering parents weekly drop-in office hours provides opportunities for informal "hellos" and for finding answers to deeper questions. Drop-off and pick-up are not good times for lengthy conversations. They are more conducive to an exchange of warmth, care, and interest or a quick check-in. If parents have bigger concerns or questions, invite them to sign up for office hours or to drop in. These office hours are much more appropriate for discussing more lengthy topics such as: learning difficulties, social-emotional health, bullying, sensory challenges, media and electronics, and the effects of our materialistic age on the students of today. Parent-teacher conferences are scheduled twice a year, and they build parent trust and strengthen collaboration. My hope is that after each parent-teacher conversation, the parents feel more love for their child than when they walked into the meeting.

Parents and educational support: expanding the triangle

Waldorf education's developmental approach to learning allows children to develop at their own rate. We must be mindful not to miss a learning disability that requires additional help and a circle of support. We must understand the early signs of a child's more serious challenges, work with specialists, and educate ourselves in how to incorporate elements into our lessons that support various learning styles.

Looking at the child's early movement patterns, speech formation, and comprehension can allow for intervention to be put in place that will support the child early on. In first grade, reversals of letters are normal to a degree, and so are reversals of numbers. But when a child struggles with crossing the midline, balance, rhythm, and language development, it is important to do something about it and to allow our well-trained Extra Lesson teachers to join our triangle to form a circle of support.

When learning difficulties arise, it is very helpful if an educational support coordinator attends a parent-teacher conference, even facilitating the meeting and taking careful notes. Before starting the journey with a class, I would spend hours reading the student's reports and meeting with the Extra Lesson teacher in order to make sure I didn't overlook a learning difficulty in a student. Observations and best practices at home and at school should be shared in such a meeting. Goals will then be set in writing and a plan put together. Communicating with the parents and keeping careful records are very important for this process.

As an inexperienced teacher, I had a troubling situation when I took over a fourth grade class. I assumed that all the children had been evaluated for dyslexia because of the serious issues this condition can pose if not dealt with. When, by fifth grade, a student was still struggled with writing and reading, the parents were up in arms. In a healthy triangle, this would have been our mutual responsibility and concern, and we would have been in constant dialogue at the first signs of a problem. This is where the parent-student-teacher triangle really shines. It is a reality check on all levels, always keeping the child in the center. By the end of fifth grade, angry and disappointed, the parents withdrew this particular student from the school. Once she received support for her dyslexia, she began to excel in academics and her confidence grew. She was much happier and learned to live and grow with her learning difficulty.

Working with anxious students and their parents

When working with parents, understanding how to support anxious children can be useful. Part of my parent work is sharing resources. For example, I recommend reading the chapter in which Köhler gives a detailed account of how to prepare a child for sleep: "Preparations for Sleep and for Starting the Day."[12] It is insightful and practical. We can be a resource for our parents, which can then influence their home life in a positive fashion. Knowing that anxious children may need additional layers of protection in order to help relieve their "soul soreness," we can find ways for them to be more comfortable in school. Anxious children may have a hard time falling asleep. These threshold fears can be eased with rhythmic evening rituals.

With overactive and anxious children, support between home and school provides extra sheathing and healing. Köhler recommends strengthening their sense of life by providing: "rhythm, continuity, nearness, protection, warmth, skin care, a carefully considered diet, comfortable natural clothing, bodily well-being, development of touch experience, and sleep enhancement, as well as giving protective shape to evening hours."[12]

After-school study hall

Working after school with students pays dividends. Choosing one afternoon a week, I prepare a snack (eventually the parents were eager to pitch in), and make myself available to anyone in the classroom who needs an additional challenge or requires extra support. Occasionally, I even have parents stay who want to learn how to academically support a child at home. Anxious students or

students with educational needs enjoy this one-on-one time with their teacher. Offering this gift of time fosters more confident students and builds a foundation of trust. It is well worth the sacrifice of a few hours once a week. Our time spent in after-school study hall is fun and supportive.

Behavior and executive skills

A student is more likely to succeed if parents and teachers agree on the goals of education. For students who struggled with executive functioning skills, I have them bring in planners that are used as a communication tool between the parent, student, and the teacher. This works well to remind the student to accomplish homework/classwork in a timely manner. The same can take place with a behavioral contract. The parents need to know if a student is not behaving appropriately, and the parent-student-teacher must agree on behavioral expectations between home and school.

Conclusion

The strongest structure in the school is the parent-student-teacher triangle. It is ideal if the parents can work things out with the teacher and vice versa. The parents must feel that the teacher is approachable, and the teacher must maintain a comfortable connection with the parents. Strong and connected triangles create a powerful geometrical form; they involve everyone directly and build a lasting foundation for learning. This vibrant class community will work and breathe together. Parent-student-teacher triangles are gems in the life of a Waldorf school. A school that is based on such threefoldness can celebrate—for a cultural impulse brings Waldorf education into existence. At the opening of the first teachers' meetings in Stuttgart in 1919, Rudolf Steiner stated:

> Waldorf education is to become the bearer of quite a special impulse. And so, first of all, we must direct our thoughts toward the consciousness that something special is to be born into the world through this education. Such a realization will come about if we do not look upon the founding of this school as an ordinary everyday event, but a festive act in the great ordering of the world.[13]

By working as partners with our parents, we invite trust and gratitude to manifest in the relationship. By studying and reading our students, we bring to life the vibrancy of our curriculum which is inspired out of a true understanding of the human being. As times change, Waldorf education must be created anew to meet the challenges of our times. We work each day with the students but also with the parents who stand as partners in this stream of time. Spiritually, we are imbued with a great heritage that helps us find living pictures and amazing answers—as long as we collaborate and listen. Between parents and teacher, the individual child can blossom into an independent thinker who participates in life in a heartfelt and active manner. We can better care for the "I" of each student, which is in a state of becoming, when a relationship weaves between teacher, child and parents each day and every night.

Our homework every night as parents and teachers is never to turn away from, but again and again turn more strongly toward our children, to see what is true, and to hear the hint of the voices that will carry their strength and light into the world. It is important that the parents stand with us and support the impulse of Waldorf education. In the words of a parent during a graduation speech:

> The door to [our] heart is open, and the room is as large as the universe. The students are mysteries to fathom as they sparkle like stars inside of [us]. [We are] not burdened by this astronomical weight; if anything [we] could say, [we] are full of light from working with [the children.][14]

ENDNOTES

1. Steiner, Rudolf. (1915, 1996). *Art as seen in the light of mystery wisdom*, lecture on January 2, 1915 (GA 275). Forest Row, UK: Rudolf Steiner Press.
2. Lawrence-Lightfoot, Sara. "The essential conversation: What parents and teachers can learn from each other." New York: Ballantine, in Finser, Torin. (2014). *A second classroom, Parent-teacher relationships in a Waldorf school* Great Barrington, MA: SteinerBooks, an imprint of Anthroposophic Press, Inc.
3. Lutters, Frans. (2015). *An exploration into the destiny of the Waldorf school movement*. "The teaching of Trevrezent" Philip Mees, trans. Chatham, NY: Waldorf Publications, pp.118–128.
4. Ibid.
5. Op. cit., Steiner, *Art as seen in the light of mystery wisdom*.
6. Auer, Arthur. "Sleeping on it, The most important activity of the Waldorf school day," an essay earlier in this book, first published in *Research Bulletin*, Vol.14, No.1, Spring 2009. Wilton, NH: Research Institute for Waldorf Education.
7. Gais, S. and Born, L. (2006). *Sleep after learning aids memory recall*, www.learnmem.org/cgi/reprint/13/3/259.pdf. See also: N. Axmacher and others (2007). *The role of sleep in declarative memory consolidation: Direct evidence by intracranial EEG*.

8 Steiner, Rudolf. (1996). *The foundations of human experience*. Great Barrington, MA: SteinerBooks, pp.41–42.
9 Op. cit., Lutters.
10 Charney, Ruth Sidney. (1991, 2002). *Teaching children to care, classroom management for ethical and academic growth, K–8*. Turner Falls, MA: Northeast Foundation for Children, Inc.
11 Blanning, Nancy. (2016). "Discipline–guiding angel style," *Lilipoh*, Winter 2016, Issue 82, Vol. 21. Phoenixville, PA: Lilipoh Publishing.
12 Köhler, Henning. (2001). "Preparations for sleep and for starting a new day," in *Working with anxious, nervous, and depressed children*, Chatham, NY: Waldorf Publications, p.72.
13 Pedagogical Section of the School of Spiritual Science. (1991). *Toward the deepening of Waldorf education*, Dornach, Switzerland: Goetheanum.
14 Leif Garbisch. (2011). Eighth grade parent's graduation speech, Hawthorne Valley Waldorf School, Ghent, NY.

Remedial training programs

Association for a Healing Education (AHE)
Sessions held at Rudolf Steiner House
Ann Arbor, Michigan
www.healingeducation.org

The Association for a Healing Education's Educational Support Training has offered programs since 1992. Covering a span of three years and designed for Waldorf teachers and professionals in related fields of education, it provides an in-depth study of child development and its relationship to developing a child's capacity for learning. A foundation from Rudolf Steiner's indications on child development coupled with current theories on the brain, movement development, and behavior guide teachers on how to address diverse learning needs in today's classrooms.

Audrey McAllen's *The Extra Lesson* and her other books are explored, along with theory and practice within the field of sensory and neurological development. These bring a repertoire of methods that can be incorporated in classrooms and with groups or individuals in kindergarten, grade school, and high school. The study includes common profiles such as ADHD, autism spectrum, and dyslexia along with best practices from Waldorf education. Certificate-level students are assigned a mentor teacher as a guide for applying the course work professionally and learning to utilize the assessment tools and activities found in *The Extra Lesson*.

The third year prepares a teacher for a profession as an educational support teacher or a private Extra Lesson practitioner. A certificate is issued to those who complete the course requirements over the three years; there is an option to audit the course.

Artistic and personal development of the teacher is supported by speech work, eurythmy, therapeutic painting, form drawing, singing, games, and biography work. Guest lecturers come from fields of specialization in the arts and anthroposophic medicine, master Extra Lesson teachers, and those working in the field of sensory integration.

Healing Education and Training (HEART)
Rudolf Steiner Centre, Toronto, Ontario
http://www.rsct.ca/index.cfm?id=40440

The Rudolf Steiner Centre offers a Healing Education and Remedial Training program. It is a three-year graduate level program that provides teachers, therapists, educational specialists, and related professionals with knowledge and practical skills to work in a healing manner with children facing developmental, social/emotional, and learning challenges.

This course is based on Rudolf Steiner's anthroposophic picture of the human being, Waldorf child development and education methodologies, and the adult development of the educator to develop capacities to observe with understanding, assess with depth of knowledge, and remediate with effective practical technique. Central to this work are Steiner's own indications for curative education as well as the depth of research conducted by those who have carried these indications over many years of practical work, including the foundational research of Audrey E. McAllen.

Remedial Education Programs at Rudolf Steiner College

Fair Oaks, California
www.rudolfsteinercollege.edu/remedial-education

The Remedial Education Program of Rudolf Steiner College (since 1991) offers a three-year, part-time intensive course designed to instruct Waldorf pedagogues and professionals from related fields in educational support theory and practice. The Remedial Education Program deepens the understanding of child development as a foundation for learning, plus offers training in practical, pedagogical approaches supportive of everyday working with students of all ages. As individual learning differences are related to each student's developmental situation, appropriate activities that meet the individual needs of students can be created—whether in the classroom, in small groups, or in individual lessons.

Rudolf Steiner's indications for child and human development, curative and Waldorf education, sources of students' learning, and behavior challenges are thoroughly explored from developmental and educational lenses and medical, neurological, and therapeutic perspectives.

Children's drawings are explored as indicators of development. Various past and up-to-date resources are considered, including educational, therapeutic, Waldorf, anthroposophic, and mainstream methods of support.

Assessments and exercises of the Extra Lesson are presented as foundation, per indications according to its developer, Audrey McAllen. Movement, form drawing, and painting are explored to support the development of the participant's own facility in each of these activities and how to use these activities in support of their students' further development.

Artistic work for personal development and training includes eurythmy, speech, therapeutic painting, and singing. Introductions to chirophonetics, rhythmical massage, anthroposophic home remedy/nursing and Spacial Dynamics are also aspects of this program, and a career development segment explores working in educational support with practical applications regarding insurance, work proposals, contracts, and so forth.

Contributors

Linda Atamian earned a master's degree in reading and a certificate from the Association of Healing Education (AHE) ; she is a Fellow of the Academy of Orton-Gillingham Practitioners and Educators. She has taught students of every age, worked with teachers in public and independent schools, including Waldorf schools, and is the Director of Remedial Services and Teacher Training at Middlebridge School, RI. Linda is the co-founder of Mariposa, a Waldorf-inspired urban early childhood center in Providence, RI.

Arthur Auer, MEd, is Director of the Waldorf Teacher Education Program at Antioch University New England. He is author of *Learning about the World through Modeling: Sculptural Ideas for School and Home,* a sourcebook for teachers and home-schoolers. His 18 years as a class teacher at the Pine Hill Waldorf School using hands-on and experiential methods convinced him that an arts-based, "action academics" significantly enhances and builds intelligence, emotional health, and motivation.

Elizabeth Auer is a graduate of the Waldorf Teacher Training program and the Remedial Resource Waldorf Teacher Training program of AHE. She is the author of *Creative Pathways* and *Learning to See the World through Drawing*, both abundant resources for parents and teachers. While taking a class through grades 1–8, she helped continue the work of the care group at Pine Hill Waldorf School where she also taught Extra Lesson. She currently teaches a variety of workshops and courses, works as a freelance consultant and educator, and teaches Extra Lesson.

Regine Bruehl-Shemroske graduated from the Pedagogical College in Freiburg, Germany, received her master's of education from Tufts University, and her Waldorf teacher Training from New England Waldorf Teacher Training. Regine has taught in Waldorf schools for 38 years. She and her husband Gary live in Boston, where she is currently shepherding a first grade at the Waldorf School of Lexington. She enjoys adult education and has taught classes in Waldorf pedagogy, music, and anthroposophy.

Dennis Demanett A Waldorf class teacher for 40 years, Dennis has completed his fourth class and is currently teaching first grade at the Pasadena Waldorf School. He trained in England, and took his first class through there at the Ringwood Waldorf School. Moving to Hawaii, he taught grades 7/8, grade 8, and grades 3/4 at the Honolulu Waldorf School. He then took his second class for eight years at Pine Hill Waldorf School. For the last 18 years, he has taught two classes in Pasadena.

Contributors

Karine Munk-Finser, MEd, is a painter and has a diploma in painting therapy from the Medical Section in Dornach. She has painted with children and adults for several decades. Karine is on the Teaching Faculty at Antioch University New England, where she has taught for 18 years in the Waldorf Program. Karine is also the Coordinator for Renewal Courses at the Center for Anthroposophy, where she has run Renewal Courses for the last 17 years.

David Gable holds degrees in music performance from the University of Michigan School of Music and the Boston University School of Fine Arts, as well as a master of education degree with Waldorf certification from Antioch University New England. Since 1988 he has been on the faculty of the Waldorf School of Cape Cod, where he has taught the eight-year main lesson cycle three times, in addition to developing and teaching a choral and instrumental music program for the upper grades.

Connie Helms has worked with children and adolescents for over 30 years as a special education teacher, Waldorf Remedial teacher and in private practice as an Extra Lesson practitioner. As a Waldorf remedial consultant, she travels to independent schools in the U.S. and is co-director of the Educational Support Training program sponsored by the Association for a Healing Education (AHE). She holds a Waldorf teacher certification from Antioch University New England and a Waldorf Remedial certification from AHE.

Robyn Hewetson After studying at Emerson College, England, Robyn received the Art of Speech Formation training from Maisie Jones in London, England. She taught in Waldorf schools as well as businesses in New England, before returning to teach in her native land of New Zealand. She currently has her own speech business called WellSpoken and gives courses at conferences.

Helen-Ann Ireland has taken two classes through the grades and was a special subjects teacher in the middle school for four years. She also took up Extra Lesson work to be able to help unusual learners within the classroom setting and to work closely with therapists and tutors. She is currently involved in a doctoral program in Educational Leadership K–12 where she hopes to join the broader educational conversation and bring the world of Waldorf education into the academic arena.

Hannah Jackson currently works as the educational support therapist at the Haleakala Waldorf School in Hawaii. She has taught for 18 years as a special educator, elementary educator, Waldorf class teacher, and Extra Lesson teacher. She has a bachelor of science in special education from Appalachian State University, a master's degree in elementary education, a Waldorf teaching certificate from Antioch/New England Graduate School, and a Waldorf remedial teaching certificate from the Association of a Healing Education. She is an Integrated Listening Systems advanced practitioner.

Contributors

 **Jennifer Kennerk** is the educational support teacher at the Cincinnati Waldorf School. She received her Waldorf training at Antioch University New England. Before becoming a Waldorf teacher, she had the privilege of being a practicing midwife, working out of the inspirations of anthroposophy.

 **Jennifer Kershaw** has a bachelor's in acting/theater from the University of South Florida, a master's in education from Wheelock College in Boston, MA, and a Waldorf Teaching Certificate from Antioch University New England. Jen has been teaching in classrooms for over 15 years, first as an artist educator, then as a middle school math and history teacher, and finally as a Waldorf class teacher. Jenn currently teaches seventh grade at Pine Hill Waldorf School and has served the school as the Care Group chairperson for the past three years.

 **Amy Lloyd-Rippe** was a class teacher at the Meadowbrook Waldorf School in Rhode Island for 18 years and continues as a faculty mentor as well as a Board member and human resource committee member. She has been a student of anthroposophy for 23 years and is a graduate of the Antioch University New England Waldorf Teacher Training program.

 **Carol Mannion** is a developmental therapist and has completed the Waldorf Early Years Therapist Course. She is also a Waldon Therapist and works with children from birth to 16 years. Waldon therapy, after Geoffrey Waldon, a neurologist, is a physical movement-based therapy, used to prompt the typical development of the infant from birth onward.

 **Patrice Maynard**, MEd, is the Director of Publications and Development at the Research Institute for Waldorf Education. Her former work includes leadership in the Association of Waldorf Schools of North America (9 years), class and music teacher at Hawthorne Valley School (13 years), and co-founder of the Maine Coast Waldorf School.

 **David Mitchell** (1945–2012) was one of those rare, super-abundant personalities who completed several lifetimes in one—all of them devoted to Waldorf education. He was class teacher and high school teacher at Pine Hill Waldorf School and High Mowing School, NH, and Shining Mountain Waldorf High School, CO. David founded AWSNA Publications (now Waldorf Publications) and was co-director of RIWE. His insights into Waldorf education and his ability to connect Waldorf education around the world have made lasting impact. His many articles, books, journals, and research studies continue to influence and promote Waldorf education globally.

 **Colleen O'Conners** completed her Waldorf teacher training in Dornach, Switzerland, in 1995, and has been in the classroom ever since: 13 years in Switzerland and 10 years in the U.S. She has taught many subjects to many different age levels, including being a class teacher and middle school specialist. She received a master's in Waldorf education in 2011, and for the last few summers has served as adjunct faculty for Antioch University New England's Waldorf Summer Intensive Teacher Training Program, where she teaches math and language skills.

Contributors

Mary Jo Oresti has been a member of the Detroit Waldorf School faculty for 30 years. her activities involve coordinating and instructing in teacher development programs in the U.S. and abroad, consulting in schools about remedial programs, and some private work with children. She serves as the director of the Learning Support Program for AHE. Mary Jo has a master's degree from Marygrove College, Detroit, MI, in learning differences and a Waldorf teaching diploma; she has also studied chirophonetics.

Kim John Payne, MEd, is the author of the best-selling books, *Simplicity Parenting, Beyond Winning,* and *The Soul of Discipline*. A consultant and trainer to over 200 North American independent and public schools, Kim has been a Waldorf school counselor, adult educator, consultant, researcher, educator, and private family counselor for 27 years. He is co-director of the Simplicity Project and the founding director of The Center for Social Sustainability. www.simplicityparenting.com

Bonnie River holds a master's degree in education and is finishing her doctoral dissertation at the University of La Verne, CA. She has worked with special needs learners for more than 25 years and as a classroom teacher and early childhood educator for the past 35 years. Trained in mainstream assessment of learning disabilities as well as in Waldorf-style assessment tools, Ms. River works with anthroposophic doctors and educators. She is a founding member of Gradalis, an adult education institute.

Maggie Scott's passion for Waldorf education began 20 years ago with the birth of her eldest of four daughters. After attending Rudolf Steiner College for both class teaching and Extra Lesson education, Maggie has worked in Waldorf schools in the kindergarten, as a class teacher, and as the director of educational support programs. She currently runs the Cabinet Mountain Cooperative School, a Waldorf-inspired program in northern Idaho.

Barbara Sim received her eurythmy diploma from the Goetheanum, Dornach, Switzerland and her therapeutic eurythmy diploma from the Medical Section Goetheanum, Dornach, Switzerland. She has worked privately for many years with students at the Pine Hill Waldorf School, NH, and with individuals at Four Winds Community for special needs, Wilton, NH.

Jane Swain is a physical therapist and a graduate of the Level III training in Spacial Dynamics. She is the associate director of Waldorf early childhood teacher education at Sophia's Hearth Family Center in Keene, NH, consults in early childhood and elementary classrooms, and works with children of all ages in a private practice.

Contributors

Jeff Tunkey is a graduate of Spacial Dynamics and is coordinator of the educational support program at Aurora Waldorf School in Buffalo, NY, where he currently teaches physical education and whole-class Extra Lesson activities. Jeff also teaches various workshops and courses and mentors teachers at many Waldorf schools. He is an instructor for the Association for a Healing Education.

Hanneke van Riel, MEd, MS CCC-SLP, has been teaching in special education settings and in Waldorf elementary schools in The Netherlands and the U.S. for the past 47 years. In addition she practiced as a speech-language pathologist. She currently teaches at Antioch University New England as core faculty in the Waldorf Teacher Education Program.

Juliane Weeks was a public school and Waldorf school teacher in Germany before coming to the United States. After completing her training at the Dorion School of Music Therapy, she received her diploma for anthroposophic music therapy from the Medical Section in Dornach, Switzerland. She has worked at the Rudolf Steiner Health Clinic in Ann Arbor, MI, as well as at the Husemann Klinik, a psychiatric clinic, in Freiburg, Germany. For the last 15 years, she has served individuals of all ages and abilities in southern New Hampshire, including many students at Pine Hill Waldorf School.

Christof Wiechert is a former Head of the Pedagogical Section at the Goetheanum. His book, *Lust aufs Lehrersein (Desire to Become a Teacher)*, has recently been published by the Goetheanum Press.

Brigitta Witteveen was born in The Netherlands, where she completed her undergraduate studies in art, psychology and family therapy. Her MFA was accomplished at the Rhode Island School of Design and her MEd in early childhood and elementary Waldorf education at Antioch University New England. Her certification in Extra Lesson work and woodworking made her an indispensable faculty member at the Lexington Waldorf School for 29 years.

Acknowledgments

Many thanks go to the authors who contributed to this compendium. They are all individuals who are committed to the education of children and have given freely of their time and efforts to make this book possible. The authors vary widely in geographical location, as well as in talents and experience. Some of the writers are class teachers and first-time authors, others are therapists. Several are Extra Lesson teachers/practitioners, some of whom are also class teachers, having completed both Waldorf teacher training and Remedial training.

A special thank you to Christof Wiechert, Jeff Tunkey, Kim John Payne, Bonnie River, and Arthur Auer for permission to include their previously published articles.

Also a special thank you to Connie Helms and Mary Jo Oresti for writing chapters and lending their support to this endeavor. They are both co-directors and instructors for the Educational Support (Remedial) Training at the Association for a Healing Education (AHE). Several contributors to this book are AHE graduates or have taught in AHE's programs, which span over 30 years. AHE offers workshops to schools across North America and is also affiliated with remedial training programs overseas. www.healingeducation.edu